Being Against the Wor

How can we save politics from the politician? How can we save ourselves? The wager of this book is to look at the example of those who leave the city and break the social contract, rebellious exiles and freedom fighters like Orestes or Che Guevara who escaped the wheel of necessity. Their aim? To come back and inspire revolt among those who have condemned themselves to abject passivity; to proceed towards politics beyond the ways of the understanding, beyond self-authorisation, and beyond critique.

Being Against the World challenges a critical standpoint that, by ruling out archaic, quasi- or obscure objects as superstitious things of the past, law and politics have been attributed the sober task of managing or controlling human interaction. Rethinking the notion of objectivity that underpins this standpoint, the focus here is upon how archaic fetishes and quasi-objects return to create social conflicts that shatter the most mature ethical senses of precaution and legal policies of prevention. The return of these obscure objects is a political event that, shattering the conventional critical standpoint, reveals a field of politics beyond critique.

Being Against the World elicits and addresses this beyond, in the domains of art, law and politics.

Oscar Guardiola-Rivera is a Lecturer in Law at Birkbeck College, University of London.

Being Against the World

Rebellion and Constitution

Oscar Guardiola-Rivera

First published 2009
by Birkbeck Law Press
2 Park Square, Milton Park, Abingdon, Oxon OX14 4RN

Simultaneously published in the USA and Canada
by Birkbeck Law Press
270 Madison Ave, New York, NY10016

Birkbeck Law Press is an imprint of the Taylor & Francis Group, an informa business

© 2009 Oscar Guardiola-Rivera

Typeset in Sabon and Gill Sans by
Florence Production Ltd, Stoodleigh, Devon
Printed and bound in Great Britain by
Antony Rowe, Chippenham, Wiltshire

All rights reserved. No part of this book may be reprinted
or reproduced or utilised in any form or by any electronic,
mechanical, or other means, now known or hereafter invented,
including photocopying and recording, or in any information
storage or retrieval system, without permission in writing
from the publishers.

British Library Cataloguing in Publication Data
A catalogue record for this book is available from the British Library

Library of Congress Cataloging in Publication Data
Guardiola-Rivera, Oscar.
  Being against the world: rebellion and constitution/Oscar Guardiola-Rivera
     p. cm.
   Simultaneously published in the USA and Canada by
     Routledge-Cavendish.
   Includes bibliographical references and index.
   1. Government, Resistence to. 2. Social conflict. 3. Revolutions.
   I. Title.
JC328.3.G82 2008
303.6–dc22   2008003875

ISBN10: 0–415–45945–1 (hbk)
ISBN10: 0–415–45946–X (pbk)
ISBN10: 0–203–93076–2 (ebk)

ISBN13: 978–0–415–45945–7 (hbk)
ISBN13: 978–0–415–45946–4 (pbk)
ISBN13: 978–0–203–93076–2 (ebk)

To Zoe
(She's about to enter the Labyrinth)

To Sylvia
My Heart in a Chest

Contents

Foreword	*x*
Acknowledgements	*xiii*
Introduction: art, politics and infinite critique	**1**

Infinite critique: the aims of this book 3
Postulation: rebels and archaic objects 9
The heart in the chest: structure of this book 16

1 Archaic objects   24

Archaic and obscure objects: Tlingit coffins, Peruvian stones and French paintings 26
Power: the model of penetration versus the model of exemplarity 31

2 Uncanny encounters   37

Evental bodies and radical connections: the contribution of cognitive science 39
Magic and the uncanny: contributions from psychoanalysis and anthropology 42
Uncanny objects in philosophy 44
Rebellion and objects: notes towards a definition 49

3 An introduction to fetishism (with a plea for materialism)   57

Political consequences of a deficient account of materiality 58
Truth and the return of the fetish 61
Impossible matter: the two aspects of the fetish 63
A brief history of the fetish 70

Call without meaning: the fetish-voice and contagion 72
A German critic in the Caribbean: Marx's fetish 77

4   The most sublime of fetishists   93

Where does fetishism come from? 95
Before psychoanalysis, the privilege of man: projection,
  desire and right 102

5   Let us make love (and listen to Death From Above):
     notes on psychoanalysis   107

Beginnings: on how psychoanalysis lost its woman 107
Lacan and his double: on contradictory objects and
  the death-drive 120
Clarification: contradictory objects are not just illogical.
  On proximity 125
The theory of drives and ontology: on substitution 128

6   The love that seeks no other: further notes . . .   132

The love that seeks no other: additional notes on
  psychoanalysis, proximity and substitution 133
The logic of substitution in the field of sacrificial
  violence 138
The slave-ship and the sailor's paradox 141
Metaphysics of time and the politics of anticipatory
  projection 148
The heart in the chest: on pirates 152

7   Horror in philosophy   168

A nightmare 168
Time and matter, series and groups: uncanny metaphysics
  and the politics of visionary speculation 173

8   Rip it up and start again   187

Ontological consequences of realism 187
Consequences of realism in politics and economics 191
Consequences of realism for the study of laws,
  natural and social 201
Consequences of realism for the study of
  globalisation 206

9   Sex, laws and rock 'n' roll: on music as an organising
    principle   220

    Rip it up and start again 220
    Anarchy in the UK: on temporary autonomous zones 223
    Law, radical choice and rock 'n' roll 228

10 Guevara's choice: on revolution as a radical organising
    principle   235

    On virtuality 236
    The path of the hero: virtuality and the sacrificial 242
    Guevara's choice 247
    Coda: in freedom 256

    Bibliography   259
    Index   279

Foreword

A pragmatology of rebellion or
In defence of res

What happens when objects start acting, dancing, entrancing, rebelling? When idols seduce people with their beauty, their simulations and reflections of the true? What kind of people believe that the non-human speak, that fetishes turn people's minds, that the res has become persona? Who believes seriously in fetishes outside those happy souls ensnared in some stiletto shoe or kinky underwear compulsion?

The fetish brings together the subject and the object, the subject in awe, seduced by the uncanny object. The 'discovery' of the fetish, its ethnography and mythology are attempts to separate the two and return the subject to its masterful dignity. Fetish-talk is a sign of modernity; it means to be a clear-headed, enlightened subject addressing a rather distasteful, decadent object and culture. Whether we call the object a golden calf (religious idol), the mask of social relations (fetishism of commodities) or a stand-in for primary psychological processes (obscure object of desire), we place ourselves in a position of knowledge and superiority against those described as idolaters, ideologically unsound or fetishists. Fetish-talk inscribes its speaker in an economy of Western rational authenticity. It proclaims the metaphysical chasm between the subject and the non-subject, object or God.

The fetish acts as cut and frontier, therefore, it separates: between epochs, geographies, cultures and selves; between the open-eyed critical Western subject and those who are ignorant, childish or simple who project on the inanimate the animus of humanity; between the superficial, transient, ornamental surface or form and the deep, permanent, substantial content. To believe in speaking objects, acting nonhumans and zombies signals some kind of pre-modern or crazed Other, still in the throes of prejudice, stupidity, Kant's heteronomy, victims of error as dangerous as it is seductive. As the Dutch missionary D. K. Wielenga put it in 1909, 'the primitives confound what which is a fruit of the imagination with the reality, the objective with the subjective, the outer phenomenon with their own spirit life'. Analysing the fetish asserts that I, the observer, can see through the desires of the other, separate the real from fantasy, subject the body to the soul.

This is the metaphysics, epistemology and politics that Oscar Guardiola-Rivera attacks relentlessly and compellingly. His tactics adopt the wide repertory of the cultural urban guerilla. The rules are clear. Pack your toothbrush and a couple of books and keep moving; there is no resting place for the underground fighter. Don't use the same weapons often and keep changing them, mixing and camouflaging them. Don't trust the philanthropists and the humanists. Make quick decisions and stick to them.

So Oscar keeps moving from suburb to suburb, from the poor barrios to aristocratic quarters, from austere to ludic places: from the sciences to the humanities, from anthropology to law, from philosophy to psychoanalysis, from culture to ontology (or should we say 'pragmatology' the ontology of things?), from logic to politics. He keeps changing his tack to confuse the enemy, using music for methodology, film for philosophical insight, advanced physics for rhetorical purchase. He sticks to the plan (both physical and symbolic) of announcing an object-led rebellion, but he understands (even welcomes) the consequences. Rebel pathways lead to ostracism and outlawry: Orestes will leave Athens (but return to Colonus in a promise of redemption); Che Guevara will travel from Cuba to Bolivia (and will enter both the hall of revolutionary fame and a million T-shirts). Oscar himself has followed a strange almost destined peregrination from Bogota to Aberdeen and London, from law to analytical philosophy, from logic to phenomenology and jurisprudence and back to critical legal studies. A convoluted route, zigzagging around the Atlantic, following the law in order to break it, in search of the semi-object (of desire).

Acting as a reverse and manic Moses, Oscar uncovers 'obscure and sublime objects such as ancient stones and rebellious angels, lost jungles and discarded humans, weird noises and uncanny fetishes' everywhere. Unlike Moses and our Dutch missionary, however, he does not smash or demystify. He returns them, according to a law of eternal return and the rhythms of fetishistic jouisance, to the places and desires they came from: Latin America and totems, Africa and pirates, cities of the red night and cocaine nights, freed slaves and fields of energy. These are the places, the tools, the images and music of the rebel, the revolutionary who left behind the bipolarities of critique (judgement and change) and the strictures of the name of the father (with all the side effects of the *beyond*, well-known from psychoanalysis, the only orthodoxy left in an age that has turned the heretical into a lifestyle choice).

This is a philosophy of the remainder, of excess and lack, what defies systematic order and orderly practice, what systematicity itself spews out, ejects. A phenomenology and politics of the 'pragma', the reject or ruin, the pirate or rebel in every system (of nature or culture, of thought or action) who (always) returns and unpicks its systematicity. We can approach these errant revenants as pre-transcendental objects, there before the 'conditions of existence' of thought and action or theory and practice took hold of the cognitive and practical fields. Oscar following the most avant-garde logic and science calls them 'postulated' objects. They open possibilities, some returning from the most ancient past, others firmly arriving as memories of the future. These quasi-objects modify space-time relations, 'interrupt the ceaseless flux' of objective reality. Posited by the rebel, political fetishes such as the universal equality principle or Guevara's 'new man' rearticulate the real towards the future beyond self-authorisation and then stick to the path, by establishing a way of moving forward, step by step, in the face of unexpected uncertainties and decisive events.

This is, then, a book where the fetish and the rebels gather together under many names and aliases, where the object and the subject are reunited. A ragtag army of philosophers, mystics, scientists, hip-hop artists, film-makers, actors, politicians and revolutionaries meet ancient treasures and black holes, omens and hearts in the chest, *signa* and *monstra*, fleeing slaves and slave-owning judges. 'My name is legion' says the possessed to Jesus and Derrida's Nietzsche repeats. My things are legion, repeats Oscar Guardiola-Riviera, opening his treasure trove, and this is the path to revolution.

Working with Oscar at the Birkbeck School of Law, at the Institute for the Humanities and in many other intellectual and political activities has been a wonderful pleasure. He personifies the perfect balance of content and form, of knowledge and finesse, of prudence and emotion, of wisdom and dilettantism. I would have said that Oscar is a true Renaissance man, only I know that he dislikes the Eurocentric narcissism of certain clichéd periodisations. The serendipitous coincidences that brought him back to London have changed our lives as much as or even more than his. I always felt a little guilty for helping Oscar come to London away from his beloved Bogota, his friends and the struggle. However, in publishing his book which joins such path-breaking contributions as those of Bill Rasch, Louis Wolcher and Johan van der Walt, Oscar helps to change the philosophical, legal and political landscape both here, in the tired West, and there, in the revolting South. We are all indebted to his rebellious *lacrimae rerum*.

Costas Douzinas
Athens/London
April 2008

Acknowledgements

Graham Harman and Bernard Stiegler. For a world jam-packed with objects.

Miguel Taussig. For a question, why do prophecies always come in riddles?

Enrique Dussel, Ignacio Ellacuría, Jaime Rubio, Jorge Hoyos. Ontology, topology, drives, and visitation by angels.

Jacques, Bruno and Ken. Two ghosts talking on a screen. One behind the camera.

Santiago Castro-Gómez. For friendship and a partnership in philosophy.

Costas Douzinas. Politics not Rights. This book would not have been possible without his commitment and passion. A true friend.

Slavoj. Perverse jokes, Marcos, Lacan and Hegel in Latin America.

Guillermo Del Toro and Gael García Bernal. Rebels. In admiration.

The School of Law, Birkbeck College.

The children of the South. May they forget the name of the father.

Introduction
Art, politics and infinite critique

We ask the social to explain the origin of things. What splendid ignorance. The origin and ultimate destiny of things is archaic and therefore beyond the scope of the social contract. The latter is based on the fortuitous convergence between technology and matter, a destructive event that ultimately produces us, but we have inverted this contingent relation, construed it as necessary and situated the cause of its necessity in human spirit. Such a conviction has turned into envy, the shortsighted notion that nothing is more worthy than to rid ourselves of the obstacles standing in the way of our future transcendence. Man's greatest right has thus become the new figure of sovereignty, an empire that requires a definition of what is to be conquered 'in the perspective of the legitimacy of this conquest' (Stengers, 2007: 9).

It demands the sacrifice and elimination of all obstacles as not really mattering: particularly indigenous knowledges, rebellious practices, entire ecosystems of persons and things, but we pretend society can rise spontaneously beyond this generalised narcissism and steer us all to paradise. The paradox is that we now know the humanist hubris, which has given the age of society its seemingly unfettered power, threatens humanity's very continuity and that of the spaces it inhabits.

For centuries, the concrete image of such coming paradise has been the well-ordered city and the politician, its architect. Immersed in the exclusivity of the social contract, the politician keeps drawing up plans, blueprints and graphs, flowcharts and poll charts; he digs, he founds, he measures, he partitions. He is the real scientist, an expert on risk management and prevention, a naturalist in the social sciences, and an artful imitator of utopias. He practises philosophy as enlargement by scale drawing, the direct expansion of a local image, and adjudicates on the proper rules of understanding. His politics are the colonisation of metaphysical sense by common sense, 'a politics that authorizes itself by allusion to modern logic' (Kerruish and Petersen, 2006: 67). He is the ultimate king philosopher.

To speak of the colonisation of metaphysical sense by common sense is to observe that politics nowadays focuses on the social and the finite, and forgets the world and the reasonable. The world is jam-packed with obscure objects: ancient stones and rebellious messengers; copies and automatons; sacred texts, prophecies and riddles; lost worlds and discarded humans; noise, voice, and music. In short, an assortment of uncanny fetishes, which have been adjudicated against and discounted by the rules of common sense and understanding.

It is also to remind us that the rules of understanding, the allusion to modern logic at the basis of contemporary politics and economics, quite simply do not give this authority, as Kerruish and Petersen observe (ibid.). Such rules do not decide the *philosophical* question that is at stake, namely how sense (logic) and world (packed with objects) are related. This is also a *practical* question: metaphysical sense includes the issue of truth and whether or not our quests for truth can set aside the world and its objects, on the one hand, and defer questions concerning declarations and procedures to a separate exercise of intellect exclusively placed in the domain of the socio-legal or the politico-ethical, on the other.

As it often happens with oppositions and borders, the drawing of seemingly unsurpassable frontiers here betrays a case of studied indifference. As Michel Serres says in relation to the standpoint of the modern politician: 'closed up in the social collectivity, he could be splendidly ignorant of the things of the world' (1995a: 74–5). Serres also contends that the politician now knows that 'global history enters nature and global nature enters history' (Serres, 1995a: 4). Like the politician we all know, but do not want to believe, there are things which are man-made but whose effect has gone global and now threaten the whole of nature: planetary warming, mass forced displacement, atomic weapons, car-bombs, paramilitary warfare – all manner of catastrophes. This is our blindness; such is the scale of the problem.

The wager of this book is to look at the example and learn from those who leave the city and break the social contract, rebellious exiles, barbarians and freedom fighters escaping the wheels of necessity. The aim is to proceed step by step, and to propose a politics beyond the ways of understanding and self-authorisation; in a phrase, *beyond critique*.

This can be done by asking whether or not problematic objects such as artificial composites, rebellious messengers and messages, and archaic fetishes, plague politics with their paradoxical DNA, that is to say, paraphrasing Bruno Latour (2004a) and Kerruish and Petersen (2006: 78), if they threaten the healthy exercise of public reason or merely contaminate the self-satisfaction of political reasoning in its blindness to its own role. The next step is to postulate these objects as constitutive of politics rather than residual or derivative; to entertain the notion that idealistic practices – messaging, thinking and discursive practices – have more-than-idealistic consequences; to map the withdrawal of such objects in modernity and elaborate rigorously, with them, after them, a transition from locality to totality – Hegel's reasonable – by means of certain procedures that can be termed 'algorithmic' in the sense given to the term by people such as Michel Serres (1983, 1996) and Xavier Zubiri (1980) among others. Finally we shall return to the city not to gain recognition, but rather, like Orestes and Guevara, in order to incite revolt among the people who have acquiesced in abject passivity and complacency.

Infinite critique: the aims of this book

Remember the last scene of *Butch Cassidy and the Sundance Kid*? The protagonists find themselves cornered in Bolivia. Outgunned and outsmarted, the two outlaws face their destiny. Surrender would be the only way to save their lives; instead, they choose to go down in a blaze. Coming out of a wooden shack, they face a rain of bullets. They choose freedom.

After Max Weber and Emile Durkheim, sociologists would interpret this episode of rebellion as a struggle against the reification of socially constructed norms and rules. Weberians in particular point out that conduct can be oriented on the part of actors towards the notion of the existence of a legitimate order. They would say that only if the orientation towards its maxims occurs because the actor regards them as in some sense obligatory for him, only then such an order could be considered valid. They would conclude that since an externally guaranteed order must also be guaranteed internally, rebellion should be understood as a case of the actors ceasing to hold on to their internal acceptance of the rules, thereby short-circuiting their external objectivity.[1]

In turn, naturalists would consider the stance of rebellion as an attitude of unveiling and denouncing the falseness of belief, order and method. Anarchical naturalists like Paul Feyerabend (1993) would favour childlike play and the time of innocence as the true liberty, a time to recover. In this interpretation, Butch Cassidy and the Sundance Kid are more like playful kids attempting to return to Mother Nature. More refined naturalists, critically enlightened by the arguments offered by sociology and the sociology of science, would add that it is society 'up there' that explains true and false beliefs in the same terms, as anchored but not shaped by nature 'out there'. From such a standpoint, the act of rebellion would consist of the rediscovery of the (pre)linguistic state of subjectivity when grasping language and practice allows one to attain freedom and creativity.[2]

Sociologists and naturalists are often portrayed as sworn enemies, defenders of the cause of two different and opposed houses: the house of man or 'society', the internal aspect, and the house of things or 'nature', the external aspect. Look closely however, and in spite of the apparent division, you will see that talk of opposition in this case is misleading. Sociologists (including sociologically informed naturalists) replace the childlike innocence of the radical naturalist with words and the following of rules, but they share a common concern with criticism, spontaneity and foundations. They remain committed to a similar notion of objectivity.

The two positions are critical in the precise sense of the term. Both maintain a sharp distinction between the internal and the external, between subjective acceptance and objectivity 'out there' (or 'up there' in the case of society and its rules) and in denouncing (the centrality of power and its sanctions, the empiricism of scientific method, a determinant big other and so on) they presuppose the existence and importance of that which is at stake.

The first aim of this book is to propose a different conception of objectivity, one that is, somewhat paradoxically, non-objective and more substantialist, in that it escapes the apparently opposed but in fact correlative codes of the internal aspect and the object out there, the critical standpoint shared by sociologists and naturalists. This basic dichotomy between inner and outer results in an understanding of reality in terms of relations and self-positing subjects; it represents the human for legal–political purposes and the nonhuman for the postulation of the same thing: a zone of objects out there taken over by the sciences under the rules of prevention and precaution.

In this respect, the critical standpoint appears to be built upon the basis of two original political acts. These acts define the two tasks of criticism: first, to rule out archaic, quasi- or obscure objects as a superstitious thing of the past, unrelated to us in the present or the future. This task is given to the natural sciences. The second task is the control and management of human interaction with time and the natural environment, under the rules of prevention and precaution. This second task is given to the social sciences and ethics. The problem is that archaic fetishes and quasi-objects *return* precisely to the realm that is supposed to rule them out, the sciences, and create social conflicts that shatter our most mature ethical senses of precaution and our policies of prevention. In other words, the return or re-entry of these obscure objects is a political act that shatters the 'original' political partition of criticism and in doing so seems to reveal a field of politics beyond critique.

The second aim of this book is to provide an answer to the question 'what lies beyond critique?' In a nutshell, what lies beyond critique is the realm of quasi-objects and reality by postulation, to use the terms coined by mathematician Michel Serres and metaphysician Xavier Zubiri, respectively. The latter, a student of Martin Heidegger, a philosopher of mathematics whose work influenced the politically engaged project known as Liberation Philosophy in Latin America and elsewhere, introduced the concept of reality by postulation to explain the ontological status of mathematical objects, algorithmic procedures, literary characters, laws posited by normative and scientific theories, and the upheaval of such norms. As the example of liberation philosophy shows, this notion can be extended to the political field with significant results not only in theory but also in practice.[3] The former, a mathematician doing philosophy of science in France, proposed the term 'quasi-objects' for entities that are not describable as naturalistic objects, not entirely an object out there nor just a relational phenomenon, but a marker of the subject that, nevertheless, is itself something in its own right (Serres, 1982: 227).

For Serres, 'the object here is a quasi-object insofar as it remains a quasi-us' (Serres, 1982: 88) which is to say that it is primary in relation to intersubjectivity. In fact, the fundamental question at stake here is that of the relationship between the community of observers and reality, rather than that between the observers themselves, and the status of both terms in the relation. Is it the case that the status of reality can only be determined in relation to what the community of observers perceive or fails to perceive? Or else, is reality precisely that which escapes such a determination in relation to perception, knowledge and observation? To put it in more philosophical terms: is it possible to come up with an ontology that is not ultimately dependent upon (critical) epistemology? If so, what does this mean for politics since the latter has been construed, after critique, as the activity of setting and policing limits, beginning with the supposedly certain divide between human observers and non-human reality? At this point, to postulate the notion of an object that is a quasi-object invites the question about an entity that is something in its own right, and the consideration of the consequences of such a postulation, beyond a thought of the limit.

The quasi-object is in fact 'that by which I am a subject, that is to say, submitted'; not just a marker of the subject but also 'an astonishing constructor of intersubjectivity' (Serres, 1982: 227). This means, as Niklas Luhmann put it, that for Serres 'the stabilization of objects (identification, recognizability, and so on) is more likely to contribute to stabilizing social relations than the famous social contract' (Luhmann, 2000: 37). The difference between Luhmann's rendition of the quasi-object and Serres' notion, is that for the latter the object 'is in the world' (Serres, 1982: 225) and makes common cause with the subject that observes it by becoming invisible to any observer. This is to say that the reality of the object is never exhausted in the act of observation or self-positing of the subject, but it is not just a residue that is left behind after the relational act of observation. Rather, this residue or remainder actively escapes the act of observation; it becomes invisible to the observer and it is precisely this activity of the object that inaugurates the gap that is then occupied by the subject. In contrast, for Luhmann 'reality is what one does not perceive when one perceives it' (Luhmann, 1990: 76), the residue left behind by observation, and thus, as he says, the observer could never be in the position of the subject for it is unobservable not to the other but only to itself.

To complicate matters, if it is the case that the subject occupies a gap, an empty space left by the withdrawal of the object, then its observation of the object does not posit itself in the place of the object, as Kant would have it, but rather, at a distance from it. Another way to say this is the following: if being observable in the world is to be marked by certain discourses, an act of discursive imposition, as the structuralists of the 1960s would say, an element exists that escapes such an imposition. The question arises: what would it mean to think such an element that is, but is not observable or amenable to discursive marking? What we encounter here is the classical distinction between being and existence (or being-in-the-world),[4] or to put it otherwise, the case of an element that is *against* the world. How to think that element without disturbing its withdrawal, at a distance, without suppressing its rebellion? How to think Being *against* the world?

In that respect, Serres is right to state that the observer must also become unobservable: 'He must, at least, be last on the chain of observables (. . .) he is thus unobservable by the observed.' (Serres, 1982: 237–8). What is knowledge then, if it is not the result of the self-positing of the subject in the place of the object, if it is not a co-relation, the result of fusion, the seizure or penetration of the object by the subject? For now it will suffice to say that knowledge is not the observation of an object 'out there', the active self-positing of an outsider upon some 'other' artefact or creature,[5] as if the object were in place, waiting to be seized by our senses.[6] In fact, if the object withdraws, then it is always beyond place, within and beyond, or as psychoanalytical theorists would say, it occupies the peculiar place of the outside within. Since the object is within only in its act of withdrawal, or *against*, and therefore it cannot be observed directly and absolutely, then knowledge can only be indirect and infinite.

In that case, knowledge can be better described as a process of substitution. In substitution, communication and causality occur through a third or vicar element,[7] and it involves a double transference that transforms the object withdrawn into something totally other than, and transcendent to, the community of observers. This is why many of the so-called quasi- or obscure objects appear to the community as 'sacred' objects. As a result of this, the community belongs to the object but the object does not belong to the community, and thus, it cannot be had or owned, but only given.

A 'gift', in the anthropological sense, is precisely that obscure object of substitution (among non-European or 'traditional' communities) which proved elusive to European attempts, during colonial times, to impose a 'Western' notion of property relative to the market economy, on the one hand, and a 'Western' notion of sovereignty relative to the alleged singularity of the point of force-accumulation, on the other. However, as Christopher Bracken (1997) explains, that object is also a blind-spot, the point where the commodity fetish became invisible to European modern colonialism or capitalism, also the point where Europe became oblivious towards forms of rule without a master. The result of this double bind between the gold-commodity of the conquerors and the gold-fetish of the conquered is 'potlatch', as the illegal object of late nineteenth and early twentieth-century Canadian law, or the 'donación' referred to by Peruvian writer Felipe Guamán Puma de Ayala in the seventeenth century. In this sense, as Bracken says, the gift is given at the moment when 'what Europe identifies as its outside bends back over its interior' (1997: 6), so that Europe gives non-Europe to itself 'by extending its limits to its outside', while at the same time non-Europe over-identifies with Europe and withdraws from it – as in the case of the Haitian revolutionaries singing *La Marseillaise* in battle against Napoleonic troops.

The insight is of course that by over-identifying with the colonist, the colonised confuses the notion of barbarity and foreignness for he cannot be barbaric if he can sing songs in French, deal with the English constitution or write novels in Spanish, as Dhanvantari explains (2004: 109). At stake in the issue of obscure objects is the questioning of the self/other, friend/enemy opposition upon which war and much of political analysis are based. Crucially, contained within the question is the improbable as a category of reality, for instance a future without subordination and difference.

Generally, these objects will appear to be more foreign than intimate, and those who make common cause with them will be seen as visitors, rebellious messengers coming from unknown or newly discovered worlds. As in many myths, both object and rebel will be perceived as returning from the outside precisely at the moment when the community of critical observers expel them or sacrifice them, thereby giving what is negated to themselves, and thus, as harbingers of disaster and the end of days, an internal sign of some coming event. The prescription to go and search for truth 'out there', and the prescription that prohibits the seizure of certain objects (and we must be reminded that everything and anything can become taboo) have a common origin in this mechanism of double transference.[8]

Serres acknowledges that to be observed is to be supplanted or substituted rather than limited or seized, and thus, as said before, if a relationship of knowledge or observation between subject and object is at all possible, it must take place at a distance, through a third or vicarious element. Knowledge is substitution, indirect and infinite. Put otherwise, to know and to observe is to invent a common or a collective, a composite set that contains at least three elements and which becomes something in its own right, without ever becoming a full synthesis of the elements within. The elements of the composite set, at least those with minimal existence, are always escaping the absolute embrace of the set, thereby abstracting or constructing new, unpredictable ones.

It would be possible to introduce a distinction here between a primordial (but still composite) set and new ones. So, in all, the total number of sets is always $x + 1$. The +1 in this figure stands for the newly postulated or created sets/entities, that is to say, those that are added to reality after the beginning of the world, a plus of reality. In one case the +1 set may contain five entities, in others one hundred or one thousand, and to each new set that is postulated another +1 set may be added. The element that withdraws from the primordial set becomes the basis for another set or collection of a higher level. At least in this sense, knowledge appears to be infinite and so are the depths of reality we cannot even start to dream of. Also, if this is the case, then it is not too far fetched to suggest that to observe, to know, involves a political act: let us call this the act of infinite critique.

Zubiri's (1963) main point, taken up by liberation philosophers and theologians, is similar. According to him, things that exist minimally, which are often perceived as a residue, cannot be counted off and should be taken into account in their own right (or 'de suyo', as Zubiri would say). However, these things cannot be taken into account within the same order that makes them a residue with minimal existence, an empty set in a particular world, for they do not have a place in such a world, even though they are within it. They are within, but are unplaceable: the outside within. For them to fully exist another world is necessary and so the withdrawal and return of these things brings about the end of the present order, a rebellion, a catastrophe, and thereby the constitution of another set and another order of counting for which they are the foundational, universal basis.

Rather than the possibility of another world, or the set of all possible worlds, what we encounter here is the infinite nature and necessity of the actual world, a necessity that is brought about by sudden irruption, noise and contingent closure. Artists such as Gérard Titus-Carmel, Doris Salcedo, Felipe Londoño or Michael Kidner have been exploring the creative implications of this relationship between void, necessity and contingent closure in their artwork.[9] We will have more to say about this in the pages that follow. For now, let us remark that, theoretically speaking, this is what Zubiri called 'the power of reality'.

This is the fact that there are depths in reality we have never dreamt of and cannot fully capture in given sets of possibilities. The act of postulation (in other terms, the enactment of a world) does not exhaust the reality of postulated objects, says Zubiri, giving as an example the case of mathematical objects in accordance to Gödel's incompleteness theorem.[10] In this case, the theorem shows rigorously that objects are not exhausted through logical deduction and have a reality that exceeds what was put into them by postulation; hence, we can go on abstracting and, in doing so, expanding our canon and the form of reality. Here, something of the Hegelian and Sartrean spirit of dialectic glimmers against critique:[11] reality is fundamentally infinite; elements escape and withdraw from the fields and networks of relations where they become present. Such spirit is perhaps the one constant in this book.

On the one hand, postulation of reality makes no sense under the traditional/critical notion of objectivity, reality and causation shared by sociologists and naturalists; to them reality is a separated zone of things, often envisioned as somewhere outside the mind and more or less passive in relation to it, or 'practico-inert'. In this perspective only the mind is active, insofar as it establishes the conditions for the unity of the object out there.

The term 'mind' can be replaced here by other, more or less socially constructivist terms such as 'intersubjective consensus', 'human nature', 'being-in-the-world' or 'scientific community', but the result is ultimately the same: objectivity is out there and it must be transcendentally guaranteed. Reality, in that conception, cannot be postulated but only found, intended or discovered. On the other hand, quasi-objects such as fetishes and global warming, but also circles and exemplars, laws and transformative upheavals of these laws, political and scientific, appear in the eyes of Durkheimian sociologists, Hartian legal theorists and hardcore Kantian realists and mathematicians as mere nonsense.

This is why to them the episode of rebellion evoked at the beginning of this introduction can only be interpreted as a more or less childish tantrum before objectivity. It does not matter if the model for that interpretation is radical and anarchic, as in the case of Paul Feyerabend (1993), or moderate, as in that of Max Weber (1954) or H. L. A. Hart (1961); in any case the result is deeply conservative: freedom as choice and the actualisation of given and surveyed possibilities, constructivism in the hands of the dominant social agent and his state, the model of the isolated monad existing side-by-side other equally exchangeable monads, critique as the public denunciation of falseness or superstition in the name of self-authorised tribunals, the establishment of common sense, prevention and precautionary principles as a guide for policy and adjudication, causation as the one-way exercise of force by one object over another and, consequently, a notion of power – including political power – which is now taken to be obvious.

Postulation: rebels and archaic objects

Postulation can be used to describe the origin of archaic or obscure objects in mathematics and art. For now, let us consider the case of mathematical objects. Chapter 1 will explore the case of art objects in due course. As Zubiri explained, these objects are real by postulation: we postulate the existence and notes of mathematical objects, as in 'Let X be a Hilbert space'. Put otherwise, we decree what all should know without ambiguity and also state that even if such declarations, positing truth, are not demonstrable in themselves, they can be verified in their consequences; thus postulation makes deductions possible ('Let X be posited, then it follows that . . .').

In mainstream understandings of deductive logic this is commonly taken to entail that the declarative order presupposes totality as the universal or homogeneous space of necessary forms (those of geometry and physics) and the highest order of generality that subsumes all localities of site, event, custom or tradition with the latter disappearing by necessity because of their accidental or merely potential nature, their 'derivative' or contingent character before the law of a constitutive *necessity*.

However, this does not have to be the final word on the matter: as Serres and Zubiri observe, the algorithmic procedural practices that Leibniz and Pascal took from Arabs and medieval merchants circulating in North Africa, the Mediterranean and the Atlantic in the seventeenth century, and theorised anew, allow the formulation of local cases and the transition to circumstantial solutions, the move from a concept to its extension, in the form of an engagement with the significance of paradoxes and problems in self-referential totalities.

The important result, that came back forcefully and shook logic and other related practices from within (with infinitesimal calculation, cut-up art, coding theory, computer calculation and programs rapidly following suit), is that postulation and deduction do not exhaust the reality of postulated objects. Rather than a cavalier dismissal of contradiction, antinomies and paradoxes, postulation calls for a heightened metaphysical sense, better and more detailed attention to what makes contradiction so unpalatable: the assumption of the validity of either/or reasoning, its formality as a method of avoidance, preservation and prevention; an assumption that leaves the question of the significance of contradiction and rebellion untouched. The point is to make sense of rebellion and contradictory objects, to take them seriously and observe that although they may set strange bounds to the power of self-reference and transformation in a given totality, the same unpalatable objects shatter these bounds, since the fact that they are discounted by that given totality becomes a proof of their constitutive character in a totality of higher level. Reality remains thus open (or more precisely, in-closed) and banning totalities, or setting limits, could not be described any longer as the task of critique and politics.

Let rebellion, even as formalised in art, literature and cinema, be the experience that remains problematic in mainstream accounts of objectivity, reality and causation. Let us describe that experience as the return, enactment or postulation of contradictory objects and let us see what follows from their return. These are objects that seem to defy the limits of critique and our most basic intuitions: they may be socially produced but their effects are natural and global; they can be measured but to forecast them is not to anticipate them; they remain unpredictable, unexpected, both within the grasp of our systems of knowledge and without. They can only be half said. This is the case, for instance, with climate change, a hurricane, atomic power, dark matter, mass displacement and famine, but also with rebellion and revolution. Since our mainstream systems of knowledge share the perspective of critique, they cannot account for and merely adjudicate against these returning or postulated quasi-objects. As suggested before, the perspective of critique is that of objectivity out there 'for us' and the sharp distinction between the internal and the external. Confronted by factual uncertainty, this perspective responds by postulating the necessity of being and certainty, of the understanding's way (Kerruish and Petersen, 2006:

61–91) and time as the transcendental ground of the structure of possibility and objective reality.

In contrast, rebellion must be understood as a decisive alteration of spatiotemporal relations vis-à-vis objective reality, or the absolute intervention that interrupts the ceaseless flux of necessary innovation or stasis of being. In this respect, rebellion has little to do with change or stasis of being since *ens* or being, as commonly posited in critical accounts, refers to the ultimate human conception that involves all the other concepts and categories and the point where the latter find their ultimate resolution. Alas, rebellion entails neither an idealistic affirmation nor a final judgement in which purely intellectual ideals are forged primarily and remain always in need of a secondary movement of realisation in order to guarantee (or prevent) their encounter with reality. These two conceptions, the activation of being for the purposes of change and difference on the one hand and the realisation of ideals on the other, belong to the same erroneous scheme that expels reality by making it part of an internal relation with human intellect, social language or effect. Its error can be seen in the fact that in this scheme the nonhuman quasi-object with which the rebel makes common cause and that stabilises social relations becomes inexplicable or nonsensical in its own right.

The arguments and concepts that follow in the rest of this book are part of an attempt to correct that error and to propose, in contrast, a politics beyond critique. This will be done by exploring and emphasising the role played by quasi-objects, fetish objects and archaic elements in different instances of rebellion, virtual – as in the case of the art-objects, films and musics evoked at the beginning of this introduction and elaborated upon in Chapters 1, 2, 6, 7, 8 and 9 below – or actual, as in the case of Ernesto Guevara and the Cuban revolution (and the allusion to contemporary Latin America) considered in the final chapter. As the case of Guevara suggests, rebels typically go on asserting the existence of some postulate, a political quasi-object such as a universal equality principle or 'new man' (that was Guevara's case) whose genealogy could not be traced back to the range of possibilities present in the previous situation and could not have been the object of a forecast, a risk-management strategy, prevention or precaution. Then, they explore the consequences that follow by proving the strength of the principle and its applicability in the face of unexpected and decisive events in the future, and establishing a method or a procedure, a way of moving forward, step by step, that extends the principle in the face of such uncertainties.[12]

This mode of operation is the true constant in revolutionary thought and practice. It entails a dynamic connection between rebellion and constitution, against the mainstream view according to which these are the two opposite terms of a linear temporal and conceptual sequence. In the latter case, as Michael Hardt says: 'rebellion is necessary to overthrow the old regime, but when it falls and the new government is formed, rebellion must cease'

(2007: xii). In contrast to this view, we must acknowledge that in fact rebellion never ceases; it returns. As Hardt (2007: xiii–xv) points out, rebellion is not just a matter of correcting the wrongs committed by the previous government, and thus neither a single event that breaks up with the past nor merely the destruction of the old regime in the name of a just one to come, but rather, the continuous, incessant reopening of the political vis-à-vis all attempts to establish politics as a fully constituted power. Revolution is infinite, in the sense that it opposes the eternal return of the rebel to the constant condition of deferral that is intrinsic to politics.

Politics, government, is not about getting things done; it is about the promise of getting certain things done and preventing others from occurring. In our times, such promises and cautions are commonly uttered in the language of rights (Douzinas, 2007). Government today is about granting rights to some and taking them from others, but what is crucial about this is to understand that both the granting of rights and the taking of them are part of the same structure of exception, the time of deferral, a game of expectations in which normality means the death of public liberty: to acquiesce to what there is in abject passivity.

To play with the rules, by following or breaking them, and being 'realistic' or pragmatic about what there is, is the sort of attitude that most modern governments celebrate. They seek a public that is participatory only at the level of consultation and the formation of contingent networks of like-minded people 'who communicate for common purposes but then withdraw when their personal goals have been achieved' (Forman, 2002: 339). Government understood in this way is about the management of expectations and risks, which are both produced and located in the sphere of the merely possible. Soon enough, this state of affairs stifles public life, which gets reduced to such practices as poll-answering, focus group-gathering, and the legitimating of authority through banal electoral mechanisms. The metaphysics that underlies such practices is one of normal progress within a linear sequence, 'in which time bifurcates into a series of successive branches, the actual world constituting one path among these' (Dupuy, 2004: 28).

Against the normality of that condition, revolutionaries of all times have stressed the need for periodic rebellion and participatory self-rule: 'God forbid we should ever be 20 years without such a rebellion', wrote Thomas Jefferson in response to Abigail Adams and William S. Smith's criticisms of the Shays' Rebellion in 1786, a mere decade after the Revolutionary War of Independence breaks out in North America (Jefferson, [1787] 2007: 35). Pointedly, Jefferson argued in favour of the eternal return at twenty-year intervals of both rebellion against government and the revision of the constitution, and referred to this circular movement in space and time as 'virtuous' (2007: 30, 32, 34). A virtuous circle then, a value-creative and reality-enhancing structure that becomes concrete and rooted in space, in Jefferson's system of wards or 'little republics', but also in the *comunas* of the rebellious Communards of 1800s New Granada, as well as in the *altepetl*, the *ayllú*-system, and the loop-form of projected time described by Peruvian writer Waman Puma in what is probably the first radical political proposal of the modern/colonial world, contained in his seventeenth-century tract *Nueva Corónica y Buen Gobierno* [1615] (1993).

In spite of their differences, both Jefferson and Puma de Ayala were writing their proposals from within a society based upon an economy of gift and exchanges, at a time when that economy was in the process of being interrupted by the emergence of a single point of accumulation of economic goods and political power: the colonial matrix of capitalism, if you like. In both cases, the emergence of that single point was perceived as a misfortune, a catastrophe that had occurred already. The name for it was 'empire'. With empire, with misfortune, comes voluntary servitude where once was freedom. Prince, king, despot or tyrant, the one who exercises power and monopolises force 'desires only the unanimous obedience of its subjects. The latter respond to his expectation, they bring into being his desire for power, not because of the terror that he would inspire in them, but because, by obeying, they bring into being their own desire for submission,' as Pierre Clastres so clearly puts it (1994: 104).

Divided between the dominating and the dominated (along axes of race, space and gender), the aim of these societies is to endure, to defer the end that would be brought about by the excluded memory of freedom and friendship, in a word, by envy. But envy is internal to this society and the key to its endurance: it becomes concrete in the disdain felt by those who command for those who obey, and the reciprocal love of the dominated towards those who dominate, and in particular the love for the king or the despot, and the love for the law. As Clastres explains, 'this love of the subjects for the master equally denatures the relations between subjects' (1994: 103–4) so that a new rule governs society: insufficient love is a transgression of the law. 'All watch out for the respect of the law, all hold their neighbour in esteem only out of fidelity to the law. The love of the law – the fear of freedom – makes each subject an accomplice of the Prince: obedience to the tyrant excludes friendship between subjects' (ibid.). Individual desire is merely the obverse of envy, which threatens society with the spectre of a total war that in fact will never come, thereby guaranteeing the endurance of society.

What then of these anti-imperialist rebellions? They could only have been perceived as an infinite threat, the highest crime and the greatest terror. People such as Jefferson and Puma de Ayala choose the end, rather than the deferral of the end, in the belief that society could reassemble as a (composite) whole in friendship, the solidarity of equals. But what could be the basis of such a belief, once the memory of freedom has been excluded and people desire their own submission? Only the negation of love for the big Other, the Prince or the Tyrant, the denial of his claim to love and possession. This is why the second part of Puma de Ayala's tract, titled 'Good Government', while on the one hand seems to accept the moral justification of the invasion as provided by the invaders themselves, on the other hand emphasises the specific fact of the donation, the gift of the Tawantisuyu (the Andean common) to the King of Spain. The key to understanding the significance of this gesture is to acknowledge that a 'donation' functions in an economy of exchanges in a way that denies the Andes were conquered in a just war (in accordance to the legal/theological categories of the times) and at the same time establishes an infinite debt on the part of the King towards his newly acquired subjects, given the surplus of this gift in relation to any possible countergift. As a result, the key to 'good government' is the recognition that the King is infinitely indebted to his subjects, and thus, infinitely less powerful than them.

In this way, an egalitarian circuit of exchanges is re-established which differs from the simple reciprocity that characterises envious relations (and vicious circles) measured by the quantitative equivalence of goods. The exchange referred to by Waman Puma de Ayala takes place in a fundamentally agonistic context in which the first concern is to create an infinite debt with the party who is receiving the gift. However, paradoxically, as anthropologist José Gil observes: 'it is the context that produces the equality of exchanges and, initially, the equality of the right to take out debts; then the circuit of debts – which began in one generation and cannot be closed except in a subsequent one, to begin again on a new footing and so on – denies the accumulation of goods, [and] disallows potency to found itself on such an accumulation' (1998: 270–1).

Can we not take Jefferson's proposal on the return of rebellion and the revision of the constitution by subsequent generations as, precisely, the establishment of an egalitarian circuit of exchanges, different from mere reciprocity and envy, in which the circuit of debts denies the accumulation of goods (and the potency of any despot) in the right to write them off, to bring closure to the circuit in order to begin again on a new footing?

Understood in this way, the aim of these radical proposals, between rebellion and constitution, is pretty clear: to learn to rule ourselves without a master. This proposal entails careful attention to what can be termed 'popular education', or more precisely, to the process through which the people constitute themselves as such: since it would be naïve to conceive that a multitude or a series, with a plurality of aims and desires, will be immediately and spontaneously transformed into a collective or a group after the rebellious event, such a transformation entails a constructive process (Hardt, 2007: xviii–xx). At stake in this constructive process is the enactment of a world, and thereby the very existence of the collective as such.

This constructive process requires the establishment of a new order of counting and a new space, the true discovery of a new world, with its own axioms and prescriptions, which declares that the previous order of oppositions, partitions and classifications has prematurely certified its place as division, and discovers what marks that space as the territory of a withdrawal: a gift, a donation, an object. In an organisation that is based upon reciprocity, substitution and redistribution, as was the case of the organisations that Jefferson and Puma write about, the gift brings forth a relationship (political, legal) that is altogether different from that of conquest, equivalent exchange or plain resistance.

In the case of Puma, in the 1600s, this also implied the projection of a utopia in Lascasian terms, a new discursive order which took into account the Andeans as much as the Europeans. Thomas Jefferson and Waman Puma concede that the series as it exists must be transformed, that it must 'recover' its memory. The point is not the recovery of a past long gone, or its idealisation. In short, this is a form of self-subversion that is at the same time a form of self-transcendence.

In contrast to what sociologists and naturalists believe, rebels do not invoke objectivity, what there is, by invoking the fight, the actualisation of some inherent potentiality. Similarly, this book does not invoke 'law and order' by speaking of rebellion as that which fights it. Rather, it places the object at the centre of politics and then explores what follows from the observable fact that the centre just so happens to be located at a crossroads. If you extend a horizontal line with the realism of 'law and order' at one end and the social constructivism of the fight at the other end, you quickly realise that there is another line that traverses and shatters it because neither the natural order nor the socially fused group, play the role that is expected of them (Crawford, 2007 and Latour, 2002).

The natural sciences do not expel all obscure objects, they keep returning as remainders, and ethics and the social sciences appear increasingly powerless to confront the challenges posited by their return. What you get is the image of a crossroads or a loop, and at the very centre of it lie the obscure objects; they are there, but not in the sense of waiting 'out there' to be intended or discovered. Rather, the objects are there, gathering other elements around them and actively enacting new worlds, simulating one another and in the process resembling what our world is made of.

This entails a different kind of relation between the elements thus put together, in contrast to that described by the critical perspective. 'Gathering' is not a case of one object exerting force over another and making it change physical position or some of its features. In fact, this conception of power cannot account for gathering, and since we all know that gathering is crucial for the very establishment of anything resembling a political field, then it turns out that such a notion of power explains the political away.

The heart in the chest: structure of this book

If we want to bring the political back, we must ask what sort of relationship is referred to by the term 'gathering'. As Graham Harman (2007a) has noticed, on the footsteps of such master thinkers as Heidegger, Zubiri, Serres and Latour, this sort of questioning opens up the issue of causality and relations once more. He explains that 'causality has rarely been a genuine topic of inquiry since the seventeenth century. The supposed great debate between sceptics and transcendental philosophers is at best a yes/no dispute as to whether causal necessity exists, and in practice is just an argument over whether it can be known' (Harman, 2007a: 172). His point is well taken: the current debates on causality remain preoccupied with the relational gap between social man and nature (even if only to deny such a gap, as he observes) and in that sense, the reopening of the issue of causality and relation means moving beyond critique and its key distinction between the internal and the external aspect, people and everything else out there, and the bifurcating image of the world. To do this, another conception of objectivity and reality is required.

The book starts by introducing and explaining some of the basic notions underlying this alternative conception. Chapter 1 starts at the crossroads, rejecting the mainstream conception of the present dominant since at least the seventeenth century, which owes so much to the belief in progress writ large, in order to prepare the terrain for the uncanny return of archaic objects in modernity. According to such a belief, the near-spontaneous convergence between scientific and technological innovation on the one hand, and ethical maturity on the other, would prevent us from descending into a situation of almost perpetual war over natural and other 'scarce' resources. Not only do people increasingly question whether or not such a belief in spontaneous convergence corresponds to reality or is just bad fiction but, moreover, *we find ourselves in a situation of almost perpetual warfare.* Any notion of the present worthy of the name can serve as a starting point only if it includes within itself these doubts and the factuality of war, religion and empire that haunts the triumph of the project of Enlightenment, rather than adjudicating against them as mere relics of the past.

The notion of the present established as a starting point in that chapter originates in the work of a number of researchers, most of them based in the so-called 'Global South', that gather together under the banner of the modern/colonial project and the decolonising turn in the humanities and the social sciences. To present a moderately adequate introduction to the work of this group, little known outside the political battlefields of the South, particularly in Latin America and the World Social Forum (although some of its participants are well known in Euro-American circles[13]) would go beyond the scope of this book.[14] For now it will suffice to say that they seek to engage with the current phase of neoliberal globalisation that involves a significant reordering and reorganisation of geo-historical units, which in their view recasts the centrality of the internal/external, West/other oppositions in a way that not only obscures their mutual constitution, but also reinstates the critical viewpoint that separates 'culture' from 'nature' and asserts the primacy of time over space as the transcendental ground of objective knowledge. This separation, it is argued, 'has the effect of producing images of society cut off from their material environments ... takes for granted the natural world upon which societies depend' and, crucially, limits the theorisation of nature and quasi-objects such as land or oil in the discussion of capitalism (Coronil, 2000a: 354).

While ongoing work in the Sartre/Serres/Latour/Badiou tradition in Europe seeks to reintroduce quasi-objects such as mathematical and political objects in order to reopen the debates on causality and relation at the level of substance/ontology, their politicised colleagues down South, together with the social actors that make common cause with the objects themselves, reintroduce quasi-objects such as land, oil and space, in order to reopen the debates on separation, division and communication at the level of culture/ontology. This may go some way to explain their differences in style: the former approach from the side of the 'hard' sciences while the latter do so from the 'softer' side of the sciences, surely an effect of geopolitics and transnational division of labour. However, it is a methodological contention of this book that the two converge, perhaps surprisingly for both camps, on an object-oriented philosophy that seems to push the boundaries of critique, traverses predominant culturalism, and obliterates the modernity divide without lapsing into anti-modernism or aloof disengagement. They are both in fact (politically) engaged approaches, and in the case of the Latin American side, very much involved in actual processes of rebellion and radical political transformation.

This is not to say that there are no interesting contributions in mathematics and the hard sciences, relevant to our endeavour, on the Latin American side. It is not to say that Northern Europeans and Americans invest little energy in politics and the understanding of culture. Examples of the contrary abound, and they are extremely relevant to the aims of this book: Francisco Varela on self-reflexivity, neuroscientist Rodolfo Llinás on anticipation, anthropologist Arturo Escobar on self-organisation and networks, Michael Taussig on fetishes, Bruno Latour and Slavoj Žižek on quasi- and 'ticklish' objects. Rather, it is to point out that in spite of mutual, sometimes studied indifference, productive engagement takes place on a scale that remains unacknowledged.

One example of such an engagement is the dialogue that took place in 1978 between two Colombian philosophers, Bruno Mazzoldi and Freddy Téllez, and the French/Algerian deconstructivist Jacques Derrida. The dialogue, which remained unpublished until 2007 when it was finally included in the issue of *Critical Inquiry* dedicated to the latter, versed on the subject of archaic objects and something called 'the thought of the remainder'. Those of us who knew about the dialogue before its publication were certain of its importance for both parties and for philosophy in general. In that encounter the participants speculate on the nature of modernity and point out that such an experience, both as mastery and enlightenment, produces a sort of leftover or 'remainder' that does not manage to reassemble itself completely (Mazzoldi and Téllez: 2007). Its self-referential structure seems to remain incomplete, interrupted by the return of that residue or remainder. They propose that in spite of the fact that such a residue is often discounted as a result of the operation of modernity, a calculus or division, it cannot be set aside and must be counted in. They suggest that the 'incompleteness' highlighted in different ways by many observers of modernity (for instance the incompleteness of the project of enlightenment, but also, of the project of decolonisation, as any reader of Franz Fanon would know) should be understood from this wider perspective that calls for a different form of calculus. This they refer to as a 'thought of the remainder'.

They question how to think of this leftover that is thoroughly modern, and yet, seemingly returns as an archaic experience, ancient and immemorial, beyond the bounds of (transcendental) experience, and offer what looks like the beginning of an answer in the form of a detailed examination of what returns, not as an experience but rather as an object: the archaic object. The participants in the dialogue conclude that in such an examination we must go beyond the substantialism of naïve realists or naturalists and the celebration of entified change that is commonly associated with constructivists and postmodernism writ large.

Not only does this dialogue offer the chance for a radically different interpretation of the work of those involved in it, more often than not mistaken as yet another variety of postmodernism writ large, but also, and perhaps much more important, it opens up the gates to a whole series of questions concerning the very core of criticism and modern philosophy as such, in the guise of the enigma posited by so-called archaic objects. More recently, French philosopher Quentin Meillassoux (2006) did just that: taking the banner of archaic objects, which he calls 'arche-fossil', a material indicating traces of archaic phenomena previous to history, as in the case of pre-Columbian objects such as those referred to by Mazzoldi in the dialogue (interestingly, Meillassoux's father is a well-known anthropologist), or even previous to life, as in the case of cosmological objects such as dark matter or the ancestral statements produced by natural science (these are the examples offered by Meilassoux), he mounts a fierce attack on the whole of post-Kantian philosophy.

Chapter 1 charters the consequences of Mazzoldi's postulation of archaic objects, which he refers to as the terms 'charm', 'fetish' and 'remainder' (in relation to pre-Columbian magical objects 'found' in contemporary art) and, together with Jacques Derrida, their call for a thought of the remainder as a 'thought of superstition' from aesthetics to ontology and back. The chapter places an emphasis, already present in Mazzoldi and Derrida's call, on the fact that such a thought of superstition also involves a thought of rebellion (the return of indigenous rebellion observable in Bolivia and the other Andean countries, in the case of Mazzoldi; *restance*, in Derridian parlance) that is crucial for the reasoning of a politics beyond critique. This 'thought of superstition', which can be understood for now as an aestheticised ontology or 'aesthetics as first philosophy', in a sense that invites comparison with the more recent work of Heideggerian philosopher Graham Harman (2007b), is given form through the development of a series of concepts such as world, function, projection, simulation and contagion. These concepts appear to be basic for the model of power – causality, communication and relations – put forward as an alternative to the model of critique – penetration, occupation, and judgement – in the conclusive part of the chapter.

The reader must remain alert to the connotations of the term 'uncanny' in relation to obscure objects and rebellious archaic practices that return and interrupt the flow of change (the time of the present), suggested early on in Chapter 1 and present throughout Chapters 2, 3 and 4 but made explicit, as part and parcel of a theoretical framework modelled upon Freudo-Lacanian psychoanalysis, only in Chapters 5–10. The propedeutic work undertaken in Chapters 1–4 is necessary for the different strands of the discussion to proceed in more or less orderly manner and gather together in Chapters 5–10. This work is more conceptual in nature and some readers may be put off by the flight to such levels of abstraction. However, let me assure such readers that the journey will be rewarding and quite pleasurable.

Chapter 2 focuses on the alternative model of power as exemplarity and the notion of transition, transference or responsiveness that is central to it. Some readers may recognise the origins and development of this notion in the fields of Hegelian logic, psychoanalysis and critical legal and political theory. In the latter field the notion has been developed further in the work of people such as Costas Douzinas and Peter Fitzpatrick of Birkbeck Law School and the Birkbeck Institute for the Humanities, in London. They both use psychoanalysis and continental philosophy in their approaches, and the former, in particular, moves in the vicinity of Slavoj Žižek's decisive contribution to cultural criticism and philosophy, half-way in between Lacanian psychonalysis and Hegelian logic.

What is most decisive in these contributions is the linkage between self-reflexivity and the (Hegelian) logic of abstraction or postulation, which has become evident and observable in popular culture (cinema and music) and the sciences (psychoanalysis, cognitive science), and the notion of a decisive cut or 'responsiveness' to what lies beyond the limits of established conceptual and practical apparatuses such as law and human rights (particularly in relation to the political question of collective self-legislation). As the chapter suggests, via an exploration that proposes to bring these developments back to their origins in Francisco Varela's work on self-organising entities, human and nonhuman, and forwards, towards the continuity between humans and nonhumans posited by Jean-Paul Sartre's phenomenology of necessity and contingency, 'responsiveness' means not some sort of moral commitment in the face of the ineffable other, a philosophy of the limit, but rather the opposite: the cut, the decisive transition beyond the limits, the crossing of boundaries and the formation of radically new 'evental' bodies and collectives. The latter entails the radical and violent reorganisation of all things, a new way of counting inaugurated by the transition of the postulated quasi-object or the fetish, to use Mazzoldi's terms, unaccounted for in the previous organisation. The spirit of reason, to go beyond the limits set to abstraction by the understanding, shines once more: a rebellious spirit for which, following transition things are not just as before. Violence and cut, the markers of things that are not just as before, are posited as the two aspects of the object of a thought of the remainder, the fetish or obscure object, as a thought of superstition, unrestricted abstraction or transition. Finally, this understanding of transition is associated in this chapter, first, with the notion of the 'breakdown' of a system introduced by the enactive viewpoint in the cognitive sciences (and in more general terms with the notion of 'catastrophe'), and second, with the idea of the necessity of contingency developed in phenomenology by Jean-Paul Sartre.

Chapters 3 and 4 further develop the two aspects of the object of a thought of the remainder, and the implications that follow for a politics beyond critique. The tone of these chapters is less abstract, closer to the more concrete approach of the social sciences, particularly anthropology, economics, law and politics. That obscure object of critique known as the fetish exemplifies quasi-objects. The two aspects of the fetish are examined through an investigation of the origins of the term in the rebellious Caribbean of the seventeenth and eighteenth centuries, the fetish-object of West African and Caribbean religious and revolutionary political practices, and its transition into the language of criticism in Feuerbach and Marx via earlier anthropological accounts, legal analysis and comparative religious studies. The examination of the two aspects of the fetish proceeds in Chapter 3 as a plea for a renewed form of materialist realism. While the main aim of this chapter is to sketch an outline of what that form of realism would be like, a sort of sublime fetishism or form-materialism, the next one explores its early presence and implications in the thought and politics of a young and haunted Karl Marx.

This paves the way for what are perhaps the pivotal chapters of this book. Chapters 5 and 6 develop further this most sublime of fetishisms and constitute in that sense the book's heart in the chest, to employ a reference that will become clearer to the reader soon enough unless, like me, she is also a cinema buff with a soft spot for Hollywood blockbusters and perverse art. The chapters start by linking the earlier reading of Marx's (and Feuerbach's) sublime fetishism, its two aspects, with the question of the double and the death-drive, the will to destruction that is also the will to immortality, postulated by Sigmund Freud in his 1919 essay on the uncanny and developed further by Jacques Lacan's notion of the primordial mother/child dyad. The key concepts of proximity and substitution are then introduced to the attention of the reader and elaborated as a more or less natural follow-up to the discussion of the fetish. These chapters bring together some of the themes discussed already in the form of a 'Mexican standoff', or more precisely, its Hollywood version. The question of the double and the death-drive is exemplified through a discussion of *Pirates of the Caribbean* and its sequel *Dead Man's Chest*, in which psychoanalytical theory and the principle of substitution are linked to instances of rebellion, violence, horror, sensuality, fascination and the standpoint of philosophy, art and politics beyond critique.

Chapter 7, aptly titled 'Horror in philosophy', starts with a nightmare and ends with a vision. Between the philosophical horror of inconsistency and the infinite multiplication of entities, acted out as necessity, on the one hand, and the politics of visionary speculation, or contingency, on the other, the chapter elaborates a metaphysics of time as self-transcendent circularity that owes everything to the notion of objectivity developed by phenomenologists during the twentieth century, but could also be traced back to the uncanny political writings of seventeenth-century Peruvian Waman Puma de Ayala. The point of this notion is the continuity between time and matter, and the series and the group as forms of gathering or organising a collective in space. The Sartrean concepts of 'nothing' and 'cut', as applied to self-reflexive structures, become here the springboard to launch a rebellious politics of visionary speculation, a politics beyond critique, ready to face the challenges of the twenty-first century: object-oriented, anticipatory rather than preventive or precautionary, realist or form-materialist. The consequences of such form-materialist realism in ontology, and in the field of knowledge comprised by economics and the study of laws, natural and social, are then charted in Chapter 8 and brought to a conclusion in the final two chapters of the book. The latter focus on concrete instances of radical choice and rebellion: the temporary autonomous zone in the case of Hakim Bey and others working in the interface between contemporary music, electronic technologies and 'anarchist' politics, and revolution in the case of Ernesto Guevara. The conclusion doubles up as a call and an opening: rip it up and start again.

Notes

1 See on this Weber (1954). All paraphrases and quotes taken from Lacey (2004: Part III, Chapter 9). For her controversial and significant insight into the influence of Weber's sociological thought on H. L. A. Hart's account of the internal aspect of rules, decisive on today's predominant conception of the law, plus evidence, see pp. 30–1.
2 The reference here is to critical varieties of naturalist scientific realism. See on anarchic naturalism: Feyerabend (1993). On the sociologically informed version: Bloor (1991) and Winch (1990). For Winch's influence on Hart's concept of law see Lacey (2004: 230). For social constructivism see Luckmann and Berger (1966).
3 See on this, Ellacuría (1990) and Dussel (2001a). For a general introduction to liberation philosophy in the context of Latin American philosophy, see Dussel (2003: 11–53). For Zubiri's metaphysics and his philosophy of mathematics: Zubiri (1999: 155 ff.).
4 See Badiou (2007b: 37).
5 For the various connotations of the term creature (*kreatur*, *creatura*, nature) in connection to the argument advanced in this book, see Benjamin (1985), Wiebering (1971: I, 204–II) and Hanssen (1998: 105).
6 The active self-positing of an outsider upon some artefact that is considered 'other' is, of course, the very definition of objectivity in most of our mainstream research practices. Take for instance socio-cultural research: how should we study a culture? From what standpoint should we approach cultural artefacts, icons, beliefs and practices? More often than not, scholars turn to the study of 'other' cultures with the methodological assumption that it is best to approach the understanding of a certain tradition 'from the outside in' (Murphy, 1994: 1). For this reference and an argument in favour of 'insider' methodological approaches, see Abímbólá (2006: 25–6). For examples of such 'insider' approaches in socio-cultural research, such as transculturation (Ortiz, 1995) or *antropofagia* (de Andrade, [1928] 1981) or what sociologist Ramón Grosfoguel would call 'situated' knowledge, see Castro-Klarén (2000: 295–322), Grosfoguel (2000: 347–74) and Grosfoguel and Cervantes-Rodríguez 2002: xi–xxix).
7 See, on vicarious causation, Harman (2007a).
8 See Girard (2003: 78–9).
9 On Kidner, see Pratt (2007: 113–24). On Salcedo, see Cerón (2007: 53–7). On Londoño and Salcedo, see Guardiola-Rivera (2007b: 59–65).
10 Kurt Gödel's incompleteness theorem is derived in classical logic for formal theories featuring consistency and containing some arithmetic. The first theorem establishes that there is a sentence in the language of the theory in question that is neither provable nor refutable in that theory. This obscure element or result is thus posited as 'undecidable'. Roughly, an undecidable is a sentence that says of itself that it is unprovable. In other words, the phenomenon present here is one of referential circularity, a self-reflexive and self-subversive structure. The second incompleteness theorem shows that the consistency of the logical system cannot be proved within the system. The surprising result of the two theorems is that a certain proposition is provable within the system for each and every natural number but is neither provable nor disprovable for the totality of all natural numbers. In this interpretation of incompleteness totalities need not be banned, and the connection between 'totalities' and 'totalitarianism', assumed by many to be of political importance, is severed since the notion of a vicious circularity or 'closed totality' can be dropped in favour of the notion of transition or alteration – passing from a predicate or a concept to its extension for the

purposes of constructing an object with reality of its own or *postulation*. Such 'surprises' keep turning up everywhere in the sciences, from mathematics to biology and cognitive sciences (e.g. the work of people such as Francisco Varela and Rodolfo Llinás) to political philosophy (e.g. Jean-Pierre Dupuy's enlightened catasthrophism). In this book, such surprising elements will be termed 'in-closure structures' and associated with so-called quasi-objects. See Díaz Muñoz (2000: 7–28). See also note below.
11 See Kerruish (2006: 57).
12 Guevara [1965] (1997: 197–214). See on these political quasi-objects, that the author terms 'prescriptions', Hallward (2005b). See also Fowler (2002). The decisive and most original development of a political framework along these lines remains that of Ignacio Ellacuría in El Salvador; see Ellacuría (1990). See also, this time in the post-Heideggerian spirit of Levinas, Dussel (2001b).
13 For instance, in sociology and socio-legal studies, such as Boaventura de Sousa Santos; world-systems theory, anthropology and global studies, such as Fernando Coronil, Aníbal Quijano and Ramón Grosfoguel (who have collaborated with Immanuel Wallerstein), Walter Mignolo or Arturo Escobar; and even in their engagements with European philosophy as in the case of Enrique Dussel.
14 The interested reader will find some of their seminal work in the issues of the journal *Nepantla. Views From South,* published by Duke University from 2000 onwards under the direction of Walter Mignolo, Alberto Moreiras and Gabriella Nouzeilles. Among its associate editors there are some recognisable names in the fields of cultural criticism and political philosophy such as Fredric Jameson and Michael Hardt. A contemporary appraisal of the group's work is available in the 2007 issue of the journal *Cultural Studies* (vol. 21, issues 1 and 2; General Editor Larry Grossberg) put together by Mignolo and Escobar under the heading 'Globalization and the De-colonial Option'.

Chapter 1

Archaic objects

This book concerns the nature and behaviour of an archaic category of elements called quasi- or obscure objects. These objects are contradictory, in that they seem to enter into and withdraw from all relations, particularly from relations with us. They can be neither described as simple and localisable particles or events, nor as fully substantive and autonomous totalities standing side by side other fully autonomous totalities, which are the way they appear to us.

Rebels are one example of this peculiar nature: they cut off all links and escape from all given relations. But let us not forget that their 'subjective' experience is entangled with the ability of objects to move in and out of relations from the very outset. There would be no Butch Cassidy and the Sundance Kid without their guns and bullets; and there would be no Che Guevara without the beret, the star or the Havana cigar, and perhaps more important, certainly not without the famous photograph. At some point, sooner rather than later, the objects take centre stage. This has implications for political philosophy and legal theory, disciplines that for the most part seem to assume a human-centred universe, which have been hitherto ignored or only partially explored.

According to this book, the most important philosophical implication is that substantialist realism, the view that objects are out there for us, and constructivist subjectivism, the accompanying view that rejects the existence of something in itself corresponding to something for us, cannot account for the form of reality of these objects.

Given the centrality of these objects for science (wave-functions, dark matter) but also for law and politics (guns, berets and stars, but also declarations, prescriptions and constitutions), the fact that criticism cannot account for their reality would entail that the realm of politics gets reduced considerably (mostly, to self-positing rules, adjudication, precaution and prevention). This is no abstract matter, in the pejorative sense of the term, for in fact we live in such a reduced world, and perhaps our inability to bring back the belief in a dream of freedom, an assertion of the reality and importance of anticipating the future, and in reaction to that, the convergence between abject passivity and violent acting out that has become the predominant feature of our daily lives, are but a symptom warning us about the perils of such reductionism.

Against such a reduced view of the world in general and the political world in particular, this book seeks to explore the political significance of obscure objects and rebellious elements. These elements, all or most of them related to radical experiences and attachments, from the pressures of non-locality and global warming to war and revolution, will become evident to the reader soon enough. They circulate and communicate in ways that no talk of globalisation could ever dream of; later on we will use the term 'contagion' in order to refer to their manner of circulation. In fact, they will become so ubiquitous that the reader may be forgiven if she concludes that this is not a specific category that refers to some special kind of objects, but rather that there are only obscure elements and quasi-objects, and that the dream of freedom is not as unreal as it seems in the present situation.[1]

For now, since one of the claims of this book is to be a relevant guide to the present situation, it would be best to start by clarifying what is meant here by 'the present'. This will prepare the stage for the re-entry of powerful objects, and will help us to explain in what precise sense they can be called powerful. After doing that, we will return to the question of the nature of relations and to the contradictory role that objects play in the formation of radical attachments. Hopefully, by then, the connection between the two topics will not be lost for the reader.

That connection is central to an idea of freedom that seems to have slipped out of view in recent times, replaced by a much reduced notion of freedom as choice that has become central to our belief in unfettered progress, both scientific–technological and moral/ethical. That notion of freedom as choice between open possibilities predominates not only in law and economics but also, with particular force, in politics, art and the observation of technology. It is perhaps 'the real' of our culture. True, people nowadays ask whether technology is out of control, 'a runaway train without steering and aim' (Kaiser, 2006: 1), whether our science no longer feels commitment to serve the public good but has become enslaved to powerful interests, and whether or not 'innovation', the drive to permanent self-enhancement and constant renewal that motivates such interests, has lost sight of solidarity and neglected the challenge of socially desirable ends. Amidst this questioning has emerged a cry for the development of 'the right moral attitudes and instruments to manage the risks' (Kaiser, 2006: 2) posited by science, technology and the drive to constant and unfettered renewal. However, this precautionary position seems powerless when confronted by the question of the drive itself and its connection with a notion of freedom as pure unleashed productivity outside the frame of the present that is, nevertheless, inherent to the present itself.

As an attempt to question this state of things, the present will be described here as modern/colonial in spite of its faith in unfettered progress or perhaps *because* of it. In this situation, a dimension of coloniality – religion, magic, superstition, empire – haunts the very triumph of the project of Enlightenment.[2] On the one hand, what is properly 'modern' is the widespread belief that through our actions and decisions we become masters of our own destiny; according to this belief, the aim of our existence is to live and die in our own fashion, following our own enlightened designs for progress. However, on the other hand, the experience of modernity – both as mastery and enlightenment – produced and continues to produce a sort of remainder or leftover that does not manage to gather itself back (Mazzoldi and Téllez, 2007: 367), to reassemble itself completely.[3]

How to think of this leftover that is thoroughly modern, and yet seemingly returns as an archaic experience, ancient and immemorial, as what is brought back from the past or from colonial and imperialist adventures?[4] Philosopher Bruno Mazzoldi introduced this question in an early dialogue with Jacques Derrida and Freddy Téllez on the subject of images, words and powerful objects (Mazzoldi and Téllez, 2007: 372). In the remainder of this chapter, let us engage with this question of the archaic object and the consequences of that question in relation to the real of the present and reality as such.

Archaic and obscure objects: Tlingit coffins, Peruvian stones and French paintings

The initial subject of the exchange between the Colombian philosophers and Derrida was a 1978 exhibition by French artist Gérard Titus-Carmel titled *The Pocket-Size Tlingit Coffin et les 61 premiers dessins qui s'ensuivrent*, and the accompanying text put together by the French/Algerian thinker, *Gérard Titus-Carmel: 'The Pocket-Size Tlingit Coffin' illustré de 'Cartouches' par Jacques Derrida*.[5]

Titus-Carmel's work is, as Andrew Weiner and Sonja Hansard-Weiner (1992) point out, 'utterly fascinating and just a bit disturbing: to be forced to see these "made-up objects", with such an intensity and so convincingly present is to forget Magritte's injunction ("Ceci n'est pas une pipe")'. As they suggest, Titus-Carmel's work reflects upon one of the problems that is essential for art and metaphysics: that of the relationship between original and copy, nature and artifice, absence and presence. Moreover, he introduces a non-representational twist to the study of this relation. In his *Suites* (Titus-Carmel tends to work in series) the artist begins with an 'archaic' model (Tlingit coffins, Narwa objects, ancient Peruvian stones)[6] and draws a sketch. From this loosely drawn 'original', he then makes a three-dimensional model. This in turn, becomes the subject of a series of carefully rendered drawings (127, in the Tlingit coffin series). Sometimes the three-dimensional model is destroyed, other times it is abandoned. We are left looking from the first drawing to its descendants at two, three, or one hundred and twenty-seven removes. For the spectator it is a question of counting and, if she wishes, tracing each consecutive drawing to its absent parent(s), missing but fascinating.

The drawings are outlines, in the sense of having the force of the stroke. Their aim is not to reproduce or serve as stand-ins for the original, but rather to trace or draw a line on the same model. They suggest a quest for origins, with a twist: the original has been smashed. The 'archaic' is gone and yet it remains fascinating. Like native rituals to the anthropologist, fossil records and found objects to archaeologists and sound artists, uncanny experiences to psychoanalysts, and very old 'made-up' texts to religious and legal interpreters. The question is: what does this absent presence say to us? To sum up, the dialogue between these philosophers takes on a very old debate: that of the relationship between words and images, absence and presence, form and matter. In more general terms, this is a dialogue on the nature of cause and relation. As we will see, this debate has had profound consequences in 'Western' (and non-Western) cultures, from art and religion to law and the sciences. It still rages on.

It is important to point out that the Tlingit referred to in the exhibition's title are an American Native people who speculate that the fundamental insight about the world is its ambiguous duality between superficial presence and hidden or absent depth. Their objects – like the coffin 'found' and 'made-up' by Titus-Carmel – are meant to stabilise relations between what is absent and what is present. Gérard Titus-Carmel came back to this question of fundamental duality, in relation to non-representational ancient Peruvian stones and objects, in his 1984 *Suite Chancay* series. 'Presented as a series of permutations based upon motifs from a lost Peruvian civilization, we find not a bit of statue, a fragment of axe, but an invitation to pass beyond' (Weiner and Hansard-Weiner, 1992: 4), like Orpheus's passage through the surface or Cocteau's watery mirror, themselves reflected in the liquid mirror scene of *The Matrix*. These objects – the statue, the axe, the mirror – are charms, fetishes, and their magical allure invites us to seek more basic realities once 'reality' has been reduced to only the void in which all things began. This involves an assertion of hope and boundary-crossing, of rebellion and passage (Mazzoldi and Téllez, 2007: 374).

Similarly, Mazzoldi argues in the dialogue that magic (by which he means the connective power associated to charms and powerful objects such as fetishes in 'pre-modern' societies, but also to the 'made and found' artworks based on archaic objects that were the subject of the dialogue) is a leftover from the experience of Enlightenment that needs to be explored in its own right:

> I'm going to say that this body of the *revenant*, what remains, what cannot be gathered back, and this thought of the remains, it could also be defined as a thought of superstition.
>
> (Mazzoldi and Téllez, 2007: 372)

He then goes on to explain that although magic has been displaced by other beliefs and practices in modernity such as law, normative religion and techno-science, and has thus become secondary in relation to them, it may still play a central role in the understanding of radical attachments, affects and actions – from the experience of the spectator of the arts to envy, theft, violence and rebellion.

He calls for a thought of the remainder, a careful consideration of the role played by objects in radical attachments, as a means to clarify the nature of such relations and perhaps also relationality as such. As Mazzoldi suggests, the aim of this focused attention upon objects themselves, rather than just objects for us (as in traditional phenomenology) would be to develop a way of thinking what remains in a different manner: neither as mere residue, the result of our operations of division and calculation which does not count and has no effects, nor in terms of a presence that remains permanent in spite of apparent modification. In more general terms, the issue at stake in this shift from phenomena to objects is that of causality and relation and the possibility of conceiving cause and relation in accordance to a different model than that of the unchanging substance and the accidental change. Therein would lie the potential for a critique of certain inadequate models of substance, but also the possibility to retrieve a repressed notion of change, revolt and resistance from within the model of substance. He elaborates thus:

> I noticed in the text that is illustrated by 'Cartouches' certain references to the charm, to the throw of luck, to something that awakens envy. The *zelōtypos* is the one who is jealous, like the spectator of Titus-Carmel's paintings, of all paintings maybe. You [Derrida] speak of the spectator precisely as someone who is jealous. 'Jealous onto madness' (. . .) But, now, the one that makes you jealous unto madness, the thing that makes you *invidus* – because *invidus* has both an active and a passive sense – that's the sorcerer. There is no way to get around this fact. Finally, the little coffin, what is it if not a magical device? So it's true, what I suspected from the first moment and also from the last is true: you [Derrida] are a magic maker. But this kind of magic never leaves reason; it is not madness. It's a way to operate, a way to get the body and the mind to function. I would like you to talk about that, precisely.
>
> (Ibid.)

Here Mazzoldi speaks of the magical device as part of the body–mind system, as 'a way to get the body and the mind to function'. The fundamental duality embodied in Tlingit objects like the coffin and Titus-Carmel's images reappears in this reference to the mind–body problem: how are these two different substances to function? How are they to connect? Is it mutual fascination with the same object? Are they there 'in order to' do something required by the object, 'for the sake of' the object, rather than the other way around? The hidden reference in this sort of talk is Heidegger's insight that all beings fall under the heading of 'equipment' (Heidegger, 1967: 105). This means to say that body and mind, for instance, are there in order to do something else but also for the sake of something else. This is to be understood not in the sense that they are inert utensils to be used, but rather, in the sense that they are plugged into one another and embedded into even remoter references. In any instant, these substances are affixed to one another in total embrace. This totality – the body–mind function – is primary and hidden from view in relation to the specific presence or presentable form of the mind and that of the body. And since this system is itself embedded into other, remoter references, ultimately it forms a primary totality that Heidegger (1967: 120) calls 'world'.[7] Function, the structure of the 'in order to' and 'for the sake of' refers to this totalising force Heidegger calls world. What emerges into view out of this world is not equipment or system, but a 'simplified' mode of the system: the mind as mind, the body as body.

The crucial point here is to understand that the body as body is not the same as the body itself, and the mind as mind is not the mind itself. Rather, the 'as' refers in these cases to a real appearance prior to any distinction between truth, semblance and falsity, or to be more precise and use the language of phenomenology, the appearance or sensual-character of reality. Put otherwise, the 'as' refers to allure and fascination (which we will later call 'reciprocal projection' or enactment), that is to say, to an aesthetic dimension that is primary or more archaic than the representational language of truth, commonality and falsity. Entities (mind, body and so on) encounter each other as appearances (appearances taken as something that is precisely the logic of magic) and never directly. Thus, in order to connect at all they need to lure each other, to invite sensual embrace. That is precisely the role of charms, images, sounds and partially apparent or quasi-objects.

How to understand appearance? The event that cuts across systemic totality (world) and allows specific entities to appear and encounter one another is one of simulation: the mind is a simulation or an idea of the body that encounters the latter and identifies its specificity only as such. In turn, the body, in its specificity, is a simulacrum of the mind–body system. In more general terms, things simulate themselves. Heidegger calls this 'the as-structure'.

It is perhaps better to understand simulation as a self-reflexive or auto-transcendent process: each entity projects itself onto a fixed point out of itself – an objectivity, let us say an image of itself – while its real self (function, totality) withdraws out of view, and encounters or identifies itself and each other only in relation to this fixed point, object or simulated image. Simulation is a process of exteriorisation; in more strict terms, it is a process of auto-exteriorisation.

The externalised image or simulated object is not merely a representation, a 'deficient' copy of the real object. We have learned this already while referring to the work of Titus-Carmel. It is not an abstract stand-in for the real object, but rather, its intermediary, a vehicle allowing it to connect with others. A simulation does not communicate with others by achieving or producing some commonality of meaning. Rather, communication between simulacra is first and foremost purely sensual, imaginative, an interplay of reciprocal projections. Simulated objects are like retroviruses, injecting back their code into everything they encounter. The proper term for this form of attachment is *contagion*, a phenomenon that is observable in biological processes (ingestion, viral infection), socio-political processes (imitation, identification, over-identification) and even inorganic processes (cellular automata).[8] Forms of contagion such as identification, 'irrational' as they may seem at first, found the stability of relations between specific terms. Contagion makes related termini similar, uniform and equal without the need for a previous community of meaning. Therefore there seems to be no reason to postulate a realm of 'meaning' – comprising dematerialised beliefs and fully meaningful commands – existing beyond and above the realm of sensuality, in order to explain collective attachments. Contagious mediation through simulacra seems to explain the formation of related collections, including social and political collectives, much better than abstract prescriptions of equality, naturalistic rights, consensus and dematerialised beliefs or languages.

The latter are, all of them, essentialised representations void of sensual character and thus incapable of galvanising attachments or totalising collectives unless they themselves become attached to (embodied in) sensual vicarious objects. In contrast, simulacra are exemplars. They are more like partial objects or partial enunciations that interpellate us, and others, without fully establishing or predetermining our responses and the consequences of such responses. They lack the certainty that is commonly associated with fully meaningful commands and precise rule-following in the more legalistic, positivistic accounts of action that make up our mainstream conceptions of collective life.

These conceptions rely upon a notion of the object that deprives it of its sensual capacities. Such notion is the result of debates concerning the nature and function of icons vis-à-vis (written and authoritatively spoken) words in early 'Western' religious contexts. It can be argued that the primacy given to the authoritative word over the icon, or in more general terms 'presence' over 'absence' in these debates, produced a 'normativist' conception of collective life that retroactively transformed (and/or actively seeks to transform) non-normative, mimetic ways. Following Costas Douzinas and

Pierre Legendre,[9] we shall conclude that the issue at stake in these debates was in fact the way in which the border between subjectivity and objectivity should be deployed. As a result, connection, cause and relation, were conceived solely in the model of presence to subjective consciousness, certainty and determinacy; that is to say as direct causes, contiguous connection and determinant relation. This is the model present in the notion of power now taken to be obvious: one entity (primary) exerts force over another (secondary) and makes it change position or character. As can be seen this is no small or purely abstract matter: the impact of these debates in such questions as the attachment of soul to body and subject to law, but also in the sciences, has been profound and durable.

Power: the model of penetration versus the model of exemplarity

The model for the notion of power described at the end of the previous section could be termed 'the model of penetration' because of its obvious associations with the assumed role of masculinity in sexuality: primary exercise of force provoking a change of character or position in the passive, secondary element. In contrast, the feminine model of exemplarity – which, in passing, could be traced back to Scythian and post-Socratic perspectives in classical philosophy[10] – relies upon a notion of the object as the scene of a perpetual tension between hidden reality and sensual presence, a self-transcendent presence which is itself turned asunder by another tension between totalisation and individuality or specificity. Instead of direct causes, causation is posited as always indirect; connections as sensual or vicarious; and relations as necessarily contingent.

In such a scenario, our task would be to trace simulacra back to their origin – an activity similar to that of 'remembering' or 'retrieving' in Platonic philosophy, but also, at least to some extent, in contemporary psychoanalytical accounts. But only the encounter with the charm, the sensual object in the structure of presentification (put otherwise, 'in time') can trigger such remembering – our recollection of the real object or true form, to put it in post-Socratic parlance. Interestingly, although this statement would remain in need of further consideration, one could argue that there is a structural homology between this notion of connectedness as 'remembering', the rebellious act known as 'defacing the currency' in Scythian classical philosophy (asking 'why' to the 'how' of the law, as Butch Cassidy and Sundance Kid do in the film) and modern feminism, and possibly also the practice of reverse engineering performed by contemporary punks, industrial pirates and hackers. They are all, in a sense, Mazzoldi's magic-makers.

This notion of magic-making, as the timely or sensual encounter through the charm that throws one back into being (totality, world) resonates with debates on embodiment and the relation between repetitions, images or sounds, and words in early 'Western' and non-Western religions, as said above. Key to these debates is the notion that the 'how' – procedure, usefulness, the state of things – can always be submitted to the 'why' – origin, foundations, the hidden function, totalisation – and that the latter is primary. At this point, it would be safe to define 'rebellion' precisely in this way: as the act of submitting the present state of things to the question 'why' and to hold the latter as hierarchically superior.

Put otherwise, to rebel is to point out that procedural or qualitative divisions are subordinate to total or quantitative divisions. In Sartrean parlance this means to submit the authority of the *group*, defined qualitatively, to the higher authority of the *series*, a notion that refers to counting, continuity and founding divisions. This is exactly what Mazzoldi does when he sees the remainder (the result of a division dismissed qualitatively) as rising over and above alleged 'primary' elements. His gesture is not to perform a mere reversal between the two terms of this qualitative situation, but rather, to submit the situation as a whole (the qualitative division) to the higher court of a new, founding division. The 'newness' of this division is not so much qualitative as quantitative or formal: another way of counting. Mazzoldi's call for a new 'thought of superstition' must be understood precisely in these terms: as a rallying-cry for a new way of counting, one that takes into account what before counted for nothing. This is the point where mathematics and geometry – the stars and the stone – touches the political. This point of convergence between geometry and politics was apparent to ancient eyes. It must become apparent to contemporary eyes once again.

Moreover, because the question of quality – usefulness, efficiency and the state of things – always leads to and can only be properly answered if referred back to that of hidden function and totality – quantity, there is a continuity internal to the division between the shape or state of things, what is commonly seen as materiality, on the one hand, and the totality or hidden function, what we often call the 'big picture' or the form, on the other. This gives place to a fundamental ambiguity of matter and form or 'form-materialism'. Once again, this fundamental ambiguity is common to several forms of magic-making, prophecy and revolt, but also – and this would matter for the purposes of establishing stronger links between science and ontology – in the case of numbers. Here too there is confusion between form and matter, the group and the series: for a number oscillates between being an empirical, topological or concrete object and a mere category, a class or a set of things. As John Milbank (2007: 20) observes, this confusion suggests that counting, tracing back to the 'why' and encountering entities (causes, relations) in time are all homologous: 'for in either case one claims that one can only fully describe something in terms of origin'.

However, as in the case of Titus-Carmel's paintings, here the original is not an unmoved mover, a *potentia absoluta* or a fixed background for the drama of becoming. Such a conception would subordinate the dynamics of becoming – the rift between absence and presence, totality and individuality – by reducing it to a question of shifting modalities of emphasis within an always/already synchronous system of relations. Not only does this conception not solve the tension present in each and every entity; by postulating 'being' and 'world' as a transcendental framework it also makes the quest for origins appear fallacious: the reversal of everything that has been disseminated into some otherworldly Being or *potentia absoluta* (Milbank, 2007: 21). Milbank argues in his cunningly titled *Only Theology Saves Metaphysics* that the question of the 'why' and the 'how' and remembering, in the Platonic tradition, are in fact central to realism – the materialist kernel 'saved' within theology's idealistic shell. In pages 21–2 he argues that in Augustine's version of this tradition, only recollection in time allows us to move from being as 'nihilistic dissemination' to its 'musical' integration. Let us emphasise the significance of this reference to music for the remainder of this book: the point is that the quest for origins does not mean to gather back what has been dispersed into some substantive cause. As we have learned before, what has been dispersed cannot be gathered back (Mazzoldi and Téllez, 2007: 372). Rather, it can be composed, cut or separated and then related by vicarious means. This is to say that any reverse engineering or 'quest for origins' composes the elements that hide from one another only 'indirectly', by interrupting their formal solitude and separating, slicing them in order to allow them to resonate materially, in sensual fascination with others. This is akin to the varied forms of the cut-up technique that are integral to musical and visual artistic composition. I will use the term 'cut-up' from here onwards in order to refer precisely to such strategies as techniques of (auto)transcendence of the contrast between form-category and content-matter.

The model of exemplarity focuses on techniques of (auto)transcendence of the chiasm between form-category and content-matter, and upon objects that embody such techniques; mainly sounds and images. In this case the image or sound, the simulacra, are not 'deficient' in relation to the authoritative word or absolute principle, but rather, the two of them – the simulacra and the word – are embraced in the unresolved drama of embodiment. Put otherwise, in this model the sharp Aristotelian distinction between form and matter and the primacy of efficient causality and design, human or otherwise, seem insufficient if not misguiding. This statement could be extended to the Aristotle/Leibniz/Zubiri distinction between natural simples and artificial composites. In their place we have formal systems exceeding any set of parts, always/already instances of a remainder. These formal (speculative or reflexive) systems are said to be 'excessive' in the sense that they are neither mere constructs or composites – artificial sets of parts – nor the product of design, human or otherwise. They are remainders, excessive leftovers, but not in the sense of being mere artificial residues or secondary features attached to some undeniable eternal presence. And we also have material objects that are in excess of (or at a distance from) all relations (formal totality) and specific differential contents (unique materiality), and appear as the ground of relationality as such. Faced with the set of paradoxes that result from these initial discoveries, we can expect little help from models of substance that distinguish sharply between simples and composites, since all objects seem to oscillate between simplicity and composition or, as Bernard Stiegler (1998) puts it, between the purity of nature and the originality of prosthesis.

Indeed, the objects that we have called simulacra appear from a certain perspective as mere prosthetic attachments to real objects, aiding the latter in their task of presentification. But from another perspective, these objects originate presence (by negating absence) and poke sensual holes through to other objects thereby enabling identification, specificity and wholeness. To put it in Heideggerian terms, the derivative nature of the as-structure (the sensual, accessible zone of presence) is now constitutive; but against Heidegger's post-Kantian leanings, there is no need to postulate the as-structure – this zone of sensual accessibility – as a uniquely or primary human feature. On the contrary, access and sensuality (the tense realm of presence/absence and relation/individuality that can be identified, after Harman (2007b) as the object of a 'first aesthetics') seem prior to design and classification, human or otherwise. Here we are faced with a truly 'archaic' realm.

Certainly, the alternative model advocated here is not without problems of its own. Its results are paradoxical in at least two senses. First, it suggests that all origins (constructions, compositions, collective foundations) necessitate the retroactive action of a prosthetic or simulated element that in turn is the product of the collective (projection, simulation, choice). Second, it points out that the derivative nature of projected or simulated objects is constitutive of relational wholes, while the latter are constitutive in a strong sense (the sense entailed by the term 'world').

These are serious questions and they need to be tackled. It would be foolish to claim that a final answer is provided in this book. For now it would suffice to notice that faced with these paradoxical results, a wider question arises: what is the nature of the form-materialism advocated here? So far we have learned that form-materialism attempts to account for cause and relation without conceding primacy to efficient causes or design-principles. It proposes that all causes are indirect and that all relations are contingent. Moreover, it suggests that the role of partial or quasi-objects, called here simulacra, is vital in order to stabilise these relations. It joins the call for a thought of these objects (charms, fetishes and so on), a 'thought of superstition', against inadequate models of substance and presence (including the modern emphasis on presence to consciousness), but also, against inadequate models of superstition.

One of the suspicions driving the arguments of this book is that these two models, that of the substance and that of superstition, are linked in their inadequacy. We should ask whether the primacy conceded to efficient causes and organising design-principles has functioned as some kind of self-imposed limitation that does not allow us to think the remainder (the sacred, magic) properly. We may even suggest that it is because of this self-imposed limitation that religious zealots and normative 'deciders' have occupied the place of a thought of the remainder. However, these characters are in fact unable to adjudicate on these matters. Not being able to adjudicate they merely reciprocate one another, thereby initiating a vicious circle of violence–terror that they, and us, unlike the rebel, cannot traverse. To acknowledge such suspicions would help us to enhance the sense of urgency attached to these questions, but of course, does not constitute an answer to them.[11]

To speak of 'indirect' causation helps to clarify matters a little. To use the example of the rebel – cutting all links with the collective situation and altering or founding the collective anew – allows us to bring these seemingly arcane questions closer to the issues of the day: the failure of our positivist/empiricist systems (normative, religious, scientific and social scientific, political) to deal with 'demands' that do not assume empiricist frameworks (post-colonial, decolonising, Islamist, retro-gardist and so on); the insufficiency of our right-democratic societies based upon 'thin' social bonds to adjudicate on 'thick' socio-political attachments (practices of enmity and scapegoating, discourses of belonging, radical attachment and purity) or produce some of their own; the absence in our times of the political imagination necessary to galvanise dissenting voices into an act of revolt. Once again, in no way do these strategies claim to solve the ensuing paradoxes or to provide a definitive answer to the wider questions. The claim of this book is somewhat more modest: to encounter and posit a genuine problem, a metaphysical problem that is also a problem for us in the present situation.

Notes

1 See Crawford and Latour (2007).
2 As Matthias Kaiser (2006: 1–2) correctly points out, some of the earliest and strongest proponents of the belief in progress writ large may be found among the enlightened *philosophes*; for instance Condorcet, whose *Sketch for a Historical Picture of the Progress of the Human Mind* (1795) lays down an overtly optimistic vision of the progress of man, both past and future, on the basis of a convergence between advances in science-technology and ethics-morality. See note above.
3 For the haunting presence that defines the enlightening turn from magic to reason, see Dolar (1991). For modern coloniality as a system of internal (fully present, viciously self-reflexive) relations defined by an element of exteriority, see Quijano and Wallerstein (1992). For 'magic' and the modern post-colonial state, see Taussig (1992) and Coronil (1997).

4 For the convergence between this problematic and that of the uncanny in psychoanalytical theory, see Freud [1919] (1953–74, vol. 17: 247–8). See also Lloyd Smith (1992), for this problematic in a Victorian context, and Gordon (2004: 50–8) for a more contemporary context.
5 A second version of this text appeared later in Derrida (1987/1987a: Chapter 3).
6 On non-representational ancient Peruvian stones, see Paternosto (1989). My gratitude to cinematographer Francesco Cincotta for bringing Paternosto's work to my attention.
7 'World' is the actual system of equipment, a determinate totality of things (within which we all are) hidden from view in its performance or function. For an illuminating commentary on this aspect of Heidegger's critique, which I follow in these paragraphs, see Harman (2002).
8 See on this Varela et al. (1974: 187–96), Varela and Dupuy (1992: 1–25); Dupuy (1998), Varela and Depraz (2000). See also Taussig (1992) and Mahmood (2004). Mahmood developed some related ideas, taken up in these paragraphs, in a paper delivered to the *Thematics: A Workshop series*, organised by Peter Fitzpatrick and Richard Joyce at Birkbeck Law School, University of London, 9 February 2007.
9 Douzinas and Nead (1999) and Legendre (1998, 1997).
10 Particularly among the Cynics, see Martin (1996).
11 The reader should be alert to the references in this paragraph to some of the ideas advanced by French philosopher Quentin Meillassoux (2006).

Chapter 2
Uncanny encounters

Provoked by Mazzoldi's intriguing suggestion that there is a connection between the Tlingit coffin, theft or copying,[1] and the need for a thought of superstition as the thought of the remains, Jacques Derrida draws the following conclusion in relation to his own work on phenomena, being and presence:

> What I'm trying to think, if you will, is what I call *restance*, the way of the rest, the remains. A philosophical habit [smiles] this *restance*. *Restance* is something that cannot be thought philosophically as a modification of substance, as a substance (. . .) I think that the rest or the remains have to be taken into account, but not in the form of substance. Yes, the chain: substance, presence, permanence, essence, and so on. The rest is not a substance and, for this reason, the rest is not, in a way. We have to try and think about the rest away from the authority of being, of the verb *to be* and of everything that depends on it: essence, existence, substance, and so on. That means to think the rest otherwise or to think the rest as another, if you will. And I think that all these phenomena are referred to as marginal, referred to as superstition, magic, sorcery, envy, jealousy, spell casting, and so on are related to this rest or remains that, in some way, exceeds ontology, which exceed the thought of being, the thought of presence, the way of thinking that determines the rest either as a residue or as substance.
> (Derrida, in Mazzoldi and Téllez, 2007: 372)

Derrida is perhaps unusually clear here: he criticises inadequate models of substance that account for causality and relations only in terms of constituent or efficient power (*causa sui*, *potentia absoluta*, presence, immediacy, contiguous contact, determinacy, permanence, certainty, Being). As suggested in the previous chapter, this notion of power has now been taken to be evident: an element (creative or efficient) exerts force over another (inert or passive) and makes it change its position or some characteristic feature. More often than not, this notion of power is coupled with a post-Kantian relational gap between humans (animate, efficient, self-regulatory) and nonhumans (inanimate, inert, subject to unchanging rules).

As a result of this coupling, philosophy (including political philosophy) has determined for itself an ever-tinier province (human self-regulation or full self-reflexivity) while all other relations are either abandoned to scientific research or dismissed as mere superstition. Indeed, whenever 'reflexivity' seems to appear beyond the realm of human self-regulation it is either treated scientifically (for instance in cognitive science, quantum physics or thermodynamics) or dismissed as a residue of archaic thought. In contrast, Mazzoldi's argument (with Derrida) should be taken as both a denunciation of efficient causality and a call to reintroduce the question of causality and relation as a genuine topic of philosophical inquiry.[2]

This is particularly relevant to political philosophy (and its offshoot, legal theory) insofar as its central question is precisely that of constituent power, often described as the decisive act or a series of reflexive acts of 'self-authorisation', self-legislation or prescription.[3] This is a foundational, creative or original act that constitutes the collective or series as a (political) collective or a group, and it entails a paradox: the efficient creator or first lawgiver, who initiates the constitution of the collective or series into a group, and gives the law that is to rule among the members of the group, can only become such if and when it is recognised by the constituted group as being authorised to issue prescriptions by them. In turn, the group can only become such if and when it is identified as such by the lawgiver, whom it authorises, and given a universal rule by him (Lindahl, 2007: 12). This paradoxical or vicious foundation sends time and space, not only logic, off its hinges: time becomes 'out of joint', divided into an archaic (the time of the founders) and a modern time (that of the civic group) which coexist but never coincide.[4]

Is there a way out of this paradox? If Mazzoldi and Derrida's (Heideggerian) critique of efficient causality is correct, the answer is no. Mazzoldi goes on to suggest that rather than finding a way out of this paradox we should embrace it, thereby transforming the question of the way out into a different inquiry that, as said before, he calls 'the thought of superstition'. As it becomes clear during the dialogue, this is to be understood as a thought of the object conceived as an intermediary that stabilises relations between coexisting but non-coincidental elements, entities that are never fully present to themselves or to one another. To repeat, the issue at stake here is that of a notion of causality and relation that refuses to conceive activity in the model of the otherworldly *causa sui* or the *potentia absoluta*.

This leads to the following question: Is there another model of activity? Or put otherwise: Is there a way to move from paradox (vicious circularity) onto change and alteration (virtuous circularity)? In this case the answer is positive. The alternative model for activity is exemplarity–reflexivity, transition, transference or responsiveness. Put simply, these terms refer to the emergence of a concrete articulation – a collective – in the active relationship of one element with another through a border or vicarious element, this relationship being specific to the element's own resources and functionality. In terms of causality and relations, this is the form of indirect causation or what we called before 'reciprocal projection'; it can also be understood as a form of affective perception. Affective perception pertains to the formation of an 'evental' body or radical connection, that is, the formation of a functional structure across gaps and borders.

Evental bodies and radical connections: the contribution of cognitive science

This model of activity has been posited as a possible answer to the mind–body/body–environment problem in the work of cognitive scientists like Francisco Varela, Evan Thompson and Andy Clark.[5] In the context of this scientific endeavour, Varela and Thompson explain that 'somatic and environmental elements are likely to interact to produce (via emergence or upwards causation) global organism-environment processes which in turn affect (via downwards causation) its constitutive elements' (Varela and Thompson, 2001). There are two nuances in this insight, which may prove relevant to the paradox of self-legislation highlighted by Lindahl, and the problem of the persistence of magic in modernity pointed out by Mazzoldi.

Let us explore that relevance in the remainder of this chapter. That exploration will lead us towards a consideration of the uncanny and uncanny encounters in psychoanalysis and metaphysics. Rather than sworn enemies, cognitive science and psychoanalysis will be presented here as continuous. The contribution of the enactive viewpoint in cognitive science, that the problem is not adaptation to a given environment but rather how it is that there is something, a specific element, which must adapt in the first place, and the notion of the in-closed loop, cut or self-organisation, will be taken as a central point in the wider debate concerning whether or not the mind/brain coincides simply and directly with the inability to resist and revolt that psychoanalysts have identified as a psychic effect of life under endlessly innovative capitalism.[6] After this, we will move onto the distinction between the group and the series, already introduced in the previous chapter, in order to re-deploy the notions of 'cut' and cut-up techniques in the vicinity of disciplines (literary and theoretical) that take the connection between magic and realism seriously, that is to say, the problem of relations across real borders that cannot be bridged conceptually or empirically or, in more technical terms, the problem of transition.

The first nuance is, as John Protevi notices in his commentary of Varela's work (Protevi, 2005), that there is a distinction to be made in the enactive viewpoint between 'environment' and 'world'. In the passage quoted above 'environment' refers to regularities or laws that are real and objective in that they impose constraints upon world making or 'enactment'. In contrast, 'world' entails totality and totalisation, that is to say, the ability of a system to project out of a multiplicity of resources and a repertoire of behaviours a (virtual) self and to enact a world (as a correlate of the projected self). The point here is to try and solve the problem posited by the fact that in principle all entities hide from each other, that they form a differential field. If they are not immediately present to each other how do they connect? Varela's answer is that within this field there emerges a triumphant, concerted, mode of comportment. These emergent regularities are constraining, but contingent. They form an environment. A breakdown in regular comportment throws the related elements back into the differential field, like broken tools. To connect with the environment or 'fix it', broken tools must project a world – a totality of concrete prototypes (like Mazzoldi's charms and objects) in which they and all others can be (re)counted. Strictly speaking, it is not correct to say that entities, tools and selves connect or relate to the world; rather, in enacting a world they connect with the environment.

The second nuance is that constitutive processes are no one-way street. A set institutionality emerges out of some concerted action. This action entails the enactment of a world (for instance, the projection of one's worldview) onto a concrete prototype (for instance, the leader or a prophet, or more strictly, a prophecy or a sacred text). The latter reacts back and affects the agents. There is a potential fallacy here: that the agents think that the prototype, the leader, the sacred text or the exemplar, has produced them. The logic of exemplarity (mimesis, magic) is based upon this possibility, but it avoids a fallacious result by introducing the inevitability of 'breakdown' into the surrounding system lived as a world. This also means to introduce the possibility of failure within the prototype: the text or the leader. For instance, although the text may be seen as 'sacred' this does not mean that it is fully present to itself. Self-reflexivity is interrupted by the unexpected. In this sense contingency becomes necessary for the functioning of the text as an exemplar: prophecies come in riddles that need to be solved, but never completely; texts and positive laws are full of gaps in need of 'creative' reading; leaders fail, turn into tyrants and are overthrown; heroes return to save the city and then disappear leaving the crowds without a clue as to the meaning of their appearance, obliged to solve things on their own. Here, hermeneutic enterprises find their *raison d'être*.

In respect to the surrounding system lived as a world, the inevitability of breakdown often takes the form of an apocalypse: that the world as we know it will come to an end. In passing, it is the inevitability of breakdown that inaugurates the problem of evil: how could a wise or divine leader (ultimately, the deity itself) be whole and wise and divine if the world is inevitably coming to an end?

It is no coincidence that this sort of question (re)emerges whenever catastrophe strikes: Cortés's arrival in Tenochtitlan, the Lisbon earthquake of 1775, the Indian famines of Victorian times, hurricanes Flora and Katrina. Take the earthquake of November 1775: it not only destroyed Lisbon but also shattered Leibniz's theodicy and inflamed a forceful response by none other than the thinker of constituent power himself, Jean-Jacques Rousseau.[7] The earthquake was interpreted as an omen, a sign or proof that the world had not been created according to the principle of maximising perfection. Just like the 2004 tsunami in Asia and the 2005 hurricane in New Orleans, those affected by it resented it as a revenge of nature, a magical omen and a divine warning. The key to these events is their indifference to any sort of moral distinction, and in this sense they are not unlike other less 'natural' and in their own ways, unique phenomena: contemporary terrorist violence, the Jewish holocaust or neoliberal terror in Argentina.

These insights coming from the enactive viewpoint in cybernetics and cognitive science may help us to correct some of the more paradoxical results of certain discoveries concerning the (auto)transcendence of scattered or disseminated elements, a 'thought of superstition', and the impurity of self-authorisation.

First, the leader or 'lawgiver' is produced by the multitude ('us', the political collective entity) even if the latter think themselves to be produced by him. Second, self-authorisation is not the result of unmediated self-positing, but rather, of projection and world-making or enactment. This entails a form of postulation or positing that is mediated through the authority of an element that is external or foreign to the established entity–environment system. Third, this means that, in political terms for instance, the legal environment (democracy) does not aim at consensus, not even normatively speaking as Lindahl puts it (2007: 16–17). This is so, not because the legal order neutralises the strange occurrence (the foreign), levelling the extraordinary to a figure of the ordinary (ibid.). Rather, consensus cannot be the political principle and responsiveness to the foreign is always radical, a more radical truth than any consensus, because the stranger, the foreign element, is always/already within and unavoidable.[8] Put otherwise, the foreign element is within, in the sense that it is a trace of the rule-environment's origin or constitution and dissolution, and not something derivative from the system. This has nothing to do with inclusion or exclusion, which always pertain to a use of truth in order to make room for a new arrangement of the marginal element and the system, either by an exclusion that is agreed upon or even wished for, or with the aim of attempting to authenticate a sense of 'self' or 'identity' that would be the most endurable and permanent in being.

Rather, 'truth' and not consensus is the principle of politics if, and only if, it cannot be used, treated and/or mistreated in its transmission to others. On the contrary, truth as a principle of politics has to do with the consistency of the other, of its determinate form as something other. The established entity–environment, a regularity, senses what is foreign to it not just as different content (that would perhaps be impossible) but senses the content in a determinate form, as something other; and this form of otherness which is not reducible to content is formality. This is to say that the foreign element, postulated in political practice, is real and not ideal; it has the formality of reality even if it is only a result of postulation or incalculable 'enactment'. Truth is unexpected, it emerges as it wishes, or more precisely, truth is the unexpected, which is why it can only be half said.

In other words, the system has consistency, in the logical sense of the term, only insofar as it designates the point of its incompleteness, where its limit is marked.[9] The foreign element or extraordinary event marks the outermost limit, what is most hidden in the entity–environment system, beyond the plane of identity and recognition.[10] Put simply, the foreign element or the surprising event inevitably embodies the 'breakdown' of the system. Thus, it cannot be included or assimilated: in order to appear in the world it must make (enact) the world anew. The foreign element is, in this sense, both within and without the system. Because of this its appearance or (re)-entry is in some way magical, apocalyptic, and portentous (it is taken to be a powerful body, a prophet, an emissary, a revolutionary): an agent of destruction set to bring about the end of days. Fourth, breakdown, rebellion, is the uncanny encounter of the system with its own foreignness. It is uncanny because it indicates that imagination (freedom and so on) is indissociable from violence in the (political) act. In this sense, rebellion is a moment of leaderless-ness without spontaneity, as marvellously depicted in the last scenes of Gillo Pontecorvo's *The Battle of Algiers*. Granted, the masses cannot say 'us' (they need an external fixed point to focus their energies) but the moment of unity and concentrated energy coincides with that of total dispersal, leaderless-ness or panic. Lastly, this moment, the advent of the stranger cannot be prevented but it can be anticipated. It is neither just a matter of optimistic militant, pre-emptive design (à la Rousseau) nor an act of God that is incomprehensible to our finite minds (à la Voltaire); hence its 'magical' appearance. Put otherwise, this is to say that the extraordinary event cannot be neutralised or minimised (by maximising compromise) without augmenting the entropy already affecting the system. But it can be anticipated in an image of hope or impending doom, in a riddle or a prophecy, one that makes 'breakdown' and 'failure' internal to its own discourse; this is why prophecies always come in riddles.

Magic and the uncanny: contributions from psychoanalysis and anthropology

Given the point made in the previous section, we may ask: What is then the nature of the (extraordinary, magical) event and its agent? As suggested before, it is that of the remainder, the rest and the uncanny. It will be argued in the remainder of this chapter that the element which does not count has a nature that is akin to that of the ghost and the haunting presence, made evident in all manner of rituals. It is both within and without, a virtual dimension haunting our imagination and waiting to be embodied. We shall now approach this strange nature by attempting to clarify the centrality of the notion of the uncanny in 'Western' ways and modes of being. We will do this with the help of anthropology and psychoanalysis, two disciplines that have taken the uncanny, in different but related ways, as their object of inquiry. Anthropology and psychoanalysis teach us that the uncanny is a borderline notion. It is already inhabited by a tension: while Western consciousness oscillates between Rousseau and Voltaire, between sovereign decision and finitude, 'the rest' appears displaced, or to be more precise, unplaceable. This tension is precisely the form-matter of the uncanny.

As Mladen Dolar observes (1991), with the triumph of the Enlightenment, magic turns into reason, and the sacred or excluded place (the exclusion that founded society) is displaced by sovereign design (law, politics, techno-science). All that was placed under the dominion of magic and the sacred becomes now unplaceable, giving rise to a new experience of bafflement and paranoia. This experience has been linked historically, politically and affectively, or in clinical evidence to wider issues: sex, class, race, identity and the fear of what is brought back (or returns) from imperialist and colonial adventures: from wars of liberation and immigration to terrorism, from unfamiliar or exotic portraits, cultures and objects to ecotourism, globalised news and charms, still unfamiliar in their very familiarity, and so on.

The experience of rebellion corresponds to such coordinates too: thoroughly modern, up against everything that seems to violate our almost intuitive sense of self-determination, our ability to project ourselves into a future that we wish determinate, and yet, strangely caught up in a repetitive circle of returning violence and indeterminacy. Furthermore, it is not an experience of (achieving) identity and particularity but rather the opposite: the obliteration of identity, that of self and other. In short, to use a term that has been and will remain central to this study even when not invoked explicitly, this is an experience of 'the uncanny'; an uncanny experience.

The centrality of this term should alert the reader towards the significance of psychoanalysis as a theoretical framework. It is well known that, within this framework, the uncanny is not simply an experience of strangeness and alienation, but more strictly, a peculiar commingling of the familiar and the unfamiliar. 'It can take the form of something familiar unexpectedly arising in a strange and unfamiliar context, or of something strange and unfamiliar unexpectedly arising in a familiar context' (Royle, 2003: 1). It can take the form of a prophecy, a riddle or a revelation of something unhomely here at home. It might arise from some eerie or mechanical repetition, a curious coincidence, a sense that things 'happen for a reason'; but also when mechanical props and objects take a life of their own and seem to run the show. It has been associated with the animated/ing photograph, with ghosts and the return of the dead and, crucially for us, with (more or less successful) attempts to create a society of sleepwalkers (Galeano, 1978: 307).

Uncanny objects in philosophy

In twentieth-century philosophy, as Nicholas Royle observes, it was Martin Heidegger who, with particular resilience, sought to pursue and develop the notion that 'at bottom, the ordinary is not ordinary; it is extra-ordinary, uncanny' (Heidegger, 1975: 54). As most of his commentators have noticed, for him the fundamental character of our being in the world is unhomely, uncanny; in this respect, he says that '[t]he "not-at-home" must be conceived as the more primordial phenomenon' (Heidegger, 1967: 233). He means not only that our being in the world is marked by the uncanny discovery that we are not at home in the world (as it occurs in heightened states of anxiety or ecstasy) but more precisely and perhaps more significantly, that the world is an ambiguous duality in which sensual surfaces conceal a hidden depth that can be brought to light only in a contingent manner and never absolutely. However, this contingency of necessity, this sensual or 'light' presence, is itself necessary. Contrary to the common notion that surfaces and contingent appearances matter less, that what really counts is the hard kernel, hidden beneath the surface and the true repository of causal powers, the point here is the opposite: the hidden depths of reality or 'being' are never absolutely present, but only slightly so. Dark depths recede from the light; causality and interaction only take place at the surface.

This is to say that at some level entities withdraw from all relationships while at another – along the shiny surface – they relate to each other. Causal powers are thus exercised at the superficial level and causal connections take place only here; hence, as Graham Harman says, 'all relationships are superficial' (Harman, 2007a: 147). He explains that 'the only place in the cosmos where interactions occur is the sensual, phenomenal realm' (ibid.). This argument brings together two well-known and widely accepted insights: Husserl's intentionality of consciousness and Heidegger's withdrawal of real objects behind all relations.

Let us rehearse the argument once more, this time with the help of Jean-Paul Sartre. He observes that in intentionality my encounter with the tree is a unified relation: 'I thought without words, *on* things, *with* things' (1964: 126 ff.). The reference is to the intentional relation as a unified whole that cannot be exhausted by phenomenological description. But it is also true that the tree and I do not fuse in one single mess, and thus the tree remains distinct from me in the sensual relation. The result of this observation is that to think *on* things, *with* things, means also that the tree and I inhabit the intentional relation; the latter is our home and we both reside in the interior of this third.

I am (and think) with things within this homely third. Being at home I am (and think) with the foreign. Foreignness is within.

Furthermore, there is symmetry and asymmetry between the elements of this relation. Symmetry: the tree and I are elements of this set/relation and as such we may stand for one another, pressed against one another. 'Serpent or claw or root or vulture's talon, what difference does it make ... I made an experiment with the absolute or the absurd' (ibid.). Asymmetry: the tree is there in a way that I cannot fully explain, precisely because this sensual tree relates to the real me, whereas the real tree is not part of this relation. According to Sartre, to be with the tree in intention (to think with the tree) is not to exhaust the reality of the tree in thought, since the real or existing tree withdraws from that relation, but rather to be fascinated with it. As he puts it, to have one's eyes 'filled' by it: 'This root – there was nothing in relation to which it was absurd ... I had not seen the seeds sprout, or the tree grow. But faced with this great wrinkled paw, neither ignorance nor knowledge was important: the world of explanations and reasons is not the world of existence... This root, on the other hand, existed in such a way that I could not explain it. Knotty, inert, nameless, it fascinated me, filled my eyes, brought me back to its own existence' (ibid.).

Sartre is clear: being is not exhausted by thought. In thought, in the intentional relation, my connection with the tree is purely sensual, aesthetic (the term he uses is 'fascination') and I am continuous or in relation with the tree in sensuality. But at the same time, I am completely discontinuous with the tree in that beyond sensuality, beyond fascination, there is no causal connection and no passage from *this* to *that*. As we will see later, it is from within this ambiguous sense of continuity and discontinuity that the distinction between the group and the series emerges in Sartrean thought. There we will locate the concepts of 'cut' and 'cut-up' borrowed from music and mathematics in order to emphasise this ambiguity in crowd theory and politics. But for now it will suffice to insist upon this ambiguity of continuity in sensuality and discontinuity beyond sensuality. Sartre writes: 'In vain to repeat: "This is a root" – it didn't work any more. I saw clearly that you could not pass from this function as a root, as a breathing pump, *to that*, to this hard and compact skin of a sea lion, to this oily, callous, headstrong look' (ibid). The point is that the existence of the tree does not entail the necessity of a causal connection with me. That necessity is contingent, and this contingency is the essential thing: 'The essential thing is contingency. I mean that one cannot define existence as necessity. To exist is simply to be there; those who exist let themselves be encountered, but you can never deduce anything from them' (ibid.).

To 'let themselves be encountered' ... this is the language of fascination and sensuality. Indeed, the truth of that encounter, if it happens – and perhaps Sartre would have done all of us a favour had he inserted in his text a parenthesis: 'those who exist let themselves be encountered (or they don't)'

– does not belong to the order of deductions but rather to that of fascinations. Truth belongs to aesthetics, not to logics. The true problem is whether to enter into or to withdraw from relations, and this is a matter of choice. But the choice is not ethical or moral; it is aesthetic. Building upon this insight it will be argued, against the present consensus, that politics – the discourse and practice of decision-making and choice – has nothing or very little to do with ethics. It is a branch of aesthetics. Aesthetics, in turn, should be treated as first philosophy (Harman: 2005; 2007a; 2007b).

Relations and choices, if they are to occur, to be made, are always sensual and since sensuality is not an exclusively human feature, not necessarily limited to humans. What type of relations are sensual relations among things or entities, human and nonhuman? They are indirect, vicarious relations. On the one hand they never directly encounter, as presence, the hidden reality of the related elements. On the other hand, if being is not presence (and not thought, either), indirect encounters are the norm. Put otherwise, if things and elements hide from one another then their encounters take place only through some sort of intermediary: a vicar, things-*mono* ('things', or things-between, in Japanese), charms or fetishes (Fukushima, 2005: 58–63).

According to Masato Fukushima, 'mono' is the ordinary Japanese equivalent of 'thing' or 'object'. He explains that it meant, originally, not only an object with shape but also every sensual object. Because of this the boundary of 'mono' also extends to ghostly existence and to speech. This would allow the translator, the analyst or the ethnographer to concoct another category: from speech and ghostly objects to 'the hauntedness of things' (ibid.). Based upon this ambiguity – the contestable boundary between living things and dead things, to a certain extent similar to the distinction between sensual and real objects that appears in phenomenology – one could consider, with Fukushima and others, the possibility of a comparative research or exhibition-project concerning ritualistic or (non-normative) 'religious' practices all over the world. Such a project would focus on the object-between, the charm or the fetish, on their deep affect or the form of their connection, as they help to stabilise indirect relations, and perhaps also to obliterate them, like guns and bullets in the hands of Butch Cassidy and the Sundance Kid. In principle, such a project would allow a sort of comparativism in anthropology, politics and law that does not start from a posited, necessary rule or norm and then searches for its exotic variations.

The sort of comparativism that starts from a necessary rule has been denounced by Michel Foucault's critique of ethnology as a science predicated on a hypothesis of sameness. As he put it, this sort of 'comparative' ethnology 'can assume its proper dimensions only within the historical sovereignty – always restrained, but always present – of European thought and the relation that can bring it face to face with all cultures as well as with itself' (Foucault, 1994: 376). In this respect, ethnology depends upon European hegemony, even if it is not always relying upon it – what cultural anthropologist

Walter Mignolo would term 'the modern/colonial geopolitics of knowledge' (1995). In fact, and we shall come back to this later, this criticism updates Marx's early use of comparative anthropology of religions, inspired by Feuerbach. Like Fukushima, Feuerbach (and Marx after him) focused upon reciprocal projection and the double nature of the fetish as an object-between. This concern was introduced into German idealist philosophy of religion (already politically motivated) via early ethnographic accounts of West African religions in the rebellious Caribbean of the late eighteenth and early nineteenth century, and transformed into a critical insight. In a sense, this uncanny encounter between West African religious practices, Caribbean rebellions and German idealist criticism inaugurated the study of transcultural political forms whose possibility is called forth by people such as Fukushima and Mazzoldi. That exploration, and its motif, are also central to literary and theoretical endeavours associated to decolonisation, psychoanalytical accounts of oppression, post-coloniality and magic(al) realism. In all cases the central motif remains the same: the invention (or colonial imposition) of figures of necessity do not explain contingency away, but merely displace it, or more precisely make it unplaceable. Inevitably, it returns as a marker for breakdown and rebellion; and in its role as the harbinger of destruction it fascinates us.

Isn't this what Sartre, himself no stranger to the exploration of coloniality, had in mind when he wrote: 'to exist is simply to be there; those who exist let themselves be encountered, but you can never deduce anything from them. I believe there are people who have understood this. Only they tried to overcome this contingency by inventing a necessary, causal being'? (1964: 131). In this paragraph, Sartre seems to explain religion (with capital R, as in the more dogmatic and legalistic religions of the book; in this case most probably Christianity) as an invention or a projection made by people who understood very well the contingency of necessity and sought to replace it with a necessary 'causal being', a prime mover or a big other. In the face of haziness and the uncanny – in a word, uncertainty – these men invented certainty, or rather, a figure of certainty: the original cause, the absolute sovereign and the founding father. In short they invented the first lawgiver, and by implication the law or a form of legality driven by nostalgia for certainty.

For Sartre this attempt to overcome contingency was vain: 'but no necessary being can explain existence: contingency is not a delusion, a probability which can be dissipated; it is the absolute, consequently, the perfect free gift' (ibid.). Sartre opposed the necessity of contingency to the false dichotomy between contingency and necessity, which dominated mainstream accounts of causality. Like Feuerbach, Marx and Heidegger, like the Japanese as well, somewhat more sensitive to the power of the fetish and its double (perhaps infinite) nature, Sartre denounced the vanity of religion and philosophy with capital letters – to overcome uncertainty. And instead of remaining in the twofold between the disavowal of uncertainty and the legalistic absolutisation of certainty, these philosophers left in search of the threefold – the third, the object-between, time and the fetish – the fourfold (as in Heidegger or Titus-Carmel) and perhaps allowed us to imagine the infinite-fold.[11]

The fundamental insight here is a form of realist materialism as form-materialism: the assertion of the infinite unfolding of reality to depths we may not be aware of. But also, a consideration of our responses to such an ambivalent reality: either the vanity of absolute certainty in law and religion, or else the deployment of charms and powerful things as exploratory drones probing the hazy boundaries between things and us, and between things themselves.

The latter entails an exploratory activity: a first-order exploration (or if we follow Fukushima, an exhibition) of the way in which charms and fetishes – the objects themselves in fascinating mode – allow real objects to appear from within their hidden depths, without relying on conceptual translation or transmutation, and without exhaustion of reality. This would be an investigation on indirect causation, and thus part and parcel of an ontological endeavour. This sort of investigation may not be necessarily or totally conceptual, but rather, as suggested above, more like an exhibition of things in the curatorial sense encompassing not only object-things but also the hauntedness of things, the boundaries of life and death, reality and sensuality, and the things-between that are inspired by, for instance, the Japanese term *mono* or West African and Caribbean practices such as *voudoun*.

The determinations of culture matter less here, not because of conceptual flight or abstract indifference, but because of the very power of the exhibition of things. By poking holes through to the sensual surface, the more foreign reality of the thing becomes intimate, it calls us to the border and once there, in melancholia, as psychoanalysts would say (Kristeva, 2000: 177) or nausea (the 'gustatory' perception of contagion, melancholia and unhomeliness), transforms into a position of revolt.[12]

Sartre writes: 'contingency is not a delusion, a probability which cannot be dissipated; it is the absolute, consequently, the perfect free gift. All is free, this park, this city and myself. When you realize that, it turns your heart upside down and everything begins to float (. . .) here is Nausea; here is what those bastards – the ones on the Côteau Vert and others – try to hide from themselves with their idea of their rights' (Sartre, 1964: 126–31). In this passage the position of revolt is described in two ways. First, as a result of the original gratuity of things. The reference is to the archaic economy of reciprocity and substitution. This is a primordial or hierarchically superior situation, in respect to the secondary nature of 'rights' (in this case, the rights to property, backed by the state's monopoly of force, invoked by 'those bastards' on the Côteau Vert). Seen from this perspective, the position of revolt consists of submitting the 'how' of rights and positive commands to the 'why' of the original position of things as 'free', floating, in-between. Second, following Kristeva, the position of revolt appears as the transformation of nausea (the gustatory perception of contagion or mimesis) into melancholia in the Freudian sense of the term: 'that is, to the subject/object, language/affect, sense/non-sense borders' (2000: 177). In short, revolt is presented as a position of borderless-ness or 'not being at home' . . . out there, away from the centres of accumulation, in some lost backwater in Bolivia, like the characters of the film or Ernesto Guevara and his guerrilla army fighting a lost cause. It is there that the subject imagines, projects and encounters freedom while traversing violence.

Rebellion and objects: notes towards a definition

We have added one additional layer to our exploration of archaic objects and rebellion: Heidegger's crucial insight is that we are not at home in the world because the world is unhomely, populated with ghostly things with which we can only make contact superficially, their vast depths withdrawing always from us. If this is the case, then the question arises: how do these ghostly things poke holes through to the surface so that we can relate to them and each to another? They must signal each other from afar, unable to touch each other directly. At this juncture, it becomes obligatory to consider the possibility that indirect relations are the order of the day in reality, as argued by traditional occasionalism and scepticism before and post-Heideggerian philosophy and phenomenology after (Harman, 2007a and 2007b; Levinas, 1997; Zubiri, 1980).

The point is that relations never directly encounter or stand in for the autonomous reality of their components (Harman, 2007a: 173–4). If so, substantive or autonomous real objects must 'inflict their mutual blows only through some vicar or intermediary' (ibid.). The other alternative would be to posit some necessary cause or privileged being (for example, god, the mind) as distinct from all the other autonomous entities in the world, infusing the latter with a dynamism that they would otherwise lack. That alternative must be rejected, and therefore, we are left with the model of vicarious or intermediary connections.

Intermediary causality is similar to the case of the formal but partial cause. Harman explains 'the formal' as follows:

> To say that formal cause operates vicariously means that forms do not touch one another directly, but somehow melt, fuse and decompress in a shared common space from which all are partly absent. [The] claim is that two entities influence one another only by meeting on the interior of a third, where they exist side-by-side until something happens that allows them to interact. In this sense, the theory of vicarious causation is a theory of the molten inner core of objects – a sort of place tectonics of ontology.
>
> (Harman, 2007a: 174)

Instead of the hard inner core of objects imagined by most essentialist theories of substance, the image here is that of a fluid core supplemented by a harder crust or surface. This surface is an appearance, which is to say that its hardness, the consistency of the membrane separating one object from the other is the result of exposure. As in tectonics, the surface is harder than the core because it is exposed to the force of the elements, it cools off and acquires solidity; but as soon as the exposure ceases it returns to the heated molten core. Two insights are crucial here. First, exposure and connection occur on occasion; it is contingent. Second, the model of atomistic materialism does not apply here. Although we speak of objects that exist side-by-side and for the most part do not relate to one another, it is not the case that they behave like ultimate, simpler building blocks or billiard balls in state of stasis. As we have seen, they are in constant tension between molten core and cool surface. They are more like particles in constant buzz, experiencing their own tension and confronting one another by proxy.

When objects move, as a result of their own dynamics, they poke holes through to the surface of another object without ever becoming confused with their intimate substance. In this sense, objects do not penetrate each other but embrace each other sensually, by proxy, through vicarious projections of themselves. These vicarious projections are ideal, in the Husserlian sense of the term, and can be distinguished from the real substances that step back, always avoiding each other. Harman rechristens Husserl's ideal objects with the name 'sensual objects' (Harman, 2007a: 176) and submits that the interplay between real and sensual objects 'provides ontology with a radical new theme' (ibid.).

Let us do some rechristening of our own and name ideal/sensual objects 'fantasy' or 'fantasmatic objects', and leave the term 'the real' for real objects. If the former are closer to the Husserlian side of phenomenology, the latter belong to the Heidegerian impulse of the tool-analysis. As Harman says, 'these two types of objects are both different and complementary' (ibid.). The tool-analysis is the start of a novel conception of technics that has remained in the margins of philosophy at least since the post-Socratics. For the latter, technics is just some derivation of theory and the contemplation of essences, which is primary, and remains always subordinated to it. Technical objects are merely bad copies, and our task is to strive for progressively more cogent visions of the original, even if the latter do not capture the original essence in its entirety. For Heidegger things are very different, for the technical–practical relation grounds theory. Like Kant, Heidegger thinks that there is a progression from the theoretical to the practical, with the latter making possible the former. And like Kant, Heidegger thinks that the practical relation is able to fully grasp the object within the relational whole of world and time.

However, the lesson that can be obtained from the 'primacy' of technics is precisely the opposite: the practical relation is unable to grasp the objects fully, man does not become a master through technology but merely its operator, and technics is all about relations by proxy with a fundamentally incomplete reality, that is to say, relations between abstract, sensual, ideal, fantasmatic objects and real objects that escape all relational wholes. Put otherwise, phenomenology teaches us that appearances and illusions do matter, and thus we may speak of the objectivity of the phantasm and the illusion at least in the sense that fantasmatic phenomena are objects in constant search of one another (Husserl), always enacting worlds of relation, while real objects withdraw from such worlds (Heidegger).

Harman concludes from this presentation of the Husserl/Heidegger ensemble that 'the only place in the cosmos where interactions occur is the sensual, phenomenal realm' (2007a: 179) and thus our task is to 'discover how real objects poke through into the phenomenal realm' (Harman, 2007: 181). This means that, on the one hand, fantasy is the realm that structures reality in terms of relations while, on the other hand, it is by traversing fantasy through to the end that there might be an entry into the real.

The use of psychoanalytical vocabulary (as in 'fantasy' or 'the real') is in this case deliberate and justified. For psychoanalytical theory nowadays these are categories of fundamental ontology rather than human-centred psychopathology, since the realm of affect – the object of psychoanalytical discourse and practice – is that of the operation of non-human forces that impinge upon the human behind or beyond the conscious level. The real remains always inaccessible to the direct grasp of the conscious, and can be contacted only by proxy, through fantasy objects. It is in fantasy that the human encounters the real, never in reality, and since this is a unified relation, an encounter, one can speak of it as a whole that resists exhaustion (for instance, exhaustive description in referential language). Put otherwise, it has reality of its own behind and beyond uniquely human capabilities such as language. The conscious me and the real inhabit this fantasy, which has reality of its own, but since the real is in fact inaccessible, there is no actual merging between me and the real. The real is too violent and traumatic to appear directly, it must do so indirectly, by proxy, and so through fantasy and projection I and the real can connect without fusion, in relative or responsible proximity, and thus, in distinction. Fantasy, an object itself, operates as a cut that divides and communicates fundamentally inaccessible real entities. Finally, since these categories refer to fundamental ontology and grant no particular privilege to human abilities, fantasy appears as a fundamental ontological structure rather than a particularly human capacity.

Now we have all the necessary elements to define a new approach. Using the example of my encounter with a tree, ubiquitous in phenomenological literature all the way up to Sartre's *Nausea*, Harman summarises thus the elements of such an approach:

> [. . .] we have a real intention whose core is inhabited by a real me and a sensual tree. In addition there is also a withdrawn real tree (or something that we mistake for one) lying outside the intention, but able to affect it along avenues still unknown. Finally the sensual tree never appears in the form of a naked essence, but is always encrusted with various sorts of noise.
>
> (Harman, 2007a: 182)

A real fantasy, a real me and a phantasmatic tree within the fantasy, a withdrawn real and efficacious tree, a phantasmatic but highly structured tree – identifiable and always allowing itself to be encountered. What matters is the occasional relation between real entities through fantasy, and the objectivity of the fantasy. This novel approach to objects provides at least two insights, which are crucial to the purposes of our discussion of rebellion. First, that their free-floating nature (the contingent 'why are these things together?') is primary in relation to any established regularity or particularity (the necessary 'how are these things gathered together'). The latter can therefore be questioned by contrast with the former. Second, projection, fantasy or world-enactment is necessary if any connection between an entity and its environment is to be made. But, in a sort of reversal, such connections and the projected worlds they depend upon are contingent. The latter can be questioned whenever their internal tension – between the projected aspect and the relative aspect – is highlighted. The overall picture is one of entities constantly falling back upon chaotic dispersal precisely when they reach out to one another.

This double insight illuminates our predicament, embodied in the situation of rebellious characters: weird solitude, being driven towards the borders between subject and object, sense and nonsense, and reach out, shattering the established coordinates of space and time; that is to say, creating the occasion. This suggests that the imaginary aspect of action (Kristeva) or 'fantasy' (my term) cannot be sharply distinguished from the violent aspect, the refusal of one element's existing links with others, of what that element is there for, and its shattering projection that creates new spatial and temporal conditions of relation and existence for itself and another.

After refusing to be a mere effect of a network, a mere potentiality – being there for – something that remains in a state of inherence until being actualised in its identity with the whole, these rebellious characters or elements attain a state that is devoid of egomania or full identity, and beyond human construction: withdrawn, liberated. And yet there is nothing otherworldly about this state. They are there, in the real, and let themselves be encountered. Let us call this a state of 'sincere exposure', a form of connectedness or 'love' that seeks no other.

As Harman explains (2007a: 183), in sincerity a real element or object is absorbed by a sensual object or element, even if the fascination is merely illusory. But the former does not penetrate or fully contain the latter since containment is the work of fantasy, which, to add to Harman's explanation, is itself dependent upon the incompleteness of reality. Fantasy provides a structure within which the sensual or projected element and the real element encounter each other in motion, that is to say, in space-time. This is not to be conceived as a fixed background structure, for it is the motion of the elements that determines the coordinates of space and time. Put otherwise, fantasy provides the elements of reality, in principle all alone and incomplete, with a closure condition, a self-reflexive form of temporality that allows for reality's composition. To the incompleteness of reality we must oppose (and supplement with) the composition of reality. It turns out that reality is a composite, made possible through fantasy, affected by contingency and anticipation (and thus a completion process that fails, at least partially). Thus, it is changing, and its laws and regularities change too; this is so not because of the participation of 'chance', but rather because in fantasy, which is no less part of reality than the real, sensual or fantasmatic objects can split from their fundamental quality leaving behind what becomes undesirable and thereby distinguishable from what is in the (sensual) object more than it, the *objet petit a* in psychoanalytical parlance.

In a flight of inspiration, Harman terms this separation between the un/desirable object and its innermost quality 'allure' (2005: 142–4). He observes:

> In the sensual realm, we encounter objects encrusted with noisy accidents and relations. We may also be explicitly aware of some of their essential qualities, though any such list merely transforms the qualities into something accident-like and fails to give us the unified bond that makes the sensual thing a single thing. Instead, we need an experience in which the sensual object is severed from its joint unified quality, since this will point for the first time to a real object lying beneath the single quality on the surface. [. . .] There are countless examples of allure. In instances of beauty, an object is not the sum total of beautiful colors and proportions on its surface, but a kind of soul animating the features from within, leading to vertigo or even hypnosis in the witness [. . .] In language, names call out to objects deeper than any of their features; in love, the beloved entity has a certain magic hovering beneath the contours and flaws of its accessible surface.
> (Harman, 2007a: 199–200)

The point here is that sensual objects may be split from their unified quality, because even such a unified quality is a composite made out of parts. Notice that the operative notion here is the opposite of atomistic materialism: there are no simpler points of matter that are more qualitatively basic than a unified object quality or the quality of one of its parts, including its accidental or residual parts. Therefore, we can continue splitting a unified object until there comes a point where it cannot be regarded as the same object any more; it has changed. This 'point' is occupied by the accidental parts, the residue or remainder, the part of no-part. These 'accidents', the remnant not deployed in the 'unified' object, are the only possible source of change since they alone can connect one sensual object to another. One can speak of the violence of the split in reference to this point where/when the unified object that was, is no longer the same.

Importantly, since real objects are also composite they too can be split up, cut up (Harman, 2007a: 204). But in the case of real objects, residual parts point towards the other side of fantasy, which cannot appear directly. If this is the case, then residual parts of real objects can come together only indirectly, through a sensual replicant, a 'charm' to use Mazzoldi's terms, and thus, only through fantasy and allure. It is the allusion to a deeper power lying beyond – the real object – what animates the encounter between real objects, rather than their sensual fusion (ibid.). The remainder of a sensual object points also towards its beyond and therefore, in contrast, it connects with another sensual object via an intermediary real object (for instance, the real intentional me).

In the end composition and decomposition, or division, take us always to the point where the object turns into its other or is substituted by it. But this is no smooth exchange within a fixed causal background or a given totality. Whenever an element steps into its border and reaches beyond, it does so animated by the pull of the other element even if that element cannot be seized directly or is not immediately evident. The effect is that of a field with the object-cause at its centre, never immediately present or reachable. It is no surprise that Harman's description of vicarious causality matches almost literally that of the object-cause in the psychoanalytical theory of the drives: 'the gravitational field of a real object must somehow invade the existing sensual field' (2007a: 204–5). The separation of a thing from its quality, the split between the un/desirable object and the object-cause, is no longer a particularly human phenomenon but the structure of all relations, including motion in space and time, explained as the violent invasion of the field of fantasy by the 'gravitational' field of a real object. But this is also to assert the centrality of fantasy as a structure of reality, a cut that establishes the boundary and in the same act, literally an act-passage, leaves behind what was before but is no longer.

In this respect, violence must be understood as a cut that divides being, but always, to paraphrase Eleanor Kaufman, too deeply or not deep enough (2005: 372 ff.). The important thing is to acknowledge that objects do not penetrate and annihilate one another, rather they interrupt each other, cut one another always too deeply and not deep enough. Their primordial condition is solitude and silence, but this solitude and that silence have nothing to do with identity, with being in possession of another object, that is to say, in a full and inescapable relationship that would allow for the clear drawing of boundaries between one object and the other, and presence. On the contrary, the condition of solitude and silence has to do with absence, the obliteration of identity, self and other, and the traumatic silence of the real. Violence can be conceived in this sense as a traumatic event, a form of systemic 'breakdown' that is necessary and inevitable but not necessarily nihilistic. At the other side of it lies freedom.

As Kristeva points out, 'this is not just a matter of recourse to a mythological metaphor to justify the violence of the Resistance fighters or terrorism against the conformism of compromises and foundations'[13] but an assertion of the inevitability of passage, the crossing of boundaries and the necessity of contingency. Later on, with Dupuy and Varela, we will see that to take this necessity into account requires a new 'metaphysics of time', at odds with the one that underlies present accounts of choice and action in the intersection between ontology and political theory.

Violence and fantasy constitute the object of a 'thought of superstition' as a thought of the remainder. As such they are indissociable, but for the purposes of analysis in the following chapters we will consider them separately. First, we will explore the nature of the projected object, what Mazzoldi calls the charm or the fetish. Then, we will explore the cut, the violent division that rips everything up and starts again. To this aim we will provide a brief genealogy of the notion of 'fetishism', and will pursue its trajectory as it enters the vocabulary of modern criticism and philosophy via early ethnographic accounts of West African religious practices in the revolutionary Atlantic.

We shall abandon Sartre for the moment, at least apparently, but will keep a broad Heideggerian outlook. Starting with Heidegger's warning about the transformation of the powerful object into a mere sign, we will consider what anthropologists have to say on the subject of our inability to think the fetish. Then, we will begin to explore some of the problems faced by a renewed thought of the object. Certain contemporary forms of materialism will serve as our guide and also as contrast. Then the focus will shift towards the writings of the young Karl Marx on religious art and freedom of the press as an exemplary moment of the return of the fetish in modern critique. Here we will highlight, with Jean Luc Nancy, what the latter calls the 'double aspect' of the fetish. We will do this in the hope of laying the foundations for a more correct understanding of materiality.

Notes

1 Mazzoldi refers in the dialogue to a revolt against the rules of property: first, in the case of Titus-Carmel's copying of the original Tlingit coffins, then smashed and copied again in 127 drawings, and then, second, in the case of Derrida's own unauthorised drawings or 'cartouches' of Titus-Carmel's drawings. See Mazzoldi and Téllez (2007: 327–8).

2 For contemporary arguments in this direction, from a perspective that is somewhat different (but related) to that of Mazzoldi and Derrida, see Harman (2007a) and D'Spagnat (2006).
3 For self-authorisation as self-positing, see Kant (1993: 170 ff.). For self-authorisation as decision and collective legislative action, see Arendt (1951: 301). For self-authorisation as collective intentionality, see the work of John Searle; the relevant insight is summarised by Petit (2001: 117). For self-authorisation as collective reflexivity, with a direct link to the (sensual) problem of representation, see Roermund (2003: 235–52). For self-authorisation as universal prescription, see Hallward (2005b). For a precise and clarifying exploration of the whole argument from Kant and Hegel to Robert Pippin and Judith Butler, see Gordon (2005: 121–37).
4 On the dislocation of space-time and legal–political foundation, see: Lindhal (2006) and Guardiola-Rivera (2006b).
5 For a brilliant appraisal of the successes and failures of present-day cognitive science and its missed encounter with the humanities, see Dupuy (2000a).
6 See on this Malabou (2004; 2005). See also Žižek (2006a).
7 Rousseau, Jean-Jacques. *Lettre à Monsieur de Voltaire*, dated 18 August 1756. This is a response to Voltaire's *Poème sur le désastre de Lisbonne* published in March 1756. Cited in Dupuy (2005: 39).
8 On responsiveness in law and politics, see Fitzpatrick (2000, 2001, 2006).
9 On this understanding of logical inconsistency, see Lacan (1991).
10 For the legal–political system as based upon the plane of recognition, see Hart (1961) and Lacey (2005).
11 On the meaning of this numerology in relation to the work of Heidegger, see Harman (2007c). My gratitude to the author for allowing me to use a copy of this appendix before the release of the book.
12 As Kristeva clarifies, this must not be confused with romantic mores: 'If there is a reason to establish such a link [between melancholy and revolt] it is not the spleen of romantic states of mind that demonstrates it but indeed this Sartrean nausea that leads subjectivity to melancholia in the Freudian sense: that is, to the subject/object, language/affect, sense/non-sense borders' (2000: 177). She also makes a reference to her previous work *Black Sun: Depression and Melancholia* (1982).
13 See Kristeva (2000: 160). See also Sartre (1947) and Aeschylus (1991).

Chapter 3
An introduction to fetishism (with a plea for materialism)

A thought of the remainder (a 'thought of superstition' in Mazzoldi's parlance) focuses on the role played by certain objects, elements and materials that may have been displaced as a result of the advent and triumph of the Enlightenment project associated with modernity. Some argue that such a displacement can be seen in modern thought's tendency to dematerialise the objects, placing in their stead immaterial entities such as beliefs, concepts, norms and world-views whose function would be to stipulate, reproduce, synthesise, command or designate, and whose mode of relation would be merely representative, as in the interplay of signs in a holistic account of language. Others prefer to argue that rather than displaced, the objects associated with the dimension of the haunted, the sacred and the foreign became unplaceable. Thus, for instance, Mladen Dolar states that:

> There is a specific dimension of the uncanny that emerges with modernity (...) in premodern societies the dimension of the uncanny was largely covered (and veiled) by the area of the sacred and the untouchable. It was assigned to a religiously and socially sanctioned place (...) With the triumph of the Enlightenment, this privileged and excluded place (the exclusion that founded society) was no more. That is to say that the uncanny became unplaceable; it became the uncanny in the strict sense.
>
> (Dolar, 1991: 7)

Whether Enlightenment triumphed and replaced magic and the sacred with disembodied reason, or whether it simply made the former an invisible element that deconstructs the latter from within as a kind of 'return of the repressed', a symptom of what was wrong from the beginning, so that every attempt at rational self-authorisation (collective self-legislation, epistemic self-positing, universal self-prescription) becomes always an impure act, the crux of the matter is that we need a better account of materiality if we are ever going to understand the role that these objects play in the formation of radical attachments in time.

The goal of this chapter is to provide an outline, a first sketch, of what that sort of materialism would be like. We will start from the notion that with the transformation of our understanding of the functionality of objects, the essence of truth and reality itself changed. Then, assisted once again by the findings of anthropologists, we will speak of the return of the fetish. This will set the stage for the question: what sort of materialism? What sort of realism? The answer to that question will occupy the rest of the chapter, back and forth between philosophy and anthropology, and will link up with the discussion of fetishism in Marx and beyond.

Political consequences of a deficient account of materiality

With the transformation of our understanding of the functionality of objects after modernity, no longer located in the realm of the sacred, but rather, as Mladen Dolar puts it, 'unplaceable', the essence of truth and our conception of reality changed. They came to be seen as holistic, present only as an effect within a network of effects, more or less like the system of language. Writing on the subject of language, Martin Heidegger observed:

> From the Hellenistic (and Stoic) period onward, as the convention becomes sheer stipulation, the sign comes to be an instrument for designating; by means of such designation, representation is coordinated and directed from one object to another. Designation is no longer a showing in the sense that it lets something appear. The alteration of the sign – from that which shows to that which designates – is based on a transformation in the essence of truth. (...) The representation of language that we have sketched here in rough outline has remained throughout manifold transformations the guiding and supporting one in Western European thought over the centuries. This way of looking at language, having commenced in Greek antiquity and ramifying along many different paths, gathers to a kind of summit in Wilhelm von Humboldt's meditation on language.
> (Heidegger, 1993: 402)

It would suffice for now to notice Heidegger's emphasis on the modern alteration of material signs and the subsequent transformation in the essence of truth: from showing to designating, from the unveiling of objects to their representation in the mind, or to be more precise, the self-positing of the mind in the world through a network of non-material concepts.

Elaborating on this account, anthropologist Saba Mahmood has argued that such a transformation might explain our current inability to understand what she calls 'moral claims', and the place of religious symbols in modern secular societies (2004; 2007). This becomes apparent, she says, in discussions concerning the use of the veil by Muslim women living in Europe or in the debates caused by the depiction of the prophet Mohammed in Danish cartoons. To add another instance of this inability, outside Europe, one could turn to the confrontations concerning the role of land, water, coca, oil and gas, which have set apart rebellious indigenous majorities and descendants of white settler colonisers in contemporary Andean countries, particularly Bolivia, bringing the parties to the brink of violence and civil war. These examples demonstrate that it is a global issue.

'We must fight for our land to safeguard the future of the children of our communities,' Hernando tells me. 'We say: Leave! All of you who have stolen our lands and natural resources!' Hernando[1] is an activist working with the indigenous representatives at the Constitutional Assembly that has been deliberating in Bolivia since fall 2006. He refers to the so-called 'Water War' that took place in 2000. An unprecedented case in the recent history of globalisation, it saw a mobilised townsfolk expel a transnational company that was trying to take possession of the natural resource. This, and subsequent events, galvanised the indigenous opposition against the Bolivian white-settler oligarchy.[2]

The latter organised as the Santa Cruz Civic Committee and the Pro-Autonomy Junta. The Committee, and the more radical fringes of the *Cruceñista* movement, have been demanding departmental autonomy in a bid to stop the Indigenous and Peasant Unity's political agenda of decolonisation, or secede, thereby guaranteeing the 'free' disposal of the natural resources of the 'half-moon' region in the global market.[3] While the Pact for Indigenous and Peasant Unity[4] marked the transition from the era of multicultural politics to the era of decolonisation, within the oppositional movement, the Santa Cruz Civic Committee, but also mainstream analysts of the region, continue to mobilise a culturalist and regionally chauvinistic discourse, which combines the issues of race and culture with a more or less explicit motif of modernisation and free trade. Such discourses are totally unable to make sense of the radical attachments between the Indigenous and Peasant Unity and its objects (land, water, gas, the coca leaf, the mantra of decolonisation) and the place of popular symbols in modern secular society, in terms other than those of 'backward' and 'anti-modernist' practices. Thus, for instance, the reputed Peruvian writer Mario Vargas Llosa, also well known for championing the cause of the neoconservative/neoliberal right in Latin America, mistakes the Indigenous and Peasant Unity/MAS movement as *indigenista*, a purely restorative movement engaged in the reciprocation of five centuries of white-settler racism with an equally 'racist' combination of Quechua/Aymará anti-modernism and political idiocy (Vargas Llosa, 2007).

Taking sides with the modern colonialist discourse of the Santa Cruz Civic Committee, Vargas Llosa misreads the demands of politicised indigenous as 'conceptually untenable' (ibid.). He argues that in the Andean countries there are only 'minoritarian "pure" indigenous [or white] groups' confronted by a historical fact: the majority of *'mestizos'* (ibid.). The argument is not new. The foundational myth of 'modern' post-colonial states, particularly in Latin America, is the notion that a *de facto* hybrid identity – mixed, integrated; majoritarian – quashes any radical claims to the political, social or moral consistency of indigenous notions, practices, and the objects associated to such practices. The latter are seen only as signs of bygone eras, mere relics of the past, and ultimately, as dangerous obstacles in the path towards self-authorised modernisation.

According to this position, the task of 'modern' politics proper is to achieve development.[5] However, once it focuses on the obstacle that acts as a stumbling block, impeding the full enjoyment of modernity, this form of politics loses sight of its end, and instead remains fixed on the deployment of the most effective means to get rid of the obstacle. The often-unacknowledged result of this 'modern' conception of the political, based on a particular sort of blindness, is the greatest violence, since 'doing evil to the other' becomes the very condition of one's unalloyed *jouissance*.[6] Vargas Llosa's position is but the reinstatement of a conventional view, which sees the disappearance of the obstacle as a 'necessary evil'. That view was already present at the foundation of modern/colonial constitutionalism (Clavero, 2000).

However, two caveats are required in order to properly understand this constitutional convention and its current reinstatement. First, the supposedly *de facto* hybridity (*mestizaje*) is not a fact, but actually, the result of the elevation of the notion of 'common citizenship' into a political–constitutional canon, which cancels the explicit recognition of the status of the indigenous *qua* indigenous, while at the same time excludes their objects *qua* common objects.[7] *Mestizaje* (common citizenship) and private property are part and parcel of the same story: the establishment of a modern/colonial power structure. Second, it becomes easier to explain and understand, from this perspective, why indigenous peoples must struggle to recover their indigenous bodies and objects, not just their 'identities', like ghosts in search of a body, and enact a world where they count, rather than being discounted as mere obstacles or relics of the past, on the way towards decolonisation, the overthrow and replacement of modern/colonial power structures.

Why do analysts like Vargas Llosa, in Latin America, or the commentators that mistake every enactment of Islamic ways in Europe for a reactionary assault on the values of the Enlightenment, remain blind to the importance of powerful objects and thick attachments in politics and society? In more general terms, why are we unable to make sense of such elements and relations, and instead adjudicate against them and wish them erased? Rendered in an obfuscating language that confuses the victims, and reduces classical modern politics, economics and choice theory to little more than a glorified version of cost–benefit analysis, such mainstream positions vertiginously slip towards the sort of short-sightedness and thoughtlessness that Hannah Arendt, among others, have correctly posited as the missing link between the idea of a necessary evil and the greatest violence (Dupuy, 2005: 70–99).

The working hypothesis is that the problem lies in a 'deficient' understanding of materiality, one that sees 'signs' in the place of powerful objects (exemplars, charms, fetishes), adjudicates against the latter as mere relics of the past and can only conceive of material relations and causality in representational terms, as co-relative to our self-positing powers.

Truth and the return of the fetish

Saba Mahmood suggests that even modern Muslims dismiss powerful objects and the claims attached to them as superstitious, or retroactively transform and displace them within a normative framework (2004). Once displaced, they cannot be dealt with but only disciplined or juridified. As a result of this, claims that do not assume a legalistic, positivist or empiricist framework (for instance, radical ethical–political or religious claims) are either dismissed as having no effects or transformed, more often than not into an obstacle, within a legal-procedural network. Since neither result is satisfactory for the parties involved, Mahmood calls for a new thought of the object in modernity, in a manner that is reminiscent of Bruno Mazzoldi and Jacques Derrida's call for a 'thought of superstition' as a thought of the remainder (Mazzoldi and Téllez, 2007: 372).

In keeping with that call, this chapter started its exploration of powerful objects in the vicinity of Heidegger's account of the transformation in the essence of truth; but rather than accepting that modernity has displaced the object, rendering it secondary, unimportant, a mere residue which does not count and has no effects, it was argued that these elements, once associated with the sacred and magic, with rebellion and the wild man (particularly in the former colonies) have become unplaceable. And yet, although unplaceable in modernity, they have effects and remain central to the creation of affective radical attachments, including political attachments. In this sense, we shall speak of the 'return' of the magical object, the fetish.[8]

Let us proceed: to speak of the return of the fetish is to contend that there is a case for extending self-reflexive capacities to the objects with which humans mesh and interact. That claim could be understood as a plea for a renewed form of materialism. What sort of materialism? This would be a materialism without any residual essentialism, but also one that does not aim at emphasising solely the reality of the world 'out there', or conversely, that of (human) relations. It could not be a 'default' materialism, one in which matter is defined as what remains after all descriptions have been rehearsed but acts, nevertheless, as the stand-in for some mysterious causal power. 'Matter' understood in this way would only be that which is posited by the failure of *our* descriptions.

The problem with that sort of materialism – recognisable in such varied contemporary philosophies as those of Saul Kripke and Slavoj Žižek – is threefold. First, it ultimately denies capacity to matter itself. Second, it uses the term 'matter' as a (realist) stand-in for some ultimate 'efficient' cause located not in matter itself, but rather in the human mind. Very broadly, the argument underpinning such uses of materialism is as follows: if 'matter' is that which remains after the failure of our descriptions, it is so only as inert matter, as some sort of thing-in-itself. However, as can be seen in Immanuel Kant's final writings, known to us as *Opus Postumum*,[9] the doctrine of the thing-in-itself is quickly superseded by the doctrine of the human mind's self-positing. 'Matter' being undescribable or unrepresentable, is quickly turned into a fantasmatic reservoir that remains in the background unless motivated by an efficient cause or a purpose: the thing-in-itself 'for us'. Third, this is no materialism but something else.

To explain further, according to this view, purpose is provided by the self-positing of the human mind among the material objects of the world, thereby providing them with meaning and sense. In a way, thus, the human mind *wills* the world of objects *anew* every time it posits itself onto them, but in doing so, it forgets that it has made gods for itself among the objects of the world and, thinking that it can simply replace them at will with new ones, it becomes a god for itself. Since the human mind is not an all-encompassing substance lying somewhere beyond embodiment, but exists in variegated form in each and every human being, ultimately men become gods to one another. The result of this metaphysics is therefore *practical*, a particular kind of violence that characterises modern times: it begins as violence against the objects and ends up as an abstract domination of some by others.

This is not the immediately physical kind of violence that we have grown accustomed to see in the news, or rapidly identify with terror and the violation of human rights (although it is never incompatible with the latter) but rather one that is less overtly corporeal or dis-incorporates. An example of this sort of violence is the abstract violence that a state or a multinational class exerts upon those who are dominated. Subject to this sort of violence and terror, the latter become more like ghosts in search of a body. To be more precise we should speak of 'the incorporeal attributes that lie at the heart of the most destructive corporeal actions' (Kaufman, 2005: 350), the disembodiment that occurs prior to, as a condition for, or on the way towards the destruction of an actual (human) body.

Eleanor Kaufman suggests that the exploration of these 'incorporeal attributes' entails a turn towards the ontology and connectivity of (non-human) bodies (ibid.). She locates the traces of such a turn in the phenomenological tradition, up to and including Sartre, De Beauvoir and

Merleau-Ponty. Placing herself firmly within that tradition she posits, after De Beauvoir, the following question: 'Might the object somehow have its own object ontology that is not even perceptible by the human as such?'[10] Such is the question that a contemporary form of materialism worthy of the name would try to answer.

Positing such a question in the form of a plea for materialism does not entail the abandonment of our concern with (human) bodies subjected to violence. Quite the contrary; Kaufman argues that insofar as this tradition explores the boundaries between the human and the nonhuman it also suggests 'new ways of conceptualising the complexity of the relation between matter and violence'.[11] Her point is that interrogating different forms of violence to objects might give us a different way of perceiving violence to humans (Kaufman, 2005: 358). This is also part and parcel of an inquiry into a superior form of realism or materialism. As we will see in the following paragraphs, the young Karl Marx identified early on this result in politics and philosophy, and the necessity to explore the complex relation between matter and violence. To this aim, he used a notion taken from the analysis of Afrological religious forms, but also from the transit of these religious practices into revolutionary political and legal discourses, first in the Americas and the Caribbean and then in Europe. That notion entered the vocabulary of the critical tradition via the slave-trade routes connecting Africa and Europe with the Caribbean, and was later made famous by the social sciences, particularly religious anthropology and psychoanalysis. That notion remains central, and should be rediscovered for the purposes of developing a superior account of materiality: it is the concept of fetishism.

Impossible matter: the two aspects of the fetish

It is often thought that the explanatory power of the fetish-image invoked by critics such as Marx has to do with the identification of an illusory appearance and a revealed kernel of reality, or 'matter'. However, as Jean-Luc Nancy observes, this is merely the beginning of a more complicated story (2001: 3–8). He explains that by conjuring up the image of fetishism Marx seems to promise us demystification, that is to say, he promises to give us the *real thing* instead of the apparent fetish. But here we encounter the first problem: by definition, demystification promises the real thing as that which is in excess of any of its presentations. Take for instance the prohibition concerning presentations or images of god in monotheistic religion. These are denounced as false gods or fetishes because the true god does not show up. In fact, the true god's higher authority and transcendence is confirmed by the fact that it cannot be reduced to any one actual thing. Here we are in familiar territory, that of (negative) theology but also philosophy: things are sorted out into substances and derivatives, the simple super-essence on the one hand and composite artifices on the other, and the latter are denied any reality of their own. However, as Nancy observes, if this is the case then demystification cannot deliver what it promises: it cannot show the real thing whose presence would take the place of the fetish, because the real thing is by definition non-presentable.

Conceived in this manner, critique leads to disillusionment. Thus, a second movement is necessary in order to avoid disappointment: once again following Nancy, to make the second move we must recognise that by denouncing the fetish as false or artificial we may be acting out our desire to explain it away so that the authority of the true essence remains unfettered. However, even if we achieve that, we do not explain the fetish at all. In this second instance the question is not 'why is there this object-fetish instead of the real thing/nothing?' but rather 'how come there is a fetish at all?'. In dealing with these 'two secrets' of the fetish, as Nancy puts it, we find out two things: On the one hand, we discover that philosophy, like theology, has a problem with the apparent, the composite and the artificial; a problem that it does not, and perhaps it cannot solve. On the other, we discover that the problem, the fetish, refuses to go away. It returns.

The problem is that of the return of the fetish; but now we can reformulate the problem in the following way: since the fetish has never really gone away (never fully obscured by the light of the true essence), the problem is that of its presence as artifice: the being of artifice, of composites and made-up objects. No longer secondary since the simple entity does not, it cannot, explain the existence of the composite, the artifice, the fetish, and hence has no priority. No longer just a mere appearance since we are not concerned with the 'real thing' behind it but with the reality, the materiality or objectivity of the fetish itself.

In reformulating thus the problem of the fetish, with Marx and Nancy, we have found yet another face of the uncanny: 'the uncanny entails another thinking of beginning: the beginning is already haunted' (Royle, 2003: 1). If the fetish functions as a beginning that is haunted, the copy in the origin, a vanishing point in the sense that as soon as we try to grab it, it vanishes (it retires into the darkness of its falsity, nothingness or absence so that the authority of the true essence may shine on in its full light) then its refusal to go away, its continuous lure and fascination, confronts us with a more general problem: that of withdrawal, or the vanishing as vanishing point (Badiou, 2007b). This is not the problem of presence in general, but on the contrary, that of the coming-to-presence of matter that is always vanishing. Put otherwise, if a 'first critique' wishes to explain away the fetish as artifice, a 'second critique' (after critique, beyond critique) is obliged to explain artifice. This is precisely the problem of production as artful presentation (produced/producing matter, ghostly matter, fantasy or 'the formal') inherited from idealism by Hegel, Marx and others.

In Kant's solution to the problem of the coming-to-presence of matter, or 'crystalization', as it is termed in the final development of the argument contained in his *Opus Postumum* (1993), and which still dominates a great deal of philosophy, the body and the world of objects are left causally inefficacious in respect to the mind's operation. They are merely made up, produced or constituted. As suggested above, this has consequences for a theory of action and practice, since we are left without the possibility of studying the connection between technical objects, body and action; as a result real-time performance, which is actually carried on through the body, is disfavoured in relation to the study of the inner and abstract determinations of action, conceived as powers of an immaterial mind. That is the principle through which a certain account of substance, let us call it substantialist idealism, in spite of its self-proclaimed realism, persists in philosophy of mind, in certain forms of cognitive science and in the theory of action, including law and politics.

This principle leads to non-realism since the particular externals of the world are conceived to be causally inefficacious in relation to the mind's operation; hence the dogmatism of the thing-in-itself. Moreover, the causal inefficacy of the world in respect to the mind allows a sharp separation between persons and objects that re-enacts the ancient categories of Roman private law at different stages during the development of a modern concept of property (crucially, in relation to the question of slavery or the progression between the technical–practical and the moral–practical). Kant's definition of 'person' (the moral/thinking subject) is composed of a network of dichotomies (such as ends/means, subjective/objective, absolute/relative) that are themselves juridical distinctions. In this manner, the form of a social relationship based upon the distinction between persons and things is introduced in the rational form itself. Here the formal idea of 'Man' as moral/thinking subject and prime mover of the objects of the world, arbiter and instance of the law, re-enacts, as Gillian Rose observed, a specific form of legality (1990: 26–7). The idealist programme of material critique, understood in this manner, takes on a purely juridical form: the Tribunal of Reason.

Kant's 'tribunal of reason' aims at establishing the limitations of human reason. He shows that to apply the concepts from our understanding beyond the limit of possible experience leads reason to paradoxical results, or 'antinomies'. Antinomies can be understood as points or moments at which reason arrives at divergent or contradictory conclusions. The image here is that of two divergent paths, with the observer being unable to travel both. Notice how, on the one hand, in spite of Kant's obvious epistemological emphasis the image suggests that the limit is not just epistemological, that the very existence of antinomies may indicate an incompleteness in reality that no effort to apply the concepts of the understanding could remedy. However, on the other hand, Kant's insistence on the determinant nature of the position of the observer entails that the issue at stake is incompleteness as a matter of observation, or at least that the incompleteness of reality is correlative to the limitations of our apparatus of observation. In any case, the ontological question is ultimately subsumed under and 'resolved' as an epistemological question.

Consider for instance the case of the Third Antinomy, the contradiction between freedom and necessity: the moment we try to reason about freedom we arrive at the contradictory result that we are both free – beyond the causal, unchanging laws of nature – and not free – subject to the laws of causality. This is to say that both freedom and necessity are true, but they cannot both be true, since we cannot travel both paths at once without ceasing to be one and the same person. Thus, for Kant, the idea that reality itself may be contradictory or incomplete is always subordinated to limitations on our part, in this case the unity of consciousness or its presence to itself. Put otherwise, although Kant hints at the possibility that we are confronted with a real (objective) uncertainty because reality itself is incomplete, he seems to stop short of exploring the implications of such objectivity.

The reason for this is Kant's commitment to a principle of unity or identity that expresses not only logical unity – totality – but also the unity of experience – wholeness – (Kant, 1993: 210). Reality itself cannot be incomplete or contingent; otherwise our unitary experience of it would be impossible. We would know the frequency of its variations so well that we could know nothing else. The solution to this problem, according to Kant, is to postulate the unity of experience as a narrative unity imposed by the observer upon a reality conceived in terms of chance and hidden necessity. Crucially, if the unity of experience is 'narrative' this means that wholeness is a matter of temporisation or 'anticipation'. This inaugurates in Kant the theme of the anticipatory or 'practical' use of reason.

Later on Kant distinguishes between 'technical–practical' and 'moral–practical' reason (1993: 210–13), thereby suggesting that freedom and legality are the result of a progression from 'technics' to 'rights' and therefore entirely a matter of subjecting ourselves and nature to technical programmes or projects, anticipatory fantasies that make the world stable, that is to say, whole. The idea here is that we give ourselves an image of the future as a whole, which contains within itself an infinite number of possibilities and therefore has no real limitations (Kant, 1993: 210 [22: 49]) or to put it otherwise, a set of all possible cases, each one representing a conceivable outcome having as much chance as the others of being chosen or realised. Then, such an infinite set or whole is given to a symmetrical or 'inert' (homogenous, unchanging) technical object, a die or a coin for instance, but also laws, which are identified here with a universal technical object – this is the meaning of the 'progression' from the technical–practical to the moral–practical in Kant (Kant, 1993: 210; also Meillassoux, 2007: 64–5). We conclude from this calculative/anticipatory procedure that a hidden necessity presides over the actual outcome or choice. As Meillassoux observes:

If the die or the coin to which such a calculative procedure is applied always falls on the same face, one concludes by affirming that it has become highly improbable that this phenomenon is truly contingent: the coin or the die is most likely loaded, that is to say, it obeys a law (. . .) And an analogous chain of reasoning is applied in favour of the necessity of laws: identifying the laws with the different faces of a universal Die – faces representing the set of possible worlds – it is said, as in the precedent case, that if these laws are contingent, we would have been present at the frequent changing of the face; that is to say, the physical world would have changed frequently. Since the 'result' is, on the contrary, always the same, the result must be 'loaded' by the presence of some hidden necessity, at the origin of the constancy of observable laws.

(Meillassoux, 2007: 64–5)

As can be seen, this account of anticipation depends on at least three assumptions: (i) That technical objects are indeed inert or homogeneous; the persistence of this assumption in the later writings of Kant (1993), in which the progression from the technical–practical to the moral–practical and the question of temporisation are schematised most properly, reveals that the anti-fetishist leanings of the first Critique remain in place in spite of the move towards the practical – anticipation and fantasy – in the second and third Critiques. (ii) That it is possible to make up an image of time as a whole, and to separate such an image from the (suspected) incompleteness of reality itself for the purposes of calculation; the assumption that persists here is that the principle of identity is not just a logical rule but also inherent in the nature of the set, that there can be only one set of all sets, cases or possibilities. After Cantor and non-classical logics, it is obligatory to enquire at this point, as Meillassoux does among others (2007: 66): what sort of infinity or wholeness is this one? On the one hand, we know after Cantor that infinities are multiple, and 'above all that these infinities constitute a multiplicity it is impossible to foreclose, since the set of all sets cannot be supposed without contradiction' (ibid.). On the other hand, the assumption of an actual infinity of all cases is not 'anticipatory' in the strictest sense of the term, but rather, 'preventive' insofar as it is postulated in order to foreclose the possibility that reality itself is incomplete, and not just our knowledge of it. The assumption of the principle of identity becomes in this case a concession to the truth-preserving nature of classical logic, which submits the case of the observer confronted with divergent paths to the necessity of either/or reasoning. The possibility that the observer can be split into two and effectively walk down both paths at the same time, or more precisely that reality itself can be split into two as a result of the shattering force of a futural or projected event, retroactively acting upon the present situation, is dismissed as simply too far-fetched. (iii) The idea that a decisive cut or a split in reality is simply too far-fetched seems to spring from the well-founded fear that such an idea would be ontologically profligate, from its apparent flouting of Ockam's razor. But this would be the case only if we sustain a conception of narrative, temporality and temporisation as a linear progression branching out into divergent paths every time a choice is made. If that were the case, any anticipation would remain an unrealised possibility that cannot be verified or falsified. Arguably, this is exactly what happens with the postulation of a temporal whole that contains the infinite, open-ended number of cases. Perhaps at this point the image of the observer confronted by divergent paths ceases to be useful, and should be replaced with that of the time-traveller, the self-reflective trajectory in which the future and the past intersect and touch one another. Here, the important notion is that of something like a time-shift, made possible by the dynamics of the technical objects themselves, which allows us to gain knowledge of events and phenomena that preceded or exceed the possibility of us experiencing them (Trotta, 2007: 152). This suggests a reality whose incompleteness exceeds the bounds of our experience, but also that the role of reason is generative, in the sense of technical creation, exteriorisation and the realisation of possibilities beyond the determination of a given programme, rather than merely preventive or preserving.

Seen from this perspective, Kant not only appears as the forefather of probabilism and prevention, it also becomes clear that his critique remains an attempt to resolve the deadlock prompted by a situation of purely epistemic or (subjective) uncertainty, which for all its practicality, would ultimately exclude the (contingent but necessary) relation between the ethico-political and mortality, or the anticipation of the end. As we will see later on, this inability to link the ethico-political and mortality results in the preeminence of immortality in politics and the social sciences – the preservation of life by any means necessary: biopolitics, thanatopolitics, the merging between 'security' and 'development' and so on – which is best schematised in the analytical theme of the death-drift or death-drive.

To sum up, although Kant hints at the possibility of the incompleteness of reality (what analytical theories term 'lack' or 'absence') his explorations of real incompleteness are at best cautious and at worst preventive. Ultimately, they are reduced to limitations of reality 'for us', that is to say, limitations of human reasoning, which, if corrected, by clearing the way of all fetishes and contaminants, might give us the upper hand over nature. This is why for Kant, at least in the *Critique of Pure Reason*, the only alternative to resolve the impasse is to set the strictest rules upon the use of concepts and so on in order to prevent reason from overstepping its bounds and engage in speculative exercises beyond the field of possible experience into weird, fantasmatic, fetish objects and ultimate questions. At this point, the decision of the tribunal is that we must abandon philosophical speculation and fetishism, the notion that matter has its own dynamic, as both archaic and a fantasy in the pejorative sense of such terms (Kant, 1996: 418).

In contrast, the argument advocated here pushes for an extension of the term 'matter' to all composite entities, human and non-human alike, once we have accepted that all entities are composite, obscure, and none of them simpler than others. Everything hinges upon this axiom: granted that there are no criteria to distinguish materials that carry more ontological weight (simples) than others (composites), the establishment of the human mind as (active or retroactive) efficient cause of inert or invested matter must be considered suspect.

The sort of materialism advocated here follows from this notion. It is a materialism of machines and artifices, of artfully presented objects that allow us to consider looking down into divergent paths, to go beyond; a materialism of projection that contrasts with all materialisms in that it does not speak of matter as either inert or atomistic, set in motion by the direct influence of a privileged cause, and therefore does not posit the power of anticipation (a power and its presentiment, as Nancy says) solely in divine or human hands (Stiegler, 1998: 158 ff.). Because of these two aspects, this materialism is both sublimely fetishist and counter-humanist.

In spite of our criticism, the starting point for this materialism is precisely the image suggested by Kant's critique: that of being confronted by two divergent paths. More than any other critical philosopher in modernity, Kant hinted at the incompleteness of reality and explored the possibility that fantasmatic projection, in the form of the technical–practical and moral–practical uses of reason, might actually hold the key to anticipation and exteriorisation. Granted, he fell prey to the chronological, logical and ontological pre-eminence that terms such as 'form', 'autonomy', 'freedom', 'totality' (*Totalität/Allheit*), 'anticipation', and 'exteriorization' induce: if one could speak of exteriorisation, this would mean the preceding presence of an interiority (Stiegler, 1998: 152). This bias must be countered by the materialist injunction that such an interiority 'is nothing outside of its exteriorization' (ibid.), and thus, that the issue cannot be posited in either/or terms (either interiority or exteriority). What is required is a thought of the composition rather than the opposition of the two terms, a common constitution that is also the constitution of the common.

This sort of materialism or 'double critique' would allow us today, as it did Marx before, to explain the coming-to-presence of the fetish, the sort of personification and reification inherent in such legal–political categories as 'commodity' or 'product' (in today's commercial speech referring to a reality – object or service), 'capital' and 'money' (which are nowadays not metallic but electronic capital and credit), and 'assembly' or 'right', in the people-vanishing constitutional language of our self-authorised democracies. In all these cases, what is called 'interiority' must not be understood as a potentiality of which 'exteriorisation' or 'objectification' seems to be the act, since in such an understanding 'interiority' appears as the expectation or the promise of objectification. As Stiegler observes, the problem is that expectation is anticipation, and thus the object appears both as the result of anticipation (exteriorisation) and the condition of all anticipation, anticipation appearing itself '*qua* the interiorization of the originary fact of exteriorization' (1998: 153). That is to say, as a gesture, as *Erinnerung*, the very moment of reflexivity or the affection of self as a return to self (ibid.). As Stiegler puts it: 'there is no anticipation, no time outside of this passage outside, of this putting-outside-of-self and of this alienation of the human and its memory that "exteriorization" is' (1998: 152). The argument could be presented in summary form as follows: the image of the observer confronted by two divergent paths must be turned into the image of the self as a return to self, or objectification, and the image of the line branching out into two divergent paths must become, in turn, that of the circle (Klossowski, 1969).

Let us now supplement this argument with a short genealogy of the reference to the fetish-object, the term 'fetishism'. Let us follow the trajectory of its entry, its return, into the language of modern criticism. This term is probably the most important contribution of Portuguese/Spanish languages, in their shattering encounter with subaltern languages, to modern metaphysics, political philosophy and theory. It is in fact an anomaly, the trace of a 'subaltern' language at the very centre of modern philosophy, and thus the basis for a modern 'perspective of the Scythian' (Martin, 1996).

A brief history of the fetish

The term 'fetish' emerges out of the transformation of the Portuguese *feitiço* into *hecho*, signifying 'made' or 'made by art'. Between Portuguese and Spanish the f often transforms into h (as in *fermosa* and *hermosa*) but the common root carries the notion of something made by human hands, an artifice, a copy, as degraded and therefore unworthy of our attention because of its disconnection from the alleged authenticity of nature. Because of this, the conditions under which an artifice becomes valuable as such become suspicious. This is why in beauty contests (proverbially popular in Latin America) Miss Venezuela and Miss Colombia are always busy trying to convince everybody else that their beauty is 'natural', no matter how many times they have been under the knife, or product-placed in gentlemen's magazines.

But there is more to the story. The term entered Anglo-Germanic languages via France, where the term *fétiche* was used for the first time in connection to the study of Afrological religious forms, in particular those of West African peoples, but also those which derived from the West African diaspora caused by the slave trade, such as *voudoun*, *candomblé* and *santería* in Latin America and the Caribbean. In the Caribbean, these religious forms were central to the formation and passage to action of revolutionary collectives during the seventeenth, eighteenth and nineteenth centuries. The language of the fetish entered political radical language and, like a virus, jumped from there into legal language (it can be seen in cases decided by judges from the American south, for instance the famous *Charles River Bridge* case) and then onto literature and cinema.

In this usage it referred to an object, a charm or an amulet, through which gods, spirits and ancestors would communicate or intervene. Fetishes anticipate their power, and actualise it. Importantly, the context of this first usage of the term is that of colonial transactions around unique gods and spaces. As anthropologist Manuel Durand-Barthez observes (2002), in this sort of situation and as a result of conflicts, alliances and conquest, social and territorial bonds may enlarge, diminish or break down and disseminate through, for instance, exile caused by chattel slavery, as in the eighteenth and nineteenth centuries, or by modern migrations, as it happens today. He explains that in these cases 'contact is kept with gods who emanate from human minds and simultaneously exert a determining influence on human beings. These can, in turn, phagocyte foreign gods, even enemy gods, whether victorious or defeated'.[12] What Durand-Barthez explains in the final lines, having in mind an encounter in 1938 between French ethnologist Michel Leiris and Cuban painter Wilfredo Lam, is the process that Brazilian poet Oswald de Andrade called 'anthropophagy' and Cuban anthropologist Fernando Ortíz termed 'transculturation'.

In Chapters 1 and 2, this process was referred to with the terms 'mimesis' and 'contagion', and was associated with Sartre's notion of nausea and Freudian melancholia. The key to these terms is the replicating/gathering/world-enacting power of the object. Subjects and characters appear as nothing but the 'choice' (projection, enactment) of an object or an issue, and equal no more than the chosen object. They lack immediate psychological or social density (against holism and naturalism) and are more like 'freedoms caught in a trap' (Sartre, 1998: 217). In fact, rather than choosing these objects or issues, the latter are projected, cut up and made present against their original solitude in being, and through these projections worlds of sensual relations are enacted. By enacting these worlds and projecting these objects, subjects are invented and reinvented. The latter do not pre-exist the enactment as an a priori agency doing the projection but are rather the result of the enactment and the projection. In this sense they *must* be invented or postulated and the force of this path and the violence of this appearance signal the breakdown of any established agency or system of relations. This being the case, the elements of contagion cannot be conceived of as rules of law or fully meaningful commands. Rather, the objects of contagion and contamination interpellate without establishing the mode of the response; the latter is not pre-given but must be provided. In this sense, and in contrast with positive legalistic commands, powerful and contaminating objects, fetishes, have the form of a call without meaning. Let us now clarify what is meant by speaking about fetishes as a form or 'call without meaning', by providing and examining some instances of contagion.

Call without meaning: the fetish-voice and contagion

Instances of contagion include the adoption of images from Western pop culture by non-Western communities in post-colonial situations, as in the case of the Cuna peoples of Putumayo, Colombia, studied and described by anthropologist Michael Taussig in *Mimesis and Alterity* (1992). Since the early twentieth century, the Cuna have modelled their traditional objects, *molas* and figurines on Western commodity objects such as the Jack Daniel's bottle or the RCA dog and included in them the well-known faces of recognisable historical Western characters. When the 'obvious' connection is pointed out by the anthropologist, the Cuna would deny that their figures have any representative or designating value. According to Taussig, in pointing out the difference between the obviousness of the representationalist connection for the anthropologist and the fact that such a connection is not obvious at all for them, the Cuna behave like critical thinkers on their own right rather than naïve receivers and reproducers of modern culture, or mere superstitious folk. Like the rural and urban workers who were the subject of Taussig's *The Devil and Commodity Fetishism in South America* (1983) by including Western commodity motifs as devilish forms in their sacred objects, the Cuna identify that capitalism is based upon the magical belief that capital is self-positing, that it works according to the logic of abstract representation, when in fact it feeds on the destruction of actual worlds. Given the latter, the Cuna are obliged to respond by enacting their worlds anew and reinventing themselves in a way that includes capitalism as an inevitable element of failure in their futural horizon. The inclusion of the inevitability of failure in one's own world-enacting, self-enacting projective practice (anticipation) is a form of over-identification or close proximity with an obstacle or a boundary. This may explain the association of feelings of nausea, melancholia and disgust which accompany these objects. Alas, these objects express and enact the necessary, violent passage through this boundary on the way to freedom.

A related instance of contagion and over-identification is explored by Françoise Vergès in her study of responses to the post-colonial condition in the Réunion Island, *Monsters and Revolutionaries* (1999). The central conception of the book is *métissage* (miscegenation) to be distinguished here from *mestizaje*, the inverted racialism that informs the 'multiculturalist' ideology of European, American and Caribbean post-colonial nation-states. In the case of the latter, the existence of racism is disavowed by presenting the historical mixture of races as the basis of the nation's identity. As such it is an ideology and discourse of national 'identity' that, on the one hand, accepts the pluralistic demand of so-called tolerant and well-ordered societies, while on the other, forecloses the possibility of non-elite claims against the nation and almost in passing erases the colonial past. Vergès' argument performs a sort of reverse engineering of this discourse, and shows it as the post-colonial avatar of the colonial racism of the blood (or *pureza de sangre*).

In contrast, her notion of miscegenation seeks to highlight the reality of the exploitation of black and indigenous women by white men and the impossibility of a self-recursive discourse on purity, which renders the state-politics of identity vacuous because of its strange accommodation of naturalist and holistic tendencies. The point of her argument is neither to celebrate local hybridity nor to return to substantialist politics. Rather, *métissage* entails another thinking of origin and remainder: that the beginning is already haunted by what remains. Put otherwise, this is to say that composition or contamination is universal and that there are no simpler elements (such as 'pure' blood and so on); only remainders, mixed efficacious elements. On this she walks in the footsteps of José Vasconcelos and Ernesto Guevara but avoids the trap of naïve transcendentalism present, to a certain extent, in the latter.

Given this universality of the remainder, no politics of liberation can be based upon a claim of purity, biological, cultural, moral or otherwise. Conversely, a politics of liberation worthy of the name can only be sustained by an engagement with and in relation to the oppressor. That is the point of introducing white faces in sacred objects or commodity figures in traditional *molas*, but also of gaining close proximity – the closest possible – with the white male coloniser (as in *métissage*). In 'identification', those who identify with the call of the leader or the 'white mask' take that call as a command that determines their response. The voice of the Other or its gaze becomes the law. On the contrary, in 'over-identification' the distance between the subject to the law (self) and the subject that gives the law (other) disappears and, as a result, the contingency of both gets revealed and the response remains indeterminate. What follows is the annihilation of both self and other. Controversially, her analysis suggests that over-identification with the discourse of domination may be a more rebellious weapon than resistance.

This result finds confirmation in the work of a seventeenth-century Peruvian indigenous writer named Waman Puma de Ayala. In 1615, the latter published a tract called *Nueva Corónica y Buen Gobierno* (1993), in which he accepted the claim of the Spaniards to the so-called New World, not on the basis of conquest, but rather on the basis of a donation given by the Inca Huáscar. Having (over)identified with the discourse of the coloniser, Puma de Ayala proceeds to detail the obligations that fall upon the Spanish Crown as a result of this donation, in the context of a general economy of gift and substitution. The whole of the Tawantisuyu, given by the Inca Huáscar, is a gift with no countergift. Therefore, the recipient of the gift, the King of Spain, becomes infinitely indebted to the Inca, that is to say, to all of the indigenous inhabitants of the New World, and thus being infinitely indebted to them, the King becomes also infinitely less powerful than them. Puma de Ayala dismisses conquest, but also plain resistance, and favours a solution that on the whole makes the potency of the King of Spain infinitely minor than that of his 'lesser' subjects. It is the lowest among the low, the indigenous, who acquire the most potency, and thus the right to use force. This is a justification of mass-scale rebellion with no parallel: it is trans-cultural, since it operates in both Lascasian Spanish terms and in terms of the indigenous logic of substitution, but also general, since the argument can be presented as a universal postulate that is, nevertheless, completely situated. It can serve as the basis of a politics of engagement in close proximity.

In contrast, resistance can be understood as a politics of distance and non-participation based on the alleged 'higher morality' of the group that claims to possess some sort of privileged access to a truth that can only be perceived as such from within the perspective of the group, guiding its actions and responses, and is being applied in every instance. The difference between resistance, understood in this manner, and proximity or 'over-identification' is that the latter entails a politics of engagement and passage to action devoid of truth in the sense, previously established, of an idea that is first present only to the faithful group and then applied. In proximity, 'truth' becomes part of the activity of world-enactment rather than previous design or prescription.

In passing, let us observe that the qualitative research of Vergès and Taussig, or the early example of Puma de Ayala, bring to mind and may provide some backup for the sort of analysis and theorisation of 'the real of the law' present in the contemporary work of people such as Mladen Dolar and Slavoj Žižek. The latter has used the term 'over-identification' precisely in this context: the necessary traversing of violence in order to engage and pass to action without a previously established truth or command.[13]

There are other, more contemporary, instances of contagion and over-identification in which peoples subjected to situations of oppression engage with the violence around them in their own way. A perhaps less obvious example is the work of art collective NSK/Laibach in Eastern Europe. Laibach is a post-punk band well-known for its controversial posturing, performance and use of cut-up techniques, which include working in very close proximity with images and sounds originated in Nazikunst and real socialist art. Faced with the violence of NATO's 'humanitarian intervention' and an already existing situation of governmental oppression and widespread terror, Laibach engaged on a tour aptly called '1994 Occupied Europe', and mimicking NATO forces, it declared its purpose to 'liberate' each visited European city. Tellingly enough, Laibach, identifying itself as an army of liberation, 'occupied' Sarajevo before NATO troops, declared the city 'liberated', founded on site the so-called NSK State in Time, issued passports and so on. Of course, neither the 'liberation', nor the 'founding' or the 'issuing' can be understood as proper legal activities, although the same can be said of NATO's actions, and the passports or the NSK state are not, strictly speaking, legal objects. However, their political intent should not go amiss: these are 'exemplars' rather than proper 'normative objects', more like calls or interpellations without meaning, structures of feeling that communicate through contagion. The affect communicated, or the challenge posited, in this case, was one of self-liberation in the face of the inevitable entry of NATO forces as liberators.

In terms of international law, if NATO's intervention in Europe during the 1990s is posited as a precedent for a newly emerging exception to the principle of the non-use of force enshrined in the UN Charter and derived from well-known customary rules, namely the use of force for the purposes of unilateral 'humanitarian intervention', then the action of Laibach/NSK helps to unmake the precedent, insofar as, together with other events, it indicates lack of an 'invitation' to intervene or, at least, a lack of identification between a sector of the intervened people with the 'self' proposed by NATO as the passive oppressed that, by its own nature, would justify its claim as rescuer and defender of Human Rights through force. It is the gap between the overidentified Laibach/Yugoslavia collective (as 'self') and the victimised 'self' imagined by NATO (as 'other') that allows one to speak of the obliteration of both self and other as the proper rebellious act.

Indeed, there was not much anybody could do to stop the occupation by NATO forces – and it may be true, as some have said, that this was the only option available – and yet the point of Laibach's performance was to highlight that it is precisely in these situations, when one has no choice, that choice and action become necessary. Perhaps it is no coincidence that the theoretical work of people such as Žižek and Dolar has been associated at times with the artistic and political efforts of Laibach and the NSK. In a sense, by over-identifying with the discourses of domination, Laibach engaged in emancipatory action before the arrival of NATO, or to put it more accurately, it questioned the self-righteousness of Europeans and Americans (and in this way, at least indirectly, the morality behind the proposed doctrine of humanitarian intervention) at the same time that it challenged the pervasive state of mind of Yugoslavians at the time: a crowd concealing the crime of its leaders and condemning itself to abjection in passiveness. It obliterated self and other.[14]

Other, perhaps more mundane but no less important instances of contagion include the Trobriand islanders modification of cricket, studied and captured on film by Jerry Leach in *Trobriand Cricket: An Ingenious Response to Colonialism* (1974); the Hauka possession cult of Ghana's Gold Coast, which is the subject of Jean Rouch's 1955 documentary *Les Maîtres Fous*; the 'ways of the Prophet' in modern Muslim communities studied by

Saba Mahmood in *Politics of Piety* (2004) and elsewhere, which are not commands but rather exemplars to be lived, made intimate through the deployment of powerful objects like the hijab, an image of the prophet or the lack thereof; but also, at a more theoretical level, the phenomena studied in crowd theory by Gustave Le Bon (1895) and William McDougall, later elaborated by Sigmund Freud in his 1922 essay *Group Psychology and the Analysis of the Ego* (1975), in which the latter introduces a distinction between 'identification' as a form of radical collective attachment through contagion and 'object-desire' in relation to the libidinal attachment between the individual and the (projected or anticipated) leader.

The insight here is that it is through attachment with objects that identification with others becomes possible; this Freudian insight into phenomena of contagion has been updated and brought to bear on the analysis of neoclassical conceptions of the market in economy and liberal political philosophy by Jean-Pierre Dupuy in *Le Sacrifice et l'envie* (1992), and more recently by Ernesto Laclau's timely study of populism in *On Populist Reason* (2005). The latter focuses, following Freud and psychoanalytical theorist Joan Copjec, on the enacting/gathering power of objects in the formation of popular political demands. In doing so he lays down the foundations for a thought of political demands outside legalistic and empiricist frameworks; in a different context, that of literature and cinema, instances of contagion through powerful objects appear in the nausea of sadness that overcomes the guests at the wedding of Pedro and Tita in Laura Esquivel's novel *Like Water for Chocolate*, adapted for the big screen by Alfonso Arau in 1992, or the plague of forgetfulness that ravages Macondo in Gabriel García Márquez's *A Hundred Years of Solitude*.

As can be seen, *fétiche*, the term for powerful objects and phenomena of contagion, is a rich and significant noun. The very fact that it entered the languages of northern Europe via an ethno-anthropological study of West African peoples *from* Portugal and/or Spain, suggests that the context of this transit is precisely that of the emergence of capitalism and the question of slavery in the formation of the world-system. This is the world that impinged upon the observations of the young German critic Karl Marx.

So what do Venezuelan beauty queens, Vodoo, *molas* and Karl Marx have in common? To begin with, the same root that nowadays informs arguments on beauty in beauty contests is present in Marx's insight concerning 'made up' gods being posited as the origin of everything (the efficient cause, in metaphysical terms) and thereby canonised and worshipped *as if* they were the real thing. Furthermore, Marx may have picked up this insight from anthropological accounts and stories concerning the destiny of social, religious and political forms in situations of conquest, encounter and oppression. When one reconstructs the genealogy of Marx's earlier usage of the term in the 1840s, what emerges is a fascinating and perhaps little known network of connections.

A German critic in the Caribbean: Marx's fetish

As Enrique Dussel observes (2006: 40), the young Marx 'discovered' fetishism while writing on the limitations on the right to freedom of the press imposed by the Prussian government. In Chapter 3 (10 May 1842) of his *On Freedom of the Press* we find the following lines:

> A surprising turn of phrase! The influence of the province on its Assembly is characterised as something external to which the conviction of the Assembly of Estates is contrasted as a delicate *inner feeling* whose highly sensitive nature calls out to the province: *Noli me tangere*! (...)[15] We will do what we like (...) Who are *we*? The estates (...) The Assembly of the estates has a province to which the privilege of its activity extends, but the province has no estates through which it could itself be active. Of course, the province has the right, under prescribed conditions, to create these gods for itself, but as soon as they are created, it must, like a fetish worshipper, forget that these gods are its own handiwork (...) We are confronted here with the peculiar spectacle, due perhaps to the nature of the Provincial Assembly, of the province having to fight not so much through its representatives as against them.
> (Marx, 1975, vol. 1: 132–81)

This passage merits careful consideration. Here Marx is referring to the nature of the Assembly of Estates, what we would call Parliament nowadays, in the language of a modern constitutional lawyer who criticises the 'medieval' conception of the Assembly that follows from the Speaker's words justifying the Assembly's privilege to publish its debates when and how it wants. This is a 'medieval' conception insofar as such a 'privilege of the estates' would stand against the 'rights of the people' (or 'province', in Marx's terms), and thus entails a misappropriation of the constitutional rights of the latter by the former. The passage echoes legal discussions of the time on the role of the people and the running of government, and contains an indictment of the notion of government having a will of its own. However, as we shall see, much more is at stake in these few but significant lines.

In order to correctly understand this passage we must acknowledge that Marx's conception of constitutional law is, at this point, miles away from what could be called 'deflationary constitutionalism'. Deflationary constitutionalism reduces the projective or anticipatory capacities of a political collective by denying that constructive future-oriented propositions make sense (that which entails irrealism in respect to the future); it 'deflates' actual reality, including future time, into mere possibility. In contrast, Marx's conception of constitutionalism, as it appears in this early text, is realist in respect to the future and seems closer to what Larry D. Kramer has recently termed 'popular constitutionalism' (Kramer, 2004).

Kramer has shown convincingly that by the late eighteenth century this was precisely the prevalent view, aided and abetted by a number of epoch-making events, particularly the revolutionary cycle in the Americas and elsewhere. As it is well known, the cornerstone of the Atlantic revolutions was an understanding of the people themselves, conceived as a 'compact', that is, a meshwork or composite, rebellious humans in alliance with their civil political machinery, as having produced a fixed point of closure in history: an anticipation or visionary speculation that had produced (retroactively) causal effects in the actual world.

Notice the terms used by St George Tucker in the appendix to his 1803 edition of *Blackstone's Commentaries*:

> The American revolution has formed a new epoch in the history of civil institutions, by reducing to practice, what, before, had been supposed to exist only in the visionary speculations of theoretical writers (...) The world, for the first time since the annals of its inhabitants began, saw an original written compact formed by the free and deliberate voices of the individuals disposed to unite in the same social bonds; thus exhibiting a political phenomenon unknown to former ages (...) The powers of the several branches of government are defined, and the excess of them, as well in the legislature, as in the other branches, finds limits, which cannot be transgressed without offending against the greater power from whom all authority, among us, is derived; to wit, the PEOPLE'.
> (Tucker, 1999 [1803]: Appendix A)

St George Tucker describes the American Revolution as a self-reflexive movement, a virtuous circle or a loop: the coming of the people to themselves. He speaks of the reduction to practice, in the past and the present, meaning what has already happened, of visionary speculations or anticipations, what was supposed to happen in some virtual, distant future. He describes 'the people' as transiting through time, seeking the circle's fixed point where the visionary speculation (on the part of the past with regard to the future) and the construction (of the future by the past) coincide. Accordingly, coming to oneself from the future means in this passage to return to the already, and thus it can be argued that the theme of St George Tucker's appendix, sovereignty and legislation, is intimately related to the question of resoluteness and fidelity, on the one hand, and the survival of the revolution beyond those who made it, those who were present, on the other.

The latter is the more essential question, since it inaugurates the theme of the revolution as something with a dynamics of its own: a thing that must be taken care of by those who are yet to come. Resoluteness projects itself beyond those who were present, first for the who to come, and second, that the who takes care of the what 'together with its becoming, projecting another horizon of what(s), affirming an infinite finality of the who-what totality, past, present and future' (Stiegler, 1998: 262). To sum up, the infinitude of the thing (the what) that exceeds the finitude of the subject (the who present) is what constitutes the possibility of resoluteness and fidelity: that the people, not just those present but essentially those to come, include the nonlived in the instant of resoluteness and the affirmation, through repetition of the 'already' of the world as much as the already of the subject. To repeat is to re-call that which precedes any identity, the event.

It is the event that marks each identity as a thrownness, a heritage from which the subject is handed over only when it comes back to it, handing it over itself authentically, to use Heideggerian parlance (Heidegger, 1967: §74). Is not this thematic of heritage precisely what Jefferson had in mind when he proposed, apropos of the American Revolution, that the rebellion return and the constitution be repeated, forgotten, at least every twenty years? (Jefferson, 2007: 32 and 35). What must be forgotten here is the self, any established identity or what we commonly call nowadays 'patriotism', which is based upon the notion that no work must be done by future generations because all the necessary revolutionary work was made by the previous ones, in favour of the sense of epochality in which 'resoluteness' and 'fidelity' consists, in its properly historical character, which has very little to do with the transcendentality of a given that would do away with its indeterminacy and contingency.

Work is, as Blanchot remarks apropos of Hegel (Blanchot, 1981: 24), to forget the self and to let one's other be, not another self or one's own 'other', but rather the other that brings with him the unforeseeable new, the true rebel. Indeed, the passage of the *Phenomenology of Spirit* that Blanchot has in mind is nothing less than a call to arms, a description of the *passage à l'acte* as a paradox that makes sense only in terms of production, artful presentation, and quite simply, of essential temporality. Blanchot recalls that Hegel is talking about the man who writes, and in more general terms of humanity as the organism that produces, when he says:

> [The man] has to start immediately, and, whatever the circumstances, without further scruples about beginning, means, or end, proceed to action.
> (Hegel, 1988, Chapter 5, section Ia)

What Hegel and Blanchot emphasise here is not so much a return to oneself, but rather, a moving towards the world, out-there into effects and consequences, which follow from the primary withdrawal from the world as a given. With Blanchot, writing designates an originary horizon of technicality, of tools and objects, which is constitutive of temporality as such (Blanchot, 1981: 33–4; Stiegler, 1998: 266). And this brings us back to the object of

Tucker's remark: the constitution as a surface of inscription, a technological object, a what, that allows the people access to history, not just in the sense of the given, but crucially in the sense of possibility that they have inherited and yet have chosen (Heidegger, 1967: 384), a shared fate: 'historizing of the community, of the people' (Heidegger, 1967: 384–5). This 'fate' is neither that of the given once and for all nor that of the mere succession of 'nows'. It is specific to the dynamic of a certain object (a technical object) and shot through by such a dynamic, from which each generation can never disengage itself (ibid.).

Here again we find an explanation for the rationality of Jefferson's proposal: that each generation forgets and repeats the constitution, the revolutionary event. As Bernard Stiegler correctly states, at stake is the question of the community of those who have nothing in common, of the default of community 'and of the community of the default' (1998: 269). That is to say, an artificial or composite collective made up of the elements that the previous organisation deselected as a residue and a remainder. Such a collective is possible as a repetition of itself in a projected futural horizon, each time specific in that it is shot through by the dynamic of a certain what, a surface of inscription: equipment and work, what Heidegger called 'the world-historial' (1967: 388) and Tucker, Jefferson and Puma de Ayala identified with the constitution.[16]

Put otherwise, the event is the key to resoluteness and fidelity, to (popular) sovereignty and legislation, but the event is inscribed in a complex of tools and materials, which are themselves submitted to a finality that itself stems from a mode of organising temporality: the mode of forgetting and repeating. Only this mode, which is also the mode of work and production, of writing, of invention in the larger sense of the radically new, allows for the establishment of a community of the default, and the survival, through rebellion and repetition, of the default of community.

Tucker's name for the latter is 'the people', but this name makes sense only in relation to the written constitution ('We, the people . . .'), or more precisely, to the indefinite task of writing a constitution, which according to Jefferson must be undertaken by each and every generation. An infinite constitution and an indefinite name, then; nothing like a 'self' or a decisive sovereign. Rather, the people are sovereign because they are indefinite, the default of community, and the commission of their task remains uncertain and contingent. Uncertain, yes, but viable, indeed necessary; one must speak here of a necessary contingency in that 'the world-historial' allows the people a resolutory dynamic and remains within ontological reach. If the vulgar understanding always apprehends time starting from the now as a moment inscribed in a flux that branches out into a number of given possibilities (Heidegger, 1967: 75, 81), all equally valid, like a decision tree, in the metaphysics that underlies the revolutionary conception of time the historial is a matter of the repetition of historical ruptures (the heritage).

The image that comes to mind is that of a loop: coming to themselves from the future becomes a returning to the already. In this sense, the people *qua* subject of repetition are futural. This is so starting out from the originary phenomenon of the future as return to the world and to heritage.[17] This movement of the subject has the character of recurrence, in that access to the future is only possible through access to heritage. Is this not precisely what connects parts 1 and 3 of Puma de Ayala's *Nueva Corónica y Buen Gobierno*, written between 1583 and 1613? Part 1 chronicles Andean ways and forms thereby allowing the default of community in the colonial Andes to access their world (their world-historial), while part 3 postulates a series of axioms for 'good government' that take the shape of a viable constitution in the future. If the latter is anticipation, this is so only in the sense that the future is being-able, having the capacity to predict it and make it happen, rather than something at hand, present or ready. The same goes for the past, which was not lived, in the strictest sense, by those to whom the *Nueva Corónica* speaks to, Americans and Europeans. This past, which is not 'lived' or 'experienced' past and that nevertheless remains, is there. The people are thrown there, and must dwell in such an inhospitable and unhomely place. That is precisely the meaning of part 2 of *Nueva Corónica*: this is the situation and these are the facts (Heidegger, 1967: 328). However, the resoluteness that is necessary in order to traverse this inhospitable place on the way to freedom can only make sense through its projection into infinitude, which is what is encountered through the very endurance of the facts of the situation, or put otherwise, through endurance of finitude into the beyond of self and other. The path of the hero and the rebel starts there.[18]

Thus, the people are heroic and rebellious, 'sovereign' is the term that St George Tucker uses, in two senses. First, in the sense of acquiring a greater power by making common cause with their 'world historial', antiquities that are still preserved, buildings and institutions, including, crucially, the legislature and the other branches whose function is to allow the people access to their heritage, and which only make sense as a prosthesis of the people, although they are in no sense secondary, and never separated as an isolated element from the compact. The potential for an excessive will on the part of these constituted powers is thereby limited, and this is of course the origin and radicality of the doctrine of the separation of powers, and thus the very heart of the constitution as such. Second, in the sense of having the power to *predict* the future and *make it happen* (deliberate voices ... disposed to unite ... thus exhibiting a phenomenon unknown to former ages).

Put otherwise, the people acquire a greater power in that they transit to or communicate, in a fashion that seems almost magical, with the anticipatory dimension. The key is to avoid conceiving the world-historial as present-at-hand, and that is why the keyword in the previous phrase is 'almost'. The people enter into a relationship with a flux that was not lived or experienced by them and nevertheless remains, a truly archaic dimension, through its material traces or residue (the world-historical, the remainder). This is not a flux of successive 'nows', but rather, a flux of ruptures and suspensions that can always be reassumed (the flux *qua* heritage, see Stiegler, 1998: 271). It is more or less in this sense that Heidegger writes: 'In the fateful repetition of possibilities that have been, Dasein brings itself back "immediately" – that is to say, in a way that is temporally ecstatical – to what has already been before it' (Heidegger, 1967: 391).

The historical flux is always broken and broken up, which is why it cannot be a succession of nows branching out into possibilities that may or may not become actual, but it is reconstitutable in that it can only be inherited as precisely this reconstitution – recall Jefferson's proposal. The problem, as Jefferson knew very well, is how to link these ruptures and recurrences; put otherwise, the problem of revolutionary politics is not so much the constitution, but rather re-constitution. Crucially, linking phenomena of recurrences is also a problem for geometry, the sciences and philosophy in general, in that these disciplines do not move or 'progress' by starting from the now inscribed in a flux (as a thought of falsifying, confirming, or denouncing previous 'paradigms' would have it) but rather as an unceasing reinauguration outside all teleology.

What gives form and consistency to this unceasing linking of recurrences, to history, that is, given that such consistency cannot be formed on the basis of the now? Only by projecting the event into the futural dimension, and in repetition, let it turn its gaze and causal power towards the present.[19] In this dimension, gods and visions emanated from human minds simultaneously exert a determining influence on human beings (crucially, through technology: in this case legal–political technology). This entails a special metaphysics of time, transition and withdrawal: the almost magical power of the people is their ability to transit or project themselves into the future and look back from there at the present.[20] In turn, this allows them to transform seemingly imposed or external conditions into internal conditions: that is, to enact the world anew and reinvent themselves.

Crucially, it is the mass of remains, monuments and records that are still accessible, which make such historical transition and reinvention possible. And so we must concern ourselves with the specific character of these objects made up as surfaces of recording (Stiegler, 1998: 272). These surfaces allow for reconstitution, that is to say, the differential restitution or repetition of what has been. Repetition is guided not by concern for exactitude, which as a name for truth reduces the latter to the mere functionality of objects (exactitude being the *telos* of instrumentality) and thus brings us back to a (critical) notion of objectivity as secondary or derivative, as means, in respect to a given set of ends. A desire to determine the undetermined, to establish a necessary being in the place of contingency, lurks behind this reduction of the being of objects as secondary in relation to an anthropocentric scheme of ends – a juridical, normativist desire if there ever was one.

The pre-eminence of this desire masks the important fact that the instrument, far from being just a means, a device for chronological measuring and subjective disengagement, is itself necessary for there to be any account of time. The object-tool, in the more general sense of being a surface of inscription, and before it can be thought of as a particularly exact measuring instrument, is constitutive of any account of time as heritage, as a common space, and thus as public. This publicity 'constitutes social programmatics' (Stiegler, 1998: 273; Heidegger, 1967: § 79). The inscription-object is thus the thing that brings stability to social relations, by making interior what is most exterior, namely the improbable and contingent. It brings forth inter-subjectivity but also intimate subjectivity in the form of what must be forgotten and repeated: programmatic publicity (ibid.). And as Stiegler observes, it is this publicity that opens truly historical space.

However, it must be added that publicity opens up historical space as the space of the improbable, beyond any given set of possibilities. Rather than imposing order and certainty, or prevention and precaution in the place of improbability by constantly deferring the end, this publicity seeks the end, it provides the collective with the ability to bring closure and fear no end. In this sense, true historical space is not the ground of pure potentialities inherent in the previous situation, which may or may not be actualised, but rather the ground that is constantly shaken, unceasingly broken and broken up.

This is what the people do, in Tucker's description (through their techno-political machinery): from the standpoint of the past/present the future is open, but in the transition to the future, from its vantage point, the forces that led to it appear to have acted with the force of necessity. Put otherwise, people choose their fate; and that is freedom. This is the point captured in the language of self-determination, prophetic 'sovereignty' and transculturation that characterised the period of revolutionary constitutionalism in the Americas and elsewhere.

Consider Haiti, site of one of the three main social and political revolutions of the time, and the only one carried out by slaves of West African provenance: the slaves did not simply invoke the avenging God of their masters that seemed to them disengaged and distant – unable to get angry nor to frighten – but rather trusted their own gods and related to them through various surfaces of inscription and anticipatory devices (charms, fetishes, etc.) in order to invade and assimilate the opposition's gravitational field. They would chant *La Marseillaise* to the French Napoleonic troops and cannibalise the Christian pantheon, turning their 'natural' distance into political engagement. Think of it in terms of reverse engineering and industrial piracy: their objects infiltrated the saints and deities of the opposing camp and split them up, separating them from their essential qualities until there came a point at which they could no longer be regarded as the same. They became something else, something different, animated by allusion to a deeper power lying beyond – beyond the present time of slavery and oppression.

That explains the awkward reaction of the French troops before these uncanny objects, chants and images, thoroughly familiar, recognisable, and yet absolutely alien. The revolutionary song of their past suddenly appeared as a call from the future threatening to swallow them. Revolutionary Haitians reverse-engineered the retentional objects of the opposite camp, thereby splitting up a historical space previously dominated by onto-theological figures of necessity and exactitude. In the process they opened up such a space to the improbable, the vision of a future without a master, *and made it happen*. What matters about the instruments of the Haitian Revolution is not their exactitude: considered as tools of chronological measure they may be quite inexact, and to view them from such a standpoint would inevitably result in a derogatory judgement of (in)exactitude in general, highly prejudicial to an analysis of repetition, memory, political restitution and the world-historical.[21]

Why so? Let us explain. First, as Bernard Stiegler observes, the world-historical form cannot be reduced to the exactitude of a measure, 'but (re)-constitutes orthographically a *having-been* in it *as such*. It is not the exactitude of measure but that of *recording*, of *access*' (1998: 274). Second, the possibility of access entails the question of publicity, that is to say, of going beyond cultural particularities and overcoming the singularities of subjective identity and objectivity 'out there' without erasing specificity. Thus, it is a question of obliterating the self (and other) as a disengaged primarity formally or 'efficiently' determining world-historical secondarity. Ultimately, the possibility of access entails questioning a notion of temporality that conceives it as a fixed background formally determinant of the world-historical, rather than materially determined by it. Third, if publicity entails the obliteration of self and other, inside and outside, the who and the what, then it is essentially a position of revolt and proximity in withdrawal (Kristeva, 2000: 160, 177). In such a position, the specific dynamic of the what in the who and the who in the what, that following Nancy will be called later in this chapter 'the double aspect of the fetish', must be taken into account.

This structure is similar to that of contagion and over-determination that we encountered before in the work of anthropologists such as Michael Taussig and Françoise Vergès among others. It appears also in a story that according to Jean-Luc Nancy was familiar to the young Marx: the narrative refers to a rather obscure bond between the conquerors and the conquered in the Caribbean. In accordance with the story, the former were fascinated by the puerile gods of the latter, golden charms and shiny fetishes, while these, in turn, became fascinated with the gold of the conquerors. The European's gold-money becomes a fetish while the indigenous perceive the power that it exerts upon the conquerors, which appears to them inexplicable and supernatural (Nancy, 2001: 4; Taussig, 1983). The conquered in the Americas went on to trust their fetish-objects, chants and visions to infiltrate the god-money of the opposite camp, and crucially the form of temporality (namely, eternity of stasis) attached to it.

Jean-Luc Nancy explains that this fetishising was parallel and symmetrical to that of the commodity itself, and that Marx's familiarity with the story goes back to his student years and his then marked interest in the analysis of religious forms. To our purposes, it matters to emphasise that this structure of contacted 'gods' or projected visions and fixed points in the future retroactively determining the present, is central to the language of popular sovereignty that emerged in the Americas and shook the world in the eighteenth century. This is the language common to St George Tucker, Thomas Jefferson, Toussaint L'Overture and Karl Marx.

What is missing (in Tucker and Jefferson, in the scholars that study the Haitian Revolution, but also in Marx) is an elucidation of the particular metaphysics that underlines such a language. Political philosopher Jean-Pierre Dupuy calls this 'a metaphysics of projected time'; and in that sense we may speak of popular or revolutionary constitutionalism as 'projected' constitutionalism. In more general terms, it is possible to identify such metaphysics of projected time as being sensitive to the direction of the unfolding of reality, the specific dynamic of the what, in order to emphasise that there is no reference here to something transcendent or supernatural.

Put otherwise, at stake here is the following question: what is it that always propels thought towards its reification? Rather than using the language of transcendence, we speak of time-matter and contend that time-matter has a directionality, and that such directionality can be conceived as the wrapping and unwrapping of forms within forms, and insist on the need to disengage the specificity of this what that propels thought (the who), and which remains unthought in mainstream metaphysics under various conceptions of 'substance' and 'matter'. In these conceptions, matter and substance are (un)thought of as hard kernel, content, or resistance to thought, but never considered as impinging upon thought, just as the tendency of thought towards its reification is never considered as anything else than an anomaly.

In contrast to these conceptions, 'matter', in the sense advocated here, is not to be understood as content opposite to form, as having a purpose imposed from without by the causal powers of men or any other necessary being, or as residual in respect to such powers. Rather, it should be understood as having a direction of its own in the structural (rather than causal) sense, as a composing/decomposing or 'infiltrating' form, folding and unfolding inside other forms.²² Put otherwise, this is to think the improbable as a category of reality.

Notice that there is no need to interpret the improbable, the sense of unfolding and the prophetic, in the religious sense. Jean-Pierre Dupuy writes in this regard:

> We would say today that the prophet's word has a *performative* power: by saying things, it brings them into existence. Now, the prophet knows that. One might be tempted to conclude that the prophet has the power of a revolutionary: he speaks so that things will change in the direction he intends to give them (...) The prophet is the one who, more prosaically, seeks out the fixed point of the problem, the point where voluntarism achieves the very thing that fatality dictates. The prophecy includes itself in its own discourse; it sees itself realizing what it announces. In this sense (...) prophets are legion in our modern democratic societies, founded on science and technology.
> (Dupuy, 2004: 27–8)

Let us now move onto prophetics, the specificity of the constitution as a what (in relation to access, publicity and revolt) and the language of German criticism that developed out of the work of people such as Feuerbach and Marx. The latter wrote his comments on the Rhine Diet less than forty years after St George Tucker's political paean to the prophetic power of the people in the Americas. Unmistaken, the point remains the same for both of them.

Marx wrote:

> *Privileges of the states are in no way rights of the province.* On the contrary, the rights of the province cease when they become privileges of the estates. Thus the estates of the Middle Ages appropriated for themselves all the country's constitutional rights and turned them into privileges against the country.
> (Marx, 1975, vol. 1, Chapter III: 132–77)

Notice how, while Tucker writes from the standpoint of someone who has experienced a triumphant revolution and thus describes the experience of being on the other side of history's closure, Marx writes from the standpoint of someone who anticipates a revolution still to come, or better still, who fights a past that refuses to let go, much like the dead do in magical realist novels.

That is the meaning of Marx's tirade against the speaker of the Rhine Assembly: 'We will do what we like ... It is truly the language of a ruler, which naturally has a pathetic flavour coming from a modern baron' (ibid.). In a sense, thus, Tucker speaks from Marx's future (even though Marx writes thirty-nine years after him) just as the Speaker of the Rhine Assembly speaks from his past (even though the Baron's speech belongs to the present). We can only make sense of this structure if we let go of our everyday metaphysics of straight time-lines as the adjoining of 'nows' one to another, bifurcating like the branches of a tree. Only if we view time in its circularity, can we make sense of the reversed structure just described.

The advantage of this notion over its opposite (straight, bifurcating timelines) is that it allows us to think of the future as *real* and material (a form that matters and remains accessible), rather than merely possible, and thus as impinging upon us, inviting us to take the sort of action described by both Marx and Tucker. But there is a difference between them: Marx has discovered the past and the future in the present (later on he will discover the dead in the living, and so on) or, to conjure up Shakespearean and Derridian ghosts, that *time is 'out of joint'*. Where Tucker sees conjuncture, Marx sees disjuncture. While St George Tucker's writing betrays a sense of progression, Marx's emphasises unevenness.

It is in this context that the question of fetishism first emerges for the latter. To begin with, Marx writes that 'in this way, the rights of the provincial Assembly are no longer rights of the province, but rights against the province, and the Assembly itself would be the greatest wrong against the province but with *the mystical significance of being supposed to embody the greatest right*'(Marx, 1975, vol. 1, Chapter III: 135–81). Where does the 'mystical significance' of the Assembly come from? This is not simply a case of taking as divine what is merely made up, but rather of a certain concreteness or embodiment of the divine that is possible because of the real presence of the past in the present and its coexistence, in one and the same present-unit, with a future that comes (embodied in what Marx calls, using the legal–political language of the time, 'the citizen').

Both the past and the future are real, and crucially, they have determinate form. They are embodied in the 'modern baron' and 'the citizen'. These are social forces appearing as embodied actors, fighting out a political and legal battle that turns out to be a battle *for* history. There are three important lessons to be learned here. First, the correspondence between social forces and legal–political forms. Second, for Marx the future (like the past) is not indeterminate or merely potential but determinate even if improbable. Time-matter becomes determinate in concrete and objective social machineries. The baron and the citizen are operators of different technical tendencies present in the social machinery: the open future and the closed past are concrete in the present. Third, if this is so, then we must acknowledge, with Marx, and after Hegel, the non-simultaneity of the simultaneous. This is to say that time-matter is uneven, that it folds and unfolds (in other forms) dramatically (Hegel would say 'logically'). It follows from this that the correspondence between social forces and legal–political forms is uneven. If there is logic in history, it is a logic of unevenness or incompleteness. More importantly, this unevenness explains action at a distance – projection, transference, revolt, proximity in withdrawal and so on – as a real possibility. Put otherwise, these are, like the improbable, categories of reality. This is the ontological basis for an analysis of social forces and legal–political forms (ultimately, history) in terms of projections, transitions, revolutions, and the role of fetishes, partial objects and affective investments in all that. This *hauntology*, to use Derrida's language (1994: 118; Derrida and Stiegler, 2002), a superior form of materialism, underwrites the understanding of social–economic forces as they fight it out in/through the legal–political form.[23]

When Marx speaks of the 'mystical significance of being supposed to embody its [the people's] greatest right' he describes precisely a form of action at a distance. He speaks of an appearance (literally a ghost from the past) that has real powers upon the living. In this case it is a 'medieval' assembly of estates that subsumes all of the 'modern' people's powers under the guise of a Constitutional Assembly. The point is not the naïve empiricism that commands us to go and find the hard kernel of truth (bygone forms and possibilities) hidden behind the appearance of modernity, but rather that appearance is the truth. It is the appearance of 'being supposed' to embody the greatest right that gives the Assembly its 'mystical significance'. And this appearance is no falsity or mere delusion, rather it is the uncanny apparition of the past in the present, a past that 'knows only of the province of the estates, not the estates of the province' (Marx, 1975, vol. 1, Chapter III: 135 ff.).

What ensues is a clash between the actual past and the actual future in the present, and the stakes of politics lie on the solution to such a deadlock, which has nothing to do with the given possibilities inherent to the situation, and which may or may not become actualised in some less-than-real future. There is a deadlock in that the forces of the past act in such a way that their action becomes a stumbling block before the people's coming to themselves. What does this mean in concrete techno–political terms? On the one hand, it means that the forces of the past are embodied in the modern aristocracy Acting as a political agent, the aristocracy blocks the rise of the citizenry by hijacking the constitution. On the other hand, the constitution must be considered as a powerful technical object, as equipment and work, or 'the world historial' in Heideggerian parlance (Heidegger, 1967: 388). The citizenry is its operator. The fate of the citizenry as a political subject rests upon the proper functioning of the constitution as a tool. The point is that by hijacking the constitution, the aristocracy renders the citizenry powerless.

The technical object involved in Marx's discussion is, of course, the constitution. By tampering with the constitution, for instance, by turning 'rights' into 'privileges' – in this case, turning the right to freedom of the press into a 'limited right' constrained by the privileges of government regarding what we would now call 'national security' – the forces of the past turn the constitution against the people. Thus Marx writes:

This plaintive rhetoric about 'inner conviction' in contrast to the rude, external, unauthorised north wind of 'public conviction' is the more noteworthy since the purpose of the proposal was precisely to make the inner conviction of the Assembly of the Estates external. Here too, of course, there is an inconsistency. Where it seems to the speaker more convenient (. . .) he appeals to the province: 'We,' continues the speaker, 'would let it' (publication) 'take place where we consider this expedient, and would restrict it where an extension would appear to us purposeless or even harmful'.

(Ibid.)

In this passage, which sounds today as relevant as it did in Marx's times, the idea that we, the people, should have, as Alexander Hamilton once put it, 'full confidence in the wisdom and virtue of government [the President of the United States] to whom in conjunction with the Senate the discussion ... belongs' (quoted in Kramer, 2004: 4), appears ludicrous. This is so because an appeal to 'inner conviction' defeats the very technological purpose of the constitution, which is to make inner conviction external. Here the constitution is conceived as a communicative device, *the* communicative technical object par excellence, whose tendency is to fully 'democratise' or make social decision-making public. So the issue at stake in this passage is publicity, the constitution as a surface of inscription that affords general accessibility, and thus temporal programmatic temporality – social and individual. As we learned before, that publicity opens truly historical space. Put otherwise, it is through the constitution that the operator, the citizen, can unleash the powers of anticipation and participate in the sense of the unfolding. As in *The Matrix*, it is not the Oracle/Matrix who needs the human, but the human who needs the matrix in order to fulfil a prophecy of its own making.

In this passage, Marx defends the dynamic proper to the technical object tending towards its concretisation, in Gilbert Simondon's use of the term.[24] In this sense, he writes that 'the Assembly of Estates has a province to which the privilege of its activity extends, but the province has no estates through which it could itself be active' (Marx, 1975, vol. 1, Chapter III: 137–81). At this point of the discussion, technical objects have taken over and the clash between the forces of the past and the present/future appears as a clash between old and new technologies (the medieval Assembly of Estates vs. the Estates of the People), but this is so in the sense that only through their own handiwork, that is, by creating gods for themselves *they, the people, stop becoming gods to each other*.

This is the meaning of the following lines: 'of course, the province has the right, under prescribed circumstances, to create these gods [the estates] for itself, but as soon as they are created, it must, like a fetish worshipper, forget that these gods are its own handiwork' (ibid.). Only when the people forget that the civil technologies [the estates, parliament, the laws, the presidency, etc.) are their own handiwork, not in the sense of being technology's efficient cause, but rather in the sense that it is through them that prophetic capacities emerge, and with them also the *performative* or quasi-magical power of the prophet, access to temporality, only then men become gods to one another.

The error involved in fetishism is not simply to take an artifice for a natural thing, or to worship 'made up' gods rather than the real ones, but rather to invest other men with the quasi-divine powers that a collective acquires only when it becomes a collective and as such gains access to temporality, in revolt, in a public manner. That is to say, through the common effort of 'arresting' time-matter through technical objects. This error occurs, for instance, when a politician is endowed with quasi-divine powers because he holds a position of government, or else when the CEO of a corporation achieves god-like status (delivering us from poverty, eradicating diseases, and so on) on the basis of the accumulated wealth produced by a collective. Thus the question is: why, if these prophetic powers (stopping floods, fighting poverty, eradicating disease) emerge through gods of our own making, shall some among us be allowed to become gods for the rest of us?

Marx understood that this problem had become exacerbated with the advent of modernity and its emphasis on equality (what he called, after Feuerbach, the 'greatest right'). As he put it, 'equality' becomes mystical when Parliament (the very vehicle for such an equality) separates itself from the people, in which case there ceases to be a people and only a 'fetish worshipper' remains, oblivious to the 'made up' character of the god it worships. Again, the problem is not that the god is made up – in some sense they all are – but rather forgetfulness of the power to make them, for such an ignorance closes general access to the already and the future, making the latter indeterminate. The reality of the future is thereby reduced or denied by the forgetful people and in doing so the people deny themselves their own becoming. That is the main metaphysical block to a better existence.

Notes

1 The name of the interviewee has been changed.
2 After the events of October 2003, when a series of protests in El Alto, Bolivia led to the resignation of then President Gonzalo Sánchez de Lozada, the division between these sectors came to a head over the 18 July 2004, nationwide referendum on the future of the country's gas reserves, and once again in 2006/7, after the victory of the MAS-led coalition led by Evo Morales (MAS stands for 'Movement Towards Socialism'). See Fuentes (2007) and McDowell (2007).
3 The 'half-moon' or *media luna* comprises the resource-rich northern, eastern and southern lowlands of Bolivia, controlled by a well-heeled civic and business group, and a handful of multinational corporations, opposed to the impoverished western highlands or *altiplano*. The *altiplano* is primarily indigenous – mainly

Quechua and Aymará – while the 'half moon' has a much larger *mestizo*, light-skinned, population. See Lora (2005). See also Ballvé (2005a; 2005b).
4 The Pact was formed in September 2004, gathering together sectors of the peasantry and indigenous peoples from the highlands, and stated as its central aim the summoning of a participative, popular Constituent Assembly, that would make radical changes to the country's modern/colonial power structure.
5 As Vargas Llosa puts it in the cited article, the task of politics proper would be to explain (and overcome) what he calls 'backwardness'. For a detailed explanation of the deployment and pitfalls of the discourse of 'development' in the post-colonial condition, see: Escobar (1995).
6 'Doing evil to the other' is a rendition of Rousseau's '*mal d'autrui*'. See Rousseau (1817, Premier Dialogue: 214). On the connection between blindness and the greatest violence, see Arendt (1994) and Dupuy (2002b).
7 This is the case, for instance, in the first Latin American independent constitution: articles 200 and 201 of the 1811 Venezuelan constitution extends common citizenship to indigenous peoples on the basis of an educational programme, 'that they understand the intimate commonality that unites them with all other citizens', while at the same time providing that 'the property of the [common] lands, that where conceded to them, and remain in their possession, be distributed'. This articulation of 'common citizenship', as opposed to their full recognition as indigenous peoples, and the privatisation of common property, is a generalised pattern of modern/colonial constitutionalism. See Otero (1965).
8 See Taussig (1983; 1996; 2005), and Dolar (1991). See also Mariátegui (1979).
9 Kant, I. *Opus Postumum*. Ed. by Eckart Forster. Trans. by E. Forster and Rosen, M. Cambridge: Cambridge University Press, 1993.
10 See Kaufman (2005: 351). To illustrate the point she makes a reference to a passage in Simone De Beauvoir's 1943 novel *She Came to Stay*.
11 Kaufman (2005: 354). She refers directly to Sartre's work. See also Verstraeten (1972).
12 Ibid.
13 See Žižek (1999: 228; 260 ff.). See also Žižek (2000: 143–60, and 2003: 117). For the call without meaning as a 'resonating voice' that commands nothing but compels one to engage, see Dolar (2006: 42).
14 For more on Laibach/NSK, see Monroe (2005).
15 Don't touch me!
16 For a detailed analysis in relation to the work of Heidegger, see Stiegler (1998: 270).
17 This follows from Stiegler (1998: 260–1).
18 There is an objection to Heidegger's negligence in respect to the beyond of the self that is implied by resoluteness as 'going out into the world'. For a more detailed account of this objection, see Stiegler (1998: 262).
19 Heidegger calls the consistent form of history 'the steadiness of existence'. He writes: 'The steadiness of existence (. . .) is not formed either through or by the adjoining of "moments" one to another; but these arise from the temporality of a repetition which is futurally in the process-of-having-been – a temporality which has already been stretched along' (1967: 391).
20 For a defence of this sort of power in our technological age, see Jonas (1985).
21 For an example of this sort of prejudicial and derogatory judgement, in relation to 'primitive' societies without state in the Americas, but generalisable elsewhere, see Nucetelli (2002).

22 For a related argument, see Harman (2002: 293). Significantly, Harman compares his object-forms to retroviruses 'injecting their own DNA back into the nucleus of everything they encounter' (212).
23 Here, the legal–political form is associated with the realm of fantasy and the symbolic. Fantasy is always an image set to work in a signifying or symbolic structure, or more precisely a frame that structures (into a narrative) what is expected of us in the social contractual situation. In that sense, it is the narrative or temporal frame of desire, which is always desire of the other, the wish to know what is expected of us in the social. Expectations are in fact structures of anticipation, focusing on the future and the past, and seeking the fixed point, or point of closure, where the past and the future converge and cause (or re-frame, in the structural sense) one another. The point not to be missed here is that a frame (think of cinema, for instance) is always a field of demarcation between inside/outside, past/present, is/ought. It demarcates a set, and establishes what is included in the set (the social contractual situation) but also what can be considered or 'counts' as a member of that set. So, to focus on the frame is to consider that which defines a boundary – space and time – within which the question 'what is expected of me?' (inclusion, belonging) can be answered, but also to consider the possibility of breaking the boundary or 'traversing the fantasy'. This would entail a re-framing of the whole situation. A focus on the legal–political form, on the social contract, is in this respect a focus on the boundary, on what is included but not a member of the framed. Then, at stake here is the very possibility of revolt.
24 On the notion of 'concretisation', see Simondon (1958 and 1964). For an analysis of Simondon's notions of 'concretisation' and 'individuation', in relation to Marx's famous 'Fragment on Machines' in the *Grundrisse*, see Virno (2004: 76–84). A more detailed and remarkable analysis of Simondon's theses, which sees them as moving away from human-centred accounts of technics, and towards unpredictability and contingency as the new central notions of (post-industrial) nature and society, see Stiegler (1998).

Chapter 4
The most sublime of fetishists

In the passages quoted from the early writings of Karl Marx in the previous chapter, it is not too difficult to see the imprint of his two acknowledged influences: the Scottish Enlightenment, on the one hand, and Hegel, on the other. It is well known that the notion of the correspondence between social–economic forces and legal–political forms comes from the endeavours of the Scottish writers, struggling to understand 'naturally' the appearance of legal forms. Marx, a lawyer himself and well placed in the *Persönlichkeit* debates of his time, would have had no problem understanding the language of Adam Smith, Ferguson and John Millar. In fact, the language of *On Freedom of the Press* sounds remarkably like that of John Millar.

With Millar, an earlier student of Adam Smith with whom he shared a lasting and intimate friendship, and later a University of Glasgow's renowned Professor of Law, 'the four stages theory [of the evolution of the right to property] and the basic "materialist" ideas and techniques associated with it become central and pervasive to an unprecedented degree' (Meek, 1976: 160). Millar was also a busy practitioner, particularly in the areas of civil and criminal law. William C. Lehmann describes thus his trial strategies and forensic skill: '[He] opposed every measure of public policy that, as he saw it, tended to create inequalities not of virtue and merit but unearned privilege . . .' (Lehmann, 1979: 29, 67). That is precisely the spirit of Marx's attack on the measures taken by the Rhein Assembly.

The Scots' influence on Marx (also on Hegel) is everything but news. It has been acknowledged by scholars from different persuasions and political outlook such as Laurence Dickey, David Spadafora, Robert Heilbroner, Thomas Sowell, Anthony Chase, Knud Haakonssen and Ronald Meek, to name a few. The latter informs us, provocatively, that 'Marx became a Communist in the 1840s through dwelling on those passages in [*The Wealth of Nations*] which draw attention to the workers being exploited and oppressed by deceitful traders and manufacturers and indolent landlords' (Simpson Ross, 1995: 417). Any reader of the authoritative Glasgow edition of Adam Smith's *Lectures on Jurisprudence* cannot fail to see in the quote 'Till there be property there can be no government, the very end of which is to secure wealth, and to defend the rich from the poor,' much more than a naïve paean to laissez-faire capitalism.

The point is, of course, to highlight the dynamic (rather than static) character of property. However, between Scottish materialism and Marx's critique of legality in *On Freedom of the Press* there is a deep gulf, a vacuum filled on the one hand by Hegel's notion of the uneven self-reflective nature of time-matter, already couched in religious–political language, and on the other, by the notion of fetishism as applied to the analysis of the relationship between social–economic forces and legal–political relations. Crucial as the former may be, not the least because of Hegel's recognition that from the point of view of the agent, social existence not only encompasses the whole of his experience, but constituted the horizon of his expectations as well,[1] it can be argued that it is the latter – the notion of fetishism applied to the analysis of social/political causes and relations – what differentiates *On Freedom of the Press* from its political economic and philosophical forbearers, and sets materialism on the right track. Neither in the Scots nor in Hegel, do we find the notion of a civil political technology left behind by its operators nor transferring quasi-divine powers onto them, which Marx sets at the centre of his reflections on the legal measures issued by the Rhein Province Assembly.

What we find in Hegel is a sustained discussion and criticism of the absolutisation of the right to property and the development, upon the basis of such a criticism, of a right to rebellion on the part of slaves and the poor. Indeed, the latter sets the stage for Marx's discussion but in no way entails the understanding of fetishism that allows the much firmer defence of popular constitutionalism, and the more nuanced analysis of the dynamics of property through legal form that is to be found in the 1840s literature. Let us then chart in the remainder of this chapter the introduction of the grammar of fetishism into the language of German criticism via Marx. It will be argued that his sources lie in the Caribbean: between Louisiana and the American south, on the one hand, and the *cimarronajes* of the islands and the coasts of South America, on the other. It is the legacy of rebellious slaves and fearful slave-owners determined to prevent the events of Haiti and Cartagena from occurring ever again; to erase them from the face of the earth, if necessary. The story of the gold of the conquerors and the conquered and enslaved, that according to Jean-Luc Nancy, Marx knew from his student years, remains central to this account of the transition of a concept into the language of critique and will serve as a background link between its different moments: from religion to politics and legal analysis, but also literature, music and even cinema, and from there on to political economy and an ideology destined to shock the world at its very foundations. The protagonist of the story is the obscure and sublime object: the fetish, the gold-coin, the heart in the chest. It is our story, that of the foundation of the world as we know it.

Where does fetishism come from?

So, where does Marx's fetishism come from? The evidence available suggests two possibilities: on the one hand, the study of Afrological religious forms, the sort of 'primitivism' which in turn influences the Gothic genre of literature that was to become so popular at the time, with its widespread use of ghostly metaphors and Frankenstein-like figures, from 'dark satanic mills' to the Shelleys' nightmarish inventions. On the other hand, and no less decisively, the use of such metaphors in legal discussions of the time concerning precisely the uneven dynamic of property and the role of the people in government, particularly in America, such as the *Charles River Bridge case*.[2] In both cases – early ethnographies of Afrological religious forms and American legal cases concerning property – there is a reference to the religious practices of rebellious slaves and other 'afrological' political forms that, by the 1840s, had become the stock of trade of revolutionary language.

The presence of such reference and connections in early anthropology and popular Gothic literature and imagery is well documented. It is quite reasonable to think that such a reference entered revolutionary legal–political discourse in America (and Europe) through the Caribbean – with the slaves, actually – and became deposited, under many layers of popular constitutional discourse, waiting to be retrieved in the post-revolutionary period whenever it became necessary to fight it out once again, this time within more or less established legal–political forms. Perhaps less well known is the fact that one can find instances of such retrieval in the decisions of the post-revolutionary Taney Court of the United States.

Consider the *Charles River Bridge case,* mentioned above: the US Supreme Court decided the case in 1837. It concerned a claim put forward by the state of Massachusetts to interfere with the terms of a charter granted to a private corporation. A decade after the Revolution, the Charles River Bridge corporation was granted a seventy-five year charter to operate a toll bridge between Boston and Charlestown. In 1828, the state Legislature authorised Charlestown merchants, grouped as the Warren Bridge Company, to build a second bridge whose property would return to the state once the investment had been recovered. The first company saw this as a threat against its value and future income and sought an injunction against the Warren Bridge Company, arguing that it had an implied right of monopoly over the collection of tolls. With thirty years left on its charter, the Charles River Company saw this as, what professor Richard Epstein would call today a 'regulatory taking' (Epstein, 2005), an intervention in the (future) value of private property through regulation. From this perspective, Charles River's charter would be abrogated by legislative fiat.

The holding of the case is a landmark example of the sort of 'popular constitutionalism' that Larry D. Kramer has identified as the most consistent and nowadays almost forgotten basis of revolutionary constitutionalism as such. The new majority of the Supreme Court, presided by Chief Justice Roger B. Taney, a man from the South and a slave-owner, ruled that neither the Contract Clause[3] nor any other article of the Constitution 'prevented the people of Massachusetts, through their elected state representatives, from authorizing construction of a competing bridge' (*Charles River Bridge v. Warren Bridge*, 36 US (II Pet.) 420, 1837).

The new Jacksonian Chief Justice argued that legislative grants should be narrowly construed, and candidly stated the social policy basis for the Court's decision. Years before, Taney had successfully argued a case on the right to freedom of the press, which involved a preacher accused of inciting slave rebellion; this time, Chief Justice Taney argued in response to the claim of implied right to monopoly with the following memorable lines:

> Let it once be understood that such charters carry with them these implied contracts, and give this unknown and undefined property in a line of travelling; *and you will soon find the old turnpike corporations awakening from their sleep,* and calling upon this court to put down the improvements which have taken their place.
> (*Charles River Bridge v. Warren Bridge*, 36 US [II Pet.] 420, 1837)

As Anthony Chase points out correctly (1997: 124), the image conjured up by Taney, turnpike companies rising like zombies from slumber in the earth, is as effective as those used by Blake, the Shelleys ... and Marx himself. But where did Roger B. Taney learn about such images, the West African religious practices they referred to and their political usage? As said before, the Chief Justice was a man of the South and himself a slave-owner. Would it be too far fetched to think that Roger Taney learned of the political usage of West African religious practices, conjuring powerful images and entities in the crevasses of the system, from the slaves themselves? We know for a fact that Justice Taney conceived the presence of the slaves as central to the life-style of the American South and lived in close proximity to them – this is how he explained his views after the infamous *Dred Scott* decision – but also feared their ability to mobilise politically rebellious forces by unleashing the power of the fetish. The events of Boik Caiman in Haiti were fresh in the memory of these men. The slave revolt which resulted in the establishment of an independent black state in 1804 had started at Boik Caiman with a *Voudoun* ritual, and the message of freedom circulated among people of colour not through writing – the majority of the slaves were illiterate, their common language, Creole, was nonscriptural – but through exemplars: songs, chants of possession, charms and fetishes (Fischer, 2004: 1–4). The contagion spread rapidly, from Louisiana and the Carolinas to Bahia in northern Brazil. White slave-owners in the South of the United States knew that among the slaves in Louisiana and elsewhere were many battle-scarred rebels who had participated in these struggles and these rituals. They feared them almost as much as they were fascinated by them. Justice Taney was one of these men.

The landmark case provoked the interest of journalists and Whig commentators on both sides of the Atlantic, who saw in this decision a rebellious attack on the sanctity of private property and the inversion of the legitimate order of things. Two of these journalistic reports appeared in the *North American Review* and in the Boston press. The *North American Review* suggested that the new majority behind the Supreme Court's decision had adopted an economic doctrine likely to cause 'subversion of the principles of law and property'. In the other one, a Boston journalist reported that after the decision, federal 'restraint would be removed from state legislatures, and investments in corporate property would have no guarantee or legal protection'.[4]

At the time Marx was an avid reader of the press, a journalist himself and had developed a keen interest in American legal–political affairs. We know that his acquaintance with American affairs dated back to 1842 and remained alive until at least 1844. During that period he considered, among other materials, three major books on the social and political situation of the United States. In 1842, as he engaged in the writing of a series of articles on the right to freedom of the press for the *Rheinische Zeitung*, Marx wrote:

> Naturalists seek by experiment to reproduce a natural phenomenon in its purest conditions. You do not need to make any experiments. You find the natural phenomenon of freedom of the press in North America in its purest, most natural form.
>
> (Marx, 1975, vol. 1: 167)

In this passage, the young Karl Marx gave concrete application to the methodological direction he had learned from Hegel's *Philosophy of Right*, which the latter elaborated more explicitly into a process in the lecture course of 1819–20: '*Was vernünftig ist, das ist wirklich*', and could be rendered as 'what can be thought is in actuality'.[5] As Domenico Losurdo explains (2004: 32–8), the contrast here is between actuality (*Wirklichkeit*) and empirical immediacy or transitory existence (*Dasein*). The point is that, as Hegel notes in the lecture course of 1824–5 (Hegel, 1973–4), not everything that exists in empirical immediacy is actual. Conversely, there are actual things which are not empirically immediate. Let us call them 'obscure' objects, since they are not directly present, but let us keep in mind that in fact they are no different from other elements, such as mathematical objects and literary characters, whose reality is given by postulation. According to Losurdo (2004: 32–8), Hegel formulates this distinction at the level of historical analysis, and it is important to keep in mind that when it comes to Hegel, historical analysis unfolds along the lines of dialectical logic. Put otherwise, all these objects constitute the world-historial.

Crucially, dialectical logic can be described as a logic that does not require the analyst to frame determinations of things in terms of either/or propositions, that is to say, as propositions of the form 'either x or not x', which are very different and have nothing to do with arbitrary (relativistic) propositions of the form 'either x or y'. This means that the analyst of logical development (including for Hegel the analytic of the world-historial) cannot isolate an object, for instance a surface of inscription operated by a social agent at a certain moment of history, as a *punctum* standing out there and side-by-side all the others, with which it would have no possible connection besides penetration (being conjoined or adjoined, as a point or a link in a chain). The issue here is that the consistency of history (and thus logic, which is about steadiness in temporality) cannot be formed either through or by the adjoining of points or moments one to another (x or not x conjoined to y or not y ... and so on) but rather, these elements, points or moments arise from a temporality which has already been stretched along, as something present which comes along, has presence and then disappears (x and not x) or futurally in the process of having-been, as Heidegger would say (1967: 389 and 391). This entails an image of time and history that is not linear (the succession of points on a plane) but rather circular, with elements reacting back upon themselves after being postulated in proximity to others, forming unexpected clusters and networks of relation, while at the same time withdrawing from such relations. Such elements would seem to possess an original ambiguity of form and content, expressed in this and previous chapters as the double aspect of the fetish, which cannot be described properly in side-by-side 'atomistic' accounts.

Roughly, in terms of historical analysis this means to say that the immediate presence of claims that are reactionary in nature, that is, time-matter from the past, coexists in one and the same present-unit with a causally productive but not immediately present future. The immediate presence of social forces from the past does not erase the profound connection of the social forces of the future with the needs of the time. Put otherwise, the contingency of the future cannot be erased by affirming the necessity of the past and so the present appears always as possessing an original ambiguity, a double aspect, as cut, split or rupture. Time is not the vehicle for the realisation of the possibilities already contained as a germ in the past, rather it postulates or creates the possible at the very moment it makes it come to pass; it brings forth the possible as it does reality on its own right (Meillassoux, 2007: 74–5). The effect of the immediate presence of the forces of the past is rather to 'deflate' reality by engaging on precautionary or preventive activity, thereby downgrading actuality to immediate empirical existence.

Along similar lines, according to Losurdo, Hegel distinguishes in the *Encyclopedia* between *Wirklichkeit* and *Erscheinung*. In a nutshell, the methodological point is to seek the causally productive future in actuality (Losurdo, 2004: 32–8; Lenin, 1961: 309). For Marx in 1842 this was America. The Americas provided the analyst of freedom of the press and revolutionary political practice with an actual case in which the dominant tendency of the times (embodied in the maxim 'learn to govern yourselves without a master') makes the claims and practices of the past unnecessary and shows the coming breakdown of the system. However, this is not to say that politics is just a matter of waiting for the right time to come. The forces of the past have to be contaminated, destroyed and transformed, *precisely because such claims and practices of the past are, nevertheless, present*. To find the 'natural phenomenon' of freedom of the press in North America, in its 'purest, most natural form', as Marx put it, means to see the causally productive future unfolding in actuality against the forces of the past immediately present to our eyes.

Put otherwise, the US and the whole Atlantic scene appeared to the young Marx as the case in which the social forces of 'projected constitutionalism' fight it out against the forces of 'deflationary constitutionalism' through the legal–political link of the network. 'Projection' should not be taken here to mean the positing of unrealisable ideas or the will of the moral subject against opaque actuality, but on the contrary, the task and capacity to find a point where the speculative vision is 'reduced to practice', as St George Tucker put it in 1803 (Tucker, 1999; Kramer, 2004: 6). As he said, to reduce a speculative vision to practice is the task and power of the people in revolt. This entails a vision of the revolutionary process as objective (rather than the product of subjective enthusiasm), and there is no better example of the objective unfolding of the revolutionary process during Marx's time than that of the Jacksonian era of legal–political American affairs, as it was impacted upon by the rebellious events in the Caribbean.

This is the 'pure case' that frames Marx's writings on the right to freedom of the press, as he himself pointed out in 1842 (Marx, 1975, vol. 1: 167; Marx, 2007). His observations of the 'natural phenomenon' of freedom of the press in its 'purest' form were aided and abetted by the critique of the providential that he had found in the study of religious forms, developed by Feuerbach and others, which compared Christianity with the archaic and contemporary practices of East and West African peoples.

Feuerbach's motto 'Providence is a *privilege* of man' in *The Essence of Christianity*, resonates with the attack on privilege unleashed by the jurisprudence of the time and echoed by Marx's writings. According to Feuerbach, the secret of the belief in providence is the privilege of man over and above nature: the economic and legal–political elevation of (human) well-being as the 'greatest right' and, in parallel, that of whomever appears to protect and guarantee such a right.

The subject that appears as the guarantor of human 'greatest right' ends up becoming a god to other men. Such a subject is produced as a projection of the collective by the collective, associated with its political and economic practices. The problem is that these practices erase the traces of postulation, pretend to exhaust their reality in given sets of possibilities, and tend to present these constructs as personified and more or less eternal. In this way, such practices become blind to the power of their own fetishes, and the latter start to run the show. The proper term for such blindness is 'envy', a sort of short-sightedness that is at the very basis of the modern malaise: in a phrase, the rest of us end up behaving like mere fetish worshippers. In comparison to the more complex understanding of the power of the fetish among contemporary West Africans and Caribbeans, an issue that immediately brings the politics of slavery, rebellion against property, and early globalisation to the fore, the Christian belief in providence (aided and abetted by philosophy, law, politics and economics) betrays a much too poor understanding.

It is striking how Marx frames his discussion on the freedom of the press, written a mere five years after the US Court's decision in the *Charles River Bridge* case, exactly in the same manner that the Taney Court framed its majority argument: as a confrontation between 'old feudal grants' or privileges and modernity, with the former bidding a post-revolutionary people to stop in its tracks. Moreover, the grander theme that arises from a consideration of the case and its preceding line of Contract Clause cases (specially *Fletcher* and *Darmouth College*) is precisely that of the desire and drive of men, with men (in this case government and/or charted corporations) becoming gods to other men, as opposed to the better understanding and reason of law incarnated in 'popular' constitutionalism. This is the same kind of problematic that Marx develops in his discussion of the legal measures taken by the Rhine Assembly; that is, as suggested above, the problem of fetishism.

A Black Marx? It is difficult not to be reminded of the fascinating scene in Ken McMullen's film *1871*, aptly titled 'Spectres of Marx', in which the father of African cinema, Med Hondo, dons the iconic white beard and appears as a ghost whispering in the ear of Napoleon III, interpreted by Dominique Pinon, the famous lines of *The Eighteenth Brumaire*. Queried on the matter, the British cinema director pointed at the striking resemblance between the Mauritanian cinematographer and London's most controversial philosopher. However, the suggestion that something else may have been operating in that scene at the level of the unconscious seems more fascinating . . . a Black Marx, the most sublime of fetishists.

Among the excerpts and ideas from other authors noted as preparatory work by Karl Marx in the Bonn Notebooks of 1842 (Marx and Engels, 1976, vol. 4/1), one finds Charles des Brosses's *Über den Dienst der Fettischgötter oder Vergleich der alten Religionen Egyptens mit der heitgen Religion*

Negritiens, or *On the Cult of the Fetish Gods, or A Comparison of the Old Egyptian Religions with Contemporary Negro Religion*, translated in Berlin in 1785, from the French edition of 1760 titled *Du Culte des Dieux Fétiches*. Marx read it in Bonn while working on a treatise on Christian art (and the censorship laws protecting Christian art) commissioned by Bruno Bauer. The treatise was also expected to double as a radical interpretation of Hegel as a critic of Christian art and religion. It was never finished. However, some of these ideas made it into the articles that form *On Freedom of the Press*. Particularly, the concept *'fétiche'* which had been coined, precisely, in the French version of des Brosses's book *Du Culte des Dieux Fétiches*.

According to Jean-Luc Nancy, it is in connection with this anthropological tract and Marx's marked interest in the analysis of religious forms (also informed by Feuerbach and the *Persönlichkeit* debates) that the story about the conquerors and the conquered in the Caribbean, referred to above, became familiar to him. This would have been the origin of Marx's famous image. Crucially, the point of des Brosses's text was to provide a comparative account of religious practices of East and West African peoples (the 'Negro' of the title) from the standpoint of 'natural history', akin to the evolutionary, materialistic stage-theory rehearsed also by the Scots. In the book, fetishism is described as the 'original' religion and thus the matrix of all religious experience, starting from Ancient Egypt all the way up to the contemporary ways of West African peoples. The latter included the West African population exiled in the Atlantic via slavery.

In his 1993 study of Marx's philosophy of art, Mikhail Lifshitz argued that Marx's reading for his contribution on Christian art for Bauer suggests that the projected treatise would originally have followed a path similar to that of des Brosses's book: from the study of the religious and fetishistic art of Asia, Africa and Greece to the Christian art of the Romantics of his own time, and would have attempted to link the latter with the former (Lifshitz, 1973; Rose, 1989: 60). Following Lifshitz's suggestion, we could argue that an investigation on the significance of religious and fetishistic production would have started in Afro-Asia and finished in Marx's own times, with the religious and econo-political forms of fetishism characteristic of Christian societies, and those more archaic that persisted through the contagion and dissemination of Afrological forms of fetishism in 'border' societies, the enclaves of emergent competitive capitalism, imperialism and mercantilism. The political significance of these archaic forms had been made clear during the Atlantic cycle of revolutions, still unfolding in front of Marx's eyes. He would have attempted to link the latter with the former. Uncannily, that is precisely the structure that readers of Marx encounter time and again, even in his most recognised and later works. In fact, such a broad outline would provide a good summary of Marx's lifetime attempt.

Moreover, the specific comments made by Marx in the *Rheinische Zeitung* articles against censorship reflect not only the study of the history of African and Christian religion intended for the unfinished critique commissioned by Bauer, but also, Marx's involvement (originated in his student years, as Nancy notes) with what could be termed a comparative study of religious forms that had, from the outset, strong political resonance (Breckman, 2001). In this respect, there are crucial aspects of the argument on fetishism that Marx could have found in the work of Feuerbach, whom he was also reading, together with the literature on the Americas, Hegel and Des Brosses in 1842. Among these aspects let us now emphasise the following: the theory of anticipation or 'projection' as the basis of art and religion, but also law and politics, an idea that has become commonplace nowadays among anthropologists and psychoanalysts. In the next section, which serves as a link between this and the following chapter, the reader will be introduced to another stage in the history of the fetish as it shatters the coordinates of critique: from magic and archaic desires to the compulsion to repeat and the will to power and blind destruction. What follows may be read as a set of initial notes on the prehistory of psychoanalysis.

Before psychoanalysis, the privilege of man: projection, desire and right

The crucial passage from *The Essence of Christianity*, published in 1841, is the following:

> Man – this is the mystery of religion – projects (*vergegenständlicht sich*) his being into objectivity, and then again makes himself an *object* to this projected image of himself thus converted into a subject; he thinks of himself as an object to himself, but as *the object of an object*, of *another* being than himself.
>
> (Feuerbach, 1957: 29 ff.)

There are at least two important elements in this passage, and both of them are entangled with the difficulties of rendering the terminology used in the original by Feuerbach into the English term 'projection'. First, notice that 'projection' is here part of a meaningful chain that includes 'objectification' and 'alienation' in the Hegelian sense, that is, as moments in the developmental history of self-referential consciousness. In this respect, 'god' or 'gods' refers to an objectified image that alienates the individual from the species, an alienation that can only be sublated by restoring the predicates misattributed to the Divine Object retroactively onto the man-species where they rightly belong. This would be the 'false' aspect of the fetish. Second, the projected object impinges upon the individual who has projected it, so that the latter emerges as an object of an object, a big or Divine Other (*another* being than himself) and anticipates or desires to be recognised by It/Him. This would be the 'true' aspect of the fetish, in that the object emerges not merely from falsification or misattribution of the individual or the species' predicates, but rather from the self-differentiation between the individual and his alter Ego.

What is at stake here is the fact that consciousness senses something not only as some-thing (content) but also as something else, as something other, and this form of otherness that completes determinate content but is not reducible to it, is formality. In developing his theory of projection, Feuerbach seems to be pursuing a Hegelian theme; he observes that in the case of human beings (Man) what is sensed is real, or put otherwise, that the formality is the formality of reality. Content and formality are part of the original ambiguity of all objects of reality. Reality is in this fundamental sense a formality, not a zone of things out there 'for us'.

Projection and postulation make sense only under this conception of reality, and only in this conception can one convincingly account for the reality of dreams, mathematical objects and, as Feuerbach suggests, also religious beliefs and value. As can be seen, in this passage we find a repetition of the same pattern present in the story of the gold of the conquerors and the conquered in the Caribbean, but also, crucially, in the coming-to-themselves of the people in St George Tucker's appendix to *Blackstone's Commentaries*.

Famously, Feuerbach did much more than simply follow Hegel's lead: not only did he invert Hegel's subject–predicate relationships, a move that would make him very popular among the Young Hegelians, Marx being one of them, but he also separated the false and the true aspects of the fetish, thereby allowing for a distinction between the crude projected object on the one hand, and the visions, feelings, expectations or anticipations invested in the object thus projected and its own reality, on the other. This would permit, in turn, a comparative perspective in religious studies that would include archaic beliefs without adjudicating against them beforehand from the self-authorised perspective of the 'last' belief-system or religion. Such comparativism departs from the mere reduction of distinctiveness to some underlying rule-pattern.[6]

In other words, it can be said that Feuerbach distinguished between affective investment or desire and the object invested upon, and even if the latter turns out to be a composite (an object postulated by desire, an artifice) he posited the object as having reality in its own right, and thus, as becoming the cause of desire. The latter may prove to be the crucial move since, as the keen reader may have guessed already, it allows for an anti-substantialist explanation of the value of things that does not melt them into thin air.

According to this explanation, objects attain their value because they are desired *by others* (their expectations, anticipations or desires) even though they are not exhausted by such desires and may react back on them, rather than because of some inherent or substantial property, just as the individual has an expectation to be recognised as distinctively valuable *by others*. Crucially, Feuerbach stated that distinctive personality 'is nothing without distinction of sex' (1957: 92). This means that there is no self-consciousness without embodiment or formality, no thought without a tendency to its reification, and thus without an always/already produced and producing 'nature' or artifice.

'Sex' appears here as the demarcation of the existence of other embodied subjects as something more, as something other, for instance male and female, as objects of desire/cause of desire (desire to be recognised as an irreducible and distinctive otherness) and this demarcation is, in turn, associated with a haunted nature that impinges upon persons in such a way that 'a personal being apart from Nature is nothing else than a being without sex, and conversely' (ibid.). It is important to notice here that 'sex' is not yet another ultimate natural point, but rather a fully relational or form-material category. 'Sex' stands for the vanishing point between a fully conscious, embodied subject, and other embodied subjects, on the one hand, and between subjects and a nature that is never fully present, on the other. More precisely, it stands for the transference-relationship (projection: expectation, value, desire) between them.

Another way to put this would be to say that in sex we not only desire the body of the other but mostly, we desire to be loved by the other (the other's desire) and so, too, desirable objects are mediated by the desire of others and become, thus, valuable. In this sense we are all sublime fetishists, or perhaps more radically, there is no other mode of relation than that described by fetishism. Objects gather value, and in doing so gather people around them. The true fetish (like the true God) is not just the result of 'projecting' essentially human attributes onto a thing, but rather it has to do with the entrapments of desire: being seduced into believing in a big Other that, as Haitian *voudoun* practitioners would put it, 'is a good-natured daddy, with whom it will be easy to manage on the last day' (Métraux, 1989: 72), for he loves us so much.

It would be easy to ascribe 'seduction', fascination and 'the entrapments of desire' solely to humans, but that would go against the more nuanced approach developed here by Feuerbach and Marx. Thus, in keeping with the more general argument of this essay on the avatars of the fetish, let us argue that the transference-relationship (fascination, allure) should be conceived as a general structure that, like fantasy/desire and contagion, comes to presence 'in destroying, transforming, and "assimilating" the desired non-I'.[7] Is that not precisely the power of the fetish? The story of the conquerors in the Caribbean, the history and prehistory of psychoanalysis, and the language of popular sovereignty surveyed in this section suggest just as much.

Furthermore, the generalised notions of transference and value developed by Feuerbach, and postulated here as the basis for a renewed form of realism or form-materialism, have an interesting impact when applied to the question of the particularity of man. The result turns out to be crucial for a proper understanding of belief, religious and political, that the reader would immediately recognise as also central to other fields of practice and inquiry such as human rights and Freudian psychoanalysis. If it is true that the latter are the last surviving ideologies of the twentieth century with a claim to universality in our times, then perhaps it is not too far fetched to say that in his generalisation of transference and value, Ludwig Feuerbach should be acknowledged as the definitive thinker of the present.

Feuerbach wrote in the *Essence of Christianity*:

> Providence is a *privilege* of man. It expresses the value of man, in distinction from other natural beings and things; *it exempts him from the connection of the universe*. Providence is the conviction of man of the infinite value of his existence – a conviction in which he renounces faith in the reality of external things
>
> (1957: 105).

Since the idea of Providence, associated to natural necessity and escape from uncertainty, entails that human well-being is the greatest right, a being who guarantees such a right must also be able to escape necessity and manipulate nature *at will*. Such a being would be supernatural and would represent the limit of history. In Feuerbach's critique of modernity's privilege of man and in Marx's political adaptation of this idea in the language of American popular constitutionalism, inspired by the re-entry of the fetish in religious and revolutionary practice, we find a precursor of Freudianism (the question of omnipotence of thought) and contemporary readings of the master–slave dialectic, from Alexandre Kojève to Franz Fanon, that could serve as the basis for a renewed sort of realism.

Notes

1 As Laurence Dickey observes (1998), this entails 'something like universality within what Hegel regarded to be as the particular social moment of experience itself', a problem whose solution would lead him, on account of the debate concerning the relation between commerce and luxury, down the path which ends with fetishism. Already Millar and Ferguson, who noticed that uneven distribution of wealth would give rise to social and political tensions between poor and rich, have argued that what was accidental to human nature, and habitual rather than essential to it, had often become an 'idol' of the mind (Ferguson, 1792, vol. 1: 134–9). Later on, in the *Ethical Life* essay, Hegel would indict the 'business class' for its fascination with property rather than 'higher things', as a result of which the 'absolute bond of the people, namely [true] ethical principle, has vanished, and the people is dissolved' (Hegel, 1979: 171).

2 *Charles River Bridge v. Warren Bridge*, 36 US (II Pet.) 420 (1837).
3 US Constitution, Article I, Section 10, Clause I.
4 For these sources, and a detailed study of Marx's early interest of the relationship between race and capitalism in America, see Nimtz jr. (2003: 4).
5 See Hegel (1983). For the same formulation, in the recently discovered manuscript of the 1821–2 lecture course on the philosophy of right (*Das Vernünftige ist wirklich und das Wirkliche ist vernünftig*, rendered as 'the rational is actual and the actual is rational'), see Becchi (1986: 251–61).
6 Crucially, Feuerbach's move announces Michel Foucault's critique of ethnology as a science predicated on a hypothesis of sameness. See Foucault (1994: 376–7).
7 See Kojève (1969: 4). The purpose of this reference is to highlight the connection between Feuerbach's post-Hegelian take on the fetish and Kojève's central notion of 'anthropogenic desire' as the source of the idea of justice. See on this Kojève (2000: § 35–8).

Chapter 5

Let us make love (and listen to Death From Above)

Notes on psychoanalysis

At the end of the previous chapter, Ludwig Feuerbach's fetish shined in all its glory. It was introduced as the precursor of Freud's investigation on the nature of the uncanny and what he called *Todëstriebe* or death-drive, but also of the sort of 'end of . . .' theory that became so popular in the last decades of the twentieth century. The fetish is perhaps the lost link associating Franz Fanon's rebellious branch of psychoanalysis with its founder (remember the question of the white mask and its seemingly supernatural omnipotence) and with Marx, but also with the return of Hegelianism in phenomenology's engagement with right, justice and the human/nonhuman continuum (as in Sartre and Kojève). In the case of Fanon, it can be said that the fetish is brought back home, in a fully self-reflexive movement, back to the Caribbean and Africa. There, in the hands of sons and daughters of Maroons and Arabs in Cuba and Algeria, the fetish would once again shake the world to its very foundations.

To trace a line from Freud to Fanon is to place before our very eyes the entire history of psychoanalysis. That would be a worthy endeavour, but one that would surely extend beyond the confines of this book. All that can be offered in its place, too little . . . almost nothing, surely not enough, are a few notes scattered here and there on the prehistory and the avatars of the fetish as it encounters (perhaps founds) the language of analysis. What follows in the next paragraphs should be read in the spirit of such initial and fragmented notes.

Beginnings: on how psychoanalysis lost its woman

Sigmund Freud published 'The Uncanny' in the fall of 1919. The essay developed certain ideas concerning archaic objects and beliefs present in 'Animism, Magic and the Omnipotence of Thoughts' included in *Totem and Taboo* of 1913, which can be traced back to his 1910 correspondence with Carl G. Jung, and prefigured the postulation of the compulsion to repeat and return (*Todëstriebe* or death-drive) found in the decisive *Beyond the Pleasure Principle* of 1920, but also the postulation of the mother/child dyad by Jacques Lacan later on. Freud's engagement with the fetish proved momentous for the history of psychoanalysis since it is here that the transition from the first to the second topographic systems of consciousness takes place, as an answer to the following question: what happens if one starts not with neuroses but with uncanny experiences?

As Avery Gordon explains, a lot happens both descriptively and in terms of analysis (2004: 50 ff.). Depending on one's point of view, it can be said that things are finally set on the right track for analysis, or else, that the interest in the fetish and archaic, 'primitive' mentality persists and is enhanced by Freud's postulation of the concept of death-drive. In any case, it seems fair to describe this as a foundational moment for psychoanalysis. Only that this would be half the story: the other half is that between the 1910 and the 1919 writings, lies the decisive contribution of one Sabina Spielrein, a young Russian woman brought to Carl G. Jung's famous Burghölzli psychiatric clinic in Zurich to be cured of a nervous disorder, hysteria or schizophrenia, who quickly became a student and an accomplished researcher in the field. Her contribution to the foundation of psychoanalytical theory was neither fully understood nor properly acknowledged by Jung and Freud, with whom she worked and corresponded, but it was decisive. It has been associated with the postulation of the death instinct, the solution to the conceptual problem of repression and, crucially, a redescription of sexual desire as an inherent tendency to fusion and dissolution that threatens the integrity of the subject. As we will see, this insight was fundamental in the move from a theory of the object of desire to one of the object of the drives, the obscure object of archaic experience, operated in psychoanalytical theory.

When Spielrein was admitted to the Burghölzli clinic, her case included a set of symptoms common at the time: concern about defecation while eating, visual hallucinations about the seemingly autonomous hand of her father about to strike, symptoms whose relationship with sexuality and eroticism was known to modern sensibilities since at least Rousseau's *Confessions* up to Krafft-Ebing's *Sexual Psychopathy* and, in the wider public domain, Rudolph Binion's biography of Lou Andreas-Salomé. Significantly, Spielrein was educated by her mother in complete sexual ignorance, a 'pure' relationship broken up by her father's occasional habit of spanking her on the buttocks with an open hand, a practice that Sabina understood and visualised from an erotic perspective in a similar manner to the one that Binion observes in his account of the life of Andreas-Salomé.

This particularity concerning her admission in the Burghölzli clinic proved significant since it coincided with the publication in 1904 of Leopold Löwenfeld's *Psychic Obsessions*, which included two articles penned by Sigmund Freud. Freud had become well reputed among the physicians associated with the clinic in 1896 when he proposed that the specific and exclusive cause of hysteria could be found in repressed memories concerning an event of a sexual nature that occurred during infancy, a discovery that he credited on a new non-hypnotic treatment that he had termed 'psychoanalysis'. Since hysteria was seen at the time as a widespread condition, the idea that so many cases would spring from a unique source was received with scepticism. Recognised experts in the field like Krafft-Ebing found Freud's thesis closer to 'a fairytale' while others accused him of instigating in his patients the so-called repressed memories of sexual abuse. The 1904 publication changed all that. Freud declared in a letter to the editor that although the importance of early sexual traumas should not be put to the side, he would now focus on the constitutive factors of hysteria and the role of fantasy and delirious phenomena in repression. This change of direction was clear enough in his contributions, and it became evident to the physicians in Zurich. Löwenfeld's book circulated among the members of the clinic during the spring of 1904 and Spielrein was admitted in August of the same year: she was hysteric, wealthy, well educated and delirious. She was the 'pure' case destined to test Freud's ideas.

In 1904, her case appears reported in an important article written by Jung and Riklin that mixes decisively Bleuler's experimental approach on language and free association with Freud's notion of erotic repression: Spielrein had become Jung's 'experimental case' and much more. Their relationship became intimate; soon it threatened to become a scandal, and the ups and downs of their affair form the very crossroads at the centre of which lies psychoanalysis as we know it. In the process alliances were made, friendships were broken (most famously that between Jung and Freud) and no less important, psychoanalysis lost its woman.

By 1905, Sabina Spielrein had recovered from her condition and enrolled at the University of Zurich to study medicine, receiving her doctor's degree in 1911 on the basis of a dissertation entitled 'The Psychological Content of a Case of Schizophrenia', which was published later in the *Jahrbuch*, the flagship publication of the psychoanalytical movement edited by Jung upon designation by Freud himself. Her work had begun in the summer of 1907 and can be found in a tract called 'The Theory of Transformation and Its Corollaries'. Its subject matter is the tendency of every composite entity postulated in mental life, of every complex, to persist in reality as an object, as opposed to the tendency of change and transformation. It is in fact an answer to a point of view that she had discussed with Jung during therapy. Her argument is that every composite object struggles to achieve and maintain autonomy, and it tends to identify sensually with other objects present in the mental life of others. This sympathetic relation provokes in the person the sensation of an objective, shared complex, and thus, of control. The complex is perceived as shared rather than just a figment of the inner mind of the person, and the subsequent feeling of relief turns into a notion of comprehension between those who share it that entails sameness and can even generate sexual attraction, such as that lived between the patient (Spielrein) and the doctor (Jung).

However, her crucial insight concerns the nature of sexuality: given that it operates at the level of the species as a whole, sexuality ultimately opposes individual differentiation. Objective sensual contact seems to conspire against the need for autonomy and separation. Because of this, it can only be conceived by the individual consciousness as something demonic and destructive. This explains why inherent resistances always accompany sexuality, as the individual struggles to keep whatever it has achieved in separation. Such resistances can already be seen in children apparently oblivious to their sexual destiny, and thus it can be related but also distinguished from the desire to engage in sacrifice for a cause that is commonly associated with youth, in that the latter involves the tendency to transformation (Kerr, 1995: 165 ff.). In addition to that, the domination and dissolution of a complex in sensual contact (including sexual attraction) is but one of the many ways that remain open to the tendency of transformation: the others are art and science, also forms of the objectification of complexes, or postulation. In postulation, the link between the art-object or the scientific object and the life of the mind is transformation, the reconfiguration of a composite more commonly known as sublimation (a mechanism that will be termed here, later on and with significant variations, substitution). In cases of hysteria, what matters, she says, is to make sure that the psycho-sexual component of the ego identity is transformed (through art or abreaction) so that its reflexive tendency to return to worldly connectivity (that would lead to identity dissolution) is curbed, broken and broken up.

Spielrein refers explicitly to this mechanism concerning sexuality as a circle that does not complete its full return upon itself, 'the component will be weakened in this way just as a phonograph that has not been wound up' (Spielrein, 1983: 165–6). In addition to Spielrein's use of the figure of an incomplete circle, later developed in psychoanalytic theory and elsewhere in the notion of a self-reflexive structure or a drive that does not achieve its set target, it is important to notice that according to Spielrein this tension is inherent to every composite entity. Coached in the language of an early psychoanalytical study on love, the laws of death and transformation, Spielrein's 'discovery' is that of the tension between absence in worldly connectivity and presence in determination, which then doubles up into yet another tension between specificity or integrity and relationality, that we have identified before as a postulate of central ontological importance in relation to a certain notion of temporality. The study contains an early appraisal of the relation between sex and death, and the solution *in nuce* to the conceptual problem of the (Freudian) notion of repression. To us it matters also to highlight the metaphysical sense of this momentous contribution.

As her diaries and the correspondence between Spielrein and Jung reveal, the two discussed and developed the notion that images of death and destruction in delirious hallucinations could be related to the threat posited to the differentiated individual inherent in sexual fusion. Spielrein had argued in her three-part study on the subject, that delirious phenomena reveal the operation of two antagonistic components of psychic reality and, together with Jung, explored the notion that such antagonism may point towards an archaic level of reality in postulated objects of thought. Such an archaic level, operative in the sexual desire to dissolution, would correspond to the 'death-drive', a term that Spielrein used, having in mind the work of Nobel Prizewinner Élie Metchnikoff. In turn, Jung perceived that Spielrein's contributions fit his own ideas on the sacrificial path of the hero. Jung's work in progress on the matter was presented at a 1910 conference in Herisau, lost to us but known to Spielrein, and was included in the correspondence between him and Freud (June/July 1910) to which the latter reacted critically if ultimately with benevolence and acceptance, hastily pursuing the composition of a parallel piece on the two principles of psychic phenomena, a project that would ultimately lead to 'The Uncanny' and *Beyond the Pleasure Principle*.

Spielrein argued that the archaic level, including mythological symbolism, was attractive to patients precisely as the sphere of dissociation in worldly connectivity: myth is a collective and trans-individual form of thought, as Jung had emphasised, adding to the nascent 'theory' the notion that the persistence of archetypical symbols in the unconscious pointed towards their phylogenetic origin and transmission. Self-sacrifice (the path of the hero) was presented not only as a key element in ancient religiosity but actually as an archaic motif transmitted phylogenetically down the generations. Jung told Freud about his 'discovery', backed by the clinical evidence put forward by Spielrein and others, in a letter of September 1910. The former schizophrenic/hysteric patient had by then become an advanced student of schizophrenia, putting forth ideas of her own and publishing results before anybody else, backing Jung's phylogenetic ideas concerning schizophrenia and Freud's initial thoughts on the subject.

During a cycle trip through Italy that year, Jung stumbled upon a statuary composition in which a snake bites the penis of the god Priappus while the latter smiles approvingly and points towards the snake. It is a rich and powerful image that has proved enduring: echoes of it can be seen in late instances of popular culture such as the 2006 B-film *Snakes on a Plane*. Jung related the image to his arguments on the iconography of mitraism, a symbol of sexuality reacting destructively on another, but he might as well have rehearsed a more profound knowledge of the archaic had he remembered that a similar image, this time depicting goddess Hera amorously receiving in her mouth Zeus' erect phallus, could be seen by the worshipper in her most majestic shrine, the Heraion in Argos. He could have found then and there a more direct 'archaic' relation between the blind necessity of the laws of death, sexuality and the self-sacrificial path of the hero. Hera is goddess of the bed, and when she makes love to Zeus on top of Mount Gargaron, the earth itself shakes and sprouts a bed of flowers for the incestuous lovers. But she is also goddess of revenge and destruction. It is in Argos that Zeus betrays her with one of the priestesses of the Heraion. In response, Hera sets in motion what Roberto Calasso has properly described as a 'wheel of necessity' (1994: 24). From then onwards all other betrayals and all other vendettas will be but mere variations on what happened in Argos, and it was precisely to Argos that the hero Orestes would return to seek revenge and inspire revolt. The love of brother and sister would be betrayed in Argos once again and the hero would choose self-sacrifice, with a minimal but decisive difference.

Orestes' revolt against the law is but another turning of Hera's wheel of necessity, but it also puts an end to the circle of revenge. Like Zeus in the Heraion, he chooses the copy, the remainder, the artifice, the minimal difference 'which is enough to overturn the order and generate the new' because it was difference and it was a remainder (Calasso, 1994: 24–5). Orestes kills his mother and traverses incestuous sexual fantasy; he turns his back on his sister, on Argos itself. The order of death and necessity instituted by Hera in response to Zeus' original choice of the remainder (a copy that in fact imitated a statue; as can be seen, the problem of the nature of sexuality leads to the inanimate) comes to an end with Orestes' exile, and with it the entire order of the gods and the age of the heroes. What Orestes institutes is the age of the technical object whose sign is the breaking up of the circular flow of vengeance and desire. The choice for the minimal difference, the artifice, leaves the destructive component of sexuality weakened 'just as a phonograph that has not been wound up'.

Instead of interpreting sexuality in the modern age as the very sign of technics and substitution in violence, in a way closer to Spielrein's view (for whom sexuality entailed the wish to die in the beloved object), Jung established a relation between inherited ideas and a two-way transmission belt between the present and the chronological archaic that is simply too difficult to believe. On her own, Spielrein pursued her interpretation of the death-drive as the gravitational pull of an obscure object (all this in the language of the Wagnerian sacrificial cycle: she puts herself in the hands of a failing god or big other, possibly Jung himself, whose predicted failure sets her free), the object of the drives. In an entry dated 26 November 1910, having already started work on a piece 'On the Death Instinct', she wrote of her fear that Jung, who had planned to mention her idea in an article originally projected for July 'may simply borrow the whole development of the idea, because he now wants to refer to it as early as January . . . I love him and hate him'.[1]

In the spring of 1911, Spielrein finally realises that her study on the death-drive contains the essence of a solution to the conceptual problem of the notion of repression. For Spielrein there were only two significant drives of instincts: self-preservation and the preservation of the species (or sexuality) and two structures of the psyche: ego and the unconscious. The conscious ego operated in response to the force exerted by the instinct to self-preservation, while the unconscious had no significant role to play in the integrity or unity of the ego. It deals with collectivity and primordial relationality, and thus imposes upon the ego tasks and aims that may differ or even threaten its individual destiny. The unconscious responds to the force exerted by sexuality, the pull towards worldly connectivity and sensual relation. As Kerr observes (1995: 300), this simple but elegant explanation entails a crucial result: if sexuality responds to the imperatives of the collective, then it will attempt to coerce or suppress the imperatives of uniqueness and individuality in cases of divergence and this counts both for sexual intercourse and so-called 'sublimation' in art and science. Sexuality is fundamentally object-driven, and does not stop to consider the 'costs' or the 'risks' involved. Ultimately, the ego reacts before sexuality with resistance since the latter threatens its unique motivations and its desire for wholeness and therefore sexual desire is always accompanied by defence formations, more often than not in the form of images of death and destruction.

Spielrein's solution is not only more elegant but also more Freudian than anything to be found in the psychoanalytical literature of the time, as it relates to and explains with minimalistic simplicity such phenomena as artistic or scientific 'sublimation' and the ubiquity of incestuous sexual relations observable in mythology and clinical evidence. It also places Freud's 1909 speculation about a 'connection between sex and death' under a new light, highlighting the widespread appearance of symbols of death and destruction in the clinical phenomenology of neurosis, as explained by psychoanalytic theory from its inception.

During her brush with neurosis, Sabina Spielrein saw spirits and fetish-animals dragging her towards death:

> In my attacks of anguish it seemed to me that an unknown force was trying to take me away . . . I often had the feeling of flying away, against my will. Animals and diseases, which I imagined in the form of living beings, were trying to 'do me harm' and drag me into the fearful darkness of death.
>
> (Spielrein, in Carotenuto, 1984: 152)

Like Zeyna, the fictional character in Ken McMullen's eponymous film, modelled also upon Leon Trotsky's daughter, Sabina believed in the prophetic powers of her unconscious and thought that her schizophrenia meant not isolation from the world 'but rather a way of understanding the world and of expressing oneself' (Spielrein, in Carotenuto, 1984: 39, 146). She attempted to provide a sound explanation of her views and in the process changed the course of psychoanalytical theory and practice forever. Her arrow was aimed at the heart of psychoanalysis.

In a letter written to Freud at the end of August 1911, Jung listed Spielrein's name as a Zurich representative to the Third Psychoanalytic Congress in Weimar (21–2 September 1911). She never arrived; she had fallen deeply in love with her analyst, Dr. Jung, who despite his attraction to her, breaks off the relationship when it threatens to cause a scandal. Spielrein then confides in Freud, Jung's father figure, who thenceforth becomes a confessor to both. She moved to Vienna and read part of her manuscript on the death-drive during a meeting of Freud's closer collaborators on 29 November 1911. In the Spring of 1911, the *Jahrburg* had included Spielrein's thesis and a piece penned by Freud in which the latter proposed a distinction between a reality principle and a pleasure principle; that piece had been inspired by Jung's account of what he called the 'two types' of mental reality in which the latter had linked his theorisation to Spielrein's results.

Following these exchanges Freud started work on *Totem and Taboo*, and conscious of the parallelism between his research on the archaic, the (mythologically) absent figure of the father and Jung's own research on the primordial mother/son dyad in mythological cycles (with Spielrein), wrote to him in August 1911 in order to pre-empt any reaction. Spielrein became a member of the Vienna Psychoanalytical Society in October that year and submitted her work on the subject to the Wednesday meeting. Freud's reaction was favourable but ambivalent, and in a letter to Carl Jung dated 30 November criticised her dealings with mythology and the archaic on the basis that she subordinated psychic materials to biological considerations (Kerr, 1995: 303 ff.). Faced with such a defence of psychoanalysis' self-sufficiency, the reader may be forgiven if she asks the following question: But isn't it Freud who turns to biological considerations, precisely on this very same point, in the 1920s' essay *Beyond the Pleasure Principle*?

Noticeably, Freud does just that in relation to the question of the self-sacrifice of the organism in order to erect a wall against excessive influences of excitation. The separation between organic 'inside' and inorganic 'outside' is postulated by Freud as being achieved at the cost of the death of part of the primitive organism itself, and it is this death that gives origin to the protective wall separating the organism from its environment and filtering out the threatening influences of the external surroundings. First, observe the similarity between this early psychoanalytical formulation of the death-drive and the notion of the formation of an 'evental' body in the enactive viewpoint in the cognitive sciences referred to in a previous chapter of this book. Second, notice how death or 'separation-in-proximity' actually gives place to organic specificity and determines both phylogenetic transmission and sexual reproduction (Brassier, 2007a: Chapter 7). In this sense at least, the inanimate or 'inert' (death, the inorganic) precedes organic life not just chronologically, but more importantly, as the primordial force driving organic life towards reproduction and death. It is in this sense that the death-drive is primordial: as the repetition of the originary sequence that gives birth to any differentiated element. However, as Spielrein suggested, this repetition is incomplete, more like a circle that does not fall back upon itself (1983: 166). This is so because the passage from the inorganic to the organic, objectified in the separating membrane, shield or wall is prior to the experiencing living organism and thus, will remain obscure to it in life and even in death.

The individual's death does not equal death as a primordial event (the moment of self-organisation of every objectivity or 'autopoiesis', in the language of enactive cognitivism) but it is the latter that has to be integrated as part of the organism's identity. Following Freud and Spielrein on this point, it can be said that the individual's psyche (its interiority as an organism) remains always divided as a result of this impossible demand to integrate an event that challenges the conscious experience and integrity of the organism. The division of the individual's psyche is the trace of the continuity with the inorganic that is written within the very wall that guarantees its unity and separation. This trace appears twice, first as a primordial or original worldly connectivity and then, once again, in the sensual embrace with every other as a 'threat' or an unresolved tension. It appears as a lost or obscure object, whose existence cannot be postulated as a result of experience but rather because of its gravitational pull. Such a pull or tension is at the very core of reality; that is the significance of the so-called death-drive.

According to Avery Gordon (2004: 40), Freud thought that Spielrein's paper on the death-drive, written more than ten years before his own seminal study on the beyond of the pleasure principle, was 'personally conditioned' (Freud, in Carotenuto, 1984: 146). Similarly, after having used and complimented her study Jung saw it as 'heavily over-weighted with her own complexes' (Jung, in Carotenuto, 1984: 183). At that point, its very point of origin, psychoanalysis lost its woman. Later on it would go on wondering: what do women want? Perhaps this is simply to point out that the questions raised by her case did not simply go away. Crucially, Spielrein's case contributed to the development of a generalised notion of transference as gravitational pull that passes on to the analytical concept of a field of transference–countertransference, a field of reciprocal projection and affective attachment, in which transference appears as a demand or an object 'that insists on being recognised as real' (Rose, 1986: 42) and shatters the previous 'original' situation – the 'original' reason for the analysis, as Gordon observes (2004: 43).

In the papers collected by Carotenuto, Spielrein puts it like this:

> I see absolutely no difference between transference to the doctor and every other sort of transference: in giving one's own personality, one takes on the personality of the Other, whom one loves.
> (Spielrein, in Carotenuto, 1984: 85)

And Freud elaborates:

> There is a complete change of scene; it is as though some piece of make-believe had been stopped by the sudden irruption of reality.
> (Freud, 1953–74, vol. 12: 162 and Rose, 1986: 42–3)

The key point is the recognition of the reality (as formality) of what is projected and enacted in connection with a primordial 'void of being', the same idea that we encountered in the previous chapter while exploring Ludwig Feuerbach's comparative approach to West African and Caribbean religious and rebellious practices, but also in Marx's fetishism. Repetition, the compulsion that Freud associated with the death-drive, emerges at this junction in the form of repetition-as-displacement or the becoming unplaceable of an object precisely in the sense that transference creates a complete change of scene and things are not just as before. At the very crossroads of psychoanalysis, its centre-point, its origin, we have found a generalised form of connection, contact or communication that has nothing to do with penetration or power in the sense of critique. Rather, it is a form of causation or contact beyond critique, in that it is both intimate and foreign. French psychoanalyst Jacques Lacan would later coin the term 'extimate' in order to refer to this form of relationality as a generalised objective field: the foreign within (which is one of the meanings given to the term 'uncanny'). This is the field of operation of the unplaceable fetish, that of identification with others and its uncertainty.

Freud says that the identification with the consciousness of others is uncertain because it relies on the assumption that it is like our own (what Kantians would call self-positing). Once that assumption is dropped or restricted, once it is recognised that things are not just out there for us but actually something else, something other, the world opens up, it becomes uncertain or contingent. This contingency turns back upon us 'as we leave our former state in which we could conceive of an intelligible, if not also enchanted connection to the world at large' (Gordon, 2004: 47). If we up-end that contingency, as Gordon suggests, that assumption, onto ourselves (which is what logicians working on unrestricted abstraction, against finite thought or critique, seem to be doing)[2] 'we must say that all the acts and manifestations which I notice in myself and do not know how to link up with the rest of my mental life must be judged as if they belonged to someone else and are to be explained by the . . . life ascribed to that person' (Freud, 1953–74, vol. 14: 120). As Gordon notices, Freud here is very close to suggesting that the unconscious is inconceivable outside of the worldly relations that structure the encounter between myself and another, the otherness of encountered humans and nonhumans or *formality*, and that bring the encounter inside as my own otherness that I cannot explain or consciously integrate 'without knowing something of the life world from which the other came' (Gordon: 2004: 47).

But this is not what Freud wants to say, as Gordon points out. The recognition of formality as primordial reality may lead in Freud's opinion to the assumption of a second consciousness, an other consciousness 'which is united in myself with the consciousness I know' (Freud, 1953–74, vol. 14: 120–1). At this point in the essay, Freud distinguishes between the consciousness of another person and that 'of which its own possessor knows nothing' (ibid.), and in doing so invents the unconscious as a self-reflexive structure without residue, a closed system that leaves no room for paradoxical objects and the traces of otherness. This result could only seem to his readers as harbouring a contradiction with the postulation of a death-drive and a generalised field of transference.

Let us explain further. In order to maintain the purity of its unconscious Freud must pay a price, that is, he must sacrifice the alien objects, formally other and external but also intimate in spite of their formality, or at least keep them at bay. He has to de-realise otherness and formality, and this is precisely the sense of his choices in the papers on the significance of the uncanny (Freud, 1953–74, vol. 17: 247–8). In the essay on the significance of uncanny phenomena, and after having admitted to the reality of archaic objects that cannot be traced back or reduced to the individual's personal, closed psychic life, Freud minimises their character and importance before the discussion even begins (Freud, 1953–74, vol. 17: 248 and Gordon, 2004: 52). Freud's choices remain ambiguous throughout the essay. He seems to veer between giving priority to the individual's desiring psyche and considering the otherness in me as an archaic basis of desire beyond the individual. However, as suggested before, at the end of the day Freud comes out in favour of a closed psyche unknown to its possessor.

In this section, such ambiguity has been traced back to the haunting presence of one Sabina Spielrein. For all his resoluteness, Freud cannot quite get away from the possibility that the unconscious may be the place where all others, the traces of otherness that we called in a previous chapter 'the world-historial', live within me, not in penetration but certainly in close proximity. In this sense, the world-historial may be understood as, in fact, the real support of one's existence as a psychic being and the means through which one gains access to existence in general, to temporality and being.

This has nothing to do with some sort of 'collective unconscious', since the postulated close proximity between one's psyche and that which is other in me is not fusion, absolute relationality with the alter as the deeper truth of my being, but rather it entails a certain distance, solitude or withdrawal. This solitude is not that of Rousseaunian subtraction from the world (Rousseau, 1979) or the unhappy solitude of the Romantic or modern artist in communication with his most hidden truth. In these cases, it is a question of minimally adjusting oneself to human society, either by an exclusion that one accepts or agrees to, or by authenticating a sense of oneself as a hidden, hard truth (Guéguen, 2006: 264–5). The aim is to bear witness to the absolute singularity of one's condition in the relationship with a benevolent, equally unique and consistent other. Here, the connection between intimacy and publicity is inverted, and the most intimate becomes truer than whatever is in the public domain in ordinary life (equipment, records, monuments, inscriptions) because it is stated. Inner conviction, taken as ordinarily hidden, replaces collective access to temporality in publicity. This is also what happens in the case of so-called 'conviction' politics, predominant today: we aim for total penetration, fusion with the innermost desires of others, we dream of wholeness and equality, while in fact this is nothing but a will to say everything, and in particular, to say what it is required of us to hide under the auspices of self-control, shame and caution – an inner fascism. In all, this would be an all too human solitude.

In contrast, the sort of withdrawal that is entailed by the close proximity between one's psyche and the archaic veers towards publicity and collective access. In this case truth is on the side of the inhuman, rather than the intimate: it appears as it pleases, not as it pleases 'us' and in this respect it has little to do with our desiring psyche. It has more to do with that which impinges upon or 'causes' our psychic life from a distance. Rather than human solitude or uniqueness, at stake here is the distance or the gap between the human and the inhuman, presence and readiness, access and direct access. The only thing that can be said about such a distance is that not all can be said about it. Therefore, the philosophically important question here is that of temporality, contact and communication in the absence of direct links, windows and totally open doors (Levinas, 1997: 178).

This is the sort of withdrawal that defines Scottie in the famous scene of the kiss in Hitchcock's *Vertigo*. When, in the love scene towards the end of the film, Scottie passionately kisses Judy, now refashioned as the deceased Madeleine, he withdraws just enough to ensure that her new blond hair is still there. This gesture reveals Judy as the ultimate archaic object, a vicar or mediating instrument that allows Scottie to communicate with the dead Madeleine. In this way, by withdrawing from Judy, Scottie gains access to the having-been and the already that would allow him, him and Judy/Madeleine in this case, to keep going into the future (Žižek, 2006e: 126).

Decisively, Scottie steps back in order to focus on the colour of Judy's hair, thereby emphasising the gap that separates her, as an object of desire, from the specific feature that makes this object desirable in the first place: Judy is a substitute, not the real thing (there is no real thing that could ever be present at hand), an inhuman copy made more inhuman by the fact that it is invested with an affect originally directed towards a dead person (which, in turn, becomes 'undead'), but nevertheless, she is satisfactory not so much in terms of Scottie's psychic desire, but rather in spite of such desire. What has to be asserted here, against Freud, but also against a certain reading of value, is the priority of the objects of inscription that sustain the psychic desire inscribed on them.

Put otherwise, it is the asymmetry between Judy and Madeleine that allows an assymetrical form of communication to take place between Scottie and the ruptured temporality of death and renewal. But it is important to emphasise that the basis of such communication, and the ability to open up temporality as a flux of ruptures and repetitions, is the object as a causally powerful surface of inscription rather than an object of desire. Consequently, the object is valuable not because it is desirable, but rather because it enables its operator to access time and history, and furthermore, to make it happen. Another way to explain this would be to say that desire must be sustained and sustainable.

In this respect, close proximity with the alter can also be understood as the sort of sensuous contact that anthropologist Michael Taussig calls 'the dialectic of mimesis and alterity' in his study of powerful objects of inscription among 'traditional' peoples affected by sudden situations of death or catastrophe, and faced with the task of renewal (Taussig, 1992). He too acknowledges, against Freud, but also against the (critical) notion of objectivity as inaccessible excess, the priority of objects of inscription over whatever is inscribed on them. For Taussig, the fetish is not something transcendent, forever eluding our grasp, but rather something that runs the show behind our backs and sustains our drive into infinity. We dismiss the fetishes at our peril, since to deny their power is to entertain the illusion that our flight into infinity can be propelled on its own. Incidentally, this is precisely the sort of illusion that lies at the very basis of contemporary turbo-capitalism in its desire for unhinged, unimpeded productivity. In the next sections, the illusion of the unconstrained productivity of desire will be identified with the desire for immortality and the will to power, with nihilism, sacrificial violence and destruction.

Let us conclude this section by suggesting that perhaps Freud did peer into the abyss of infinity, and scared by what he saw, or the depths he could not even see, simply backed away.[3] At this point the risk is that psychoanalysis loses the world and its objects (it has lost women already), and one cannot help but wonder whether or not it is precisely at this point, from within this ambiguity, this flaw in the theoretical edifice of analysis, that the Lacanian revolution took off. Indeed, the Lacanian revolution took the side of the obscure object, the double and the propelling archaic: this is the theme of the contradictory object known as *objet petit a* and the death-drive.

Lacan and his double: on contradictory objects and the death-drive

At the end of the previous chapter it was argued that the transference-relationship, the gravitational pull of the obscure object – a mode of vicarious connection for which we may use such terms as seduction, allure or fascination – could be construed as a general structure of relationality and causation, more general perhaps than our common critical notion of power as immediate contact changing the nature or position of what is contacted. It was said that within such a structure elements destroy, transform and assimilate one another. This structure was associated with phenomena of contagion, whose widespread nature appears to be accounted for in the evidence put forward by anthropologists and other analysts interested in the role that projection and sensual objects play in the organisation of material reality, most famously German critics such as Ludwig Feuerbach and the young Karl Marx, but also in the work of anthropologists such as Michael Taussig.

The form of the transference-relationship – destruction, transformation, assimilation – was present in many of the instances referred to by these critics and anthropologists. It was said that in the case of Karl Marx, a great deal of his interest in fetishes and projections could be traced back to a story concerning the peculiar bond between conquerors and conquered in the Caribbean which, following Jean-Luc Nancy, had become familiar to Marx during his student years (Nancy, 2001: 3–8). According to that story, conquerors and conquered became inextricably linked via a common fascination with gold: noticing the effect that gold had on the Europeans, the indigenous used it to lure them, destroy them and assimilate them. In the process they became closely related, mimicking one another, enticing one another, seeking each other's recognition just as much as they tried to destroy and assimilate one another. It could be said that such a process continues to this very day. It is at the very heart, the heart in the chest, of imperial hubris and turbo-capitalist globalisation.

What sort of relationship is this? Can it be described in more detail? Is it a bivalent relation between mimesis and alterity, as Taussig suggests? Does it hint at the reality of being haunted or fascinated, rather than penetrated and completely altered by worldly contacts? Or else, should such a possibility be dismissed, as Freud ambiguously did, in favour of the concept of a self-positing, object-altering consciousness paired with a fully enclosed unconscious only accessible to a certain kind of analysis?

In the latter case, the assumption is that analysis may bring into focus with clarity and transparency something that the mind could not see in the previous situation, while the world of objects and the world-historial remains out there, more or less inefficacious in relation to the workings of the mind. To contrast, in the former case, that of the dialectic and the priority of sustaining objects of inscription, communication is posited as a form of indirect access, as the ability to locate things that appear and disappear without seizing them or intervening them in order to realise their 'hidden' potentialities. Indirect communication seems more capable of dealing with improbability, the sort of phenomena that go beyond given sets of possibilities and cannot be witnessed directly. Since nothing can be presented as a stand-in for this kind of phenomena, the only way to deal with them is through vicarious means. Vicar elements do not penetrate the intimate realm of phenomena, but rather operate in the frontier between inside and outside, allowing for boundary-crossing and an active relationship with temporality. From this perspective, time is not some fixed background that determines everything else, but rather it is determined materially. From this standpoint the improbable appears as a category of reality, and it becomes possible to shatter all the possibilities, rip them up and start again.

In what follows, let us focus on the tension between these two possibilities, and in particular, upon the sense of rebellion brought into the history of psychoanalysis by the work of Jacques Lacan. If the fetish shines aloof with the light of divine glory in the criticism of Ludwig Feuerbach, a light so powerful that it blinds us, it can be said that in Lacan's discourse of the analyst (but also in that of Franz Fanon, only alluded to here) the return of the fetish from the heavens of critique bursts open the chests of capital and colonialism, and in the darkness of our times, it shows the beating heart hidden within. Afterwards things are not just the same.

In lieu of this allusion to blindness, it seems that we must consider more closely the nature of the sort of darkness that haunts the forms of communication opened up by the fetish. The reader might remember that in Chapter 1 we encountered the spectator of the arts confronted by the archaic object (the charm) as something that awakens envy (Mazzoldi and Téllez, 2007: 372). Crucially, the term 'envy' refers to a certain kind of blindness, a visual impairment that could be rendered into the English term 'short-sightedness' or, with a nod to Hannah Arendt, 'thoughtless-ness'. Commentators of the work of Arendt have highlighted the connection between 'short-sightedness' and the sort of evil characteristic of modern forms of violence, as a constant in her thought (Arendt, 1958 and Dupuy, 2005: 77). Her controversial point is that the evil which inhabits the monstrous crimes committed in modern times is not the product of some malign intention, an otherworldly design (or lack thereof) which serves as proof of our intrinsic finitude, but rather an instance of envy, the sort of 'jealousy onto madness' that Mazzoldi identifies as a central aspect in the experience of the contemporary spectator of the arts. Anthropologist Michael Taussig would speak of 'fascination with abomination' quoting Marlowe in Joseph Conrad's *The Heart of Darkness* (Taussig, 2008).

These writers bring to our attention something that modernity's logic of transparency and representation disavows. This logic is exemplified by the primacy given to the eyewitness in art and politics, under the assumption that direct access without remainder is possible and that loss of information is somehow external to the act of communication. The disengagement of the eyewitness is supposed to guarantee the purity of directly accessed information. In contrast, the writers referred to in the previous paragraph seek to emphasise the most destructive side of transference and fascination, by pointing out that the latter is indissociable from blindness in projection and transference.

According to them, the privilege of the eyewitness is undermined by the fact that the witness inevitably falls prey to the eerie compulsions generated by the projected or (re)presented object, the fetish or the image. The witness finds itself in complete solitude and direct contemplation of the other, an alter ego, with which she wants to identify but at the very same time fears and wishes to reject. The result of this scheme is the hysterical identification of self and other with the truth, taken as that which is most intimate and ordinarily hidden, and which is supposed to become 'more true when it is stated than whatever is given to public view' (Guéguen, 2006: 265). The fascination with (an abominable) truth would thus be of a kind with the will to say everything (ibid.). Self and other, the witness and the addressee of the testimony (the spectator), the victim and the persecutor, become identical in the effort to highlight that which makes for the absolute singularity or intimacy of a subject: the human condition.

This is the theme of the double: the victim or the pursued locked in an eternal search for its persecutor – an other, perhaps evil external force – that in the end turns out to be identical with the 'intimate humanity' of the victim, or not. In the latter case it appears as something 'inhuman'. Let us call this the theme of Lacan and his double or 'the Lacan effect' for short.[4] Among Freudians, Jacques Lacan focused with particular strength on the act of communication and passage, but also on the truth of the intimate experience, and sought to distinguish between the significations generally given to that which is intimate and that which is also the most hidden, not because it should be hidden (for reasons of modesty, shame or caution) but rather because it remains as a limit of expression, the subject/object limit.

At stake is an effect of duplicity without original 'which perhaps is what the diabolical consists of, its very inconsistency' (Derrida, 1987c: 269). Thus for instance, by stepping into the shoes of the observer (the ethnographer) and the persecutor (the US-backed paramilitary), Guatemalan indigenous human rights activist Rigoberta Menchú (the proverbial victim) attempted to contain, to make present within her, what was before a purely external force; she tried to assimilate her devilish alter ego and destroy it. In doing so she risked becoming fascinated with the violence ensuing around her – and the same is true for the US academics that accompanied or rejected her quest (Menchú, 1985; Arias, 2001).

This effect of duplicity is inextricably entangled with the instinct for mastery and the will to power, that is to say, the desire to maximise life beyond the limits imposed by reality upon our quests for pleasure, to enjoy without hindrance (Freud, 1973–86, vol. 11: 418). In general, the idea is that we possess efficacious barriers against external stimuli that are understood by Freud as reality-related limits to our desire for pleasure. However, as he suggests, in certain cases there can be excitations from outside that are powerful enough to break through the protective shield. We become fascinated and entrapped by them, even though we cannot represent them. This fascination goes beyond the notion that the goal of life is to maximise pleasure. In the clinical literature, this phenomenon becomes evident in accounts of people affected by war neuroses (Freud, 1953–74, vol. 17: 205–10) and in more general terms, it assumes the form of a wish present in every entity 'to die in its own fashion' or according to its own design (Freud, 1973–86, vol. 11: 312).

Freud sought to make sense of these affective phenomena in terms of a protected inside and a threatening outside. However, if one abandons this rather simplistic way of sorting out the objects of memory, temporality and retention, one can see that all this talk of trauma points in the direction of an illusory conception of time, the already and the has-been, as an unhindered flux. The latter would be entirely non-material, a purely abstract flux running unconstrained and unimpeded. Put in this way, it is perhaps easier to understand the effect of duplicity associated to mastery and power as an illusion to return to a time before traumatic events made us the specific individuals we are, facing a specific history in the present and projecting ourselves into the future. In this respect, the illusion or blindness is retrospective: it 'aims at the past, at a time before the subject found itself where it is now, embedded in time and moving towards death' (Copjec, 2003: 33).

This is also the phenomenon referred to earlier on in relation to the Freudian theory of the death-drive. The primordial state of harmony or inertia postulated by the theory, which is often identified with the inertia attributed to objects, is read by Freudo-Lacanian theorists in terms of a primordial duality (the mother/child dyad) 'which supposedly contained all things and every happiness and to which the subject strives throughout life to return' (ibid.). Once again, we encounter in this Lacanian figure of the dyad or the double the notion of an ontological difference or fundamental duality between a brutal totality that encompasses everything in its fullness

(Heidegger's 'world' and/or 'readiness to hand', Sartre's 'being and nothingness' or 'series'), an invisible depth to which all elements withdraw, and a visible surface of specific elements seducing one another, making contact, becoming related (Heidegger's 'presence at hand'; Sartre's 'group').

The illusory entrapment is not the belief that things withdraw from the conflicts of life and other people (or other objects) into the void they came from – they do – but rather, the notion that such withdrawal is the end of the story, the end of history, or its pure beginning. The actual search for such an end-point, in which I am preserved in the intimacy of my self, fully present to myself through relations with others, and/or all objects persist quietly side-by-side, would lead towards nihilist violence. For it is an illusion, a case of short-sightedness, to believe that such a withdrawal would put an end to the contradiction between the invisible depth and the sensual surface that sets ablaze each and every object. That contradiction is real, and it is lived or confronted by every object, without end. Reality unfolds driven by the dynamics of such ruptures and contradictions, and this unfolding is what we call time or history, but also the thought of time or history.

Moreover, that fundamental contradiction is merely the beginning of a more complicated story. We must add to it, at the very least, yet another tension between the specificity of every object and its relationality, its ability to enter into sensual relations with other objects without losing its consistency. Notice however that in this case the demand for consistency cannot be interpreted to mean the persistence of the same in the realm of contingent appearances or connections, nor the universality of an all-encompassing 'form' in different applications or 'contents', but rather, a constant process of renegotiating the boundaries (between self and other) or, to be more precise, as an act of boundary-crossing precisely at the point where the limit seems to preclude such a possibility.

The last consideration brings us back to the question of the object that crosses boundaries and takes flight from established paths. We must ask ourselves what would be the nature of such an object (the fetish-object, in the parlance used in previous chapters). To repeat: the point was that, if we recognise the contradiction between the consistency of the object (its specificity, guaranteed by a limit or boundary) and its ability to relate to others (across such a boundary) as a real contradiction that takes place within each and every object, in addition to a more fundamental clash between withdrawn totality and individual presence, then we must also consider the possibility that at some point the object is able to go beyond the limits it has set for itself, the limits that guarantee its consistency without becoming fully inconsistent, and that this ability is part of its nature as much as the ability to limit itself. Put otherwise, we must consider the possibility of the truly contradictory nature of objects.

This in-between-ness of objects, a quality that was identified above with the nature of the remainder and the fetish, inhibits the tendency present in all objects to withdraw into the void and/or achieve fullness (to set unsurpassable limits, to be fully present to themselves, absolutely self-reflexive) and simultaneously cuts or breaks that tendency and cuts it up, curbs it, bends it, thereby driving the tendency in a circular movement towards a point of closure which is nevertheless different from its aim. This is to say that in their basic reality objects are reflexive, but at the end of their circular journey they do not find themselves; rather they find the other in themselves. Put otherwise, each element in reality seems to be caught in a loop but what returns is never the same, and what accounts for the difference is a minimal failure, an almost insignificant inconsistency. Like Rigoberta Menchú, it seems we too are obliged to include some inevitable minimal failure in our accounts of activity. In this sense, perhaps it would be better to describe the theme of the double as an exploration of the avatars of the act of boundary-crossing, the latter being understood as the minimal inconsistency within a general demand for consistency.

Clarification: contradictory objects are not just illogical. On proximity

Some readers may find this talk about consistency and minimal inconsistency simply obfuscating. They would promptly observe that logic dictates the illegitimacy of this sort of talk in the following manner: this ontological phenomenon – the crossroads, the minimally inconsistent result of a demand for consistency, contradiction – provided it can be observed in reality, cannot be said without breaking some fundamental rule of logic. The ineffability of being is required by logic, as Heidegger himself noted (Heidegger, 1959: 23) when the fact 'that he could speak of being, that is, nothing, albeit inconsistently' stared him in the face (Priest, 2002: 247). According to this received notion of logics, either our description of being and objects (as contradictory) must go or else logic does. Confronted by this either/or choice, the option seems pretty clear.

However, as logician Graham Priest points out, there is an alternative: to allow our more precise descriptions of being to redescribe our received notions of logic (Priest, 2002: 276, 295). Another alternative, championed by logicians Valerie Kurrish and Uwe Petersen, would be to restrict some of our assumptions concerning either/or reasoning. This is not the place to enter into the detailed differentiation of these alternatives. In any case, both seem to contend that to deal with contradiction (rather than dismissing it right away) is not to say that we can or should do away with consistency and logics. Rather, it means to point out that consistency has a lot to do with incompleteness and observation, and that a logical system of observation is consistent if it does not exclude its own problematic nature. It also means to say that there must be something in reality that renders certain contradictory or problematic elements and statements true. The composite object that has been identified throughout this book with the fetish-object, the technical object and the projected 'fixed point' of minimal failure, would be an example of such real elements and the object of such problematic statements.[5] To clarify, this is not the same as saying that the objects that constitute reality are contradictory, which would be a category mistake.

Let us explain further in what sense to propose dealing with contradiction is not to say that we can do away with consistency and logics, by means of an example. The aim of projecting a fixed point of minimal failure into the future is to establish that to every element or event that has been, there exists another one, literally a double, which is equal but not identical to the original one. The two elements or events can be postulated as concepts. Viewed from this standpoint, as concepts, it would be true to say that any object that falls under one of them also falls under the other. In this sense, they are equal and exchangeable. But the two elements or events can also be conceived as objects, with reality in their own right. Viewed from this standpoint they cannot be exchanged for one another regardless of context. In logical terms, this means to restrict the classical doctrine of extensionality, which also operates as a principle of identity (against bivalence), according to which 'if two concepts subsume the same objects under them, then they become exchangeable *salva veritate*'.[6]

The point here is that consistency has less to do with the 'true' reflection of the world ('it is/is not there', as if philosophy and/or science were simply mirrors pointed at the thing-in-itself, a thing-in-itself 'for us') or with an absolute principle of abstract identity (the validity of either/or reasoning applied to the values true and false), and much more with selection, that is to say, with establishing the relevant 'reference class' of observers, designating the limits of this set, the problematic nature of such limits, and the specificity of the elements selected for observation (Trotta, 2007: 153, 168). If the observers, us humans or an alien inorganic life form, are making the same observations, provided we and they use the same logic, then our inferences and theirs, or the outcome of such inferences, must be able to form a certain connection that does not disturb the specificity of the observed entity. Observers in the same reference class cannot connect with the world in a different way or, put otherwise, the observed entity has got to be an entity on its own.

The term for this sort of connection is 'proximity'. Consistency entails a form of approximation that keeps a certain distance from the approximated object (of observation). In logical terms, this means to abandon the way of the understanding ruled by the principle of abstract identity. Consistency does not mean here the repetition of the same in the same, as if my sameness had to be identical with the sameness of the other, the observed (or another observer). Consistency is not about the identity between observer and observed, but rather the specificity and uniqueness of the observed entity, an object that has to have intrinsic properties of its own, perhaps common to other entities in the same selected or collected sample, which 'cannot be processed at will by interaction with different observers of the same reference class' (Trotta, 2007: 155). It is not the case that the observer can exchange itself for the object of observation, or present itself as the object's witness and stand-in. On the contrary, consistency demands that we acknowledge both the uniqueness of the object observed, its positive being, and the fact that there is a gap, a void of being, a negativity that belongs also to the object and that the act of observation, made possible through technologies of this or that kind, cannot fill or fully cover. Only on the basis of such an acknowledgement can different observations by different observers in the same reference class be consistent.

Consistency entails thus a critical distance, but since such a distance is neither aloofness (indifference to the object) nor fusion (the observer becoming identical with the observed) it is better to speak of a 'minimal' distance beyond critique. To speak of a minimal distance in this way does not seem repugnant, and it should not fill us, or philosophy, with horror – the horror of arbitrariness, relativism and/or infinite reduction. On the contrary, the point of such talk is to emphasise the uniqueness of entities; that they have a substance of their own, which every observer in the reference class of observers has got to agree upon (ibid.). To avoid misunderstanding: this has nothing to do with intersubjective agreement or heuristic pragmatism,[7] but rather, with the recognition of the void of being that lurks behind a fundamental principle of our received notions of logic (extensionality) once the latter is not supplemented by a metaphysics of identity, expressed as indifference or fusion and conceived as a form of necessary determinacy.

Ultimately, questions of consistency, reality and the scrutinising power of any scientific methodology have to do with the 'creation' of a particular state of nature. The key question here is not to allow one to be tricked by the more transcendent connotations of the term 'creation'. In fact, what is at stake is the distinction between a natural system (ruled by laws which are natural laws) and a highly artificial or created environment. Since that distinction cannot be clearly drawn, because of the cohabitation, within each entity, of pre-individual or 'natural' elements and individuated or artificially engineered elements (Simondon, 1958), then we must admit that there is something in reality that allows scientific statements, beyond the Copernican Principle, beyond the idea of the impartial observer who sets up an experiment and sits back to simply describe what follows from it, statements that refer to partially withdrawn and partially related entities, to be true. Put otherwise, this is to affirm the existence of contradiction, that is to say, of contingencies that are improbable.[8] If that is the case then we may not have to deny, as Heidegger and Russell did, the fact that is staring us in the face (Priest, 2002: Chapter 15).

And it does: when contemporary psychoanalytic theorists postulate the existence of partial, composite or contradictory drives and contradictory objects, they are aware that their descriptions and categories are not regional but rather belong to the field of general ontology (Copjec, 2003: 34). As Ernesto Laclau observes, these writers tell us that 'the theory of the drives in Freud occupies the terrain of classical ontological questions' (2005: 114). He also points out that the genetic character of psychoanalytic arguments can be recast in more general, structural or metaphysical terms.

After having clarified that contradictory objects are not just illogical, let us now turn to the manner in which the theory of the drives postulated by psychoanalysis (and the obscure objects postulated by the theory) entails a general reworking of some mainstream basic ontological assumptions. This is yet another chapter in the history of the fetish, its more contemporary phase; as we will see with the help of Ernesto Laclau and Joan Copjec, two researchers that use psychoanalytic theory to upend their efforts in political and feminist theory, respectively. The fetish returns; after it does, things are just not the same.

The theory of drives and ontology: on substitution

Political theorist Ernesto Laclau explains in reference to the work of psychoanalytic theorist Joan Copjec on the death-drive, that 'the mythical wholeness of the mother/child dyad corresponds to the unachieved fullness evoked – as its opposite – by the dislocations brought about by the unfulfilled demands. The aspiration to that fullness or wholeness does not, however, simply disappear; it is transferred to partial objects that are the objects of the drives' (Laclau, 2005: 114–15).

We need not be concerned here with the particulars of Laclau's use of psychoanalysis vis-à-vis his theory of political hegemony and popular demands. What matters to us in the passage quoted above is to notice how the psychoanalytic theorist has to postulate the existence of contradictory objects if the operation of the drives in reality is to be accounted for. 'Death-drive' is not just some regional anomaly or the result of a disconnection between thought and being. It is rather a fundamental structure: the lost model (world, withdrawn totality, mother, the original) is a lack of being, a void that cannot be filled by any representative. In logical terms, it cannot be exchanged for some other entity regardless of context.

If this were the case, it would seem that, in ontological terms, we are left with an inherently porous reality whose elements would forever remain separated in isolation unless a force of necessity, an efficient cause or *potentia absoluta*, posited above and beyond the whole scene, brings them together. Furthermore, the elements comprising such a reality would be merely derivative in respect to the causal force that brings them together. However, there is an alternative to the view that posits a necessary being or 'big other', in psychoanalytical parlance, as the efficient cause of reality: that the elements themselves bridge the gap that separates them through vicarious, equally derivative means or elements which *frame* rather than *cause* (in the sense of efficacy) the whole scene.

In the first case, that of the postulation of necessary being ('providence' or 'big other') we are obliged to explain how it is that the absolutely necessary, constitutive force or entity can make contact with and bring together merely derivative elements. And since such an explanation does not seem available or satisfactory, for it does not verify the postulation of such a necessary being, the only option is to affirm the merely derivative elements as constitutive, capable of drifting towards the limit and once there take the next step, to connect, and thus as contradictory: derivative but constitutive, limited but auto-transcendent; beyond finitude, or as Japanese philosopher Kojin Karatani would say, 'trans-critical' (2005: 1 ff.).

According to the Freudo-Lacanian explanation put forward by Copjec and Laclau, the drive is transferred to a partial contradictory object and the latter assumes – in its specificity, in its contingency – the place and the role of necessity.[9] This is not to say that it operates as the representative of necessity. We must distinguish here precisely between exchange and substitution. In the case of exchange, the object functions as evidence of something else, a support-model. In contrast, a substitute object makes evident exactly the opposite: that 'other' or 'formal' objects exist without the need of a support-model. As we have seen, the idea of a support-model entails the postulation of a necessary being as the efficient cause of all the other merely derivative elements of reality. Since such a postulation cannot be verified, reason suggests that the best way to proceed is to drop the notion of a support-model.

Partial or contradictory objects do not function as evidence of something else, a Thing existing elsewhere, but as evidence that the elements of reality act without the support of a model, be this a model for action or a causal model – like the drawings in Titus – Carmel's series referred to in the first chapter of this book. This raises the following question: If the correct notion of the activity of objects is not that of the approximation towards a determinant (commanding, supporting) model, then what is it? The wager of this book is that a better notion of activity would conceive objects as crossing boundaries in order to connect with others, bridging the gap that separates them and making themselves noticeable, visible and alluring to one another through some sensual mechanism. If this is the case then enactment and allure, fascination and seduction – in a word, aesthetics – may be posited as an absolutely primary level in the constitution of reality (Harman, 2005 and 2007b).

Objects appear in their own way, and their appearance is their nature. They do so by poking sensual holes through the porous fabric of reality.

They tear boundaries apart and violate the isolated peace of all the other objects. If this is so, then the reciprocal sensual activity that characterises relations across boundaries (let us call it reciprocal projection) is indissociable from some kind of violence. Psychoanalytic theorists conclude that the blindness that accompanies mutual projection as a tendency (the illusion of fullness, the actual search thereof) may lead towards destruction, and that it must be curbed if the spread of violence is to be contained. Psychoanalytic theorists, as well as anthropologists studying sacrificial practices and rituals of victimage (Girard, 1977: 3 ff.) discover here the mechanism of substitution as an antidote to the spread of violence.

'Substitution' is a way to escape the blindness that is tendencially present in reciprocal projection, that is to say, the illusion of full reciprocal presence, penetration or 'nihilistic violence' strictly speaking. It is true that violence in general, the violation of the isolated peace of an object by another, cannot be avoided if contact is at all possible. But the object of violence can always be substituted or, put otherwise, it always withdraws (at least partially) from the relations it enters into, and thus it can be said that its unique substance is never fully penetrated.

Underlying the phenomenon that has been named 'substitution' is the notion of the uniqueness of every substance. If every substance is unique then one can never be exchanged for another or, put otherwise, no principle of abstract strict equivalence can be justly applied to the objects in reality. This is so in the sense that no object, no substance can be fully absorbed within a relational totality. To claim that an object can be absorbed completely within a relational totality, and that within such a totality it can be exchanged for any other (as is done in mainstream accounts of the market-system or the language-system, for instance) is in fact to obliterate the object, to subject reality to a form of nihilism.

If this is the case, if no substance can ever be exchanged for another, how can one substance connect with or open up to another? How can one portion of the world make contact with another? This question is known in philosophy as 'the problem of communication'. In the next section, let us explore an interesting, truly original answer to the question recently proposed by post-Heideggerian philosopher Graham Harman. Although an admirer of the work of psychoanalytical theorists such as Slavoj Žižek, Harman does not develop his arguments within such a framework. His work belongs to the field of tool – and object-oriented ontology. However, as we have seen already, ontological questions are not only a central concern for psychoanalysis, but also the latter now sees itself as occupying the terrain of ontology and metaphysics. Thus, in spite of the apparent change of tone and language, we remain in the vicinity of the encounter between the fetish and analysis.

Notes

1 See Spielrein, in Carotenuto (1984: 35). Carotenuto's book *A Secret Symmetry* (1984) contains Spielrein's diaries from 1909 to 1912, her letters to Carl G. Jung written between 1911 and 1918, her letters to Freud, and his to her. Gordon makes extensive use of these materials (2004) and so does Kerr. For an analysis of Spielrein's relationship to Jung and Freud and the hidden history of psychoanalysis, which I follow in these paragraphs, see Kerr (1995).
2 See Kerruish and Petersen (2006: 61–91).
3 For evidence supporting this claim of a 'superior fetishism' in Freud, see Freud (1953–74, vol. 14: 120 and vol. 17: 248).
4 Nicholas Royle uses the term 'Lacan effect' in order to refer to the 'regime of hallucination' that affects Film Studies. The film student mirrors Mazzoldi's spectator but also the psychoanalytic patient: as witnesses, they are both peculiarly blind. See Royle (2003: 80).
5 See on this Virno (2004: 101, also 78–80). See also Simondon (1958 and 1964) and Stiegler (1998 and 2001).
6 See on the doctrine of extensionality Leibniz (1966: 123). On its restriction, see Kerruish and Petersen (2006: 89–91). I have followed their argument in the previous paragraphs.
7 For a critique of heuristic pragmatism, see Meillassoux (2007: 55–81).
8 For the distinction between forms of contingency that may be subject to the laws of probability and those forms of contingency or unpredictability that may not, see Dupuy (2004: 15–16). Also Meillassoux (2007: 63).
9 See on this Laclau (2005: 114–16) and Copjec (2003: 37–8, 60). Quoting Lacan's definition of sublimation, according to which this phenomenon involves the elevation of an ordinary object to the dignity of the Thing, Copjec postulates that this elevation does not entail a representative function (exchange) but a form of transference (substitution).

Chapter 6

The love that seeks no other

Further notes . . .

In the context of an examination of post-Heideggerian ontology, in this case the work of Emmanuel Levinas, philosopher Graham Harman describes the problem of communication in the following manner:

> In a world where things are always more than any access can grasp, the question arises as to how we can gain access to them without gaining *direct* access. This evokes the traditional problem of occasionalist philosophy, to which Levinas is often sympathetic elsewhere (namely, in his theory of time). For occasionalism, no two substances can touch directly, but must interact by means of a third term: God. Despite the undeniable presence of God in Levinas's philosophy, communication is not the specialty of his deity. Instead, Levinas finds that *proximity* is the site of my communication with the other. In this respect, proximity is a kind of pre-contact or pre-relation from which all relation must emerge. The problem of communication is clearly visible in Levinas's own thoughts. Perhaps echoing Leibniz's monadology, Levinas asks: 'Can openness have another sense than that of the accessibility of entities through open doors or windows?' Sincerity, illeity, or proximity are designed to enable communication without doors or windows – communication without full contact. And surprisingly, this communication is always asymmetrical. The things are proximate to me without my being proximate to them.
>
> (Harman, 2007b: 21)

The key term in this passage is 'proximity'. Proximity, says Harman evoking the work of Levinas, 'forgets reciprocity, as in a love that does not expect to be shared.'[1] Understood in this manner, proximity is not just contact without penetration, but also an *asymmetrical* form of contact or communication. As Harman puts it, 'my fascination with the other does not entail the other's fascination with me' (2007b: 20).

This is relevant to our analysis of projection, blindness, violence and substitution, since this asymmetry may be interpreted as entailing the break-up of the circle of reciprocal fascination. Structurally, this is the same phenomenon we observed before when we considered how psychoanalytic theorists understand the break-up of the drives (and thus also of the will to destruction or *Todëstriebe*). Let us pursue the subject in the remainder of this chapter in order to further the discussion on rebellion (boundary-crossing) and violence inaugurated by the re-entry of the object and the shattering of the coordinates of criticism.

This purpose is not merely abstract or academic. As we will see, it also concerns our way of life. After dealing in more detail with the notions of 'proximity' and 'substitution', introduced above, in relation to sacrificial violence and politics, we will enquire whether or not it is possible to speak of the inherently violent, perhaps even fascistic or nihilistic nature of certain fetish-objects. The chapter veers towards the end with a proposal for a different model of political projection, following research done by René Girard and Michael Taussig in anthropology and fetishism, on the one hand, and Jean-Pierre Dupuy in political philosophy and rational choice theory, on the other. Then, we will conclude the chapter with an extended commentary of the Hollywood film *Pirates of the Caribbean* and its sequel *Dead Man's Chest*, which not only re-enact the story of the gold of the conquerors and the heart in the chest for a twenty-first century audience but also, uncannily, doubles up as a radical fable about rebellion and the drive and origins of capital and empire.

The love that seeks no other: additional notes on psychoanalysis, proximity and substitution

According to the psychoanalytic theorists that we encountered in the previous chapter, the break-up of the drives occurs because they 'content themselves with these partial objects' (Laclau, 2005: 112). Partial or contradictory objects appear in the empty space left by the withdrawal of the lost 'Thing' (for instance the lost mother, or the archaic past). Psychoanalytical theory contends that the lost 'Thing' is not merely the result of some epistemological defect but an ontological uncertainty, a void of being, a non-existent object or an event that is not even amenable to the laws of probability. It is a truly archaic thing, rather than an unknown unknown. If this is the case, then the postulated objects appear in the place of the void, not in the sense that they represent whatever was lost, but rather in a reversal of the common understanding of the phenomenon known as sublimation, in the sense that they *substitute* themselves for the void or the 'Thing'.

Substitution is different from exchange and representation; the relationship in question is not one of 'witnessing' or making evident the other object that was lost and remains absent, unknown, somewhere else, but rather one of standing before the other object that is not there *responsibly*. In more general terms, substitution entails taking responsibility for non-being.

The use of the term 'responsibility' in this case should not confuse the reader, leading her to believe that we have now abandoned, without warning or direction, the discourse of ontology (and psychoanalysis) and moved on to ethical discourse. Put simply, 'responsibly' means here being adjacent in proximity, and in that sense the term has no immediate ethical flavour. Furthermore, it does not mean 'adjacent' as in the indifference of spatial contiguity. Rather, the term refers to a form of relation that goes only in one way: 'from me to the other', in Levinasian parlance. To stand responsibly before non-being means to acknowledge that the relationship between concretely existent objects and the void of existence cannot be a direct causal relation. Therefore, postulated objects that have no concrete existence cannot be taken as causes. In this respect, there can be no relationship 'from the other to me'.

In this sense, substitution or responsible proximity is like a love that does not expect to be shared or corresponded. To paraphrase Harman, it entails a form of exposure to the other object, 'from me to the other', without the expectation that the other will react back, in the causal sense of the term. To be proximate and responsible is to acknowledge, before the other, that the other cannot be responsible for me. This reveals my existence as an act for which no one can replace me. And yet, although in existence I am not exchangeable, this does not rule out communication and understanding of non-being.

What would be the form of this communication? Let us first state what it is not. It is not 'alterity', understood as the interplay of differences and abstract commonality. Strictly speaking, alterity is characterised by exchangeability. In alterity, each element is determined through all and all through each. This interrelational scheme entails the existence of a bond between two elements under the passive pressure of a third, and insofar as the last element determines the relationship of the other two, the bond is this element itself in its passivity or otherness. This (relational) whole, the being of alterity, is what every element causes the other to become, as its identical double, and always submitted to the action of another object.

Such passivity, or the totalisation of otherness which for Sartre characterised the formula of the series (Sartre, 2004: 267–9), is entirely absent from our description. First, we are not assuming matter to be practico-inert in the sense of being passive, secondary or 'composite' in relation to a superior simplicity. Second, the bond we are describing here is one in which an element is in the place of the whole in its uniqueness, rather than being interchangeable with any other. Third, insofar as we have given up the fantasy of direct causation, the common being of two elements in a relationship is a third element but not an abstract or conceptual element that would be standing in for something present elsewhere (as an other that is my id-double and passively determines me and the other element); rather it is there in the place of a void, a lost object or an absence. In this sense, the fetish or vicar element is not a representative or an id-double.

Let us explain further. First, it is not some remainder of the lost object, but the remainder of the operation of substitution that retroactively establishes the dimension of non-being (Zupančič, 2000: 190). Second, it does not produce the unity of concrete individual elements from outside, or determines them in separation. Third, it does not represent the whole as the sum of all individual elements and the relations that would make them exchangeable. In contrast, it simply connects the existence of concrete elements, in their self-referentiality, with the non-existent. Put otherwise, the vicar element is like a riddle: there is no god behind it whispering the truth, in this case the truth of my existence (or that of any element, for that matter) and yet it is that very lack of ultimate support which provides existence with its truth, that every element must venture its answer.

The difference between substitution and representation can also be explained in psychoanalytical terms: 'it is not that the mother escapes representation or thought, but that the *jouissance* that attached me to her has been lost, and this loss depletes the whole of my being' says Copjec (2003: 36). She explains that the partial objects that cut the drive or *jouissance,* no longer follow the noumenon/phenomenal representation schema, in which one object is exchanged for another or acts as evidence and support of another object existing elsewhere, but act as substitutes (2003: 37). As we have seen, substitutes do not speak for another(s), but let the others be themselves while also transmitting messages to one another from afar (Harman, 2007b: 22–3). Put otherwise, they are part of an act of exposure, or in Sartrean parlance, allow themselves to be encountered. 'Exposure' entails the elevation of ordinary, contradictory or partial objects to the dignity of the lost 'Thing' or void. It is as if, for a moment, such objects appear to embody the whole world, all the other objects or a set of related elements, but in fact this moment coincides with the point when they escape from the relational totality, from being absorbed in being-in-the-world. Like Butch Cassidy and the Sundance Kid in the eponymous film. If so, then the posited 'elevation' should not be understood as entailing the function of representation or exchangeability but rather, as Copjec says, that of substitution (2003: 38).

Substitution entails the exposure of one object to another in a unique and irreplaceable way, when it takes responsibility for the other while escaping the totality of relations. Later on, in the next chapter, we will learn that substitution describes the sort of response (an act) that characterises indirect contact through prosthetic means, that is to say, technologically mediated gatherings, much better than passive seriality or communication through alterity (Sartre, 2004: 270–6). Invoking the context of today's electronic mass media, the internet in particular, we will refer to relations of substitution with the term 'virtual presence' and will argue, following Hakim Bey among others, that virtual presence entails the potential for a form of unique exposure, taking responsibility for the other, that is also an escape from the totality of relations (Bey, 2003: 106–14). This is the kernel of truth present in early twenty-first century fantasies about rebellion in cyberpunk music and literature, and made concrete in the proposal to build actual 'temporary autonomous zones'.

In more sociological terms, this means to abandon the language of seriality and passiveness in relation to such categories as class, race, community, family and gender, and the self-authorising spontaneity of the fused group (the transcendent party or the illuminated vanguard) in favour of the future-oriented exposure of the substitute 'band', the revolution of the senses through contagion and the active 'return' of the part-of-no-part.[2] Interestingly, anthropologists studying sacrificial practices and political philosophers interested in historical catastrophes refer to this point of convergence between totalisation and uniqueness with terms such as 'panic' or 'engagement' or 'mimesis and alteration', and argue that this is the foundational, (auto)-transcendent moment of a collective.[3] In all of these cases (panic, confrontation, withdrawal, mimetic sensuality), the relevant point is what Laclau calls 'the radical discontinuity between an object and the one next to it' (2005: 119), and the establishment of a relationship that typically involves the irreplaceable engagement of each element without abolishing their uniqueness or that of all other elements (Zubiri, 1974 and Ellacuría, 1990: 317). This 'escape from relational totality' through (object) substitution is the radical act proper, which puts an end to the seemingly endless cycle of nihilistic violence while at the same time inaugurating the possibility of transformation.

Concrete instances of substitution include the band and the apache commando, the emissary and the scapegoat; the Christian son of God and the ritualised warfare observed in pre-Columbian Mexica culture and in the twentieth-century Yanomamo peoples; the gathering against a common enemy and the sacrifice of the founding father in the story about the inception of the law and the origin of the community told by Freud in *Civilization and Its Discontents,* but also the event of insurrection and rebellion, the construction of temporary autonomous zones, and the intensification or enhancement of reality and everyday life, alas the central element of magical realist art (Bowers, 2004: 10–19) and magic criticism (Bracken, 2007).

As Laclau says, the logic of substitution is the mechanism that better explains radical attachments, connections and investments: the substitution of an ordinary object for the 'Thing'. The transference of affect to a (partial) object is the very essence of investment, while its contingent character (the fact that affect can be transferred again and again on to other objects, for no object is the complete object) accounts for the radical component of the equation (2005: 113–15). For him, politics is about the making of a common cause with the partial object. In that respect, Laclau's most recent refinement of his theory of political hegemony must be seen as part and parcel of an ontological turn towards the objects, even if its vocabulary (featuring such terms as discourse, meaning, representation, self-reflexive signifiers and so on) still betrays its dependence upon the model of linguistics. Beyond that once but no longer liberating model, lies the terrain of the object as embodiment of the drives and the key to ontology (2005: 115).

The object becomes the embodiment of some mythical foundation (as in Freud's *Civilization and Its Discontents*) or some mythical fullness (as in the promise of harmony, self-realisation and autonomy in some versions of systems theory). As such, it becomes also the embodiment of collective violence, as it comes to be viewed as an obstacle. Put otherwise, in replacing a victim it becomes a scapegoat but also a site of violence. It is in this sense, for instance, that the Saharawi people of Western Sahara, under occupation by Moroccan forces, commonly refer to the violence done to the objects first and then to the violence done to them, thereby waking up to the fact of their objectification. Then, and only then, the Saharawi consider the issues of rebellion and counter-violence in a highly original way, through their self-objectification. At this point, we may want to consider a possibility that Laclau himself does not explore although it seems to follow from his premises: that the objects themselves may transfer the violence directed against them upon other ordinary objects. Put otherwise, the logic of substitution may allow for a return of the circle of violence from one object to another.

It may be true as Joan Copjec says (2003: 34) that a complete will to power or destruction may be unrealisable but it does not, however, simply disappear (2003: 112). Rather, it is transferred to other ordinary objects that are the objects of the drives. If so, how are we to stop this re-commencing of the cycle of violence, marked by reciprocity and blindness, the short-sightedness that sees in the other the limit to one's full enjoyment?

On the one hand it seems that this other-as-obstacle must be sacrificed precisely because, as the embodiment of universal violence and death-drive, it appears as the ultimate stumbling block to full *jouissance* even if it is just a partial, incomplete object. In this way, the sacrifice of the partial ordinary object would inhibit the completion of the drive to destruction (from engulfing the whole system of relations) and prevent it from achieving its aim. The point of including violence within our accounts of the activity of objects would be precisely to enable us to deflect it from achieving its set target (Girard, 2004: 60–1). But, on the other hand, there is no reason to assume that the substituting thing (the scapegoat, the partial object) will simply remain passive; if it embodies the drives then it has drives of its own and instincts of self-perseverance that will kick in. Here we are facing the re-initiation of the sacrificial cycle. Can it be escaped?

The logic of substitution in the field of sacrificial violence

In the previous section, we learned that the logic of substitution seeks to explain the incompleteness of the drive to destruction but also the foundation of the collective in the act of sacrifice/substitution, the formation of radical attachments or subjective 'investment' and self-objectification. While on the one hand the self-referential character of the drives explains their tendency towards completion (self-justification and self-reproduction regardless of sacrifices), on the other hand the possibility of object-substitution, the inscription of the drive on the surface of partial objects, entails that the self-critical character of the drives, its extension or self-objectification, outweighs and curbs the sacrificial will to completion.

This means the possibility that the violent sacrificial cycle can be escaped, because partial objects can substitute the sacrificial subject. In political terms, this is to say that the ultimate desired goal may not be accomplished, for its accomplishment would generally require untold sacrifice, but it can be substituted by the achievement of partial yet satisfactory demands (Laclau, 2005). Crucially, a 'demand' of this sort would entail the gathering of many around some (partial) object, and thus it seems everything turns around the quality of the object involved and/or its capacity to gather and embody or contain the drive to destruction present in the collective. Put otherwise, the collective is made up on the basis of a radical attachment to a certain (fetish) object that embodies the potential for sacrifice and contains it.

But what guarantees the containment of violence and sacrifice in the (partial) object? What allows us to affirm with certainty that the established constitution of the state, the prime example of a partial object in modern politics, will not spread the violence it contains, not only in its application but also in its self-justificatory and self-reproductive capacity? It seems relevant to consider once more such a relationship, such radical attachment, from the point of view of the object. If the object is not practico-inert (something that follows from the premise of the embodiment of the drives) and cannot be changed at will, then it is important to consider the choice of the object in the relationship. It is perhaps not too far-fetched to think that the directionality of the common cause with the objects is not merely given to it by the user's programme (be this a worker, a capitalist, a soldier, a revolutionary or an artist), but rather that in some sense the objects are inherently determinant in the relations they enter into, or at least affect such relations from their very inception.

This does not mean to say that objects have definitive sets of unchangeable properties or function as the efficient cause of the relation, but rather that they also frame the relation. The object is contingent and there is nothing in its materiality that predetermines it (or something else) to function as a whole or as the determinant part in a relation but, as Laclau says, 'it is most certainly not indifferent – it cannot be changed at will' (2005: 115). Laclau speaks here of objects of investment, objects of transference, objects of the drives, as a refinement and reiteration of what he terms a 'hegemonic relation', after Gramsci. A 'hegemonic relation' is one in which a certain particularity assumes the role of an impossible universality (ibid.). It is a form of responsible proximity to non-being. In that sense, although partial, these particular objects are also the embodiment of some mythical fullness.

It is important to emphasise that whatever is transferred to them becomes part of their body (objects are not supported by models, they support one another through relations of transference), they are not just 'made-up' or invested upon but also 'found', and inject back their DNA into everything they encounter. This is to say that, for instance, in the soldier–weapon relation, the property 'deadly' is not meant solely for the soldier, but rather that the weapon (which points at, designates, names, kills and thus gives property and takes it away) is inherently a deadly object in spite of its partiality.

Crucially, what characterises modern constitutions as such is the principle of the monopoly of the use of force in the hands of the state. Literally, the idea is that the state holds all the weapons, or at least the most powerful. What can stop the state, or a group that seeks to place itself in the position of the state, from using such weapons in order to secure its survival? The short and brutish history of the twentieth century suggests that the answer is 'very little . . . almost nothing'. Furthermore, the state might be blind to its own sacrificial origins, they may have become mythical, and in this sense it would be appropriate to speak of a mythic violence that inhabits the modern state legal order (Benjamin, 1986: 279 ff.). This raises the different but related questions of 'structural violence' (*Rechtsgewalt*), law-making and/or law-preserving, on the one hand, and 'counterviolence' (*Gegengewalt*), law-destructive, on the other. The point here is that in the end, as Walter Benjamin suggested, sacrificial violence testifies to the paradoxical position of the technical or substitute object, elusive to containment within a means/end scheme, and in a sense it enacts 'the slave rebellion of technology' portrayed in many a Hollywood blockbuster (Hanssen, 2000: 24).

If this is the case, then Mike Davis's suggestion that certain objects 'are inherently fascist' should perhaps be taken more seriously (2007). His example of a partial technical object is the car bomb, which in its capacity to rewrite every textbook on the physics of demolition and undermine the popular support of a cause, seems to condemn all relations it enters into by making them politically reactive and regressive. According to Davis, the car bomb has an uncanny ability to invite the mobile phone, the handheld camera and the internet into its meshwork of sacrifice and horror, and to turn the image itself into a viral weapon of reaction and blind reciprocity relayed a thousand times by a thousand different media outlets around the globe. Put otherwise, the car bomb does not gather people and structures but simply blasts them.

If Davis's suggestion is correct, then we should not turn a blind eye to the role of objects in politics or reduce it within a means/end scheme. We should consider whether or not the money/private equity meshwork is inherently destructive and politically malign.[4] Similarly, to use another concrete example, we may need to produce a political model for the examination of self-replicating nanoscale machines or devices, and the release of such machines in natural environments.[5] In more or less the same vein, a radical politics of liberation may wish to consider carefully its objects since in some way they define the direction of its activity. Is the AK-47 a tool of liberation, as so many used to think in the 1970s? Back in the 1970s, these automatic rifles became a symbol of liberation during the anti-colonial struggles in the Third World and determined the direction of the Third Worldist project. Today, there is evidence that things have changed.

Take for instance the case of the Saharawi people, referred to before. The Saharawi live under Moroccan rule, aided and abetted by France, in the illegally occupied territories of the Western Sahara. As activist Aminattou Haidar and photographer Patrizio Esposito explain (2007), by focusing on the violence done to their objects by the Moroccan army, and turning their handheld cameras and mobile phones towards themselves, the Saharawi wake up to the fact of their objectification by a sadist regime, thereby preparing the terrain for rebellion and revolution, as was the case in the *intifada* of 2005. Here, the mobile phone and the handheld digital camera appear more effective than the AK-47. In the present situation, they are faced with the challenge to avoid the handheld camera and the car bomb from getting together in the same political meshwork, and to (re)affirm the UN-supported ceasefire in spite of the studied indifference of the UN and the international community at large, unable or unwilling to enforce their own measures against an illegitimate occupation. This is a most serious challenge, and all one can say is that here, passivity is not an option.

Another instance of necessary choice concerning objects in concrete struggles for liberation pertains to the situation of the politically active indigenous peoples of Southern Colombia. They prefer to confront the heavily armed far-right paramilitary (and their sometimes accomplice, the national army, but also the FARC left-wing guerrillas that have now morphed into some sort of parallel state and invested in the capitalist economy of drug-trafficking) with their wooden *bastones de mando*. Which of the two objects, the AK-47 or the wooden *baston de mando*, is liberating and dignifying, which one less lethal? The point here is not the wholesale and moralist rejection of violence in favour of abject passiveness, based on a means/ends dichotomy that misunderstands the ontology of objects, but rather a concrete wager against terror and violence that nevertheless makes it clear that one is not afraid of them (Žižek, 2007b: 28).

How to understand the sense of this apparent paradox? The next section proposes that one way of making sense of it is to consider the importance of two important insights, obtained from the historical study of the role of the slave-ship in the 'human' history of anti-slavery and decolonisation. First, if these objects come to embody the cause or the demand and at the end of the day it is they that remain, and not the support-model that is always lost, then to make common cause with an object means also to acknowledge its own dynamics. Second, to acknowledge the dynamics of the object involves both a new conception of objectivity, one that accepts the object's composite and bivalent nature, and crucially, a different conception of thought, one that takes into account the paradoxical results of its self-objectifying activity.

The slave-ship and the sailor's paradox

In his book *The Slave Ship*, historian Marcus Rediker proposes to consider the slave-ship as a technical object as much as a social system (2007: 4 ff.). He argues that the slave-ship was first of all a gunship, and as such it embodied the tendency towards the monopoly of potency and the use of force characteristic of modern state-based constitutionalism, and thereby the ability to harness and use fear and terror for the purposes of creating and maintaining social order. But it was also a factory in the modern sense of the term: it featured wage-based labour, its form was that of the enclosure, and it embodied the capacity to reach the entire globe for the first time in history. These forces were essential to the make-up of the slave-ship; they also explain the human history that emerged from within the slave-ship as it carried 12.4 million souls through the so-called 'Middle Passage' across the Atlantic (Rediker, 2007: 5), and in particular, the paradoxical coupling between the denial of violence and the denial of fear of violence that would characterise the politics of anti-slavery, first, and then the planetary project of decolonisation.

The larger picture that emerges out of the work done by Rediker, but also from his work with Peter Linebaugh (2000), takes us from the commons to the enclosures, and then from the mobile enclosures (the coloniser and slave-ships) to the global spread of the enclosure-based system of politics and production, including the factory, the city and the modern nation-state. This is the wider picture of the formation of empire and capitalism, but also, and this is crucial, of the emergence of the modern 'people', in the revolutionary sense of the word, and the global project of liberation. These are real forms or structures rather than mere types or signs, in that they frame ordinary life and reality at a global scale. But it is important to acknowledge that the real character of these forms depends upon them being inscribed, embodied, in the same technical objects (the ship, for the long eighteenth century) which then become the site of a struggle, a battleground, which is political as much as ontological.

The consequence of philosophical importance is that such a struggle defines the ontology of the object, that it is one with its nature, rather than determining its being from elsewhere. This struggle takes place on the surface of the technical object making it a composite entity, and this composite appearance is its nature. This is to say that there is no such thing as a simpler kernel behind composite appearance that would be the true essence of the object. Rather, appearance is of the essence and it is the substance of the object. However, such appearance, and the tension and struggle that takes place at such a level, do not exhaust the reality of the object. The latter conserves the ability to withdraw from the relations it enters into and become part of yet other composites and other meshworks. It is the ability to enter into and withdraw from relations, always tense, contingent and superficial, that makes up the substance and the very essence of an element. To sum up, it matters to realise that the elements of a relationship are always (am)bivalent, always in a state of tension, and that the relations they enter into do not exhaust their reality.

Rediker emphasises that although the slave-ship produced, first and foremost, labour-power it also produced new and entirely unpredictable 'categories' of race, kinship and allegiance. Some of them will become the very make-up of the emerging trans-Atlantic colonial/capitalist structure that sociologist Aníbal Quijano and others term 'the coloniality of power' (Quijano and Wallerstein, 1992). Other categories, new forms of diasporic kinship, antinomian religiosity and cosmopolitanism, will become the basis for new and unexpected sites of resistant struggle, the building of temporary autonomous zones and the projection of radical transformative projects around the globe. How to explain this ambivalence?

Rediker notices that the violence and terror present in the make-up of the slave-ship, and later on transferred on to the very core of global capitalism, cannot be expressed or explained sufficiently by quoting the statistics on mortality rate, survival and forced displacement related to the slave trade. Important as these statistics are, for they are evidence of the drama that unfolded thereafter, they cannot convey the magnitude of the tragedy (Rediker, 2007: 5–6). According to him, violence was part of a dual system of terror that was directed against the sailors and the enslaved. Sailors would be flogged to death by their captains in front of the captives; their rations were poor, wages low, and the mortality rate of the crews of the slavers as high as that of the enslaved. As a result of this situation, sailors and captains clashed repeatedly. At the same time, sailors acted towards the captives as part and parcel of a system of terror. Following orders from their captains, they whipped the enslaved, force-fed them, raped the women and, in short, slowly transformed them into commodities for the international labour market (Rediker, 2007: 7). The question arises: were the sailors victims or perpetrators? Following from this, could sailors and other wage workers ever form an alliance with the enslaved themselves, all of them people of different classes, ethnicities and genders, thrown together in the horror-filled decks of the slave-ship, and rise against the terror as one? Furthermore, can the formation of such an alliance against terror signal the end of the repetitive cycle of violence?

Rediker's work suggests that to frame such problems as either/or questions might not take us very far. At first glance, it would seem more consistent to deal with the entity 'sailor' as either a victim or not a victim. Here, the demand is to accept that either the object quite definitely belongs to a set or else it quite definitely does not (Sainsbury, 1990: 252). This seems a matter of simple logic, but its consequences for political analysis can be momentous: if sailors are merely perpetrators (that is, non-victims) their use of violence makes them one with the colonial/capitalist enterprise, part of that set, a part of the whole system of terror, determined by such a system to act above and against the no-part. The no-part are, in turn, pure victims. They are characteristically impotent, in the sense of having no recourse to violence, for if the enslaved use violence they also become perpetrators and hence part of the system of terror against some 'new' no-part. In this way, impotence is made into an essential character of the oppressed, and therefore the latter are precluded from rebellion and revolutionary agency.

From this 'either/or' standpoint there is no escape from the cycle of violence, no true revolutionary event. Whether the conflict is interpreted as a class struggle, along the lines of Marxist doctrine, or as a massive human rights violation, along the lines of liberal-humanist ideology, the result is the same: politics as a matter of either/or choices between friend/enemy, citizen/foreign, known/stranger, civilised/barbarian. Submitted to this form, political analysis can only be conceived as a matter of boundary drawing and preservation, and boundary drawing and preservation (including the preservation of truth/life as an absolute, that which includes the absolute negation of life as one of its conditions) as somehow sufficient for the purposes of analysing political entities. However, as will be argued in the remainder of this chapter, to follow Rediker's suggestion to the end requires something different from us: the acknowledgement that boundary drawing and preservation are insufficient as a form of analysis, and that this is particularly so in politics because, looked at more closely, the elements of politics and political sets are essentially (am)bivalent. To deal with essentially bivalent objects would require the weakening of the idea that the correct use of reason is to establish stable limits and boundaries, to know the finite; and this, in turn, demands a different use of reason that insists in its capacity 'to know the infinite', to put it in Hegelian parlance (Hegel, 1969: 56).

Put otherwise, the question is whether or not it is problematic in historical and political analysis to proceed on the basis of well-conceived sets (wholes, totalities, systems, classes, groupings, nation-states and so on) and whether or not a well-conceived set requires stable boundaries. The twin questions of the stability of boundaries and well-conceived sets (for instance, so-called 'well-ordered societies' in legal and political analysis, or well-defined 'agents' in historical analysis) have to do with a set of assumptions which is called for by the suggestion, implicit in the use of the term 'problematic' in the lines above, of an authoritative rule regarding the proper way to gather elements and present them as objects, not only as objects of knowledge but also as objects of desire and the reversals of such desire. The implicit suggestion is that of an 'authority' in the use of reason, stable and unchanging, or justified (von Wright, 1980: 408).

In general, authority can be understood as an effective 'power of determination which lays claim to being justified. If it manages to bring that claim within its power, it gains a self-justifying, self-reproducing quality which strengthens it to a degree such that, at least as regards political authority, the need for a standpoint from which challenges to a constituted authority are made is widely acknowledged' (Kerruish, 2006: 42). Notice that the problem we face here is not entirely dissimilar to that of the drives, the self-referential character of the drives, and the self-reproducing quality of the drive (death-drive) in psychoanalytical theory. We learned before how in that case it was necessary to curb or cut (and cut up) the pure self-referentiality of the drive by means of its transfer onto certain objects. Similarly, the point here is to insist that reason is not merely self-justificatory and self-referential but that it is also, first and foremost, self-critical. And this self-criticism, which curbs and cuts reason's self-referential and self-reproducing quality, is equivalent to its self-objectification.

Reason's ongoing activity, the activity of the finite and embodied beings that we are, seeks to grasp that activity as a process in its excess, 'by thinking the infinite' as Kerruish puts it in Hegelian mode (2006: 44). Thought gives to itself objects which then take a life of their own, which are ambivalent and seem to challenge the strength of all established boundaries, the sort of objects that have been called 'fetishes' in this book, including that which Hegel called 'the infinite' or 'the reasonable' and its contradictions (1969: 56–7). However, it has been the wager of this book that such objects are actual rather than merely potential or (im)possible, in that they satisfy the demands of what is currently known in theory and practice, or desired. And in that sense, the term 'fetish', as commonly understood, is perhaps a bit of a misnomer. Be that as it may, the point is that Rediker's conceptualisation of the sailors and the slaves in the slave-ship (2007; 8, 222–306) as an (am)bivalent, actual form of infinity (infinitely creative: fashioning new languages, new cultural practices, new bonds and a nascent community, in short, able to communicate even if the possibility of communication was non-existent or improbable) corresponds precisely to that sort of objectification.

In other words, this is to affirm the objectivity of responsible projections and the necessity of contradiction inhering in the determinations of reason 'as the principle of intelligibility of objectivity and necessity' (Kerruish, 2006: 50), but it is also to argue for a conception of the use of reason 'against the tendency of constituted and instituted power to bring the justification of its determinative power within the ambit of that power' (ibid.). Furthermore, taking into account the (am)bivalent nature of objects, which is so important a part of this argument, seems to invite a renewed conception of the relation between world and logic, in which the latter is not attributed 'authority' in relation to the former and this, in turn, the world and its objects, holds the capacity to withdraw from the established sets and relations it/they enter into on their own or as a result of subjective activity. The affirmation of such a capacity results in the recognition of the existence of entirely new situations, improbable as they may seem from the standpoint of the previous situation.

If so, then another question arises: what happens to reason, thought and its assumptions, when faced with an entirely new situation? It seems that this renewed conception of objectivity throws into question the classical idea that an assumption, once used in an act of inference, supposedly holds in future situations. Rather, it may be used up and no longer available, 'like a dollar spent' to quote Kerruish once more (2006: 51) and no longer available in the new situation reason finds itself in. At stake here is the improbable as a category of reality.

To attribute authority to a certain use of reason or logic may be problematic, it is often part of a rhetorical use of claims to necessity that neglect of the relativity of any such necessity to a certain system of logic (Kerruish, 2006: 42), but it is important to acknowledge that such an attribution points towards the uneasy relationship between theoretical reason and practical reason, which is the legacy of critique in philosophy and the humanities at least since Kant. In that legacy, the dispute over the boundaries between theoretical and practical reason, or in the empiricist tradition, the 'is/ought' controversy, results in the idea that reason cannot think the infinite (Kerruish, 2006: 43) and consequently, that the standpoint from which the claims of a determining power to being justified can be challenged is also unthinkable, together with reason's self-critical character.[6]

In terms of the political relationship between rebellion and constitution, this legacy plays on the side of the post-Kantian notion that once established (through the proper means) the constitution cannot be questioned and so rebellions should be treated as impossible or anomalous events, which come from some other-worldly 'outside' or 'beyond'. Against such appeals to an outside, one would have to take sides with the 'absolute' form of Hegel's logic that weakens limits and boundaries by stating that, formally speaking, there is no outside or beyond. The standpoint of the absolute (that is to say, of the experience of memory and retention in time taken as a whole) allows a thinking of technical objects (including mathematical logic) as crucial for the retention of experience, all the while retention, the 'suspended' but never cancelled experience of thinking subjects in time, is considered to be, strictly speaking, a subjectless process. From this standpoint, the crucial insight is that the recollecting totality (that Hegel's journeying consciousness knows itself to be), that is to say, 'technics' (after supplementing Hegel's phenomenological observation with the self-reflexive/critical character of mathematical logic) can hardly be thought to have learned or to recollect anything at all 'if it thinks its ground will not again be pulled from under its feet' (Kerruish, 2006: 49 and also Stiegler, 2001: Chapter 6).

To conclude, we need not abandon the definition of sets as a basic task of historical and political analysis even if history and politics deal with (am)bivalent objects and improbable events such as revolutions and so on. However, we may have to weaken or drop, in Hegelo-Lacanian manner, the idea that sets have sharp and definite boundaries. It is important to notice that definiteness is attributable not to the conception of a set but to a rule in the reasoning that classical logic formalises, according to which the possibility that presuppositions and assumptions may be 'used up' in the act of inference is excluded (Petersen, 2000). This treatment of assumptions is consistent with ideas of unchangeable truths and a certain metaphysics of time that does not take into account the role of technical objects but reduces the latter to the status of means to an (always deferred) end. Importantly, that rule, which also excludes bivalence, can be and is restricted in many non-classical logics (Kerruish, 2006: 58). Loosing the rule, a boundary can be unstable (Yatabe, 2006a: 1 and 2006b).

To sum up, the mainstream way of dealing with bivalent objects is to gather them within sets with definite and sharp boundaries, and to insist that set theoretic definitions can only represent definite concepts pertaining to definite objects. You are either a victim or a non-victim; if the latter, then you are part of the system of victimisation. Political and historical analysis is then conceived as the activity of drawing sharp boundaries. Bivalent objects and elements, self-objectifying reason and its contradictions, would have no place in such kind of analysis. As a result, for instance, the sailor and the slave would remain condemned to solitude and incapable of finding a common object and a common cause.

However, logicians have shown that such definiteness and sharpness is a result of certain rules and assumptions, rules that can be weakened or dropped, and not of the nature of the sets themselves (Yatabe, 2006a: 6). Such rules are consistent with ideas of unchangeability and eternity (either they support the ideal of an eternal truth or are a formalisation of such an ideal) and ultimately, a conception of time as fixed background or absolute necessity that determines objects rather than being determined by them.

Our blindness, connected to war and the will to power, is to buy into this or any other notion of absolute necessity as a total boundary or obstacle, necessitating the sacrifice of some 'other', or as a reified figure that evokes or represents necessity and brings about the reign of certainty, harmony and wholeness, and determinant relations for all time. Against that notion, it is important to recognise that the (technical) objects do not simply reproduce at a secondary level, that of sensuality, composition and the remainder, a primary wholeness and certainty that could be made present, and appropriated, in a direct way. Rather, the function of technics, composition and sensuality is absolutely primary in the constitution of reality.

This is a very important idea that deserves further consideration: sensuality, what we have called before indirect causation and responsible proximity, is a complex behaviour. It may not be reasonable to assume, as a practical matter, that all forms of such behaviour are describable or calculable in their totality without ambiguity. In some cases this may be possible while in others, such as the case of the technical objects (methods, strategies, surfaces of inscription and of retention) omnipresent in contemporary life, it may not (Dupuy, 2004). In the latter case, the simplest way to describe behaviour is to describe the structure that generates it. Under these circumstances it would be meaningless to argue, as philosopher Jean-Pierre Dupuy observes (ibid.), that such behaviour can be embodied in an object that is absorbed into a stable network of relations, since it would be impossible to define the behaviour other than by describing the object itself and its relations.

The question of complexity emerges at this point. At stake is the explanatory power of certain holistic, relationist and constructivist approaches that reduce an object to an effect or a function, and the function or effect to a structure. Such approaches, which still struggle with the legacy of post-Socratic philosophy, Aristotelian logic and critique, leave two questions unanswered: first, the question of what an object is capable of, and second, the question of what a complex or composite structure is capable of. Alas, these are in fact the same question given that there is no good reason to assume that some objects are simpler than others, but rather themselves complex structures (Harman, 2002).

Notions of determinate design ('to live and die in its own fashion') can be associated after Derrida (1987c: 358–9) with the law of the proper and with property, but also with other related concepts such as finitude, certainty, harmony, frailty, ignorance, precaution, 'cost–benefit', risk and prevention. Policies developed on the basis of such notions seem ill suited to respond to the challenges posited by the sort of objective uncertainty brought about by complex phenomena and objects. In short, they seek to produce an event while at the same time denying the reality of any truly changing event. In seems that there is a notion of temporality as a somewhat fixed background underlying these notions and the policies developed on the basis of such notions.

In the following two sections, we will occupy ourselves with this set of issues. First, in the next section, we will follow political philosopher Jean-Pierre Dupuy as he proposes an alternative model of political projection based upon a metaphysics of time that leaves room for changing rules and truly transformative events. It will be argued that such a model is much better suited to face the challenges of today's complex world, than the models based upon the law of the proper, prevention, risk-assessment and precaution. The question of 'blindness' introduced above will return in the analysis of this proposal. Then, in the following and final section of this chapter, we will pursue Jacques Derrida's suggestion of a link between the Freudian notion of the death-drive and a law of the proper (economy and economics) that regulates the search for a proper event characteristic of the modern age. It will be argued after him, and in the context of the playful narrative that is *Pirates of the Caribbean*,[7] that in today's world, the world of empire and risk-capitalism, the dynamics or 'economy' of life and death is subsumed under this law of the proper. The point is that rather than a choice between life and/or death, politics has now become a matter of calculating and producing death according to our own designs: the elevation of man as 'the greatest right' has the calculation of 'proper deaths' as its condition. The tone of the discussion will be more concrete; we are now dealing with the question 'what is to be done?' posited at a certain level of generality.

Metaphysics of time and the politics of anticipatory projection

In reference to the sort of uncertainty that is characteristic of today's world, overcrowded with complex objects and phenomena, Jean-Pierre Dupuy observes:

> We are not dealing with a random occurrence either. Neither random, nor epistemically uncertain, the type of 'risk' that we are confronting is a monster from the standpoint of classic distinctions (...) Our uncertainty regarding the behaviour of complex systems has thus nothing to do with a temporary insufficiency of our knowledge, it has everything to do with objective, structural properties of complex systems. On the other hand, this uncertainty is not the kind that is attached to random events and it is not amenable to the concept of probability. The key notion here is that of informational incompressibility, which is a form of essential unpredictability. In keeping with von Neumann's intuitions on complexity, a complex process is defined today as one for which the simplest model is the process itself. The only way to determine the future of the system is to run it: there are no shortcuts.
>
> (Dupuy, 2004: 16)

The Sartrean metaphysics of time advanced here by Dupuy engages the concerns posited in the previous section. Interestingly, following Hannah Arendt he assimilates the situation brought about by contradictory objects and complex systems, the situation we are in, with a sort of blindness:

> In cases where the uncertainty is such that the uncertainty itself is uncertain, it is impossible to know whether or not the conditions for the application of the precautionary principle have been met. If we apply the principle to itself, it will invalidate itself before our eyes.
>
> (Ibid.)

His point is that unleashing complex processes and contradictory objects is itself a contradictory activity that demands foreknowledge and limits it, presenting us, precisely, with the sort of ethical and political challenge that we have identified before with the experience of rebels: to choose, tearing established boundaries apart, precisely at the point where it seems there are no available options. At the centre of his endeavours Dupuy places the question of 'radical choice' in dialogue with orthodox theories of rational choice, liberalism and cognitive science. However, his results are anything but orthodox.

The solution to the dilemmas of uncertainty comes in the form of a radical shift that re-frames the whole scene: in the place of the indeterminacy of the future (a void of being) he says we must posit an ordinary object, a minimal failure (or the image of an inevitable catastrophe accompanied by a contingent or minimal failure) projected into the future which can retroactively act back upon the present. The figure is that of a temporal loop or continuity (accompanied by a minimal 'cut') between future and past, an inclosed self-reflexive structure that according to Dupuy formalises 'a metaphysics of projected time' (Dupuy, 2004: 21).

This sort of metaphysics has a lot to do with the notion of 'speculative visions reduced to practice' that St George Tucker placed at the centre of radical thought and constitutional practice in revolutionary America. Insofar as it mobilises a politics of anticipatory projection, in the form of a loop in which the world-historical and the incalculable future converge productively, Dupuy's account of temporality resonates with the proposals of Thomas Jefferson and Puma de Ayala, but also with the observations of the young Marx about the laws concerning freedom of the press in Prussia, based upon the insights gained from the study of revolutionary political and religious forms in the Americas. What these accounts of temporality have in common, in spite of their differences, is a conception of the improbable as a category of reality coupled with a realist understanding of technologies of retention.

Dupuy's conception has nothing to do with the temporal metaphysics of straight lines forking into branches that the orthodoxy conceptualises as 'futuribles' or mere 'possibilities', and which underlies the sort of normativity proper to the calculus of probabilities, cost–benefit analysis and the legal–political systems of risk and risk-prevention so common nowadays in fields apparently as varied as financial markets and anti-terrorism policy.

The key difference between these conceptions of temporality is that the orthodox approach assumes the open diversity of possible futures as a given, explained by the ontological indeterminacy of the future, and arbitrarily derives the same multiplicity as the inevitable reflection of our inability to know the future with certainty, or epistemic uncertainty. From the standpoint of the metaphysics of projected time, the one advocated by Dupuy and others, both the assumption and the consequences of such assumption rest on an error. The error is the confusion between ontological indeterminacy and epistemic uncertainty, a serious mistake that renders all strategies of prevention and risk-management self-defeating since it means that in the end, these strategies seek to emphasise the importance of the future while at the same time denying its reality.

In contrast, the temporal metaphysics of projection starts from the recognition that the future, improbable as it may be, has the ontological status of a real entity. It is important to notice that this is also what the Sartrean reflection on the dynamics of the group and the series presupposes. To quote Dupuy one more time, this time speaking a clear Sartrean/Heideggerian language: 'seen from the present the future was open, but seen from the vantage point of the future, the path that led to it appears to have been necessary. We are free to choose, to be sure, but what we choose appears to have been our destiny' (2004: 21–7). That is precisely the sort of experience and situation that has been identified from the very beginning of this book with the experience of the rebel.

But before we move onto the Sartrean analysis of the dynamic relationship between the group and the series, which presupposes projected time as having the form of a loop, a self-reflexive structure affected by a closure condition or a minimal failure (a projected fixed point, the object of foretelling or 'prophecy') we will take a step back and return for a moment back to the story of the gold-fetish, this time as retold for a twenty-first century audience in the Hollywood blockbuster *Pirates of the Caribbean*. The aim will be to consider once more the relation between the outcast peoples of the earth (pirates, slaves, indigenous women) that Marcus Rediker identifies with the 'motley crew' of the slave-ship, and their powerful technical objects, the fetishes, as having precisely the form of a loop where an expectation (on the part of the past with regard to the future) and a casual production (of the future by the past) actually coincide. In general, this relationship is rendered in terms of a prediction, a prophecy or a riddle (Dupuy, 2004: 27).

Why do prophecies generally have the form of a riddle? As the story of the gold-fetish reveals, the answer to this question lies in the fact that the relationship between the future and the past, made possible through powerful retentional or technical objects, has the form of a loop in that it entails the engagement of the operator of the technical object in the present, the predictor, in the absence of a clear blueprint of what is to be done. Put otherwise, prophecies are self-referential in that they include within themselves the future event of their own failure. They are like some sort of half-command that necessitates the answer provided by the operator, the addressee of the command, which enables its enactment. In this respect, prophecies are not too dissimilar from the ritual use of the voice in post-traditional societies attached to 'the letter of the law', which performs such a crucial function (Dolar, 2006: 112). This is a function related to the opening up of a public space, aimed at codification and publicity as a supplement to the hidden foundations of a collective. Dolar speaks correctly of a 'division of labour' between the voice and the letter in this case, between the ritual that ensures the proper authority of the letter and the super-ego attachment that places such authority in a hidden code (2006: 113). In any case, the point here is to enact and preserve authority by establishing and maintaining more or less well-defined limits and divisions.

To contrast, in the case of political prophecies the required voice or answer puts into question the letter of the law and its enactment, that is, authority. In this case the voice appears limitless, infinitely extending into the future rather than enacting its own boundary as foundation, but also as 'the source and immediate lever of violence' (Dolar, 2006: 114), which collapses the distinction between life and disposable life in an economy of sacrifice.

But this is not enough; understood in this way, the voice of the prophet might be confused with the voice of the sovereign. An understanding of political prophecy that stops at this point would reaffirm the notion that, for all their irreverence, rebellion and revolt are still far too reverent towards their object. What is missing in this overt submission to the terrestrial father, the sovereign, is that his command is not only indeterminate and fragmentary but actually null (Girard, 2004: 94). It is null insofar as it seeks to produce an event here and now, in the fascist version, or ensure that nothing happens, in the Stalinist. This entails a non-realist stance towards the future, in which the latter is de-realised in favour of some form of fixed background, the immediate present in the first case, the laws of history in the second. The ensuing radical paradox annuls the effects of the prophetic and makes it self-defeating. This is why there is an additional element in the notion that prophecies must come in riddles: they cannot tell what the future is going to be like, only that it is not fixed and it is very real, and therefore, to the enunciation of the prophecy one has to supply the (political) statement and take on board the counter-factual consequences of such a statement. Put otherwise, because prophecies seek their confirmation in the future they must also include the event of their own failure. The prophet can seek no release from his desire.

The story of the gold-fetish helps also to illustrate this notion, the idea that 'the predictor, knowing that his prediction is going to produce causal effects in the world, must take account of this fact if he wants the future to confirm what he foretold' (Dupuy, 2004: 27). Before modernity this was the role of the sacred (the prophet, the seer); once magic and the sacred became unplaceable, this role got multiplied rather than disappeared. It became uncanny in the strictest sense, and therefore connected to everything the modern uncanny is connected to: from the rebel and the revolutionary to the futurists and the gurus, from the re-entry of women to what returns from colonial and imperialist adventures, and from the return of the religious to the virtual world of cinema, computing and new technologies (Royle, 2003: 21–6).

The heart in the chest: on pirates

Let us take as the point of departure of this section the peculiarly repetitive nature of the story about the gold of the conquerors and the conquered in the Caribbean. That strange repetitiveness will be associated in what follows with the generic form of the transference-structure (destruction, transformation, assimilation) via a reading of the last instantiation of the story in the Hollywood blockbuster *Pirates of the Caribbean* (Gore Verbinski, 2003) and its sequels *Dead Man's Chest* (Gore Verbinski, 2006) and *At World's End* (Gore Verbinski, 2007). The protagonist of the story is the fetish, the powerful object, its allure, its boundary-tearing power.

Following the work of psychoanalytic theorists such as Joan Copjec and Ernesto Laclau, we have learned that this form of relationality across boundaries should not be understood in terms of a restricted economy of exchange and property, but rather in a reversal of the common understanding of the aesthetics of sublimation, as a form of contagious transference or 'substitution', a general economy of play that contrasts with the restricted economy of the proper (the proper name, the proper event, property).

This commentary will argue that on the surface these films may be seen as a typical Hollywood morality tale of greed and desire, but that surface (and there is no attempt at deception, this is a genuine Hollywood film) is supplemented by a no less superficial concern with imperial hubris and the insistence, repression and disavowal of the 'death-drive' that accompanies the emergence of capital and empire in Western culture.

The association between cinema, technics, the drives, and the repetitiveness of the gold-fetish story at the heart of this and the previous sections is far from gratuitous. On the one hand, repetitiveness – the 'constant recurrence of the same thing' (Freud, 1953–74, vol. 18: 356) – is the notion that leads Freud to his theory of the 'death-drive' (*Todëstriebe*, or death-drift) according to which 'death is not simply the termination of life (that being the mystifying banality by which we live) but life's driving force, its animating, dynamic principle' (Dollimore, 1998: 192). As Jonathan Dollimore points out, from the earliest times 'death has held out the promise of a release not just from desire but from something inseparable from it, namely the pain of being individuated (separate, differentiated, alone) and the form of self-consciousness that goes with that' (1998: xx). As we will see, that is precisely the common thread underlying the re-telling of the gold-fetish story in this film: the promise of a release from desire, individuation and self-consciousness attached to death-drive; escape into the void and immortality, embodied in the Aztec Gold, in Davy Jones's heart, or the impossible 'filling' of the empty box, and the imperial hubris of the East India Company.

On the other hand, cinema brings to the fore the dynamics between representation and magic (contagion) to the point where 'the entire cinema industry might be defined as a palliative working to repress the uncanniness of film' (Royle, 2003: 75). Indeed, if on the one hand photography appears as the ultimate support of a new positivism, a fact that is made clear in the convergence between film and human rights based on the privilege conceded in the latter field to the eyewitness (Bronkhorst, 2003), on the other hand, photography has been experienced as an uncanny phenomenon that undermines the unique identity of things and people, the restricted economy of the proper and the original, by endlessly repeating them and thereby 'creating a world of phantasmatic doubles alongside the concrete world of the senses verified by positivism' (Gunning, 1995: 42–3). The privilege of the eyewitness in law, human rights and metaphysics – based upon the uniqueness of her identity, which is dependent upon the notion of an original event and a support-model – is interrupted by the peculiar solitude and blindness of witnessing that is revealed in filmic experience. This is particularly true of the filmic (and literary) experience known as magical realism (Bowers, 2004: 109), to which the film that is the object of this commentary pays more than veiled homage.

The main feature of the story told in *Pirates* is the status of the group of outlaws commanded by Captain Barbossa, and in *Dead Man's Chest* Davy Jones and the crew of *The Flying Dutchman*: they are all 'undead', they are all immortal. This is the result of a curse that in both cases is the contagious effect of coming into contact with and getting to own a fetish-object (gold, a heart in a chest). These objects are but embodiments of the will to power and the drive to immortality. As suggested before, it can be argued that immortality, Freud's contention that 'the organism wishes to die in its own fashion' (or death-drive) entails a relationship with power and the laws of the proper and property. Imperial hubris and capitalistic drive, so central to the re-telling of the gold-fetish story in the film, are intimate to the full sway of self-preservative instincts that define the modern subject as a proprietor. Jacques Derrida elaborates on this, by way of the Heideggerian notion of *Ereignis*, when he says that:

> [The organism] is nothing other outside this demand and this order: let me die properly, I am living so that I may die properly, and so that my death is my own ... [Freud is here] pronouncing the law of life-death

as the law of the proper. Life and death are opposed only in order to serve [this law]. Beyond all oppositions, without any possible identification or synthesis, it is indeed a question of an economy of death, of a law of the proper (oikos, oikonomia) which governs the detour and indefatigably seeks the proper event, its own, proper propriation (*Ereignis*) rather than life and death, life or death.
(Derrida: 1987c: 358–9)

What is referred to in this passage is not so much a case of opposition and synthesis, but rather the economy or dynamics between that which Feuerbach called 'providence' – the privilege of man, the subject of presence – and Marx 'the greatest right' on the one hand, and the 'myrmidons of death' on the other. The controversial claim advanced here is that the guardians of life and presence (human rights, democracy and so on) carry out orders from elsewhere, an elsewhere that is everywhere and nowhere, diabolical, already at work in processes of group-formation: death, which weighs 'on the living brain of the living, and still more on the brains of revolutionaries' (Derrida, 1994: 109, n. 7; Freud, 1973–86: vol. 12, 157–60).

Put simply, it is violence, war and panic, responsiveness towards the dead, that drives the life instincts to take the form of 'providence' – the positing of the human as the highest value – and 'the greatest right' – the establishment of a legal framework for the protection of human value. If this is the case, then 'value' should not be understood as inherent to some sort of human nature (an aloof and allegedly privileged subjectivity) but rather as the result of the objectification (projection, alienation) of man; a process that has been parallel to, rather than exempted from, the process of the objectification–commodification of all objects. In this sense, it is the violence ensuing from the commodification of reality – violence towards the objects – that drives and explains the violence against man, and subsequent to it, the emergence of a legal–political system for the protection of man: Freud's 'guardians of life', Marx's 'bourgeois rights', our 'human rights'.

This particular convergence between violence towards objects and violence towards man, which inaugurates political modernity as the epoch that posits the human as the highest value, finds its most striking and original instantiation in the body of the slave. The slave is a ghost in search of a body, an instantiation of the more general case in which the subjects, operating under the law of the proper, are looking for themselves in the objects but can no longer find themselves in them. Men can no longer recognise in the (now commodified) objects the social character of their own labour (Derrida, 1994: 155). The key term in this 'abnormal play of mirrors' is the mysterious character of the commodity form, the aspect of the fetish that turns its operator into a ghost, 'these ghosts that are commodities transform human producers into ghosts' (Derrida, 1994: 156).

The slave becomes the embodiment of the original violence towards objects, 'what happens with the commerce of the commodities among themselves (. . .) the phantasmagoria of a commerce between market things' (Derrida, 1994: 156–7), because it is always ready to exchange not only soul, but body, with each and every other commodity. Put otherwise, what happens in the slave-ship is a becoming-commodity, a case of original prostitution or 'mutual' support (Rediker, 2007: 46 ff. Derrida, 1994: 162) between Europe, Africa and America.

All the while the slave's objects – the fetishes – become the embodiment of theft, understood not just in the sense of the appropriation of somebody else's goods, but rather, in the more radical sense of the destruction, or the fantasy of the destruction, of the norms of property that have become the pillar of the legal system for the protection of the human.

As writers like Derrida and Stiegler explain, at stake here is not just the re-appropriation of the religious, so evident in the case of human rights and international law, but also, and no less important, a certain deployment of technology and science that obliges us to think, beyond the opposition between life and death, of another (virtual) space for justice (Derrida, 1994: 169; Stiegler, 1998). If in the new world order (that of the mutual support between Europe, Africa and America) the slave is but a mere residue, a virtual ghost, for her to become existent another world, a virtual or fantasmatic world, must become actual. The space of justice is that of the actualisation of the virtual, rather than the possible or the merely potential; a case of anticipatory projection and retention 'reduced to practice'.

The first thing that the slave had to steal (to subtract from the system of rights) was her body and her name. The slave lacked a body, not a spirit or its modern equivalent, mind, the universal concept of humanity. In this sense the slave has been from the seventeenth and eighteenth century onwards a ghost or undead supplement, the remains, something that exceeds and therefore lacks. Her status was, strictly speaking, that of the virtual. The slave has been 'the rest' that cannot be counted in and exceeded the count or the account, the ratio (Mazzoldi and Téllez, 2007: 372–3). It is not a coincidence then, that the ways of the slave – his or her relationship with the objects, her common cause with the objects themselves – were deemed superstitious and adjudicated against by the dominant *ratio*.

The connection between theft, magic and superstition is 'the rest', the struggle of the slave (black, indigenous, sailor, female, exile, pirate, outcast) to acquire, to steal a body and a name by making (inventing, fantasising, re-enacting) common cause with the objects. Social scientists get it wrong when they see in the common cause between outcast peoples and their objects the sign of an unfinished pre-modernity. On the contrary, most of what now passes as superstition is more likely to have originated in the attempt of the slave to steal her body back from the clutches of the econo-legal system of rights and capital sweeping her worlds with the force of a design from the heavens; neither a hangover from primitive beliefs nor remainders of a more authentic culture, but rather political strategies born out of the effort to re-enact the world and connect with a changing environment. By making common cause with the objects, the slave was able to identify the logic of capital, to reduce it from being 'a design from the heavens' to a monstrous practice that could be destroyed, transformed and assimilated. Looked at from this perspective, the practice of the slave appears as a model for critical thinking and radical political practice (Taussig, 1983).

Armed with this conceptual arsenal, let us now subvert the re-telling of the gold-fetish story in the Hollywood film *Pirates of the Caribbean*. The first thing to notice is that the true protagonists of the film are neither Captain Jack Sparrow, modelled upon The Rolling Stones' Keith Richards, nor the fantastic crew of undead pirates led by Captain Barbossa. Rather, the protagonist is the fetish in the form of Hernán Cortés's Aztec Gold, the cursed ship The Black Pearl or the mythic heart in the chest. As said before, the film is actually a re-telling of the story we encountered while considering the genealogy of the term 'fetish' in German criticism: the conqueror's gold becoming a fetish for the conquered peoples, who, after having noticed its effect among the Europeans, used it in order to 'infiltrate' the gods of the opposite camp. As the story goes, the Aztec gold taken by Cortés carries with it a curse: the object injects itself into the nucleus of everything it encounters, destroys it, transforms it and assimilates it. This is how the Black Pearl gets cursed, and its crew with it.

During the entire film, the legendary Jack Sparrow longs to be recognised as the 'true' captain by his fellow pirates, His Majesty's Royal Navy and, mostly, by Miss Elizabeth Swann. He is the very embodiment of narcissism, the absolute being, interpreted by none other than the latest Hollywood incarnation of the object of desire itself, Mr Johnny Depp. He wishes to be freed from the constraints of necessity (his natural lack of maritime talent, the curse) and to be recognised as a distinctive individual; hence his antics and mannerisms. This explains his proverbial solitude, that of the rebel (he is, literally, cut off from humans and nature, for as we learn later in the movie he himself is cursed), but also the central role that sex plays in what is supposed to be a film for kids. The sexual tension between Sparrow and Elizabeth Swann (Keira Knightley) reaches its apex when they find themselves stranded on a deserted island, and as it happens in all great Hollywood films – starting with *Casablanca* – we are led to believe that nothing occurred, that sexual intercourse never happened, but left in doubt, or at least fantasising about it. Sex is overtly present in its very absence.

Incidentally, this is the true magic of cinema. It does not matter whether or not 'it' really happened, what matters is that we get caught within the entrapments of desire: the film about fetishes becomes thus a fetish itself and we are seduced, cursed, like the pirates of the story. This is why it is not just a simple error, born out of naïvety or ideology, that we treat film actors as gods or 'stars'. They are gods in more than one sense: isolated from all that is 'natural', we made them, like Jack Sparrow, into absolute beings. Cinema is our true religion.

Sparrow is the personification of an impossible object (money, Aztec gold): he was lured towards it and was then cursed just like his fellow pirates, the Royal Navy and ultimately the emerging Empire itself. The backdrop of the film, the emergence of a Christian capitalist Empire through predominance in the seas (the Caribbean being the historical site of this battle for hegemony) comes to the fore and becomes the true subject of the story. This is made evident in the sequel *Dead Man's Chest* in which all the elements of the story are brought to a climatic cliff-hanger that, tellingly, takes place in the shack of a *Voudoun* priestess (possibly in Haiti or Louisiana). In the sequel we learn that Sparrow's lack of maritime talent has to do with his indecisive nature (which is why his compass, yet another magical object, misleads him). We also see the sexual tension between him and Swann spiralling out of control, much to the chagrin of William Turner (Orlando Bloom) who has been, yet again, used as currency in the transactions between Sparrow and Davy Jones, the magnificent squid-like Captain of the pirate ship *The Flying Dutchman*, and his crew of uncannily beautiful sea-phantoms, one of them Turner's long lost father.

At this point of the story the reference to desire and its avatars has multiplied tenfold (Turner's desire for his absent father's recognition, the emerging affair between Swann and Sparrow, the latter's 'sacrifice', the over-sexed Voodoo priestess, Commodore Norrington's turn to piracy ...) but there are two instances of it that become crucial: first, the heart of Davy Jones (Bill Nighy) locked and buried in the chest that lends the film its title, and second, the East India Company's bid for global hegemony.

True to its origins in desire, lost love and mourning, too literal to be symbolic, the heart in Davy Jones's locker has become the most powerful fetish. It embodies separation from a cruel nature totally oblivious to one's desire, and the distinctiveness of the suffering that separates Jones from all mortals. Davy Jones's transformation from dead man into an immortal creature has been caused, apparently, by his withdrawal from the cruel necessity that took his beloved one away from him. Later on we learn that his beloved is no other than the goddess Calypso herself, formerly Tia Dalma, which means that the enjoyment that this character contains was, as an impossible object of desire, always ready at hand and yet, at the same time, always totally out of reach.

Now we know why Davy Jones took his life by ripping his own beating heart out of his chest (yet another reference to the Aztec archaic realm). Unable to sustain his status as the subject of desire, he gives ground relative to his desire (Lacan, 1997) as he escapes into the void in an attempt to sacrifice his beloved, or more precisely, to run away from the inescapable dissatisfaction that she/it produces. But as the narrative of Davy Jones's death underlines, the subject cannot simply run away from the object-cause of desire, for the consistency of his world depends entirely on the absent presence of the unattainable object. At this point in the film, we realise that Tia Dalma embodies every other 'femme fatale' in Hollywood cinema: the object that sustains the subject's world through its resistance. The minute Davy Jones escapes into the void, by ripping out his own heart, the ontological consistency of his life of desire breaks apart and becomes contaminated by fantasy. Not even the ultimate escape, death itself, provides refuge, and the contamination takes place in the form of assimilation into the fantastic object itself, *The Flying Dutchman*, and enslaved immortality, the 'undead' heart.

As it happens in most Hollywood films, in *Pirates* the worlds of desire and fantasy are carefully drawn apart. That is the point of the oppositions between night and day, darkness and light, world and underworld, which are so central to the mise-en-scene of the first instalment of the trilogy. This is consistent with the signalling of the breakdown of the barriers between fantasy and desire that takes place in the third instalment, in which the careful editing and separation is disrupted by a classical shot/reverse-shot sequence where Jack Sparrow talks to several versions of himself. This sequence indicates on the level of the editing that the distinctiveness of the two worlds – desire and fantasy – is breaking down. Consequently, the normal progression of the narrative goes haywire and we get to see ancient creatures from the past fighting it out, at the same time, with the characters of the present and a future of impending doom (the end of the world of hydrarchy and piracy, the beginning of the world of capitalism and empire).

It would be tempting to connect the return of the archaic in the third instalment with the archaic nature of the two most important fetish-objects in the trilogy: the gold of Cortés and the beating heart. Interestingly, the two point in the same direction: the symbolic and imaginary ancient world of the Mexicans. Both objects function as exemplary emblems for sacrifice, and thus can be creatively conceived as the representatives of a self-reproducing social and economic system 'whose survival depended upon its organization as a culture of sacrifice and death instituted by way of socially constructed symbols' (Kemple, 1995: 94).

Following Jean-Luc Nancy (2001), we learned before that the young Karl Marx was familiar with the story of the gold-coin of the conquerors in the Caribbean. He was also most familiar with the figure of the sacrificial pyramid:

> With kidnapping, slavery, the slave trade and forced labor, the increase of these laboring machines, machines producing surplus product, is posited directly by force; with capital it is mediated through exchange (...) Use values grow here in the same simple relation as exchange values and for that reason this form of surplus labor appears in the slave

and serf modes of production etc., where use value is the chief and predominant concern, as well as in the mode of production of capital, which is oriented directly towards exchange value, and only indirectly towards use value. This use value may be purely imaginary, as e.g. with the Egyptian pyramids, in short with the works of religious ostentation which the mass of the nation in Egypt, India etc., was [forced to undertake]; or it may be directed towards immediate utility as e.g. with the ancient Etruscans.

(Marx, 1973, VII: 769)

In the *Grundrisse*, just cited as rendered by Thomas Kemple (1995: 92–3), Marx uses the figure of the pyramid in order to distinguish between 'imaginary use value' and 'use value directed towards immediate utility' (1973, VII: 769)). Such a distinction occurs in the course of a discussion concerning modes of production based on slavery and the slave trade, in which 'the increase of these laboring machines, machines producing surplus value, is posited directly by force' (ibid.), and capitalist modes of production in which 'it is mediated through exchange' (ibid.). In spite of the apparent contrast, here Marx emphasises here the continuity between the two systems of production: the term 'this form of surplus labor', that is to say, machines producing surplus product, refers to the emergence of a single point of accumulation that upset the existing (primeval) form of social exchanges in such a profound way that it produced a fundamental void or a lack, a catastrophe of enormous magnitude or a huge misfortune, in the language of French polemicist Étienne de la Boétie in the sixteenth century *Discours de la Servitude Voluntaire*, in the social fabric.

The existing social fabric, based upon the regime of exchanges, gifts, reciprocal obligations and substitutions that early colonial chronicles and legal orders in the Americas termed 'potlatch' (Bracken, 1997) and '*behetrías*' (Sarmiento de Gamboa, 1999: 37) embodied a circularity in which everything – products, resources, potency, but also, crucially, the tools of thought – is used and used up in the very act (of consumption, violence, thinking, etc.). This entails the deliberate impossibility of unending consumption, indefinite accumulation and monopolised potency. This presupposes, in turn, a conception of time and temporality as affected by radical change, a projection that takes the form of a loop in which past and future determine each other and intersect in a point of closure. To this conception of projected time corresponds a conception of the act of thinking, in which thought abstracts, producing an image or an expectation on the part of the past with regard to the future that is then projected into the future and fixed there. Thought moves towards that image, or with equal precision, is moved by it, seeking the loop's fixed point in which the expectation and a causal production coincide. The result is the ability to reduce to practice a visionary expectation, a return of self to self, and therefore a situation in which no self arises as a 'big other' to every other self and contains them within its false infinity. This would be a situation of equality and freedom from the subjection of any master; the kind of situation referred to by early conquistadors and Spanish chroniclers of the ancient Inca and Mexico as *behetrías*.

The loss of that freedom leaves behind a void of being, a fundamental trauma or a wound so deep that it would require the reworking of society from top to bottom: thereafter, the task would be to dissolve and annihilate ancient and traditional relations in order to establish in their place, the void, quite new relations. Such a task would be given to a new subject, a 'big other' capable enough to stand in for all the other subjects and the objects of the world, and to fill the gap, to satisfy the lack that has appeared in the world (Gil, 1998: 264). However, if it is true that the loss opens up a void in the social fabric then nothing can in fact stand in for the lost object (freedom) in relation to all other subjects and objects.

The conclusion is that there is no such thing as a whole object, the sort of total (*Totalität/Allheit*) object out there for us devised by Kant (1993: 248) as a form of pure reason (the total set of beings in the totality of time, but also the moral law embodied in the unquestionable constitution of the state), but rather only the objectification of reason in its journey through time, into the future and back to the past, in a loop, complete with its reversals, antinomies, paradoxes and failures. Not a whole object then, but only a partial object providing partial satisfaction. If there is to be a state, and after the demise of the regime of exchanges proper of traditional societies the rise of the state must be thought of as a fatality, it is to be always the subject of a debt (to its subjects) that cannot be repaid, all the while it claims to be all-powerful and all-embracing. It is in this double-aspect, as partial substitute and total stand in, that the secret of the new form (the state-form, but also the money-form) lies and can be deciphered.

In this respect, its double aspect, the new form is merely a refinement of the more traditional fetish and of the system of relations (production and so on) to which it was central. And so, capitalism has much more in common with kidnapping, slavery, the slave trade and forced labour than it would be ready to accept and recognise. There is only a minor change in the nature of political and economic power. Where the sacrificial pyramid stood for the Inca and the Mexica, now stands the Sovereign in Parliament and the money-form. This is to say that the latter are affected by the same malady as the former, a paradoxical result of bounty and indefinite self-invention amidst unending wars, continuous mass destruction and untold sacrifices. But only in this respect, that of blindness in fantasy; in every other respect, the 'other' aspect of the fetish that Nancy emphasises, its loop form, its technical-anticipatory aspect, the new form stands light years away from its predecessor. It thinks of itself as anti-fetish, as a more or less infallible calculator of the future, as an unstoppable march forward. And similarly, perhaps in consequence, we all think, right and left, that we can get rid of it even though we never stop believing. The only atheism that is possible under the new form is disbelief in what we know: that the future will finally catch up with us. This we know, as we know of climate change, nuclear holocaust and massive transnational inequality, but do not believe.

Just as for the Egyptians and the Inca, after the fall of the ancient *behetrías*, and also for us moderns, imaginary use value and purely utilitarian use value merge into the total object, the sovereign and the money-form. As Kemple remarks (1995: 93), these distinctions and the suggested merging may not be marginal. When read together with Marx's critique of the old idea of 'work as sacrifice' put forward by classical political economy and legal philosophy (1973, VI: 610–11), these observations 'appear closely tied to the broader theory he has developed concerning the symbolic use of those imaginary, non-utilitarian, and apparently arbitrary constructions that organize social relations generally' (Kemple, 1995: 93). The point is to emphasise, among Marx's many concerns and (mis)judgments, his interest in the force of postulated, imaginary objects and forms. From within such an interest, it is possible to develop a theoretical framework concentrated on the analysis of projection, postulation, the dynamics of technical objects, the antinomies that plague state politics and money economics, and the self-reflexive form of reason. In short, this would be a theory of the objectivity of fantasy and sensuality, rather than a theoretical critique of an objective illusion.

Although Marx's thought seems to remain within the confines of the theoretical critique of an objective illusion, namely commodity fetishism, his commitment to develop a larger critical framework was made evident, as Kemple says, in the opening comments in the 'Chapter in Money', where 'he had analysed capitalism's need for an apparently arbitrary symbol, cipher, or character that in reality could wield monumental powers for the accumulation and expansion of wealth' (1995: 93).

Thus the exemplary emblems of sacrifice – the gold-coin, the beating heart, the pyramid (which among the Mexica was precisely the site for the extraction of beating hearts out of the chests of an army of 'labouring machines') – draw our attention towards the sacrificial basis of the self-sustaining programme of socio-economic systems, and to the fact that such a massive sacrificial programme becomes acceptable only when sacrifice is portrayed and widely perceived as 'necessary' through a network of social symbols and fantasies. In ancient societies, and to a certain extent also in ours, monumental architecture operated as precisely such a central symbol of collective unity in necessary sacrifice to ward off uncertainty and contingency. This is the idea suggested by Peter Berger when he points out, this time in relation to Mexican pyramids, that 'to see Cholula is to understand the relation among theory, sweat, and blood. For the pyramid was not designed for aesthetic purposes, as an exercise of *l'art pour l'art*. The meaning of the pyramid was provided by its sacrificial platform, the theory behind which was cogent and implacable: if the gods were not regularly fed with human blood, the universe would fall apart' (1974: 3).

Mexican pyramids were technologies of prediction, or more precisely, of prevention. They were designed to defer the end of time, out of fear of the end. And as such they were the focus and the symbol of social unity and universal law and order, 'and thereby embodied the material relations of power, knowledge, and wealth that establish a society's dominion over space and time, as well as over life and death' (Kemple, 1995: 95). Absent monumental architecture, in modern capitalism it is the money-symbol that embodies, like its ancient counterpart, the infinite set of possibilities and imaginary functions in the self-reproduction of a culture. Marx analysed money in precisely such terms, progressing from the restrictive economical operations of selling and buying, and lending and borrowing, to its symbolic character 'as a potentially unlimited and generalizable economy of wealth, power and knowledge' (ibid.). That is to say, as harnessing the potential for immortality and plenitude, or as Kemple puts it 'bounty and life, but amid squalor and destruction' (ibid.).

What needs to be emphasised, for the purposes of our discussion, is the connection between restrictive economic operations such as lending and borrowing, credit, on the one hand, and a metaphysical conception of time as potentially unlimited, on the other. Credit and the establishment of the value of an asset or a commodity depend upon an image of the future as always already an unrealised possibility, particularly so after the globalisation of finance and trade make the notions of risk and risk-prevention central to the operations of lending and evaluating. Risk and risk-prevention depend on positing or 'predicting' a catastrophic scenario or, more accurately, all possible scenarios and submitting them to more or less sophisticated forms of consequentialist and probabilistic analysis. The underlying idea is that actions in the present will decrease the possibility of catastrophic events occurring in the future; if we take action now what would otherwise have happened never happens. As a result, any practice of lending or evaluating, but also state policymaking (e.g. the doctrine of pre-emption), boils down to a glorified version of cost–benefit analysis caught in a time warp. The time warp ceases to be a problem only if we assume the infallibility or perfection of our knowledge of the future and/or the unlimited, self-correcting nature of our development in the future.

Marx's progression from the gold-coin to the pyramid, and yet further, to the metaphor of the colonial *Treibhaus* and the centrality of slavery (the army of 'labouring machines' we see in the swamp at the end of *Dead Man's Chest*), expresses the impressive development of capitalism into a global and seemingly unlimited, pre-cogniscent, self-sustaining system (1973, II: 225; V: 517–48), and turns that very same potentiality against it. This converges neatly with the narrative of seemingly unstoppable progression and confrontation against all odds that unfolds in the *Pirates* trilogy.

Remember also that pyramids are liminal sites as well, solid but imperfect foundations (*Grund-risse*) embodying the porous boundaries between life and death, stability and change, and in the case of ancient pyramids, also signs of the contingent nature of otherwise seemingly self-sustaining and potentially eternal social contracts. As the example of Cortés and the Mexica reminds us, pyramids include the real possibility of systemic breakdown. To approach critically the money-form of modern capitalist/imperial society is thus to theorise social fantasy and symbolism, its efficacy and the contingent sense and transformation of the laws regulating that efficacy just as well, but also the possibility of systemic breakdown that the money-form and the value-form, in their dependence upon an image of the future, strive to prevent and de-realise.

In the *Pirates* trilogy, this systemic breakdown is accurately portrayed in the fate of the two most fantasmatic and distorted characters, Jack Sparrow and Davy Jones. If in the first and second instalments of the trilogy Sparrow's object of desire, Elizabeth Swann, was still available and enjoyable, by the third instalment we are forced to realise the failure of their sexual relationship. Something similar occurs to Davy Jones when we are told that his was an impossible relation between a mere mortal and a goddess. The entire fantasy-scenario (a male fantasy, being stranded on a desert island with a beautiful woman, being the lover of a fifty-foot-tall goddess) was there in order to sustain the possibility of the sexual relationship, a self-sustaining mechanism. Immersed in their fantasies, the two main characters are unable to see the contradiction of the emerging world order – bounty and life amidst squalor and destruction – and the political ideology that supports it, until it is too late. Although this may seem strange for a Hollywood blockbuster, even self-contradictory, the *Pirates* trilogy does not ignore the perilous side of fantasmatic projection and fantasy, that is to say, blindness.

In fact it seems to emphasise it: Davy Jones's withdrawal into the void where all things started becomes an overbearing lust for others, whom he devours both as his debtors, reduced to eternal slavery, and ultimately, literally, as it happens with Jack Sparrow, himself blinded (literally, he cannot see where he is going), via the creature that Jones commands (the ancient Kraken, last of the Titans who created the ancient world). The conclusion is forthcoming: the emergent world of capitalism and empire is predicated upon sacrifice and blindness sustained by fantasy, just like the ancient. But perhaps the ultimate wager of the films is far more intriguing: the trilogy suggests that only by traversing fantasy all the way through to the end, the world's end, we may gain entrance into the real of the world (Lacan, 2001: 326), a traumatic point of non-sense, symbolic unrest and boundary breakdown (Kristeva, 2000) that is the very condition of rebellion and transformation. Rather than insisting upon the inherent ethical–political implications of the drive and obsessive devotion to the lost cause, à la Žižek

(1991: 272), the possibility that emerges from this analysis of Hollywood's latest output, is that of the implications of the political act of going beyond the fantasmatic by insisting on it until the very end (Zupančič, 2000: 232).

What does it mean to insist on the fantastic until the end? Remember that fantasy employs narrative and is thus a temporal form; it exists within a temporal structure and moves with time. To put it in Kantian terms, the secret of fantasy (for him the technical–practical and the moral–practical) is motion (1993: 256). And the illusory fantasy of capitalism is that of becoming a machine of perpetual motion. Now, as Todd McGowan explains in the context of an analysis of David Lynch's cinematography, 'male fantasy stops too quickly, [while] female fantasy inevitably goes on too long (. . .) the male subject experiences the real as always futural while the female subject experiences it as past, an experience of loss' (McGowan, 2007: 213). The key point here is the characterisation of male fantasy, which is what is at stake in *Pirates* and its mock-history of the emergence of capitalism and empire, as containing a form of enjoyment that always remains a potential enjoyment. Male fantasy holds back, or to put it otherwise, it is preventive. To extrapolate from this onto the nature of capital and empire, for the most part a masculine project, one could argue that at the very core of capitalism is the notion of an experience never quite achieved. In this case, the shortcoming of fantasy is not just its capacity to blind us from the truth but also, no less importantly, its ability to reduce the futural dimension to a fantasy of prevention, of refusing to give ourselves entirely to the object, and fear of the end. It is not the case that capitalism has become a perpetual motion machine or organism, but rather its cautiously pervert and catastrophe-ridden proximate cousin.

Withdrawn into metaphysical isolation, Jones's life of immortality acquires the form of debt and credit; it is a matter of keeping the future event at bay, to control it.

The heart in the chest entails the possibility of projecting and controlling a providential being whose eternity (the immortality of Jones and his crew of sea-phantoms is but a side-effect of the immortality of that ancient god, the Kraken) indicates the ultimate possibility of going beyond the vicissitudes of fate and nature while at the same time subjecting the future to one's own design, even if this is achieved at the cost of countless sacrifices. At this point the film's focus on desire reaches the outer limits of the 'death-drive'. Whoever possesses the heart controls a god, a destroyer of worlds, and by doing so becomes a god himself, an observer and designer of all possible futures. That is the goal of Cutler Beckett (Tom Hollander) acting as an agent for the East India Company.

Dead Man's Chest's cliffhanger suggests that by entering into possession of the ultimate fetish, Davy Jones's heart, the East India Company would gain unfettered power over the routes of the Atlantic thereby emerging as the dominant force of the future. As we know, this is exactly what happened: By controlling the Atlantic routes, the East India Company gained control of the world, Britain became an Empire and Christian capitalism the 'end' of history. And it is to the end of history and the world that the third instalment takes us: at the dawn of a new world order, all the outcasts of the peoples of the earth gather together for one final confrontation with the emerging anti-world of debt and slavery. They have no choice, they know their cause is lost, and yet they do not surrender. Facing a rain of cannonballs and bullets, they come out in the open. They choose freedom. It is not just that they did not give up upon their fantasy, but furthermore, that they take their fantasy to the end. When the men seemed ready to hold back, the women (Dalma/Calypso, Swann as Captain) lead them too far, all the way to the point where the past and the future causally intersect each other. There is loss, we know that the world of piracy and freedom in the seas is gone forever, that the magical objects have retreated, never to come back in the same form, but for a brief moment at least, both the characters and the spectators are able to sustain contact with the moment of loss and thus free themselves from the illusory promise that enjoyment derives from the unending struggle to manufacture environments for profit (Marx, 1973, VII: 745–78), have more, live more and discover more (McGowan, 2007: 219). The rebels withdraw from the emerging world of order and empire, thereby liberating themselves from the promise of full enjoyment through (capitalist) accumulation, sacrifice, unending debt and risk-aversion. A system haunted by the spectre of its own death. Importantly, they do not withdraw into the past, but rather project themselves into the future and from such a privileged standpoint look back at the present, at themselves as the subjects of future anthropology.

At the end of the third instalment, we see Jack Sparrow sailing towards the horizon in search for the Fountain of Youth and Will Turner, now in command of *The Flying Dutchman*, returning to his wife and adolescent child several years later. Not only does this suggest a new beginning, as it is customary with Hollywood films, but also that the dominant system as we imagine it to exist, imperial and supreme, has failed to reproduce itself in terms of the subversive logic of traditional symbolic exchange. It persists only as a broken fetish sustained by its irrational belief in its own superiority and supernatural immortality (Baudrillard, 1975: 143).

Of course this is nothing more than a fictional explanation for the rise of greed and imperial hubris. But is not fiction often a vehicle of truth? As all Hollywood films must have a moral, this one is no exception: the lesson here is to refrain from excessive desire and greed. However, scratch under that surface and you will find something much more enticing: a consideration of the desire to be freed from nature and a take on religion and our present situation as belief in providence, unending creativity and immortality, with relevant political undertones. All of them are presented in the film as manifestations of the subject's narcissism, its preventive attitude towards the future, and its attempt to be freed from and manipulate time and nature at will: to live and die according to its own designs. Psychoanalysts use the term 'death-drive' to refer to this ultimate entrapment of desire. In the end, that attempt leads to men becoming gods to other men, certain that their well-being is the greatest right.

The superficial blockbuster doubles up at this point into a radical history lesson on the emergence of modern capitalism and empire. It is 'radical' in at least two senses. First, just as Feuerbach and Marx, it suggests that subjective narcissism reaches its climax in Christian, imperial capitalism, with its emphasis on the individual that turns him/her into a god, in front of whom all other creatures and nature (all other peoples, all other territories, all things) must kneel down and worship. Second, it hints at the rebellious politics embedded in the life-style of piracy, transcultural religiosity, fantasy and rebellious slaves.

One of the most beautiful scenes of the second part of the trilogy shows a group of black folk with candles, half-immersed in the swamp that surrounds the shack of Tia Dalma (Naomie Harris): Who are they? An army of maroon freed slaves? Are they the outcast peoples that continue to haunt and fascinate white Europe and America, as they did once Chief Justice Taney? Perhaps even the Haitian army? Is Tia Dalma a stand-in for Mawu, Jesus's black sister in *Voudoun* theology? Be that as it may, the film associates slavery with debt, and makes the latter no less worse than the former (it is 'eternal'), thereby re-describing slavery for the age of credit and consumerism.

Indeed, Johnny Depp may have not been altogether off the mark when modelling his character upon a rock-star. Pirate Bartholomew Roberts has been quoted saying that in the merchant service 'there is thin Commons, low Wages, and hard labour; in this, Plenty and Satiety, Pleasure and Ease, Liberty and Power; and who would not balance Creditor on this side, when all the hazard that is run for it, at worst, is only a sower Look or two at choking. No, a merry Life and a short one, shall be my motto' (Linebaugh and Rediker, 2000: 168). As is well known, a short and merry life, as in 'live fast, die young' is the very code of the iconic rocker. Alas, rockers are modern-day pirates. Through them, through their music, through their 'Sympathy with the Devil' we can connect with the moment of loss, with hydrarchy and the free maritime state, with the struggle of slaves, their chants and charms, and with voodoo as a political weapon, with the fetish, but also with an indictment of contemporary Christian imperialism and capitalist neocolonisation. Even if the rocker himself has sold his soul to the devil.

Notes

1 See Harman (2007b: 20). Harman quotes Levinas (1997: 82).
2 See Bey (2003: 102–3). See also Watson, van Noord and Everall (2007). See in this collection the essay authored by Alberto Toscano on the revolution of the senses and Marx's 'lost' aesthetic.
3 See Dupuy (1998: 335–47), Girard (2003: 3–30), Taussig (1992), Laclau (2005: 118–20), Zubiri (1974: 12) and Ellacuría (1990: 317).
4 The term 'meshwork' was coined by philosopher Manuel de Landa, in reference to Felix Guattari and Gilles Deleuze's distinction between strata and self-consistent aggregates. It refers to an articulation of heterogeneous elements. See De Landa (1999) and Deleuze and Guattari (1987: 335).
5 See US Nanotechnology Research and Development Act, November 2003.
6 Kerruish presents the standpoint from which self-justificatory claims to authority can be challenged as the Hegelian 'infinite', or in her Hegelian terminology, 'the reasonable' (2006: 44) and relates this postulation to the acceptance of a plurality of different systems of logic and frameworks of reasoning that is at the heart of contemporary (mathematically based) reconstructions of logic. She remarks that such openness is 'specially fragile and vulnerable to the normative closures of pluralism and pragmatism' (ibid.) but emphasises that the crucial insight here is the banality of attempts to remove the contradictions that reason encounters when it reflects back onto itself from the reasonable. The result is a plurality of notions of 'the universal' within logic, whose consequences in political theory have been mapped most interestingly by such theorists as Judith Butler (but also Laclau and Žižek) among the most attentive contemporary readers of Hegel. She adds to their insights that reason's self-conceptualisation, 'its self-objectification or extension' (ibid.) should not be excluded from a project of re-staging the universal by too limited a view of abstraction. Importantly, to her mind this is a technical question (ibid.) as it involves logic and mathematics as a technical object, and thereby, all the unresolved questions that accompany the consideration of the technical object (Stiegler, 1998). The 'formalism' of classical logic that separates content and form, matter and thought and so on is then opposed to another formalism or form-materialism (of the Hegelian kind, supplemented by mathematics) that points towards, first, the demiurgos-like character of the agency of reason (pursued in this book under the rubric, after Nancy and Marx among others, of the 'double aspect of the fetish') and second, a rethinking of the notion of objectivity that goes hand in hand with a thinking subject that knows itself as implicated in, rather than opposed to the objects, 'a subject constituted in the experience of a range of attitudes to its desires and its reversals', a 'suspended' or barred subject, to put it in Hegelo-Lacanian terms, whose place is taken by technics (Kerruish, 2006: 44–8).
7 On playful narratives and a general economy of play, see Küchler (1994: 113).

Chapter 7

Horror in philosophy

A nightmare

One morning in 1664, Baruch Spinoza woke up from a nightmare. He was haunted by the image of a South American man, a slave, standing motionless before him. A ghostly apparition, the battle-scarred rebel would say nothing. His presence was terrifying. Why had he so frightened Spinoza?

Philosopher Baruch Spinoza lived at a time when the transport of people, merchandise, commodities, money, sales orders and bits of information, became the order of the day and started to cover the entire surface of the planet. Himself an exile, internal and external, he was keen to point out that to this incessant flux of things within a network, corresponded another equally incessant flux of intellectual and affective exchanges. The flux of affects, he observed, is as incessant as that of everything else in nature (Spinoza, 2000: Part III).

More often than not this potentially infinite flux bewilders humanity. However, in a few interstices where the network's links are weak, strange entities may allow a seeker to discern their existence. In every place where human activity is interrupted, where there is a blind spot, a crevasse in our carefully reasoned intellectual grids and mental maps, archaic objects and inhuman things crouch huddled threatening to throw into disarray the entire order of things.[1] Spinoza saw the black rebel standing in the entrance to one of such interstices, and it horrified him.

On 20 July 1664, he reported the dream in a letter to Pieter Balling, a merchant involved in trade with Spain and the Spanish territories in the Americas:

> When one morning just at dawn I awoke from a very deep sleep, images which came to me during sleep were as vivid to my eyes as if they had been real, in particular the image of a certain black and mangy Brazilian whom I had never seen before. The image disappeared for the most part when, as a diversion, I fixed my eyes on a book or something else; but as soon as I turned my eyes away from such an object while looking at nothing in particular, the same image of the same Ethiopian kept

appearing with the same vividness again and again until it gradually disappeared from sight.
(Spinoza, quoted by Montag, 1999: 123)

Warren Montag ventures that the image of the slave stands for a certain blindness at the centre of the political and legal philosophy that flourished in the seventeenth century: in terms of what we have learned in the previous chapters, this would be the violence and injustice done to the nonhuman which spills over into violence against the body of slaves, commoners and women in the Atlantic (Linebaugh and Rediker, 2000). He also reminds us that the emergence of modern legal and political philosophy coincided exactly with the rise of the transatlantic slave trade, but 'the great philosophers had nothing or almost nothing to say about it, perhaps because it came too close to suggesting that property rights and the system of accumulation they justified depended on violence, whether in the first or last instance' (Montag, 1999: 123).

This is an exciting suggestion, one that is worth pursuing. However, let us focus for a moment on the strange relation between the book as a powerful object and the image-entity of the silent Negro slave that appears in Spinoza's rendition of the nightmare. According to him, when looking at a book or another object in his room the slave disappeared. What was this book? We will never know for sure, but we can speculate that it was an object familiar to his surroundings, perhaps the Bible or a treatise on optics or geometry; in any case the surface of inscription of the laws of the human and the non-human; the very embodiment of reason and enlightenment against superstition. If we are to believe Spinoza, these objects had the power to dispel the image of what he and seventeenth-century Europeans feared most: black rebels and battle-scarred Indians, women, sailors, slaves – the outcasts of the nations of the earth, gathering around fetishes and monstrous objects (perhaps dancing to some African beat in a voodoo ceremony); in a phrase, the remainder whose voice the philosopher seems to deny in a dream.

What is the status of these objects? As said before, on the one hand, they seem to function as counter-fetishes, representatives of modernity countering the presence of the archaic, the unaccounted for slave and his objects. But on the other, these objects present in Spinoza's room, in his mind, could not be anything else than the result of a weird mixture between old Orientalist ways – kabbalah, the *marrano* sources of his rationalist philosophy, going back to the work of Uriel de Costa – and regression into seventeenth-century 'fundamentalism', the originalism of the Sephardite Jew community in Holland, an immigrant community confronted by the task of disciplining its members in matters of religion and liturgy (Albiac, 1997). We know that Spinoza himself was an outcast, both in the sense that his Hispanic family had been expelled several times from Spain or Portugal and France before settling down in Holland (according to some accounts Spinoza spoke Spanish before mastering Dutch), and an excommunicated member of the Sephardite Jew community. His existence is marked by a double retreat, a double exile, being lowest among the low. Is then the black slave from Brazil his enemy or his double? Is there a difference?

The presence of this element, lowest among the low, subverts the tolerant rationalism – the planetary embrace – that characterises the times. Put simply, our speculation is that the presence of the object, the book in Spinoza's dream, amounts to a double retreat from the historical present. It is an implicit affirmation of the uncanny character of the apparently obvious counter-fetishist spirit of the times.

If this is the case, if the book and other elements function in Spinoza's nightmare as a sort of 'unconsummated symbol' (Langer, 1942: 240 and Cook, 1998), an element that is in excess of the global meaning of the dream experience, then it is not simply the case that such a meaning could be uncovered through rigorous interpretation. The term 'unconsummated symbol' refers to the fact that an absence of voice, or silence, makes a communicative device lacking in assigned connotation. It creates a sense of mismatch with an image or a dialogue. In the case of this dream-sequence, a key reference in Spinoza's rendition is the silence that accompanies the image of the slave. Silence, the absence of noise or music, creates a sense of mismatch so that the relationship between meaning and context is not one that clarifies communication.

Rather, the very relation between meaning and global context appears to be inverted: it is not the historical or global context that gives us the meaning of the dream (the triumph of reason over superstition), since the latter seems suspended between its own contradictions and the former is nothing but a collection of mismatches or random encounters. We know there is or *has to be* a meaning, but we do not know *what* it is exactly. What is to be done? As Žižek and others point out (Žižek, 2006a; Varela and Dupuy, 1992: 1–25; Karatani, 2005) the only radical solution here is to shift the entire perspective and to render problematic what seems to be clear: far from being a sign of denial, the relationship between the book and the slave, cut through by silence and invisibility, entails that things go bad for modernity's anti-fetishism from the very beginning. It is not the case that the peace and quiet of the room (the library) guaranteed by law and science, are disturbed by the appearance of the archaic, and that we only have to go back to the library in order to contain the horror of the fetish (the ghostly slave). Rather, the horror that enters into Spinoza's soul after the appearance of the mangy Brazilian acts as a symptom of what was wrong from the start. Looked at from this perspective, Spinoza's nightmare and the horror that it brings into philosophy appear as a call to reject in it what has become too familiar, too false: its disdain for the objects, the fetishes and their weird causality, and the connection between this disavowal of causality and the violence that founds modernity as the epoch of humanity's 'greatest right'.

What about the slave's objects that Spinoza does not mention but are entailed by his account, the slave's powerful fetishes? Are not these objects – fragmented textiles, figurines, Tlingit coffins, meaningless sounds and images – that organise patterns of affect around themselves and circulate them, interrupting, forming and transforming the sphere of the globe, the system of justice, the reflexivity of the self whose phenomenology we have inherited from Spinoza and his readers as the very basis of our political and legal critiques? Is there a language to speak of these objects, fetishes and counter-fetishes?

In previous chapters we have learned that such a language would not be the language of the subject. The language of the subject inevitably degrades the power of these objects and reduces them to composites or artifices, secondary elements in the order of things. This language speaks of dematerialised beliefs, pure meaning, disembodied signifiers and concepts; this is the language of representation, pre-emption and prescription. As anthropologist Saba Mahmood points out (2004), such a language has produced a normativist conception of law and politics that, in turn, retroactively transforms or actively seeks to transform non-normative ways, moral and political demands that do not assume an empiricist framework. Unable to deal with such demands, our legalistic frameworks dismiss them as superstitious or turn them into legal claims to be arranged within a wider system of general consensus. In doing so, she says, our democratic legal systems seem to contradict the pluralistic axiom of so-called 'tolerant' well-ordered liberal societies and remain blind to the violence that spreads in and around them (Mahmood, 2007).

Instead of the subjectivist frame that has dominated until now our critical and mainstream theories of economics, politics and the law, in the previous chapters we started to lay the foundations for an approach to the objects, the fetishes themselves. Following Mazzoldi's call for a thought of superstition as a thought of the remainder, and Sartre's injunction to think with the object, we embarked upon an exploration of sensual objects and projective imagination. In doing so we gained insight into the centrality of objects for the projection of political demands into a causally productive future, and their role in processes of contagion. Anthropological evidence of the widespread nature of these processes added to the growing recognition that, through the fetish, political thought may gain privileged access to certain aspects of insurgent political action, forms of violence, and the formation of collective radical attachments hitherto ignored in our more human-centred, normative, holistic and substantialist accounts.

Thus, for instance, in Karl Marx's early understanding of revolutionary and anti-revolutionary practice in the Americas and Europe, projection and enactment become central and indissociable from the violence that accompanies the choice of the future over the past in actuality. We find ourselves back in full circle, facing once again Kristeva's realisation of the indissociable nature of imagination and violence in politics (Kristeva, 1982 and 2000). But this time, such a realisation is joined by a deeper understanding of the entrapments of imagination in identification and desire. Violence to the objects with which we identify appears as the key to understanding the more obvious forms of violation of (human) bodies, but also the less obvious, more abstract and widespread forms of violence that characterise capitalist production and global circulation. In what follows, the aim will be to build upon such an understanding in order to clarify and extend our knowledge of anticipatory vision in relation to the vast and inhuman reality of the future. The argument will be that a better understanding of the basic nature of anticipation and the futural dimension may help us expose and exorcise the fear that animates modern talk about law and politics; the effect that so shakes Spinoza. This fear has become, in the post-modern reign of capital and terror, coextensive with our ordinary lives.

Let us start with the lesson we learned from Sartre: the only philosophy worthy of its name would be one that starting from the conviction of the absolute futility of human aspiration, nonetheless affirms an unassailable faith in the transformative powers of anticipation. To bring the point back home, such a philosophy would be utterly materialist and object-oriented, and would stand at the opposite end of the subjectivism and moralism that contemporary philosophy inherited from its seventeenth-century forbearers. In contemporary philosophy, legal and political philosophy in particular, there is no place for thinking of the object and the good fetish. Because of this, there is no way we could make sense of the strange relations between the human and the nonhuman; we are left unable to grasp our relations to the objects in their complexity.

As Sartre pointed out (1976: 262), there is a connection between the complexity of our relation to the objects, inorganic matter, and the notion of the future as possibility or something else. The point is that we tend to think of the future as a set of rigid possibilities which are 'inorganic matter itself insofar as it is non-adaptability' (ibid.). Here the inanimate object and a form of the future are related at the level of their being: 'these rigid possibilities are inorganic matter itself' (ibid.). This entails a metaphysics behind our common conception of time.

What is this metaphysics? Notice first that Sartre relegates both terms ('rigid possibilities', 'organic future') to a secondary and inert (potential, non-adaptable, not fully realised) status. This move entails a second distinction between potentiality (inertia, non-adaptability) and actuality (full realisation) that is common among philosophers since at least Aristotle. Building upon this distinction, the future is conceived as a set of potentialities that may or may not be realised. As a result of such a conception the future becomes indeterminate. In turn, we may respond or not to such possibilities and it is always the case that we might act or respond otherwise. The latter is the basis of our common and very modern belief in free will: we are the agents of our own destiny, striving to realise our wish to live and die in our own fashion.

The problem starts when we move from free will to inertia, when we derive the conclusion that the future is not real from our belief in free will. In analytical fashion, this is to say that we hold propositions about actions taken by a free agent in the future to have no truth-value; they are neither true nor false, just possible. In this sense, there is nothing certain about what will happen or not in the future, or about what we can do in respect to such a future. If the future is not real, it is not something that can relate causally with the present. Ultimately, as Jean-Pierre Dupuy says, if the future is not real 'even if we know that a catastrophe is about to happen, we do not believe it: we do not believe what we know. If the future is not real, there is nothing in it that we should fear, or hope for' (Dupuy, 2004: 19).

Our common non-realism in respect to the future is the very opposite of the metaphysics of projection that underlined St George Tucker's description of collective action in the nineteenth century. In the context of the American Revolution he wrote: 'the revolution has formed a new epoch in the history of civil institutions, by reducing to practice, what, before, had been supposed to exist only in the visionary speculations of theoretical writers' (Tucker, 1999). Paradoxically, it seems that in the face of unequivocal evidence concerning climate change, a future nuclear holocaust, and the planetarisation of slums as a consequence of greedy consumerism, aggressive neoliberalism and imperialist terror, what we require is a form of visionary speculation that can be 'reduced to practice'.[2] In that situation, the notion that there is nothing in the future that we should fear or hope for becomes a serious stumbling block for survival, the survival of humans and nonhumans alike. This is the place where our tendency to drift towards death is located today.

Time and matter, series and groups: uncanny metaphysics and the politics of visionary speculation

Can we build a model of political action that includes a sense of anticipation and responds to the challenges of today, from terrorist violence to neoliberal violence, from climate change and nuclear holocaust to the already post-atomic landscapes of the slums of the planet? The positing of this question entails that the need for a thought of the remainder (the element that does not count in the present order) as a thought of anticipation (the reduction of speculative vision to practice, the projection and enactment of a world into a causally productive future) has now become a matter of the utmost urgency. It is not merely an abstract problem, but a concrete one. However, the way to solve this concrete problem seems to start from a thoroughly abstract, that is to say, metaphysical concern.

In the previous section, an instance of horror in seventeenth-century philosophy served as a point of entry to a metaphysics that relates the objects and the future at the level of being. Although in Sartre inanimate objects and the speculative dimension of the future appear as secondary and not fully realised elements, this is nonetheless achieved, as Eleanor Kaufman observes, by a willingness to describe the nonhuman in a way generally reserved only for the human. She explains: 'This is the double movement of Sartre's work, that in the process of making rigid distinctions he inadvertently opens a way to go beyond the limitations of these very distinctions' (Kaufman, 2005: 353).

Her point is that Sartre does provide the tools for thinking a strange continuity between humans and nonhumans, in spite and in fact because of the sharpness of the distinction he argues for, in a way that goes further than that of the thinkers who followed him in merely imagining that continuity at the phenomenological level – Merleau-Ponty, Deleuze and Guattari, Donna Haraway, Rosi Braidotti and others.[3] Sartre, she says, envisioned a scenario in which the human may *be* pure matter, a matter inextricably bound to violence and time in the sense of the historical, future or speculative dimension (Kaufman, 2005: 354).

Let us approach the scenario envisioned by Sartre indirectly. First, we will consider an instance of it in the context of magical realist literature. Taking the scenario constructed by Alejo Carpentier in *La Guerra del Tiempo* as a thought-experiment, we will gain a couple of insights concerning projection and continuity. This will then serve as an introduction to the Sartrean distinction between 'series' and 'groups' and the mathematical interpretation of this distinction that Kaufman elaborates with the help of Richard Dedekind. We will culminate with a critique of Sartre's hierarchical organisation of the elements distinguished as series or groups in an attempt to emphasise the actual centrality and causal importance of the future and the nonhuman.

Consider Carpentier's superb short story *La Guerra del tiempo* (1987): in the story everything occurs backwards, in a loop. The Marqués first dies and then grows younger and younger, until he disappears in the womb of his mother. With the passage of time all humans are gone and we, the readers, are thrown into the strangest of worlds, that of ordinary objects. This world is strange only because it has other terms for self-realisation perhaps not even perceptible to humans. This world is presented as a self-recursive loop. The narrative structure is also that of a self-recursive loop, but there is always a minimal failure that stops recursivity from being fully present to itself. In this aspect, Carpentier's story could be seen as a sort of reversed Hegelianism (rather than being anti-Hegelian).

It could also be taken as a thought-experiment: Imagine that time runs backwards. What we witness is the obverse of creation, that is, destruction: from life to death, from organic to inorganic and so on. The specific realities expressed in such terms as 'life', 'death', 'organic' and 'inorganic' seem to shade away and give place to something more basic but also more difficult to grasp and locate; some sort of Ur-place that is unplaceable. This 'third' place between life and death, organic and inorganic, sameness and difference, distance and proximity, is both more encompassing and neither here nor there; it is everywhere and nowhere. Strictly speaking it is *nothing*.

In modern logic 'nothing' is a quantifier phrase, not a noun phrase. However, there is no confusion in the above usage of the term since it may also function as a perfectly legitimate noun-phrase (as in 'Heidegger and Hegel talked about *nothing* in different ways'). In spite of that, we seem to run into trouble here since 'nothing' is by definition the absence of all objects. Can we not say something about *nothing* for to do so would involve treating it as an object? This seemingly intractable question matters to our discussion because it is akin to moving from something that is 'singular' (nothing, like being, operates on itself) to something 'specific'; a move that some philosophers would consider problematic for logical reasons (Hallward, 2001). But perhaps the problem is not the one envisioned by these philosophers: there are limits thought cannot cross, and yet it does. In each of these cases (and they tend to be legion in the history of philosophy) there is a totality (all things expressible, all things locatable and so on) and an appropriate operation that generates an object that is both within and without the totality, such as the slave in Spinoza's nightmare, the 'exception' in Giorgio Agamben's philosophy of thanato-politics (1998), Laclau's partial object (2005: 110–16), or the 'parallax object' in Slavoj Žižek's already familiar subverting inversions (2006a and 2007c).

The first situation is known as 'self-reflexive closure', while the second may be termed '(auto)transcendence'. Arguments for closure and (auto)-transcendence use generally some form of self-reference, a method that is, as Graham Priest observes, 'both venerable and powerful' (2002: 4). In fact, as he points out, it may characterise philosophy itself. Bringing a conceptual practice to reflect back upon itself is often a form of establishing closure and autonomy. A social system of law, for instance, which processes its own information using its own language, would be an example of a closed system. Mere 'transcendence' is established by arguments of a more varied kind but, as Priest affirms, they often entail the application of a self-reflective theory. Thus, for instance, Aristotle's arguments concerning 'prime matter' famously present it as some sort of zero-level substance, with no form, and thus unsayable and 'unknowable in itself' (Priest, 2002: 17–20).

Arguments concerning the existence of boundary-crossing practices or elements seem more problematic: the received notion is that crucial concepts like 'truth', 'validity' or 'rationality' require consistency, and the idea of an element that is truly contradictory seems to threaten that value. However, as we saw in Chapter 5, such received notions do not mean that we have to abandon our more precise descriptions of being, which would include the contradictory experience of limit-tearing, or else logic would go. If true contradictions are possible (for instance, to speak of being, that is, nothing, as Sartre does) and observable in reality then we should allow our observations to redescribe our received notions. This is exactly what happens in the contradictory metaphysical scenario that results from our (Carpentier's) thought-experiment, and there is no cause for horror in this move: neither relativism nor *reductio ad infinitum* or the image of multiple universes are entirely outside of the realm of any possible experience.

This metaphysical scenario could be best described as an entanglement or a woven fabric. Let us call this nothing which is nevertheless more basic *the porous texture of the world*: this is the place of mixture and relation, the crossroads (Gordon, 2004: 193–208 and Serres, 1982 and 1995b), the moment of doubt in translation (Fukushima, 2005: 58–63), of prophecy and *métissage*: 'You say we are – monsters, beasts, insane – and yet we are your equals, who are you?' (Vergès: 1999: 245).

The experiment moves backwards, rather than maximising property (towards accumulation) it goes the other way, ending in poverty. It ends in the objects, which own themselves, or nothing, and not in the accumulated reserve, capital, which owns everything and thus turns everything against everything by making everything exchangeable. What is the property of the object deprived of all properties? Its nature is that of the remainder. The objects themselves as residual property: the monster, the charm, the poor and his tunic. Nothing.[4]

In this thought-experiment, the world folds and unfolds into ever more gigantic or minute forms: it proceeds ontologically, in a circular movement, destroying mode and circumstance in order to reveal the object in the subject (the poor and his tunic) or rather, the minimal difference, which is always a first object, a primordial site more political and encompassing than a political assembly.

Let us keep two insights from this thought-experiment. First, humans are latecomers, projecting themselves into the future against the backdrop of a non-human archaic that precedes them. Second, there is an uncanny continuity between time (the archaic and the future), humans and non-humans. What is so uncanny about this continuity? Is it that the objects which quickly take over when time is set backwards cannot articulate their existence, or else, that the Marqués (like the narrator) is unable to formulate an object ontology or a time-ontology on anything other than human terms, which in any case always misses the mark? Is it that in considering the possibility of this continuum we peer with horror at the abyss of infinity? At stake is the strange continuum formed by time (the archaic and the future), the Marqués, and the objects around; an odd ontological slippage, where the Marqués, the builders, his mother and all the others *are* the inanimate house, the rocks that dismantle themselves and return to the ground, and time.

What comes to mind while reading Carpentier's story is something akin to the strangeness of Sartre's concept of the *series*, a complex formation in which the relationship between the elements is purely passive and constituted externally, which the French philosopher opposed to the authentic, self-regulated *group*. In the latter, the relationship between the elements obeys an internal logic, they act together and are thus, Sartre argues, properly practical and historical. A series is 'practico-inert', while a group belongs on the side of activity and praxis. This is the central distinction that structures the argument in *Critique of Dialectical Reason* (1976: 253–346) unfolding into a system of further distinctions that includes 'anti-dialectic/dialectic', 'practico-inert matter/practical activity' and 'rigid future/adaptability'.

The notion of the series is explained through the example of the ordering procedure that corresponds to the situation of a number of people waiting for the same bus. The point is that these different individuals are gathered together as a set externally, by the fact that they wait for the same bus, rather than because of a proper act or self-authorised choice. Their relation with one another is, allegedly, passive. The people waiting for a bus are equivalent or exchangeable only insofar as they have taken a number in advance that determines their place on the bus, and are thus related to each other by their difference of number, as Eleanor Kaufman explains (2005: 352 ff.). Sartre writes:

> On this basis, it is possible to grasp our relation to the object in their complexity. On the one hand, we have effectively remained general individuals (insofar as we form part of this gathering, of course). Therefore the unity of the collection of commuters lies in the bus they are waiting for; in fact it *is* the bus, a simple possibility of transport (not transporting all of us, for we do not act together, but for transporting each of us).
>
> (Sartre, 1976: 262)

In this passage Sartre explains serial relations as relations of inter- or exchangeability, and the being of the elements thus related as a being-outside, that is to say, determined by the temporality of the future object (the bus, in this case). The ticket that each potential passenger takes refers to a temporal determination, however Sartre argues that 'it is not a practical temporalisation, but a homogeneous medium of repetition' (1976: 261). This means that the future temporality allowed for each commuter waiting for the bus by taking a ticket has the form of a given order, it is rigid or determined from outside, rather than by the group of commuters themselves. In this sense, it is not practical or 'self-authorised' because it is the result of an external force (scarcity, in this example the scarcity of places in the bus) embodied in the object, which as a future object makes time appear as completely external. Put otherwise, the unity of this relation appears determined by pure alterity and the exchangeability of the related elements.

Since the cause of the gathering is external ('it lies in the bus they are waiting for') and remains 'a simple possibility' (to be associated with the alterity of practico-inert matter), the gathering or set thus constituted is merely a series rather than a group. Furthermore, according to Sartre there can be no concept of a series because in the series each element has no uniqueness of its own: 'in the series everyone becomes himself (as Other than self) in so far as he is other than the Others, and so, in so far as the Others are other than him' (1976: 262). Put otherwise, this is to say that the nature of the elements of a series, just like that of whole numbers or integers, is due to the fact that each element stands in the same relation to the one that precedes it as this one does to the one preceding it. 'Being' is, for elements and whole numbers, having a place in the given order and considering such a place (which is the result of alterity) irreducible.

The key in both examples, people waiting for a bus and whole numbers, is non-adaptability or rigidity. Conceptually, this rigidity is expressed as a commonality (for instance, any whole number can be represented by the symbol $n + 1$), but in the series this becomes a rule of differentiation associated materially with the rigidity of inorganic stuff and the future as a set of non-adaptable possibilities (Sartre, 1976: 262–3). The unity of the elements in a series is apparent but material, a mode of being for individuals both in relation to one another and in relation to their common being, the passive action of an object.

Notice first that this definition of the series recalls the distinction between 'identification' and 'object-love' made by Freud in *Group Psychology*, in the context of an explanation of the constitution and passage of a crowd from passivity to activity. Since Sartre also rehearses his set of distinctions in the ambit of crowd theory (sociology), it is interesting that Sartre locates the dynamic between relations to one another and relations to an object, just like Freud, in the context of a representational relationship (alterity, exchangeability, rigidity). What seems to be missing in Sartre, as in Freud, is the more radical consideration that the object may act not as alterity-representative but as substitute, the reversal of the notion of sublimation that can be found in Lacan (the elevation of the object to the dignity of the Thing). Having said that, it should be noticed, second, that Sartre does point out that the relation of all elements to their common being (the object-other) 'transforms all their structures' (1976: 266), and if this is the case, then it could not be argued that the object as common being is purely other or passive.

On the contrary, for the transformation of the structure of the elements of the series to take place, the individual elements must invest (affectively) on their common object and communicate in this manner (although indirectly) with the other elements in their uniqueness, rather than merely receiving orders from without. There is a form of communication at work here, already at the level of the series, which is not simply false (the inorganic object eroded by serial flight, or sealed exteriority) but, as Sartre himself puts it, the elementary condition of possibility for the members of the set to become a (fully internal, destiny-driven) group (1976: 345).

Although Sartre remains trapped in a schema that he himself has made suspect (full realisation v. potentiality) and the argument clearly presents the series on the side of passivity (or, at best, as the potential for true activity) what is interesting in this set of distinctions is how active a role inorganic matter plays in Sartre's conception of the dialectic, as Kaufman observes (2005: 352). This ambivalence becomes even more striking once we notice that Sartre concedes the possibility of grasping 'our relations to the object in their complexity' and connects this superior account of relationality with the problem of the reality of the future.

The notion of complexity that is operative in this argument is precisely the same that is present in the thought of people like John von Neumann or Jean-Pierre Dupuy, that is to say, the point where the structure or being of an object becomes simpler than the description of its properties. Thus, Sartre not only says that 'the unity of the collection of commuters lies in the bus they are waiting for' but actually states that 'in fact it *is* the bus' (1976: 262). The point is that at some level (at the threshold of complexity) the being of the commuters gathered together by the bus and the being of the bus is indistinguishable, and the reason for this is not just the passivity of the commuters, but rather that to describe the properties of the composite set or collection (external, passive, separated, anti-dialectical) is in no way a better definition than to describe the complex structure itself (the bus). Although Sartre's aim is to describe and subtract an ontology of praxis, of action as solidarity, common destiny – formulated in the quasi-contractual form of the pledge – and service rendered to others, it is clear that the connective force and relationality he speaks of is at work in the structure of seriality/sensuality as such, and thus, it belongs to a striking ontology of objects.

As Julia Kristeva points out (2000: 185), the attempt to establish clearly cut distinctions between passive and active relations corresponds to Sartre's relentless disparaging of what she calls 'the imaginary' (that is, sensual connectivity or substitution) in favour of pure political action in the period after the 1950s. But deprived of its sensuality (the enticing action of the sensual technical object) political engagement is, as she forcefully observes, fleshless, and lacks in fact the means to abandon the abstraction that accompanies the search for a 'localized' agent of history. It becomes equivalent to a permanent calling into question pursued with the suspension of the force of sensual connectivity. But is not the critical 'quest for origins', as has been suggested throughout this book, a matter of making a common cause with the object in search of the 'why' of the present situation?

This becomes particularly true in an epoch such as ours, characterised by radical technological development (especially in the realm of digitalisation), since the latter would tend to marginalise political groups that strived for a political praxis 'purified' of all relation with sensuality, substitution and imagination. On the face of it, Kristeva concludes that as soon as the political is cast into the spectacle (the digital image, the handheld camera filming a car bomb or an airplane exploding against a building, the World Wide Web relaying the image and the sound to infinity . . . ripping it up and starting again) the question of the sense of the sensual in politics is re-actualised, and with it, that of our common cause with the sensual object (Kristeva, 2000: 185–6).

This explains the importance of emphasising the ambivalence deeply seated in the distinctions proposed by Sartre. At stake is the possibility of assembling a politics of speculative vision for the digital/slums era. It is at the point of his odd ontological slippage – where the collection of commuters *is* the bus, and the possibility of the bus *is* the realisable future – where the metaphysics of projection into the future for the purposes of looking back from there at the present emerges. Indeed, in the passage from the *Critique* that follows the one in which the unity of elements (commuters) *is* the bus, Sartre introduces the temporal concept of future possibility and equates it, as Kaufman points out (2005: 353) with inorganic matter:

> And whatever ordering procedure is used, seriality derives from practico-inert matter, that is to say, from the future as an ensemble of inert, equivalent possibilities (. . .) there is the possibility that there will be one place, that there will be two, or three, etc. These rigid possibilities are inorganic matter itself insofar as it is non-adaptability.
> (Sartre, 1976: 263)

Tellingly, in this passage Sartre identifies seriality, the future and nonhuman matter. And in spite of a language that still condemns the nonhuman to secondary status, and conceives the future as mere potential (alternatively, this could be read as some sort of time-intuition grounded in activities like counting, breathing, singing, dancing, music in general, and so on) it connects time, inanimate objects, humans and concepts at the level of being. In a reading of the term 'rigid possibilities' as a series of equivalent successive branches or non-actualised possibilities, any sort of projection into the future would be futile since the object projected, say an image of catastrophe or hope, would retain the status of a mere possibility, not in the sense that it would still be possible for it to take place, but in the sense that it will forever remain true that it could have taken place. The point here is that there would be no fixity in this notion of the future (the doom-monger announces it in order to avert it) and hence no need for any loop to close upon itself: the announced future does not have to coincide with the actual future, since the forecast future is no future at all but a possible world that, à la Leibniz, is and will remain inactual (Dupuy, 2004: 28–9).

However, in these passages Sartre is not talking about what it would have been had we failed to take the appropriate preventive measures. Rather, he speaks of 'rigid possibilities' in relation to a form of counting which is non-adaptable or 'fixed'. Rather than an ordering procedure with no closure (a metaphysics of occurring time in which the latter is structured like a line bifurcating into branches, the actual world constituting one path among them), Sartre describes a situation in which the people waiting for the bus are (in spite of their alleged passivity) capable of seeking out a fixed point in the future. For them 'the event' (that there will be one place in the bus, or two, or three) is fixed and does not depend on their subjective designs, and thus the future is (from their perspective) real. They can explore the fixed points of the temporal loop that links the future to the past (their present) and then to the future again. They can predict that if the bus only has one place, then the people with numbers ranging from two onwards will not get on the bus, and act in accordance to such a prediction.

This is the sort of operation that Alexei Grimbaum and Jean-Pierre Dupuy call 'ongoing normative assessment' (Dupuy, 2000b: 323–45). It is a matter of obtaining (through investigation and the deployment of exemplars) an image of the future optimistic enough (to be desirable) and credible enough to trigger the actions that will bring about its auto-realisation. As Dupuy observes, here coordination is achieved on the basis of an *image* (of the future), that is, a sensual object powerful enough to contaminate, fascinate and provoke the sort of contagion that would mobilise a collective, thereby creating a closed loop between the causal production of the future and the self-fulfilling expectation of it (Dupuy, 2000b and 2004).

Notice that in these passages of Sartre's *Critique* the self-realisation of the future is associated with the self-realisation of practico-inert matter, with its imperfection (non-adaptability) and thus de-linked from the pure practicality of the group. Not only that, Sartre explicitly referred to the projection of object-forms or object-causes into the future, which he variously called 'the positing of an end' or 'project' (Sartre, 1969: 436–7). He explained that 'just as the future turns back upon the present and the past in order to elucidate them' so does the ensemble of such projects 'which turns back in order to confer upon the motive its structure as a motive' (Sartre, 1969: 437). Thus it can be argued that Sartre introduces here the form of temporality as a backwards loop affected by a minimal failure, a closure, as an interruption or 'cut'.

In Sartre's usage, this term refers to a cleavage in being, the sort of continuity/interruption that in previous chapters we identified with the (am)bivalent object that inhibits the drive from achieving its aim. Furthermore, for Sartre this cut is made-up, itself an artifice or a construct that, as suggested before, has political implications. In *Being and Nothingness* he explains that it is not the result of a simple withdrawal of consciousness in relation to the world, but rather a withdrawal of consciousness from itself and from the world, and therefore the consequence of an act of self-objectification (Sartre, 1969: 436 ff.).

In fact, Sartre speaks of the making of an object-motive of radical political action:

> It is the organized form ... which must be surmounted and denied in order for it to be able to form the object of a revealing contemplation. This means evidently that it is by a pure wrenching away from himself and the world that the worker can posit his suffering as unbearable suffering and consequently can make of it the motive for his revolutionary action. This implies for consciousness the permanent possibility of effecting a rupture with its own past, of wrenching itself away from its past so as to be able to confer on it the meaning which does not have.
> (Sartre, 1969: 436)

Building upon the insights provided by mathematician Richard Dedekind on the nature of division,[5] Eleanor Kaufman proposes a reading of Sartre's 'cut' that presents the French philosopher of the 1960s as providing us with the tools for thinking a continuity between the human, the nonhuman, and the future, 'even in fact because he is simultaneously arguing for their radical separation' (Kaufman, 2005: 353). She explains that throughout *Critique of Dialectical Reason*, Sartre emphasises the parts of the text that suggest a continuum between the humanised matter of material ensembles and the dehumanised men of the corresponding human ensemble, even while he qualifies or dismantles that continuity (Kaufman, 2005: 355).

In pages 180 and 185 of the *Critique*, Sartre introduces the notion of an 'indissoluble symbiosis' (between the human and the tool) that anticipates the sort of analysis associated with Merleau-Ponty, Deleuze and Guattari or Rosi Braidotti. However, as suggested already in a previous chapter, he goes further than any of them. Sartre writes:

> If materiality is everywhere and if it is indissolubly linked to the meanings engraved in it by praxis, if a group of men can act as a quasi-mechanical system and a thing can produce its own idea, what becomes of matter, that is to say, Being totally without meaning? The answer is simple: it does not appear anywhere in human experience. At any moment of History things are human precisely to the extent that men are things.
> (Sartre, 1976: 180)

While such writers follow Sartre in trying to imagine the human–nonhuman continuum at the phenomenological level, the latter postulates a limit situation where the human actually *is* a thing, a model of temporal continuity between human and nonhuman, the present and the archaic. That is precisely the sort of uncanny continuity at the heart of Carpentier's magical realist story and Dupuy's 'ongoing normative assessment'.

This can be extrapolated, according to Kaufman, from Sartre's notion of the radical break constituted by the act of cutting, introduced at several important passages of *Being and Nothingness* that deal with nothingness as the crossroads between past and present/future. Already in the first chapter Sartre observes that:

> If we consider the prior consciousness envisaged as motivation we see suddenly and evidently that nothing has just slipped in between that state and the present state. There has been no break in continuity within the flux of the temporal development, for that would force us to return to the inadmissible concept of the infinite divisibility of time and of the temporal point or instant as the limit of the division. Neither has there been an abrupt interpolation of an opaque element to separate prior from subsequent in the way that a knife blade cuts a piece of fruit into two (. . .) What separates prior from subsequent is exactly *nothing*.
> (Sartre, 1969: 26–7)

As Kaufman observes, here Sartre constructs a model of temporal continuity that is continuous, an assemblage, precisely because nothing intervenes to separate previous from subsequent, a model that is not different from that of the object (the knife) doing the cut. Later in *Being and Nothingness*, Sartre points out once again the indifference between the model of temporal assemblage and that of the assemblage of (virtual) objects, this time in the context of a discussion of freedom:

> Just as the future turns back upon the present and the past in order to elucidate them, so it is the ensemble of my projects which turns back in order to confer upon the motive its structure as motive. It is only because I escape the in-itself by nihilating myself toward my possibilities that this in-itself can take on value as cause or motive. Causes and motives have meaning only inside a projected ensemble which is precisely an ensemble of non-existents. And this ensemble is ultimately myself as transcendence.
> (Sartre, 1969: 437)

'Elucidation', the act of consciousness, stands here for an act of cutting. In this paragraph the knife, the causally productive future and the ensemble of non-existent (virtual) objects – projections, images, causes – are strictly speaking continuous in their negativity. And this ensemble of 'negative' objects is ultimately ontological transcendence. This is not just technology doing the work of the negative, but rather technology as the work of the negative or 'negative technology'. In a sense, technical objects bend time, and in doing so, provide their operators and perhaps also reality in general with a form of auto-transcendence. However, and somewhat paradoxically since they possess a dynamics of their own, technical objects seem in fact lacking in material substance; they are nothing.

Crucially, since for history to continue nothing must separate past, present and future, then 'nothing' must be the name for the cut that breaks up the straight line so that the continuity of time can logically be established. 'Nothing' is the cutting-up activity that allows us to envision continuity, and thus infinity (not only finitude) as an attribute of being, without establishing the direction of the continuity or the sense of the unfolding as an immanently fixed, potentialist logic.

Potentialism is the doctrine that makes of every possible a potentiality or novelty and sees that novelty (or its elements) as existing already in a past situation, even if just in potential form or lesser degree. Although at times it seems that Sartre remains within the potentialist scheme, our reading of the cut, or nothing, into the set of distinctions that make up Sartre's metaphysics of time, aided and abetted by Kaufman and Dedekind among others, should allow for a different (non-potentialist) interpretation: a model of time in which novelty is radical, in the sense that it is not simply the actualisation of certain potential conditions present in the past to a lesser degree. Rather, as in the case of Carpentier's thought-experiment, since no future/present novelty can be traced back directly to a time before their emergence or, as Bruno Mazzoldi would have put it, since it cannot be gathered back,[6] then we must accept that in every radical novelty time brings forth a point of closure within an auto-transcendent temporality.

This form of destiny that comes from the future, to use Sartrean language, challenges the mainstream notion of time as the medium by which what was already possible becomes actual afterwards. That mainstream notion assumes the pre-existence of a multitude of possibilities ('futuribles'), in some sort of more or less inaccessible multi-verse; at best, such possibilities may be amenable to the law of probabilities, at worst, they appear as completely outside of *any* possible experience, bar that of a Leibnizian divinity.

In accordance with such perspective, relations, actions, choices and withdrawals simply manifest one path out of the many pre-existing ones. On the contrary, in our perspective, any calculus of probabilities could not have forecast the point of closure that comes from the future. However, it is part of the experience of the elements in this universe since it is they who have projected it into the future in order to look back at themselves from that vantage point. Thus there is no principle superior to their projective power, by means of which *they enact the world anew*. Strictly speaking, since novelties cannot be traced back to their potentiality in the past or some

Horror in philosophy 185

parallel universe, then they disrupt what is possible and emerge afresh, together with the world. Understood in this sense, time is not a vehicle for realisation, but rather it belongs to the forces that disrupt the flow of the drive, rip it up and start again.

Carpentier's procedure in *La Guerra del tiempo* is, in this sense, warranted. We should add that there is a strict homology, at the structural level, between Carpentier's thought-experiments with time and the Caribbean ritualistic practices that he and Wilfredo Lam (but also Michel Leiris, after them) observed in political and religious radical practices in Haiti and elsewhere, but also in the musical tradition that emerged in these autonomous sites.[7] What matters to us here, at least for now, is to emphasise the rupture brought about by allowing the has-been and the will have-been, the high and low, to enter into contact.

After an encounter with Cuban painter Wilfredo Lam in 1938, anthropologist Michel Leiris analysed one of his paintings titled *Eternal Presence*. The image depicts two women. First a female-creature with two mouths and razor-sharp teeth, a monster which represents the *métissage* between West and Tropics and emphasises ingestion and sexual activity. Second, an African female figure depicted in the manner of Changó, with knife and thunder, a Yoruba god central to *Santería*, an Afro-Caribbean practice that is akin to *Candomblé* and *Voudoun*. On the one hand, the painting is a reflection on the impact of colonisation and chattel slavery, on the other, a serious exploration of the reality of time and its connection with freedom: the sharp teeth, and the knife and thunder of Changó are objects, fetishes. But the fetishes are presented here as tools for cutting and slicing, activities which are associated with ingestion, sexual activity and rebellion. The fetishes are cutting objects that radically break the flow of time and break it up or 'ingest' it, preventing it from reaching full self-reflexivity and take the shape of an eternal vicious circle, the endless return of the same. The painting depicts the return of difference.

If coloniality and slavery appear as destiny, the cutting objects in the hands of the two women are weapons of liberation, that is to say, of withdrawal from a destiny of oppression and a set of relations and forms of subjectivity that blind men towards the novelty of the future. It is thus very fitting that the two figures are female, since their very gender makes us grasp what is signified by the impossibility of tracing the reality of a new time to a phase previous to its emergence, even if that phase appears to the eyes of those who live it as having the force of legality, stopping time in its tracks, preventing the realisation of its immanent possibilities. The female characters with monstrous teeth and cutting fetishes in Lam's painting are a figure of radical novelty in the face of an undesirable fate, of cut and continuity and thus of the reality of time and the real possibility of liberation, rather than mere potentiality and endless return.

The sharp objects, but also the women in the painting and the painting itself, an ensemble that embodies radical acts of ingestion, sexuality and rebellion, permit continuity and thus also survival in the form of anticipation in respect to a real future by cutting up the past and the present. These are forms of separation that take time seriously and allow a thinking of real novelty. That is precisely the point of realist ontology and a politics of visionary speculation.

Notes

1. For the source of these paraphrases and sampled fragments, see Houllebeq (2006: 45). For the source of the story of Spinoza's nightmare see Montag (1999: 87 and 127).
2. On the need for a radically new ethics to rule our relation to the future, see Jonas (1985) and Dupuy (2002a).
3. See Merleau-Ponty, M. (1968: 130–55), Deleuze, G. and Guattari, F. (1987), Guattari, F. (1993: 155–227), Haraway, D. (2000: 291–324), and Braidotti, R. (2006).
4. See Carpentier (1976: Chapter 7, s. 23). See also Serres (1995b) for the reference to the poor/slave philosopher and his tunic, that is, to the 'non-Greek' Scythian/Cynic tradition of Anacharsis and Diogenes, and the connection between poverty and logic.
5. Richard Dedekind set out to construct an arithmetic proof to explain continuity. He argued that only by conceiving a radical break in the chain of rational numbers or along the straight line it would be possible to account for the existence of gaps while at the same time ascribing completeness to the line. He wrote: 'If all points of the straight line fall into two classes such that every point of the first class lies to the left of every point of the second class, then there exists one and only one point which produces this divisions of all points into two classes, this severing of the straight line into two portions.' This he called 'the cut' precisely to emphasise that, as such, the point was neither an element of a more substantial kind nor a void, but just the act of cut put in the place of the void. See Dedekind (1909: 10–11). See also Badiou (1990).
6. See Mazzoldi and Téllez (2007: 367).
7. See Carpentier (2001). See also Bey (2003: 122–5).

Chapter 8

Rip it up and start again

Ontological consequences of realism

In the previous chapter, the reader was introduced to a model of temporal continuity between the nonhuman and the human, the archaic, the future and the present, that attempts to steer clear from the mainstream notion that all possibilities are there, before us, and all we have to do is choose one and actualise it. That idea of freedom, thought and action, the image of the decision tree (a time line bifurcating into branches, the actual world being just one among them) was found wanting, based upon a spurious metaphysics that moves confusingly between ontological indeterminacy and epistemic uncertainty, and condemned as non-realist in respect to time, future time and virtual communication or sensuality.

With the help of Sartrean metaphysics and the literary and visual experiments of magical realists, the reader was invited to envision a limit situation where the human, the nonhuman and the future are connected at the level of being. A situation in which, as Sartre puts it, the human actually *is* a thing, and time is the force that shatters the calculus of probabilities and the multi-verse of potential futures. After Sartre and others,[1] it was argued that time and actualisation (our common cause with the object, and of objects among themselves) are a matter of world-enactment *out of nothing*, instead of being the medium for the realisation of possible futures.

To define time in such manner may seem counter-intuitive at first, but in fact this notion is more in keeping with our knowledge and experience that there are really new cases emerging in the human and non-human cosmos. The alternative would be to posit a pre-existent universe of all cases, a given set of all possibilities or, to sum up, a fixed background of space and time. This alternative would entail the background-dependency of the elements of reality, with the elements being unable to define or intervene space and time in any significant manner. Such an alternative seems non-realist,[2] since it results in the elements of reality being governed by an atemporal principle (a common notion of legality that has survived the dethronement of onto-theology) and reality itself being defined as merely one path among many with *equal* rights to existence. In the end, the human–nonhuman continuum is defined, under such a perspective, as a collection of all possible universes still amenable to survey, investigation or theorisation. As Dupuy observes (2004: 15), perhaps only God, conceived as some sort of infinite calculator, could conduct such a survey. That road is closed to us. More recently, Quentin Meillassoux has shown that the theoretical road is also impossible.[3]

If so, then we must accept that the notion of interruption or 'cut' is central to a correct understanding of time, that legality has nothing to do with background-dependency (rather, laws are temporal events not amenable to the calculus of probabilities), and that the human–nonhuman continuum is better described as the bringing forth of radically new objects and cases that cannot be forecast from the perspective of the initial, given universe of cases, but rather 'prophesied' in a self-realising enactment or projection.

This changes entirely our common notion of freedom, thought and action: instead of a 'caged freedom' – conceived as the advent of one of the cases permitted by the initial universe of the established framework – what we get is the possibility of changing the framework itself and its laws by cutting the ties that bind us or any other element to the established situation and seeking the fixed point projected outside of that framework. Put otherwise, our present notion of freedom, thought and action belongs to a 'metaphysics of chance', as distinct from contingency, that is deeply suspect because of its postulation of meta-legality and multi-versality.[4] In contrast, a 'metaphysics of time' and contingency would ground a notion of thought and freedom as the radical act of escaping the established set of relations, liberating time and legality from any subordination to hidden command or necessity, and thus allowing for real novelty, proximity and responsibility.

Rather than trying to imagine the human–nonhuman continuum at the phenomenological level, or exploring the spectral possibilities that pre-exist any actuality, the argument advanced in this book challenges us to consider a limit situation in which an act *is* the thing and the actual event comes out of nothing. This model – a metaphysics of circular time, a politics of speculative vision – is based upon a realist conception of time-matter, the future in particular, and the positing of sensuality and proximity as the primordial, excessive, realm of relations where objects and all other elements escape from (relational) totalities. Put together, these two notions make of continuity through nothing (or 'cut') the central concept of a non-metaphysical rationality, one that rejects full self-reflexivity as much as (relational and non-relational or 'absolute') totalisation as a correct account of power, cause and relationality as such.

Now it is time to consider some of the consequences of this realist model. Let us start by pointing out that if we are going to take time seriously, that is to say, if we are going to accept the reality of radical novelty and the future, then we must confront the excessive aspects of the human and nonhuman cosmos. These are 'excessive' in the sense that, in them, through them, the world is enacted out of nothing and reality adds to itself 'of itself' or *de suyo*, to use the language of metaphysician Xavier Zubiri (1980).

Zubiri argued that our common notions of reality as 'what there is' owe too much to the distinction between existence and essence that arises historically only with the onto-theological doctrine of createdness (1980: 47). Our tendency to read 'existence' as an obvious factual state of occurring rather than not occurring is a result of this distinction, but also the distribution of the elements of reality between those which may occur and be perceived, on the one hand, and those which may not occur, on the other, which is at the basis of probabilistic reasoning, current ideas of choice under conditions of uncertainty or 'risk' and a certain, nowadays common, notion of the subject as 'rational chooser', object as 'passive/given/chosen' and freedom as 'caged freedom'.

In contrast, Zubiri's language (terms such as 'of itself' or *de suyo*, and *realidad propia* or 'physical reality') is the result of an attempt to clarify that the question of the existence of an element has nothing to do with createdness – the notion that there is a disembodied essence in some world or multiverse outside of any possible experience and some remote causal agent who may bring it into existence or may not do so. In contrast, according to him, the question of the being of an element has to be described as the element's real enactment of itself amidst the system of the world (ibid.). In each element there is a tension between its consistency or stability, on the one hand, and its sensuality and specificity, on the other. Here 'stability' has nothing to do with a law of permanence given by a creator (a deity or a maker) but rather, with the changing nature of the laws that regulate the transit between appearance and withdrawal, but also between what is apparent in perception and what is absent. Laws and meta-laws do not put an end to this dynamic, but rather emerge out of this dynamic and operate within it (not from without). In more general terms, as stated above, this allows for a more serious consideration of radical novelty.

According to this argument, the stability of the world does not come from the unchangeability or rigidity of legality – social laws or the laws of nature. However, the abandonment of the idea that the laws or meta-laws of the world are unchangeable does not have to lead to the conclusion that all the elements of the world would then fuse into one big mess. The thought that opposes such a result requires a notion of simplicity and complexity co-existing in one and the same entity, what Zubiri called 'physical reality' and Hegel termed 'concrete universality'.

We are thus invited to consider the notion of a world not subject to meta-constraints and thus capable of producing its own constraints out of nothing: this is to speak of the genetic function of noise and disorder, or 'auto-transcendence' in the language of writers such as Francisco Varela, Michel Serres or Jean-Pierre Dupuy, whose work we encountered in previous chapters, rather than any religious notion of createdness or *creatio ex nihilo*. As Zubiri suggests, the error that results from interpreting the existence/ essence distinction as the result of the original activity of a creator (divine or otherwise) is the denial of the self-enacting capacities of the elements of reality, with the latter being explained through the postulation of an immanent tension between simplicity and complexity. As a consequence of such denial, reality appears as supported from elsewhere, an altogether other-worldly realm or principle of legality posited outside of any possible experience and theorisation. In turn, this multiplication of realities entails the positing of a series of objects and elements which are definitely, by construction, outside the domain, not only of our experience of time, but of *any* experience of time. Not only is this move ontologically profligate, it also leads towards non-realism in respect of (indirect) causality and relation because it confuses the origin of an object or element with its manner of reality (Zubiri, 1980: 129; Harman, 2002: 249).

Against this option one can argue, after Sartre and Zubiri, Harman and Meillassoux, and others, that a world capable of anything, capable of adding to itself reality 'of itself', which submits every law to the disruptive power of time, must also be capable of not 'reducing to practice' everything that it is capable of (Meillassoux, 2007: 76). What follows from that is an enhanced notion of reality, temporality and relations. We are challenged to take time seriously, beyond our geometric conception of laws as fixed or 'background' boundaries, and to explore the consequences – aesthetic, legal and political – of the centrality of radical novelty.

If we accept this challenge, if we take time seriously, then we must ask whether the world as it is, is hospitable to beings capable of producing more than can be accommodated in any geometric framework. As Brazilian philosopher and legal theorist Roberto Unger observes (2005), the relation between these two aspects of the question – moves within a geometric framework and the extraordinary plus of reality – is not mechanistic: there are moves and accommodations of what is within existent geometrical frameworks, but there are also extraordinary moves to transform or transcend these frameworks. To paraphrase Dupuy, this is to say that for every action taken in actuality a different landscape of objects and values emerges whose genealogy could not be traced directly to the potentialities contained in a time before their emergence.[5]

Throughout this book we have learned that this second aspect – the extraordinary plus of reality – is central in ontology and aesthetics, science and politics. We have attempted to examine this aspect of reality in its many appearances – as uncanniness, noise, rebellion or disorder – and found that in each case there is a basic mode of operation which could be described as follows: given any self-recursive relation (often known as systemic or 'reflexive' relations) there is always an element or a structure that cannot be appropriated by the system or the relation, does not belong to it, and thus, interrupts it. This element is both external and internal to such patterns of relations, foreign but also intimate. It is uncanny, less a rigid or geometric boundary between the relational system and its outside, more like an element with the capacity to enter into and to withdraw from such a system of relations. This is the element that is responsible for change and transformation; it is not a paradoxical object, although it may seem like it from some perspectives, but rather the heteronomic break in which the system cannot recognise itself, that is to say, alteration and radical novelty, an objectivity in its own right.

Following on the footsteps of other pioneers on this subject, we have identified this object as a sensual object, a thing-image (a projection) or a thing-sound (a voice). This explains why most of the materials used here in order to alert us to the presence of these strange elements relate either to music or to the visual arts. Having coined and sampled such terms as 'in-closure' or 'cut' in order to refer to the operation of these objects and their effect on self-recursive structures, we considered them from then onwards as in-closed structures. Roberto Unger refers to such structures in his line of questioning and argumentation, cited above. These structures seem to hold the key to explain hitherto ignored or unexplained phenomena such as evolving laws and radical change.

Consequences of realism in politics and economics

In social life, the presence of these structures is not a 'fact' but a consequence of political action. However, political action must not be understood here as the result of the extraordinary capacities of human beings. It may be that human beings have some extraordinary and singular capacities but change is not one of them. This is to say that the social history of human beings cannot be told in isolation from other things, as the common use of such terms as 'creativity' seems to imply. Moreover, it is the transformative nature of these relations with things that counts. In this sense, metaphysical discussion is always connected with politics.

There is an alternative to accepting that the world (as it is) is sufficient. This is to affirm that there is significantly more to the world than what there is. But this is true not only in the sense that things in the world have the potential to be other things in the future; rather 'it is also the case that the current actuality of things extends down into depths of which we have never dreamed' (Harman, 2003: 9), never seen and never heard. It is this level of invisibility, proximity and unheard noise that matters. To sum up, objects stabilise the world, including the world(s) of social relations, and not our purely subjective moves.

Consider capitalism. It is often conceived as 'the way things are', as the only game in town, as a plentiful world that constrains the emergence of any other real possibility. Our common conception of capitalism in the early twenty-first century is perhaps the best example of the acceptance of a world (as it is) as sufficient. In contrast, others have referred to that situation, capitalism in our time, as the conception of a social universe that can be wordless (Badiou, 2003; Žižek, 2006a: 318). That is why it can be global, 'a truly econo-symbolic machine that operates with Asian values as well as with others' (Žižek, 2006d: 196). But this is true not only because it provides people with no meaningful cognitive maps to navigate possible futures, but also, and perhaps more important, because it can only conceive the future as an array of possible *futuribles* which may or may not occur, and every single actual world as one possible path among others. This is why capitalism is wordless in the strictest sense: because it deflates actual reality and the anticipated future by reducing every single actual social world to what it can be in a pre-given potential future. In this sense it de-realises the future, it deems it inert and fixed in the same way it does with other objects.

This is evident in the perceived inevitability of capitalism, as much as in the ubiquity of the slogan 'another world is possible'. In both cases, time and action are reduced to an exercise of surveying the set of all possibilities, real or imaginary, and choosing the one that maximises a given function (efficiency, liberty, happiness and so on). In this sense, what matters is to recognise that the de-realisation of time, objects and social worlds is the operation that allows capitalism to establish the financial value of things, and that such an operation is thoroughly nihilistic. The question arises: What makes the establishment of the financial value of things an inherently nihilistic practice?

Let us explain: the establishment of the financial value of a thing depends upon the use of probabilistic reasoning applied to the laws of development of the economy, and ultimately to the laws of nature itself. The central notion in this sort of reasoning is that certain phenomena whose stability can be observed in the present may be construed as a figure of legality, deterministic or aleatory, which would allow the observer to dismiss or reduce the complexity, contingency or uncertainty of the future by subjecting it to the laws of probability.

The observer, say a risk-analyst or a trader in the City of London, works under the assumption that change must be infrequent in the future, or else the frequency of change would make the economy, ultimately the world, absolutely unstable. However, as Quentin Meillassoux and others have shown,[6] this passage from frequency to contingency and from ontological to epistemic uncertainty is unwarranted. The passage from frequency to contingency is based on the fallacious notion that probabilistic reasoning would still make sense as a method to survey open futures. The passage from objective to epistemic uncertainty is based on the equally fallacious idea that the future is absolutely open, indeterminate or non-real, that is to say, exhausted in the actualisation of all possible cases. Time is, in this perspective, non-efficacious or non-real, since it can only effectuate what was already included within the set of possibilities but cannot modify it.

Such a mode of reasoning, predominant nowadays and presumed by our dominant ideas of activity, freedom and choice as free will, boils down to a mere refusal of complexity. This refusal of complexity, contingency and objective uncertainty allows the observer to maintain that the phenomenal stability of laws compels everybody to suppose their necessity. The risk-analyst or the trader in the City apply probabilistic reasoning not only to the events that unfold in the market subject to certain laws, deterministic or aleatory, but also, by analogy, to the laws of the market themselves. Put simply, the establishment of the financial value of a thing has come to depend upon an image of the future as a set of possible cases that always remain open or possible: time, the future, is then conceived as bifurcating into a series of branches which may or may not become actual, the actual case constituting one path among these (Goodchild, 2005: 127–52). This mode of reasoning hinges upon the postulation of a legality, whether deterministic or aleatory, which would extend into the prospective future; that is to say, a future that is, by construction, amenable to forecast, risk-assessment, pre-emption and prevention.

Such a postulation of legality assumes as a given the open diversity of possible futures. The exploration of that diversity by probabilistic means (scenario planning, future studies, risk analysis, cost–benefit) is supposed to be the task of the observer/analyst establishing the financial value of an asset in the City of London. However, since (a) the construction of such a set of possible worlds violates reason in attempting to constitute the ultimate set of all cases, and (b) such a set would exist beyond the bounds of, not only our experience, but furthermore, *any* possible experience, then the postulated notion of law (and the form of reasoning based upon it) can only operate against reason and experience, *any* experience, that is to say, sensuality, proximity and responsibility as forms of causality and relation in reality. Ultimately, since such reasoning cannot be justified, because it would not be possible, either empirically or theoretically, to construct and survey the set of all possible worlds and choose among them reasonably, this reality over that one, that reasoning and the set of practices informed by it are nihilistic, actively subtracting reality from the world; they render the world world-less.

Quentin Meillassoux, from whose arguments the previous paragraph freely borrows and samples, has correctly described such practice. It is worth to credit him by quoting his description in full length:

> To apply a probabilistic chain of reasoning to a particular phenomenon supposes as given the universe of possible cases in which the numerical calculation can take place. Such a set of cases, for example, is given to a supposedly symmetrical and homogeneous object, a die or a coin.

> If the die or the coin to which such a calculative procedure is applied always falls on the same face, one concludes by affirming that it has become highly improbable that this phenomenon is truly contingent: the coin or the die is most likely loaded, that is to say, it obeys a law (...) And an analogous chain of reasoning is applied in favour of the necessity of laws: identifying the laws with the different faces of a universal Die – faces representing the set of possible worlds – it is said, as in the precedent case, that if these laws were contingent, we would have been present at the frequent changing of the 'face'; that is to say, the physical world would have changed frequently. Since the 'result' is, on the contrary, always the same, the result must be 'loaded' by the presence of some hidden necessity, at the origin of the constancy of observable laws. In short, we begin by giving ourselves a set of possible cases, each one representing a conceivable world having as much chance as the others of being chosen in the end, and conclude from this that it is infinitely improbable that our own universe should constantly be drawn by chance from such a set, unless a hidden necessity presided secretly over the result.
>
> (Meillassoux, 2007: 64–5)

In economics and legal philosophy, the classical name given to such hidden necessity is 'the invisible hand', 'sympathy' or more precisely 'value'. But now we know, after Meillassoux, that this 'hidden necessity' is merely the result of postulating a figure of legality that consists of giving ourselves a set of possible cases and then submitting such a set to a supposedly symmetrical and homogeneous object. The establishment of value is in fact a form of collective coordination in which an object is invested by the many; it turns into an object of common desire and is projected outside of the collective (into the future), thereby becoming a homogeneous, opaque and external point of reference for the collective. This mechanism, the externalisation and fundamental opacity and homogeneity of financial price or value, is at the very origin of the idea of general economic equilibrium, as presented by Leon Walras, Milton Friedman and A. Schotter among others.[7] Agents acting within the economic system assume such prices as a given – as if they were established by a transcendent legislator or a *deus ex machina*, as Schotter puts it – in such a way that, from the point of view of the observer, it is they who, collectively, create value *ex nihilo*.

Mainstream Marxists consider this double status of the homogeneous, external and opaque object (price, value), external and internal at the same time, both a contradiction and the source of blindness (or 'alienation'). This is only partially correct: in fact, as we have seen before, within the Marxist arsenal there are tools and notions such as the 'double aspect' of the fetish, which could do a better job at understanding the riddle of value. According to such notions, the external and homogeneous aspect of the fetish-object is merely half of the story. The other half is collective projection, contagion and heterogeneity, the power of fetishes themselves as organisers of the many into a series. It is the misunderstanding of the heterogeneity of the fetish-object (and the series) as merely practico-inert that allows Walras (but also Marxists, Sartre for instance) to conceive the mechanism of economic exchange as a purely spontaneous and automatic, opaque, and absolutely external stabiliser of relations, beyond intelligent experience or proximity.

What follows from such a mistake is an account of freedom and action as total distance from rather than proximity to others. In accordance to such an account, being free is to be free from others, as Walras puts it (but also Sartre, to an extent), that is to say, to operate as an individual in complete isolation of the sensual evaluation of another individual. As Dupuy says, egotism – the incommensurability of individuals – becomes then the basis, the principle of freedom, politics and justice. From this perspective it becomes necessary to impede any sort of contagion, not to allow individuals to compare, to substitute one another. The operative notion is that substitution and proximity (sensuality, equality, contamination) can only lead towards distrust, jealousy and suspicion. These violent affects are deemed contagious and must be, therefore, neutralised; hence the belief according to which the (free market) economy, by submitting the series to an opaque and homogeneous object, is the remedy to all human (and nonhuman) evils.[8] The emphasis on the homogeneity and opacity of the external object (price, value, money) against the acknowledged, but still mysterious, endogenous aspect, functions as a blockage of the interplay of sensuality and reciprocal projection, and the potential of violence and panic that follows from it.

Because of this, the model of equilibrium transposed by Walras, Hayek and others from the sphere of economy into the sphere of legality and political institutions attempts to (re)create society as a decentralised automaton, a purely spontaneous multitude; but it can only do so by re-introducing the figure of the original, transcendent lawgiver and a transcendent form of legality, in the guise of a homogeneous, fully transparent object – egoistic man and his 'greatest right' – that becomes the principle of (probabilistic) calculus and forecast of the future.

In the sphere of legality and political institutions, this fully transparent object comes in the guise of the total leader or, in democratic parlance, the 'exceptionally' strong Executive who, as the decider in times of uncertainty, transcends the radical investment of his subjects or, to put it in psychoanalytical language, loves only himself.

But of course, as psychoanalytical theorists would tell us, such an absolute narcissism, such complete independence, is precisely what the multitude *envies* about its leaders, but also why they are the object of such strong attachments. The paradox of the uncanny object is resolved when it is revealed as a figure of (auto)transcendence. As Dupuy puts it, it is in the negation of itself in the figure of the leader that the multitude finds its unity and identity

(1998: 337). This is to say that, in methodological terms, we must renounce the strict opposition between the series and the group, as suggested already in the chapters above.[9] Following Sartre to the point where he moves beyond liberals and some Marxists, it is in the uncanniness of the external object that the series ceases to be practico-inert or, to be more precise, it is because seriality cannot be assumed to be the absolute opposite of the practical group, since the cut introduced by the external object is in fact a cut that the series has introduced on itself of itself, where the multitudinous series transcends itself and faces the future, without forecast, without the false promise of stability that is couched nowadays in the language of probabilistic reasoning in its many guises (surveys, referenda, consultation methods, media placement, pre-emption).

Put otherwise, the phenomena we have been considering thus far in law and economics are in fact self-reflexive structures affected by in-closure, that is to say, given to a heterogeneous or partial object. The multitude produces or projects into the future, in sensuality and proximity, a fixed object, while it conceives itself a product of the fixed endogenous object (Dupuy, 1998: 339). From this perspective, what explains the central position of the decider and the money-maker has nothing to do with their assumed 'exceptional' characters (charisma, narcissism, energy, talent) but rather, with the process through which a set of elements (a series, the multitude) closes upon itself. 'Narcissism', 'charisma', 'intrinsic value' are in this case nothing but illusions, since there can be no other value than that of collective radical attachments and free radicals. Similarly, the opposition between object-desire and narcissism or 'identification' may be replaced by a generalised principle of mimesis and alteration – substitution, contagion or over-identification. Thus, for instance, the decider loves only himself because he approximates and imitates the love that others invest in him, and conversely, the others love him because they approximate and imitate the leader's love of himself, as Dupuy says (1998: 340). The 'exceptionality' of the leader and the strong decider is not the cause but an effect of the organisation. Thus an alteration in the order of the organisation (the framework, its manner of counting) will forever transform the centrality of the leader by putting in its place the remainder, the element that did not count in the previous order. Once again, the mechanism at work in this process of alteration is one of substitution.

In the establishment of financial value in today's economy, as in the instantiation of justice in the present situation, we are in fact facing a situation of collective self-legislation, a reflexive drive, but one in which the alleged homogeneity or fullness of the object would allow for a complete drive, a fully reflexive case of collective self-legislation, pure and transparent,[10] and therefore also, remember the psychoanalytically informed distinction between homogeneous and partial objects in relation to the death-drive that we encounter in Chapters 5 and 6 above, a complete, *realisable will to destruction* (Laclau, 2005: 172). Aware of this connection, the reader may be forgiven if she falls prey to the temptation of associating Meillassoux's 'homogeneous object', the gold-coin, and the curse linked to the gold-coin in the old stories about the emergence of modernity, with money and terror in our imperialist, late capitalist situation.

Value and justice are instantiated or institutionalised in the present situation as an opaque, external and homogeneous object. And this is why they are both – value and justice – operative, as Žižek has suggested, at the level of the real (2006d), but the latter, justice, ultimately yields to the conditions of liability and evidence that back up the former, value. This poses serious limitations on any ethics or politics of principled, generic, possible justice *beyond* experience. As has been suggested in this book, behind this notion of the possible lurks confusion between ontological multiplicity and epistemological indeterminacy, and beyond that, the deflationary account of reality that has become a common feature in contemporary thought: the naturalistic illusion that *physis* (the 'real' world) is neutral and indifferent, coupled with the glorification of probabilistic reasoning.

This movement of the political towards its last frontier, namely the frontier created by humanity 'upon its self-constitution as a total ethical system of relations' (Moreiras, 2003: 104) is but the other side of the autonomisation of the economy, completed today under the auspices of globalisation, and that of a notion of private law based on the recurring polarity between 'two heterogeneous spheres "namely, ethics and economics, intellect and trade, education and property" (...) now autonomous domains' (ibid.) that can no longer be identified with the legality of the state.[11]

One symptom of this movement is the progressive naturalisation of the division between objectivity as a system of non-relations characterised by practical inertia (the side-by-side doctrine of natural reality) and subjectivity as the exclusive realm of action, anticipation and relationality as such. Another symptom is the postulation of probabilistic reasoning as the only game in town. Against the attempt to construct humanity as the ultimate set of (ethical) relations stands the figure of the rebel, the outlaw and the freedom fighter – the remainder, the element that escapes from the system of relations.

The 'will to escape' referred to here has nothing to do with the singular characteristics of these characters, but rather with the movement of the collective itself, what Varela and others would call a 'systemic effect', as it takes distance from individual moves without becoming 'simple', that is to say, remaining as nothing else but a composite of relations that, nevertheless, cannot totalise all of its constituent parts. Thus, to the notion of *systemic effect* that we have learned from Francisco Varela and others, we should oppose (or supplement with) the notion of the *withdrawal* of the remainder-element from the system of relations. In other terms, this is to assert the impossibility of the ultimate totalisation of all parts in a set or a whole.

In conversation, Žižek has clarified that he identifies capitalism with the Real not in the sense of a last-instance determinant force, saturating the space of relations and absorbing them within a complementary whole, but rather as a nihilistic power impacting on the very structure of material social processes. Whether or not this entails a reformulation of his views in the face of criticism, the point is that in this reading capitalism is a 'spectral' or excessive object precisely because it cannot be reduced to the set of material relations among people; it also entails – as Phillip Goodchild has pointed out correctly – a particular relation between people and the future (2005: 127–52). Put otherwise, the Real, even within capitalism, cannot be exhausted by actual social relations since there is always more to these relations – understood as modes of reality on their own right – than what they are.

What seems to be missing in both Žižek and Goodchild is a clarification of the way in which this relationship with the future remains 'spectral', as they put it. Let us then proceed by means of clarification: on the one hand, there is more to the future than epistemic uncertainty, on the other, precisely because there is more to the future than mere uncertainty (or 'open' possibilities) it contaminates the alleged current universality of capitalism, its pretension to become the set of all sets, the only game in town. Put otherwise, capitalism is a contaminated universality from the standpoint of the particularity of a future, a real future, it cannot master. Perhaps this is why contemporary capitalism has come to depend on its ability to produce 'catastrophes' that it can master.[12]

But in order to see this we must avoid a double confusion: that between ontological multiplicity and epistemic uncertainty, on the one hand, and the assumption of a determinate set of possible futures that can be tamed or surveyed, on the other. The power of capitalism as a system of credit, innovation through disaster, and speculation is based upon this sort of confusion. It is this widespread confusion that produces as a result the basic idea according to which the radically different future never comes. Goodchild has explained the connection between this basic idea and capitalism in the following terms:

> Financial value depends on an imagined future. This imagined future is transcendent to current reality and, furthermore, the future never comes. For, even if there is a stock market crash, the value of any asset still depends upon projections about its future. In this respect, financial value is essentially a degree of hope, expectation, or credibility. Being transcendent to material and social reality, yet the pivot around which material and social reality is continually reconstructed, the value of

money is essentially religious. To believe in the value of wealth is to believe in a promise that can never be realized; it is a religious faith. Yet one only has to act as though one believes in it, and by some miracle, it becomes true – for others may treat money in the same way, accepting it in exchange.

(Goodchild, 2005: 133)

This is a paragraph worth quoting; setting aside the false consciousness model that animates its still 'anti-fetishistic' critique, the point is well taken: based upon the idea that the future is not real, our projections can only take the form of an aleatory or deterministic hope ('only a god can save us'). Worst still, since we know – even if we do not believe – that god is not coming any time soon, we then forfeit our responsibility (we know it is up to us, but can we really make a difference?) in the name of a misplaced faith in a miracle. The problem is not religious superstition, not even the fact that capitalism has a religious structure, but rather the way in which our capacity to act in the face of ontological uncertainty is tainted by our everyday actions within a capitalist structure that forces us to believe – every time we perform a credit transaction – that the future will never come: the phrase 'Buy Now, Pay Later!' was the object of irony of rock band Van Halen in the 1990s; it is now the motto of Nat West, one of the main banking institutions in Britain: 'Don't Wait. Have it Now!'

This is also the major shortcoming of Al Gore's call to arms in his doom-mongering *An Inconvenient Truth* (2006): Yes, we know that catastrophe is upon us. Yes, we know that it is up to us. And yes, we know that we can make a difference! Why then don't we do it? Not once in the film does the person who used to be the next President of the United States ask this question. He suggests that this is not a political but a 'moral' issue, right? Wrong, it is a political issue. If, in spite of the fact that I know all that the good ex-next President says is true I do nothing, then there must be an objective force (not merely a false belief) that obliges me to do nothing in the face of impending doom; and perhaps I cannot see that force, the force of the external opaque object-fetish, but surely I can feel its effect every time I go to the shop or, if need be, use violence in order to get the money that will allow me to go to the shop as is the case in the many slums of this planet of slums. Incidentally, the resultant ethical aporia is the subject of so-called New Latin American Cinema from *Amores Perros* to *City of God* and *Tropa de Elite*.

In short, we do not do it because we cannot (which means that in principle, we are not ethically obliged to do it) and we cannot do it because the most basic operations of our everyday life (eating, moving, sheltering, having sex and so on) are thoroughly affected by a power that makes the future unreal; and since the future is made unreal, whatever catastrophe we are threatened with (from terrorism to climate change) or whatever hope we entertain (from development to liberation) remains uncertain. As a result we will continue to argue on the merits until it is too late. The missing link in Gore's case is capitalism.

Put otherwise, what we face is a true ethical aporia: we have to act ethically, we have to transform our present mode of reality, but in principle we are not obliged to act ethically because we cannot; therefore, the problem is – if we want to avert catastrophic climate change for instance – that we have to act even if we cannot. That is a proper ethical aporia: as Dupuy puts it 'we do have an ardent obligation that we cannot fulfil: anticipating the future' (2004: 18). And the proper ethical act is to carry on and do it even if we cannot. How can we do this impossible thing? First of all, we have to lift the force that introduces the notion into our mode of reality that the future is not real, namely fallacious probabilism, for the reality of the future (rather than its practical inertia) is the condition that would make our anticipating it possible.

As suggested above this entails a political act: to liberate ourselves from debt (our enslavement to a non-real future) not by re-paying it (one can never pay, as we know very well, and not simply because one does not make enough money, it is more the case that money is never enough – a state of *radical* poverty) but rather, by lifting the conditions that create debt in the first place. As in *The Fight Club*, our dream is to 'erase' debt, but unlike what happens in the film we will not achieve this simply by blowing up credit institutions; that would not suffice. We may have to blow up some buildings, but before we go into that a major change in metaphysics is necessary: we require a superior realist materialism that can allow us to lift from our current metaphysics of temporality the notion that the future is indeterminate and the feeling that our action fails to add anything to reality.

French philosopher Jean-Pierre Dupuy has insisted on the first point, let us now emphasise the second: as he says, in the current state of our ontologics propositions about action taken by a free agent in the future are held to have no truth value; he has also explained why the derivation from free will to the unreality of the future entailed by this move is a sheer logical fallacy (2002a). Indeed, the notion of the future as comprising an irreducible multiplicity of *futuribles* (ontological indeterminacy) and the same multiplicity interpreted as a reflection of our inability to know anything about the future (epistemic uncertainty) are locked in a confused embrace. What Dupuy does not explain is that this embrace would not be possible if ontological indeterminacy is affirmed in a way that does not lead to confusion. That is to say, if we abandon the notion that contingency equals open diversity given to chance, the calculative procedure proper of a symmetrical or homogeneous object, and the notion of legality that follows from such a procedure.[13]

Consequences of realism for the study of laws, natural and social

The postulation of such a form of legality, whether deterministic or aleatory, entails the identification of the world with a set of sets, a universe or multiverse of all possible cases indexable in principle and thus, pre-existing their ultimate discovery or actualisation. According to this notion of legality, the world becomes a set of possibilities existing side by side, and the elements, objects or parts of that world nothing but mere potentials. The latter are denied any powers of their own outside of the legally established network or 'world of worlds', and remain there only to be chosen, activated or actualised by a maker (human or divine) with the exclusive power to transcend, somehow, the possibilities existing side-by-side and view them, as it were, from above.

As can be seen, this form of legality would survive even in a post-theological world in the guise of an anthropocentric principle that distinguishes sharply between the sensible and the intelligible, and submits the former to the regulatory powers of the latter. This is of course the sort of distinction associated with the so-called Kantian 'revolution' in philosophy and the basis of the separation between the House of Man and the House of Nature that dominates our scientific, artistic and political endeavours to this day.

In this distinction, Man becomes the stabiliser and adjudicator of (a more or less passive, perhaps in fact aleatory) Nature, and thus its centre. The argument, familiar to the reader of *Critique of Pure Reason* and refined in the so-called *Opus Postumum* by Immanuel Kant, is that of the necessary self-positing of Man upon Nature if the latter is to conserve the stability of its laws as a condition of our knowledge of them. Philosophers of science have been pointing out since the late 1970s that this is but an argument of 'good sense' against the contingency of laws, natural and political.[14]

They observe that such an argument is based on at least two problematic moves: first, an exacerbation of probabilistic reasoning and second, a conception of the world as time-symmetrical. If laws were contingent, so goes the argument of 'good sense', they would change so frequently that we would never be able to grasp anything whatsoever, because none of the conditions for the stable representation of objects would ever obtain. Hence the question 'how must the world be for our representation and knowledge of it to be possible?' and the reply 'it must be stable, either because the objects themselves are subject to laws of stability, or else, because we posit such laws, and posit them upon the objects, as a condition of experience'.

Our positing of the laws that make experience possible simply means that we extend the chain of perception from the observable present back to the conditions that determine this perception in respect of (past) time or forward into the conditions that will determine this perception in respect of the (open) future.¹⁵ But we cannot in fact prolong the chain of experience from our contemporary observations to a real past or a real future, since in a *real* past (say, the time of the first ancestors or geological time) or a *real* future (say, beyond human history) the conditions of observation and experience would not be present. The result is a world without real change or multiplicity; such a world is conceivable only as an all-pervasive token monism without structure, in which time is somehow de-linked and assumed as (metaphysically) prior in respect to space, and undifferentiated in character and extent. This is the kind of pervasive empirio-idealist world described by J. L. Borges in *Tlön, Uqbar, Orbis Tertius* in which different perspectives and the notion of space are unthinkable as well as the signature of an author.¹⁶

It is very fitting that Borges includes in his short story about the undifferentiated world he calls Tlön a lengthy reference to a series of objects termed *hrönir*. These objects are strictly co-relative objects: they are produced through thought, suggestion or hope. They become effaced and lose their details when they are forgotten. Notice, first, that these objects are the exact opposite of the sort of objects that populate and make up the world independently of any relationship we may happen to have with them, and which are described or altered by art and science. For instance, the fetish-objects obtained by the Cuna or the Tlingit and 'found' by the anthropologist or the visual artist have an autonomous existence, which is why they function or make common cause with the indigenous peoples, as much as with the anthropologist; to put it plainly, they 'ingest', stabilise or define spatio-temporal relations. Second, these objects cannot be construed as background-dependent, they are not a mere function or an effect of a fixed spatio-temporal background which already contains all possible objective alterations.¹⁷

Thus, the problem with the transcendental line of questioning that has become a commonplace in philosophy and elsewhere since Kant, and the answer given to it, is its legalistic nature. This problematic nature can be described as follows: (1) the passage from contingency to frequency can only occur under the assumption of the extraordinary *improbability* that the laws should remain constant rather than being modified at every instant, as Meillassoux has observed (2007: 66); (2) this entails not only the postulation of a set of all possible alterations, as the French philosopher points out, but furthermore, the identification between that set and the totality of time as a fixed framework or background and a condition of experience that is supposed to be constitutive of the objects themselves; in short, a certain form of legality; (3) the postulation of space-time as a form of legality, an ever-present support of changing objects and relations, and of the objects and their relations as a mere effect of that legal framework, invalidates all art and science, as Borges says.¹⁸

Faced with the potential invalidation of all art and science we must firmly assert that the elementals of ontology (time and space) are not the ever-present support of transforming appearances (discrete entities) but unstable point-centres of mutual influence with objective reality that intervene space and time.[19] This leads to the realisation that the traditional corpuscularian/mechanistic world-view that seems to have survived in philosophy and certain forms of probabilistic reasoning is untenable (since action at a distance or 'proximity' renders the postulate of action by contiguous contact between atoms conceptually incoherent). Hence, absence must be considered to have absolute and relative physical priority over presence. In turn, this entails at least ontological bivalence (being–not being) if not polyvalence, multiplicity. Probability is a matter for an observer that gives himself a set of possible cases, each one representing a possible case with equal potential to become actual, and concludes from this that it is infinitely improbable that the actual case should be constantly drawn by chance from such a set, thereby postulating a hidden law amenable to discovery. This is in fact the sort of procedure that Kant described as subjective self-positing in the *Opus Postumum*. Both the transcendental question and the answer seem to assume some sort of necessary connection between human experience and nonhuman existence or, to put it in more precise Kantian terms, the rigidification of fluid matter by means of categorical thought, an anthropocentric assumption that has become the reigning *doxa* of 'post-metaphysical' philosophy.

In accordance to this *doxa* the idea of objects subsisting independently of our relation to them and sensually manifesting themselves to one another is an absurdity and therefore, the only way to make the idea of a world or an external reality intelligible, is to make it something independent 'for us'. Furthermore, the denial of indirect, independent causality (proximity, action at a distance) involved in this idea renders the world world-less, that is to say, lacking in processual character, merely a set of discrete entities standing side-by-side and communicating with one another via penetration and contiguous contact, or merely coordinated alongside and successively (Kant, 1993: 160). This already presupposes space and time as background subjective forms, and the subject (the maker) as the active principle of objectivity, not what objects are in themselves but what they are for sense (ibid.).

This refined billiard-ball scenario posits the formal element of intuition as prior to the material, and identifies the formal element with the subjective element in the figure of a maker that is able to predict the movement of forces and combine them, or posit them, into a unity within itself (Kant, 1993: 162). The maker chooses a world, this world, or more exactly, makes it or posits it, and likewise all the objects of this world as sense-objects. The maker is not receptive in respect to the things and forces of the world but spontaneous, and the spontaneity of the subject, the formal principle of composition of simple materials, is analogous to the framing of the things and forces of the world as if it were a picture. This entails a conception of the viewing subject (the maker) as being set apart and unconnected with the framed object.

Such conception is problematic for a number of reasons. First, it presents the viewing subject as if the viewing took place from a position that is set aside and, at the same time, interactive. Second, it makes the viewer absent from the picture and takes no account of the viewer's encounter with the picture. Third, the relative absence of the viewer/maker results in a poor account of making or 'technics' that merely repeats the Aristotelian assessment of the technical object as being infused with a dynamic principle from outside, by a creator.[20] Consequently, this is not an account of making, in the sense of 'technics', but rather, of creation (and of consciousness as creative), that is to say, the realisation of a possibility in accordance with a previous programme or design. Finally, this results in a deficient account of prediction, anticipation and temporalisation.

In accordance to this account, anticipation is the mode of operation of a system of knowledge that imagines the forces of (external and internal) nature in sensation and in the construction of concepts – philosophical and mathematical – before it experiences them (Kant, 1993: 161). Therefore, anticipation entails 'exteriorisation', which would mean the presence of a preceding interiority. It is said that this preceding interiority contains subjective forms that are the principle of the possibility of the combination of the plurality of outer manifestations into a systematic unity with the consciousness of an absolute totality or universality. The location of an object in space and time, in terms of causes and relations, becomes a question of its being posited by the subject within such an absolute totality or the universe of all possibilities. Predictive propositions are possible because we can give ourselves a universe of all cases, we can give ourselves an image of space and time and their synthetic unity in one space and time, an image of persistence, that is.

Meillassoux (2007: 64–5) has argued that behind this affirmation of the persistence and necessary constancy of laws there is an argument of probability applied to the laws themselves, rather to events subject to these laws. He locates a similar argument in the Kantian transcendental deduction of the categories in the *Critique of Pure Reason*, where the German philosopher infers from the contingency of laws the necessary absolute frequency of their changing. This passage from contingency to frequency assumes that there is an infinity of last resort, of all possible or logically thinkable worlds, which reinforces the improbability that one world among the many and the correspondent set of laws should remain constant rather than being modified in every way at every moment. If they were modified in every way at every moment, frequently, frantically, then we would no longer know anything because 'none of the conditions for the stable representation of objects would ever obtain', and since such conditions do obtain then one must conclude that the world and the constancy of its laws are the result of some 'hidden necessity' (2007: 65, n. 3).

There is a problem here, in the deduction of this 'hidden' necessity out of a connection between probability and frequency of outcomes based upon the notion of a set of all possible worlds posited *ad hoc*. That connection is limited, and in particular, it does not cover the case that is at stake here, that of unique laws born out of unique events. The point here is that certain events in nature and the social are by definition non-replicable, and so they are unique. To 'repeat' them in time (as Jefferson asked in relation to the set of political laws born out of a revolution) is to betray them, since what returns is never the same. Something similar holds, perhaps even more strongly, for the case of the laws of nature. The events involved happen only once, they effectively cut the universe into two, so to speak, and thus are not covered by the notion of probability as frequency. This is the thought that does not occur to Kant: that of an event which cuts the world into two. For him, frequency of outcomes is given to absolute chance and thus gives us no ground for apodictic judgements (1993: 167) unless we posit a form of necessity supporting the event. An event is for him necessary in the sense that it remains constant in all future cases, that it can be replicated, not in observation or experiment, but rather in the presupposed totality of all possible cases, that it is 'true' in all possible worlds. This is why the thought of an 'archaic' event, which happens only once and cannot be replicated, together with the notion of changing laws and transformation beyond a given programme, escapes the limits of transcendental critique. It is the unthought in modern thinking.

This affirmation of the persistence and necessary constancy of laws from the standpoint of a subject, survives virtually untouched in our mainstream accounts of law, politics and economics; it is the basis of our idea of freedom, causality and action. In these accounts, 'freedom' means for the subject to choose or realise a possibility out of the multiverse of cases according to previous design. 'Causality' entails necessity and penetration, the execution of a force by one agent upon a passive object that moves the latter causing it to change direction, and creating a branch, a fork in the path of occurring time. 'Action' is the execution of such a force for the purposes of 'radical' transformation, an effective power of determination which is 'justified'. Since the latter is confirmed by replication, so that nothing remains really 'external' to or independent from it, it manages to bring its claim to justification within the orbit of its power, gaining a self-justifying, self-reproducing, self-persistant quality which strengthens it to a degree such that time-shifts are deemed unnecessary if not dangerous and, at least as regards political authority, 'the need for a standpoint from which challenges to a constituted authority's claim to justification are made is widely acknowledged' if not actually foreclosed (Kerruish, 2006: 42). In this manner, anthropocentrism, or at least the strong correlationism that posits the observer as maker rather than operator or selector (Meillassoux, 2006 and Trotta, 2007: 152–5) leads towards non-realism in respect to indirect causation (contact between objects themselves without fusion), causal action at a distance, absence or withdrawal, actual transformation, knowledge of 'archaic' events, and external reality independent from us.

Confronted by this non-realist dead-end, our best alternative is to abandon the side-by-side doctrine that denies the existence of objective structural properties, and the form of sorting out things between the houses of Man and Nature that follows from such denial. This is why the notion of transformation or alteration must be redescribed in relation to the reality of processes, the shattering force of time, and the ability of objects to enter into and escape from relational totalities: neither the One-All of Platonism (however inverted that Platonism may be), nor the prime mover of Aristotelians.

Consequences of realism for the study of globalisation

At the end of the previous section on the consequences of our realist reformulation of critique for the study of laws, natural and social, it became clear that the Kantian legacy of our current approaches to law, politics and economics leads us to a dead-end. It was said that our task consists in introducing a notion of alteration that takes into account the possibility of real time-shifts and transformation with no relation to a previous programme or design. This included taking into consideration the capacity of elements to enter into and withdraw from given sets of relations. What does this entail, philosophically? The trick is not to postulate *qualias* or attributes as secondary in relation to essence or being, to avoid starting from being as some sort of *terra nullius* – an uninhabited country – or the (epistemic) void in respect to all modes of being. In contrast, the emphasis must be on the modes of being rather than on Being as general onto-critical equivalent.

Similarly, when it comes to politics and economics the emphasis should be on the modes of establishing value rather than on Value as general equivalent. The present section develops this theme in relation to the study of capitalism in its global phase. The starting point is that the emphasis on Value makes all objects subordinate to value as generally equivalent, interchangeable, and ultimately subordinate to an unreal image of the future.

The subordination of the objects themselves to a legalised image of time has consequences: their actuality (the fact that they are always more than what they are) is replaced by an illusory notion of what they can be in the possible future. And since that future never comes, things are always emptied-out of their actual reality, obliterated and destroyed. The violence done to things constitutes the very core and the ultimate limit of capitalism, pointing towards the more visible violence such a system imposes upon humans.

It is often believed, even by Marxists, that capitalism is a system of production; after the previous lines it may be better to qualify that statement: capitalism is a system of destruction. It is deeply nihilistic.

What does it mean to say that capitalism has acquired nihilistic tendencies? On the one hand, the co-dependence between the establishment of value and the positing of a de-realised image of the future as legality results in a form of economic theorisation and practice that effectively enslaves the present to eternal debt, credit and prevention. On the other hand, the marriage between contemporary understandings of capitalism in its global phase and risk-prevention entail the reduction of politics to prevention policy. The present is not taken into account for what it is (its excessive actuality) but always counted as potentially 'other'.

This tendency, utopian but regressive, because restorative – it realises only what was already the case in the precedent situation – provides capitalism with its 'innovative' face, its capacity to extend beyond borders and obstacles without ever really changing. But it also hides the profoundly destructive nature of such an endless process of innovation. Perhaps we should be more precise and speak of 'renewal' rather than 'innovation', because in fact capitalism crosses frontiers and inner limitations without really changing itself, it merely renews itself by transforming everything it touches – objects, peoples, entire cultures – into a case of its own rules. It abhors radical novelty and replaces it with a spurious belief on a pre-given set of open futures that it can survey and, allegedly, actualise (a preventive, de-realised image of the future). Unable to deliver on its promise it turns imperial, casting its shadow over the entire globe, policing the frontiers of its centres in order to prevent – like a medical de-contamination unit – the spread of any project of radical innovation that might threaten its reign. It is ready to swallow every foreignness on the condition that it does not have to contemplate the foreignness within, its murderous face projected onto every 'other' that it mixes up with and assimilates.

In other words, during the twentieth century a new social contract emerged which entailed not only the globalisation of capitalism to previously uncolonised places and social systems 'but also the revaluation of what survives or must be revived from premodernity' (Kemple, 1995: 153–4; cfr. Offe, 1984: 38 ff.; Habermas, 1975). The point is made clearly by Joseph Schumpeter when he explains that inasmuch as the seemingly unstoppable march forward of capitalism is nevertheless haunted by ghosts and 'survivals from its precapitalist past' (Kemple, 1995: 153), everything hinges upon the way in which it is able to contain such spectral appearances and include them, without ever being contaminated by them. As a result, capitalism is nowadays in the position of having to use death, or the risk of death, in order to rule the living (Schumpeter, 1951: 98). In such a situation, the democratic values of equality and fraternity can be upheld for the very reason that such ideals are treated as mere unrealisable potentials.

In the new social contract, the legal status of persons may be upheld or suspended through the redefinition of liberal and radical rights in preventive and epidemiological terms (Kemple, 1995: 152–3; Donzelot, 1981: 8), 'thereby substituting the right to political participation and control for the right to "work-satisfaction" (. . .) The costs of upholding such values as health, education and welfare are then treated not as matters of civic responsibility (. . .) but in the context of the relation of individuals to their productive work, and thus within the parameters of the capitalist legitimation process' (ibid.).

Furthermore, in the twenty-first century it has become clearer that the right to 'work-satisfaction' must actually be understood as the right to get rid of the obstacles standing in the way of a much more generalised injunction to get satisfaction, so that every 'right' is redescribed as the right to unending 'X-satisfaction', in which the X stands for pretty much every demand imaginable under the sun. As a result of this, the new social contract has the paradoxical form of a rule that upholds more or less absolute 'rights' and 'prohibitions' while at the same time allowing for the exception, the prohibition's obscene (unending) transgression, aimed at the assessment and avoidance of any threat to satisfaction. Thus, the new rule of the social becomes in fact a subtle command, an injunction to enjoy yourself that is conditioned upon your implicit 'consent' that the system engages in mass sacrificial projects at home or elsewhere, whose purpose is, allegedly, to get rid of the obstacles which may stand in the way of your full enjoyment, thereby 'guaranteeing' your satisfaction.

In the post-1970s global political economy, capitalism becomes 'a social system refueled by value sources from its past or from cultures viewed as marginal to its "normal" path of development' (Kemple, 1995: 154; Hardt and Negri, 1994, 2000; Coronil, 1997, 2000a, 2000b) that it has to contain, both to include and keep apart. This is why the language of the new social contract is plagued with a highly medicalised form of double-speak: palliative or 'supplementary citizenship' instead of world citizenship or full nationality in the case of migrants, 'pleasure in work' instead of free time and political control of your own life, 'pre-emptive action' instead of re-colonisation in violation of international law, and 'development with security', 'liberal peace' or 'democratic security' instead of self-government in the case of the former Third World, which has now 'moved' into the former First World and vice versa. At the centre of this momentous transformation lies the scientification of risk (or more precisely, the risk-ification of science) and the desire to recreate all reality – objects, subjects, cultures and so on – in the image of a perpetual motion machine; in short, what animates the system nowadays is a deep-seated fear of the end.

In more concrete terms, capitalism has become global but it is no longer necessarily expansive or inclusive. Rather, as it spreads throughout the entire planet it turns it into a quarantine zone, constantly guarding itself in order to cleanse itself from any risk of contamination. Indeed, the best analogy one can obtain here in order to explain the sort of knowledge and world-view that underlies the practice of contemporary capitalism is with epidemiology. Policymakers in national governments, donor states and international financial institutions, but also private transnational corporations, need to know what in general decreases the risks of disaster, conflict and transformative events (rebellion, the formation of non-liberal complexes and so on) that might threaten their survival and equilibrium. At stake here is the possibility of determining the broad parameters of prevention policy.

Like epidemiology, current approaches to conflict and eventuality, most of them making use of econometric methodology in order to establish correlations between conflict and a variety of potential causes, seek to determine the factors that increase or decrease, in general, the risk of shattering conflicts and events. Once the initial optimism of the post-Cold War era gave way to the sober realisation that globalisation has its perils, the objectives of preventive knowledge, economic growth, survival and equilibrium began to entail the necessity of intervention and transformation of entire societies under risk or in danger of becoming risks themselves.

The same de-realised image of the future that allowed the establishment of value in contemporary capitalism now enables it to posit the 'future value' of actually existing social worlds in terms of their potential otherness. In the jargon of economic policy and rights-based international relations, the term that describes the realisation of this potential otherness is 'development'.[21] Development, understood in this way, has nothing to do with the desire for economic independence that motivated the Third World project since at least the 1970s up to the early twenty-first century. Rather than 'de-linking' in order to re-link (the so-called 'New International Economic Order' that set an alternative agenda for transnational relations via the General Assembly of the UN), 'development' as the becoming-First of the Third world is all about links without a chance to escape. Its most ominous and well-known instantiation is of course the mounting scale of e(x)ternal debt and IMF-driven globalisation, but underlying these widely perceived phenomena there is a less visible confusion between development and security, on the one hand, and potentiality and stability, on the other.

Through processes of 'innovation', 'modernisation' and 'structural stabilisation' or adjustment, global capitalism actively engages in the 'othering' of such actually existing social worlds: from charity and aid, debt and debt-relief, to global governance, intervention, occupation, nation-building and so on. As Mark Duffield explains (2001), war has now become part of development discourse. This becomes evident in the widespread commitment of donor governments and aid agencies to conflict resolution, and in the debates concerning novel conceptions of the use of force and the duty to protect in international law. He argues correctly that the very notion of development has been radicalised in the process and now requires the direct transformation of Third World societies. This entails the confusion of prevention and the future in a thoroughly new understanding of temporality and history. In this new conception the task is not to make history happen but rather, in a reversal of sorts, to prevent it from happening at all by any means necessary.

Duffield writes:

> The optimism of the early post-Cold War years that the world was entering a new era of peace and stability has long since evaporated (...) During the mid-1990s the need to address the issue of conflict became a central concern within mainstream development policy. Once a specialised discipline within international and security studies, war and its effects are now an important part of development discourse. At the same time, development concerns have become increasingly important in relation to how security is understood. It is now generally accepted that international organisations should be aware of conflict and its effects and, where possible, gear their work towards conflict resolution and helping rebuild war-torn societies in a way that will avert future violence. Such engagement is regarded as essential if development and stability are to prevail.
>
> (Duffield, 2001: 1)

Crucially, as he says, the shift in aid policy towards conflict resolution and societal reconstruction must be analysed 'not merely as a technical system of support and assistance, but as part of an emerging system of global governance' (Duffield, 2001: 2). The changing nature of North–South relations now entails that the capitalist world system is no longer necessarily expansive and inclusive, no longer a process of ingestion, but rather a corrective process of containment and de-contamination more akin to aesthetic surgery than to a reflexive practice on ageing and mortality (cfr. Taussig, 2006).

Since the 1970s we have witnessed the concentration of 'formal trade, productive, financial and technological networks' within and between 'the North American, Western European and East Asian regional systems at the expense of outlying areas' (ibid.). Since the inclusion of the South within the conventional global economy can no longer be taken for granted, the nature of security has been reinterpreted so as to focus on the fact that 'underdevelopment has become dangerous' (ibid.).

Duffield explains how 'the threat of an excluded South fomenting international instability through conflict, criminal activity and terrorism is now part of a new security framework' (2001: 2–3). Within such a framework, underdevelopment breeds all sorts of unwanted contaminants that should be contained and kept at bay. The notion of development is radicalised along these lines: conflict resolution, containment and social reconstruction are incorporated within aid policy, while aid policy is made to stand in for the lack of any political resolve to end conflict, a move that amounts to a commitment to transform societies as a whole. On the one hand, this results in humanitarianism becoming 'the lowest international common denominator' (Duffield, 2001: 79), while on the other hand, persistent conflict and the subsequent flow of conflict-resolution aid get together in a confusing embrace. Societies outlying the formal global economic network come to depend upon persistent conflict and conflict-prevention aid to maintain links with the centres of such a network, while the centres relate to the peripheries in the mode of de-contamination and containment units.

Persistent conflicts are often the consequence of a much feared and poorly understood 'shadow globalisation', but the latter is recognised or announced only in order to be prevented or averted. Thus prevention and intervention become the very form of the relationship between central and peripheral nodes of the global network. In this landscape, politics and economics become a branch of epidemiology. Consequently, projects of transformation and radical intervention are conceived upon the basis of epidemiological models. In such models, the notion that grievances play no role in causing conflicts, particularly armed conflicts, is central. These models are developed on the back of much-quoted findings in a number of major econometrical studies, in spite of the fact that econometrics has no way of directly measuring grievances and other attitudinal variables such as fear, envy, humiliation or hatred. Sometimes income inequality is used as a proxy for grievance in these studies. Where it has been used, the studies found no relation between inequality and civil war (Mack, Humphreys and Weinstein, 2004; Humphreys and Weinstein, 2007), and this result has become a mantra in the newly emerging field of development and security studies. Rather, war is a matter of risk-taking and risk-prevention. According to these models, even former rebels such as the Revolutionary Armed Forces of Colombia behave like reasonable economic agents. It is hoped that they will react accordingly to projects of radical intervention, containment and prevention.

Such projects are at work in Iraq as much as in Colombia, and as we now know, after Iraq and Afghanistan, individual Northern governments cannot carry them out. No matter how powerful they may be in military terms, it is beyond their capabilities and legitimacy: 'in this respect, the changing nature of North–South relations is synonymous with a shift from hierarchical and territorial relations of government to polyarchical, non-territorial and networked relations of governance' (Duffield, 2001: 79). Replace 'polyarchical, non-territorial and networked" with concrete assemblages between Northern interventionist governments, Southern anxious elites, fearful but mobile populations, NGOs, military establishments and private companies, and you obtain a very precise picture of the world we live in.

When in November 2007 the far right-wing government of Colombia, under strong criticism for its poor Human Rights record and alleged links to paramilitary forces, engaged in a subtle and more or less focused PR campaign throughout Europe, particularly the UK, it soon became clear how such a strategy revealingly exemplified the changing nature of North–South relations. The then Colombian Deputy Minister of Defence presented to a mostly European audience a nightmarish future scenario in which 'poor' illegal migration routes from Africa to Europe turn into 'rich' drug-smuggling routes, aided and abetted by former Colombian rebels now morphed into drug-trafficking entrepreneurs. Unwillingly or not, the Minister, and afterwards the Vice-President of the South American country, projected an image of doom in order to avert it. The aim was to get their potential European donors frightened enough so as to make them go into their pockets and help fund the 'democratic security' policy that, allegedly, would stop the future scenario from becoming a reality. Grievances, whether political or historical, played no role in the announced globalisation of Colombia's civil war, just as they played no role in the internal conflict itself.

There are at least two problems with the strategy and the argument underpinning it. First, it makes 'democratic security' policy unverifiable, since the fact that the announced scenario of doom does not take place neither confirms it nor falsifies it; it remains an unrealised possibility with no chance of mobilising us into any other form of action than mere acting-out or immediate passage-to-act. The result is sacrificial inaction. Second, it neglects or actively downplays the wider context of the argument: the fact that Northern governments now command their Southern equals to become 'self-reliant', a demonstration of the fact that the model of capitalist globalisation as inclusion has now been abandoned, and all that remains to do for 'Third World' countries is self-victimisation, doom-mongering and begging. Indeed, the more immediate context of the Colombian government's plight to the Europeans was the drop in US military-related aid in the hands of a Democrat-led US Congress.

To conclude, the lesson of globalisation is not that of the seemingly inexorable march forward of capitalism. That might have been the consensus until the 1970s but it is no more (Hirst and Thompson, 1996). From this period onwards, 'while market relations have continued to deepen in core areas, the future of capitalism as a globally expansive and inclusive system has been increasingly questioned' (Duffield, 2001: 3; Hopkins and Wallerstein, 1996 and Wallerstein, 2002). An extensive review of the existing quantitative information about global economic influence, cited by Duffield, reveals that in general, and with the exception of the emergence of some east Asian countries, the loci of economic power and influence in the world 'have remained remarkably stable for the past several hundred years' (Duffield: 2001: 3–4; Hoogvelt, 1997: 69–89).

If this is the case, then, to abuse Žižek, the lesson of globalisation is obtainable only at the level of a meaningless truth taken as the master's voice. It is not true to say that capitalism organises the world, or traverses all possible worlds, because it does not take into account noise, contingency and disorder (the changing nature of laws, the variety of a world cut up into forms): it is neither order nor disorder, but mere void taken as command, or void and stasis as a programme. This becomes evident in contemporary aid policy, which in general and in relation to the new wars of containment, continues to exhibit a mechanical and quasi-Leibnizian view of reality: a perfect clockwork machine governed by fixed mathematical laws, within which everything can be determined, predicted and reduced to a case within the given set of all possibilities. The key terms in such policy are 'democratic security' or 'liberal peace', which combine and conflate 'liberal' and 'democratic', on the one hand, with 'security' and 'peace', on the other. As Duffield observes (2001: 11), the first pair of these related termini entails contemporary liberal and economic tenets, while the second represents policy predilection towards conflict resolution and social reconstruction.

Ultimately, this is an altogether medical operation – to heal suffering, to quarantine contaminated areas, to mobilise rapid de-contamination units, to rehabilitate and provide immediate relief, to prevent the return of the repressed. Prevention looms large in this new medicalisation of politics and policy, embodied in a political humanitarianism that emphasises the reconstruction of the social fabric (*tejido*, which in Spanish refers also to the body's muscular tissue), the promotion of the rule of law and security sector reform 'in the context of a functioning market economy' (Duffield, 2001: 11).

Paradoxically, this new medicalisation of society and the world seems to aim at normality and stasis via a radical developmental agenda of transformation. The radical sense of this paradox is tamed through the investment of developmental tools and strategies with palliative, 'ameliorative, harmonising, and transformational powers that, it is hoped, will reduce violent conflict and prevent its ocurrence' (ibid.). As can be seen, new humanitarianism presents us with a 'preventive hope' rather than a 'projective hope'. The problem is that, as has been argued in this book, 'preventive hope' is a self-defeating and immobilising notion both in theory and in practice. If we hope that something will not happen, the fact that it does not happen cannot be taken as a confirmation of the hope or the prediction it entails. It merely remains an unrealised possibility; as Dupuy puts it, 'the event must be possible for us to have a reason to act; but if our action is effective it will not take place' (2004: 29). We act, but our actions become, at best, a form of cost–benefit analysis caught in a time warp, and at worst, suicidal.

Building upon Dupuy's insight, it is possible to explain the paradox that lies at the heart of globalisation. The paradox entailed by the idea of a preventive hope, which is central to the current merging of development and security in the context of globalisation, derives from the failure of the past prediction implicit in the hope and the future event to come together in a closed loop. For all its investment in the future, capitalism does not need a future world and it does not create one. It empties all of them, virtual and actual. Contemporary imperialism must be understood, in this respect, as the emptying-out of worlds and the evacuation of time. From this perspective, liberal imperial command appears as an in-built necessity of capitalism, derived from its denial of mortality and contingency: whenever capitalism is faced with actual social worlds that project themselves, actively seeking radically alternative futures, it replaces them with an image of unrealised possibilities.

Put otherwise, liberal imperial command announces that for every existing social world there is 'a plan', an open diversity of possible futures that always remain unrealised possibilities or else, conversely, an undesirable catastrophe that must be averted. Since in none of these cases there is need for closure, the result is a hope or a forecast that does not have to come true, for the announced plan or hope is not in fact the future at all, but a possible world that is and will remain inactual (Dupuy, 2004: 29). So, it is not only the case that capitalistic time is devoid of world, rather the time of capitalism makes worlds void.

In order to understand that there is more to these paragraphs than mere ideological posturing, we must abandon the notion that the only transformation that counts is subjective transformation (an active agent, choosing one out of manifold possible worlds), that the future is potentially open, and that there is no world and no future outside thought, language and calculation. These notions continue to presume that the world 'out there' is practico-inert and appeal to fixed conceptions of necessity, contingency and possibility as what may or may not occur. Consequently, they freeze time and represent it as bifurcating into a series of successive branches, the actual world being one among them. So-called 'cognitive mapping' becomes in this scenario an exercise in forecasting. Language and probabilistic calculus are its medium, doom-saying becomes the weapon of choice: to announce the future in order to avert it. However, as said before, the announced or forecast future is no future at all, but merely a possible world that is and will remain forever non-actual. What is needed, in contrast, is to include space-time, contingency and the activity of objects independent of our experience of them – the thing-sound, a call from the past; the thing-image, a riddle that comes from the future – in our discourses and actions, and in the analyses of such discourses and actions.

The claims of the linguistic/probabilistic turn in philosophy were once but are no longer liberating. The problem of truth is not simply how to establish something – a common language, a non-contradictory logics, a law-like explanation – that remains the same in all possible worlds, against, say, postmodern relativism (the allegedly irreducible multitude of worlds, bodies and languages). This probabilistic notion of truth freezes time. It says: if something is true, it is true for all time, and in particular, probabilistic/mathematical truth is true for all time – the sort of 'Platonism' denounced by people such as Roberto Unger and Lee Smolin (Unger and Smolin, 2005; Smolin, 2006: 30–5). As Unger and Smolin put it, if law-like explanations are posited and expressed in mathematics, and mathematical truth is deemed eternal, so must be laws and law-like explanations (he calls this mathematics a 'poisoned gift' to physics). Similarly, if laws change, there must be a rational account of how and why they change. This account becomes, in turn, unchanging.

After them and others, we may argue that what is needed is a non-Platonic, or rather non-Pythagorean account of truth, a mathematics that liberates itself from the clutches of probabilism, and ultimately from the isomorphism between being and thought (or mathematical ideality) and brings forth the force of time rather than arresting it. Philosopher Quentin Meillassoux and others locate this possibility in the 'Cantorian revolution' (2007: 64–9) and the reinstatement of intuition, but we may also require a more assertive way to de-link the object and legality from their mathematical inscription. To reinstate the rights of intellectual intuition will simply not do the job, as Brassier and Harman have argued.[22] If so, then we must ask: how can we de-link laws and the object from their ideal inscription without falling back onto a transcendental divide between sensible and intelligible, between reality and ideality?

For now, all that can be said in relation to such a question will have the form of an initial and incomplete exploration: rather than conceiving laws as prescriptive in relation to objects, as their fixed background existing at a meta-level (that of ideality) we could think of the objects as background-independent, that is to say, capable of escaping from the law-like system of effects. In this case, the objects themselves define the background, the legality, and the latter varies as a consequence of the alteration in the position of the objects covered or indexed by it. It is not the case that laws are the 'ideal' or meta-physical indexing of discrete objects and cases, but rather that the indexation is an effect of real objects moving in and out of sets and systems of relations. 'Thought' or conceptuality (the indexation of the cases and objects under rules and the exceptions related to these rules) is an effect of the movement of the objects themselves, as they approximate and escape one another; it is actually a form of sensuality rather than an exception to sensuality. To say this is to entail that thought cannot assert its rights over and above the sensuality of objects, that it occupies no position of exception in respect of being and can be distinguished from it only as an indexation of the current (or virtual) effects of an object upon others, or as generative of ideal/sensual objects probing the depths of sensuality and loosely connecting real objects themselves. Put otherwise, this is to conceive thought as primarily engaged in objectification, as self-reflexive but incomplete. In turn, since the objects are always more than what they are, always hiding in invisibility while sensually fascinating other elements, their being is always more than the sum total of their (sensual) effects. Thought and mathematical ideality indexes the sensual effects that objects have upon other objects, and generate (or postulate) sensual objects that separate a thing from its quality, thereby allowing for connectivity between objects without exhausting their reality since the latter goes beyond their presence in relation.

In this sense, perhaps it is not too far-fetched to propose that the relationship between an indexical law and its object has the structure of an in-closed loop: the postulated law is verifiable only to the extent that it refers to the sensuality of an object, its presence-in-relation, but since this is a phenomenon that does not pertain to the law or concept itself (it is not 'created' by it), to be entirely truthful, the law or concept must include within itself the possibility of minimal failure, that is to say, the improbable, the absenting or withdrawal of the object-reference. Put otherwise, a concept is not a case of pure self-reference (the case of a concept that indexes an 'in-itself' that becomes present for the sake of the concept) but rather a self-reflexive structure that must include (to be 'truthful') the inevitability of a minimal failure, corresponding to the alteration of the indexed set of relations that follows the withdrawal of the object.

Put otherwise, objects do not enter into sensual relations (leading to indexation, legality and concept-formation) for the sake of the concept, but rather as a consequence of their own unfolding, their inner tension between presence and absence, relationality and specificity, and it is this process which defines a (changing) legality or conceptuality. In turn, the concept is 'true', only if it includes, within itself, the inevitability of variation and the absenting of the object from relations. Concept, legality, thought, all of them are true only insofar as they stand up to the 'foreignness' within themselves: the absenting reality-object. Legality neither supports nor constitutes reality, but indexes or frames variations thereof.

In music, literature and the visual arts, the equivalent of the in-closed loop is the cut-up technique. More generally, we could speak of a world cut up into forms, or organised according to a cut-up technique, on the condition that these are conceived as at least partially invisible forms, forms unheard of, which withdraw from other objects and relations 'even while inflicting wounds upon them' (Harman, 2002: 9). These forms may be partially invisible or unheard of, but they are compelling. We could speak of the laws of such a process (of forms unfolding, wrapping and unwrapping themselves within forms), but in the sense of evolving laws that are not just rooted in some more or less static meta-law or prescriptive background.

The true problem is how to include time variation in our relational and law-like explanations of reality. The bulk of the matter is that it is easier to grasp the notion of the totality of nature by stating the laws of nature, as Unger points out, but to state the laws of nature, or any other postulated totality, is not to explain all possible histories or prescriptions that remain the same for/of all possible universes. This totality and its laws, any law-like explanation, is only relatively different from the narration of a time historical sequence. It is not the set of all possible historical sequences, which is impossible. The totality/law-like explanation only emerges in actuality, the one time-historical sequence of a natural singularity or object. It is what is more in the object than what the object is, an alluring real object, not only in the sense that the object has the potential to become something else in a possible future, but rather in the sense that alteration (its own alteration) is always/already the case in the current actuality of the object, even if we can never dream of such depths and their call (or 'allure') remains meaningless to us.

Relations are graspable only as changes or alterations in the current actuality of objects, as the split of an object from its quality, and therefore, as vicarious. That is why anti-fetishist critique has run out of steam: it is not enough to denounce the incarnation of a relation in a thing or a person as fetishism, irresolvable paradox, or reification. That once liberating sort of criticism is now in danger of becoming insufficient and irrelevant. It is becoming irrelevant because it misses the fact that we, the observers, make common cause with fetish-objects, for they stabilise our relations. And it is becoming insufficient because it sets aside the power of fetishes on their own, their ability to enter into and escape from relations (also relations with us). Such a criticism appeals to fixed notions of necessity, contingency and possibility which are simply confusing. It is time we dispel that confusion, and one way of doing so is to understand that paradox is not always irresolvable contradiction, but also alteration.

Such a perspective is still marginal, but its time is coming. Although popular contemporary critics such as Slavoj Žižek do not always oppose the perspective of critique as anti-fetishism, it may be argued that the second perspective (that of our common cause with objects) exerts upon them a stronger attraction. This perspective has explanatory powers of its own, which do not cease to emerge and alternate with the other model, against the taboo established by a certain differential relationism upon variation, noise, disorder and the veiled performance of things. Repeating Plato, the latter condemns phenomena such as sensuality and noise as the prime cause of unwanted behaviour. In doing so, it forecloses any investigation on the emergence of order out of disorder, of worlds organised according to a cut-up technique, of time-varying laws and fetish-like objects, and flattens the space of political and aesthetic experimentation.[23]

Notes

1 See Zubiri (1963) and Meillassoux (2007: 76).
2 For the elements of a critique of such a form of non-realism see Bhaskar (1997; 1990). See also Vernes (1981).

3 See Meillassoux (2006). I first came across this path-breaking study of the 'probabilistic fallacy' through Graham Harman, after having finished this manuscript text. The resonance between the case presented by Meillassoux, some of the arguments advanced here and the criticism initiated in the 1970s by Rom Harré and Roy Bhaskar among others, in the analytical philosophy of science, is obvious and striking. The more interested reader would surely benefit from considering these arguments together.
4 For the distinction between chance and contingency referred to here, see Meillassoux (2007: 70–2). The term 'caged freedom' is his.
5 Unger's observations were made in the context of a wider discussion between cosmology and socio-legal theory on the subject of time and evolving laws. The discussion took place in a workshop at the Perimeter Institute for Theoretical Physics on 16–17 August 2005, convened by Roberto M. Unger and cosmologist Lee Smolin. The audio record of the workshop is available online at www.perimeterinstitute.ca/activities/scientific/cws/evolving_laws/agenda.php. Notice how Unger's and Smolin's observations converge with Jean-Pierre Dupuy's defence of counterfactual reasoning in ethics and also with Meillassoux's insights about radical novelty. For the source of the paraphrases in this paragraph, see Dupuy (2004: 8).
6 See Meillassoux (2007: 64–81), Dupuy (2004: 19), Zubiri (1974), Ellacuría (1990) and Dussel (1998).
7 See on this Friedmann (1981) and Schotter (1983). See also Dupuy (1998). All quotes taken from Dupuy.
8 This is the argument to be found in Montesquieu, Hume, and Steuart. See Dupuy (1998: 332–5) for some of the lines of thought followed in these paragraphs.
9 See also Dupuy (1998: 339).
10 For an argument against the possibility of a pure act of collective self-legislation, see Lindhal (2007).
11 Moreiras is quoting Carl Schmitt (1996: 67).
12 This in reference to the argument put forward by Klein (2007).
13 See Meillassoux (2007: 64).
14 See Bhaskar (1997) and Meillassoux (2007: 55–81, at 65, n. 3).
15 See on this Kant (1929: A485). See also Russel (1921: 159), cited by Borges (1970: 27–43, at 34).
16 See Borges (1970: 33–4 and 37). Borges observes, tellingly, that 'this monism or complete idealism invalidates all science'.
17 I am indebted to Graham Harman for this crucial point.
18 See note above.
19 To quote Ilya Prigogine: 'In conclusion, elemental particles are unstable; almost all of them. They are far from constituting the permanent support of transforming appearances, as they were thought of by atomic theories. Contemporary cosmology obliges us to face a history of the universe and a consequential display of structures, which are higher in complexity every time. Finally, traditional macroscopic phenomena, in particular those studied by chemistry, biology and hydrodynamics, have changed their image. Everywhere we discover the causal and the irreversible.' See Prigogine (1983: 221–3). See also Prigogine and Nicolis (1997).
20 Following Stiegler, 'technics' is understood here as 'the horizon of all possibility to come and of all possibility of a future' (1998: ix), but also in the sense of 'technical entities' or composite objects that, according to the philosophical canon, do not have any dynamic of their own. It is well-known that the origin of this canon is a political debate in which the philosopher accuses the sophist

of instrumentalising *logos* as a tool for power to the detriment of knowledge. This is the inherited context in which the philosophical *ēpistēmē* is set against the sophistic *tekhnē*, whereby all technical knowledge and production is devalued, as per Aristotle: 'Every natural being has within itself a beginning of movement and rest (. . .) [whereas] no one product of art has the source of its own production within itself' (1984: Book 2, I: 329). This paragraph is quoted by Stiegler (1998: 1). See also Simondon (1958: 35) and Leroi-Gourhan (1993: 114–15).

21 The leading work on the destructive function of the discourse on development is that of cultural anthropologist Arturo Escobar. For a more recent appraisal, see Escobar (forthcoming).

22 For the problems Meillassoux runs into while abandoning Pythagoreism in favour of the claim that being is inherently accessible to intellectual intuition, see Brassier (2007b: 15–54), See also Harman (2006).

23 On the cut-up as a form of politics and jurisprudence, see Geary, A. (2005).

Chapter 9

Sex, laws and rock 'n' roll

On music as a radical organising principle

Rip it up and start again

The most recent example of the cut-up technique in popular culture is *Take Me Out*, a song composed and performed by post-punk Glaswegians Franz Ferdinand. The video-clip, which in this case is part of the performance rather than just a vehicle for the song, is a montage of early twentieth-century avant-garde images in the style of Russian Constructivism and Bauhaus design. They are reminiscent of the way Hans Arp used to tear apart his drawings, throw them up in the air and then glue the fragments on a surface in the order they have fallen on the ground. They also remind us of Franz Radziwill's city landscapes, cut-up in the painting's composition but also by carpet-bombing.[1] The same goes for Franz Ferdinand's music: just as it occurs with the imagery and the iconography, their music follows the pattern established in the last century in literature and the visual arts by avant-garde artists in Europe, Latin America and the likes of William S. Burroughs and Bryon Gysin in North America: to refrain from following the straight line, to interrupt the vicious circle of self-referentiality, via the random rearrangement of text, sound and image.

According to the cut-up principle, 'refrain' and 'randomness' allow us to decode the hidden meaning of a text, a sound or an image. Such a 'hidden' meaning is political, but not in the sense that politics is the *true* or 'transparent' meaning of a given text or an image. On the contrary, political meaning is skewed, curbed, interrupted meaning or meaninglessness – nothing like the faithfulness of straight or 'truthful' talk, understood as the transmission of information without deformation. Mladen Dolar has coined the term 'enunciation without statement' for this dimension of the political. His gesture is not unlike that of Peruvian avant-garde poet César Vallejo, who coined the term 'spoken cough' ('*toz*') in order to refer to a practice of interrupting or splitting talk. A voice split from its quality allows for an interesting political and poetic effect: reverse engineering, copying and transformation.

The practice of interrupting talk, text or sound and starting again allows, on the one hand, the (re)grouping or aggregation of several disparate parts or demands into one (the process known in law and politics as 'legitimate representation') and on the other, the converse process of disseminating the one into several. In this respect, the notion of interrupted talk or 'enunciation without statement' conveys the idea of law's inherent alterity or necessary contingency, and permits a distinction between an excessive dimension without meaning that compels us to take a stance, to engage and provide new meaning out of nothing, and the positing of fully meaningful commands that exclude our engagement and appear as the static meta-level that supports our more or less blind actions. The space marked by these related but different modalities of voice and sound – the excessive call and the posited command – entails the possibility to refrain from following a straight line by randomly rearranging the text or providing an unexpected meaning or content to a call *out of nothing*.

It is well known that the randomness of Burroughs is one with a very limited definition: the cut-up is random only as far as its results are unintended, that is, if there is no *a priori* principle or immanent teleology establishing the form of the resultant object. That is different from chance coincidence or spontaneity; rather, it pertains to some inherent obstacle that simultaneously *breaks* the flow of talk, discourse or performance (music, images, etc.) and *breaks it up*, curbs it, thus preventing it from reaching itself as its end. The result is novelty. In conclusion, the performance finds its accomplishment in the retroactive articulation of partial sounds, words, objects or images. The same phenomenon is at work in the political constitution of a network of demands. In this book we have gone further, daring to postulate this phenomenon at the level of ontology. It entails rendering historical time mutable or, more precisely 'entangled', and its laws as changing laws. Rather than sorting out the elements of reality into matter and reasoning (the basics of the centuries-old theories of reflection), 'the way things are' may mask a more fundamental layer of reality: that of evolving forms or 'information', to use the language of the digital era.

Franz Ferdinand is retro-garde and modernism *avant la lettre*. In this respect, their performance shares something with the majority of counter-cultural expressions of the last three decades: counter-culture has produced its own DIY engagement with the machine world of cultural capitalism and network democracy 'at a level at once frighteningly Futurist and retroactively Avant-garde'. Van Veen, whom I just sampled, explains it thus:

> The digitization of information rendered history immanently mutable, and thus, forgettable. *Musique concrete* had become just another email attachment to the virus of history. But this self-executing message sold a promise, and it was opened by others, at least to allow the virus of history to take hold of the potential that the machine promised. Areferential sound could promise the plug-in of ahistoricity, and it defined the ambiguous historical moment of this emerging post-subculture.

This mix of post-subcultures that we shall recognise as mediatized micro cultures of technology.

(Van Veen, 2002)

What is most interesting about the sound art of the last three decades is precisely its refrain from historicity but, allegedly, only with the advent of (digital) technology artists have been able to recognise and develop its radical novelty. As the name of the band indicates (Franz Ferdinand was the Archduke of Austria who died in a political bombing by anarchists in Sarajevo, signalling the start of the First World War) there is a retroactive reference to a time of explosive creativity geared to radical political struggle and ordinary mass violence – a bit like ours. This was the time of revolution, also the time of an amazingly intensified investment of productive energies in the creation of new and unexpected means of expression. The more cynical reader may ask: is the gesture of these musicians mere nostalgia, or rather an act of radical innovation in the history of avant-garde refrain in sound art?

As suggested above, rather than avant-garde we should speak of retro-garde.[2] According to Van Veen the avant-garde returned to music as an exploration of what he calls the a-referential, that is to say, the aesthetics of minimal failure and interruption (as a break-down in composition). This 'return' is evident in the performance of other sound artists such as Punk Jazz musician Matthew Bourne or Jem Fine, also a member of punk band The Pogues. In their work, the return of a-referentiality becomes an unforeseeable innovation. There is a moment in *Take Me Out* in which the composition breaks down, is ripped apart and starts again. This would be equivalent to exploring the moment where software and hardware fail, or in politics, to examine the emergence of political demands as a result of the failure of the legal–political machine. But in contrast to the theories that conceive failure as a dysfunction of the system that can be sidelined in the present and corrected in a possible future, these new explorations see failure and inherent alterity as the very foundation of the socio-political and aesthetic field.

What applies to music, also applies to the field of politically engaged philosophy: 'to explore the point where the transactional moment produces the unexpected glitch (or ghost) in the Machine', as Van Veen puts it (2003: 4). The ghost in the machine is the remainder, the part of no-part whose recombination or alluring power allows alteration and radical innovation beyond 'history' (conceived as the given set of all cultural possibilities). As he explains, when 'history', that is to say, the possibility of innovation, was found wanting or 'ending', it was thought that one could only do genealogy, deconstruction and social movement micro-politics. As Van Veen explains, the downside of this shift from political counter/sub-cultures to ambiguous micro-cultures tendency is that for all their apparent radicality, the burn-out effect of new social movements, deconstruction, rave culture and the crash of the Dot-Com industry provoked a retreat into a-historical formalist politics, philosophy and aesthetics. To some, this retreat was a welcome return to formalist art, proper philosophy and institutional politics that had been abandoned or were neglected in the era of counter-cultural politics.

Van Veen thinks otherwise; speaking between politics and music he observes: 'the micropoliticos had in fact come full swing, as Kim Cascone notes, to dig through the high-art tradition of electronic music. Names such as Pierre Boulez, Morton Subotnick, and John Cage began to resonate in the non-academic circles that once dosed E and danced all night to slamming techno. Marinetti, Russolo, the Futurists and *musique concrète* were in; dancing was out' (ibid.). He asks: 'What was forgotten while skipping in that way over the history of subcultures?' (ibid.) The answer is the relationship between outsider cultural resistance, the underground understanding of the concept of resistance through movement and in movement (that is, the kernel of truth in so-called subcultural politics) and, most important of all, 'the forgetful place in which the prior avant-garde becomes reinscribed' in the contemporary music and cultural moment.

Van Veen points out that in the shift from counter-culture to microcultures we skip over the ways in which the political came to be remixed, in music and elsewhere, as a mobile fight not only against State and Capital, but also in opposition to other institutional frameworks, such as law and gender relations, that attempted to define and enforce the boundaries of high culture, high politics and their history. Arguably, this is not news: Plato had already identified the mobile nature of rebellious politics when he condemned music as feminine, illicit and leading towards unbound enjoyment and decadence. However, the important point is that by forgetting subcultural history, we also forget the way it challenged and interrupted these supposedly self-sufficient frameworks; and by forgetting the challenges of the prior avant-garde, we ahistorically posit the new experiments in political and cultural theory, as well as in music, as both radically innovative and yet the return of history (Van Veen, 2003).

Anarchy in the UK: on temporary autonomous zones

A biographical note posted on the website of Franz Ferdinand is indicative in this respect: perhaps the band's most important creation to date has not been one of its hits on the charts, but rather, a place called The Castle, a location of which one cannot speak in positive terms for it is a trans-critical *topos*, an enunciation without statement, a space for intercultural transposition and critique.

At one point The Castle was a derelict building in a part of Glasgow surrounded by extreme poverty and social deprivation, populated, to use the band's own terms, by 'vermin'. It is here – in this outside – where the collective effort coalesced, bringing together different forms of artistic expression whose fusion forms the basis of their cultural output. Even though music has become the more obvious means of expression of this collective to outsiders and consumers, it is clear from both the history of the band, its versatility and its references, that it is actually just one of the many elements put together in the concoction. To bring the point back home, this articulation is not merely aesthetic, in the pejorative sense, but also political. This explains the reaction of the Clyde police to what quickly became a meeting point of creative forces in the socio-economic margins of Glasgow.

According to the story, which can be found on the band's website, it took the police over a month to find The Castle. After weeks of driving around in circles, following rumours and noise, the police finally stormed the place. Not only does this show how a well-ordered society functions on the basis of the enclosure of the commons, following a logic of de-contamination, exclusion and inclusion; it also demonstrates how a partial object can become the substitute of a universal declaration of freedom and how the logic of substitution works through the formation of partial identities. In this case the partial object is The Castle (as disseminated in a dozen songs, exhibitions, performances, etc.). Incidentally, objects of a similar kind can be found in the work of other resistant communities attempting to create a space of liberation (even if limited and temporary), for instance the fantasy location known as Aztlán, which is also the transcritical place of origin of the urban and ambivalently included Chicano community in the United States.

It is the ambivalence of the inclusion that matters here. Chicanos and other Latino/a identities are fully included in the present order of the United States, but are not treated as members that count in that order. Identities become politically mobile, rather than all-inclusive, because they are entangled with the ambivalence of inclusion in today's cultural capitalist and network-democratic society. Put otherwise, what matters is not identity politics but identity in politics, as cultural anthropologist Walter Mignolo has observed.

As the story above suggests, The Castle has only a family resemblance with 'squatting' in post-1970s Britain. The point is not to take over, but rather to carve out a space and de-link it from the existing network of relations. In this case the occupants mixed legal and extra-legal arrangements (yes, they did have an arrangement with the landlord but, no, electricity and other utilities were not being supplied with the knowledge of the providers) but were still being perceived as an obstacle interrupting the desire of law-abiding citizens to full peace and happiness, to law and order. The legal framework set in motion by the police involved in this case the laws of licensing, criminal laws related to the running of a bar without appropriate authorisation, disturbance of the peace, and other legal forms associated with peace and security, social order and tranquillity; in short, the set of laws whose aim is the cleansing of 'vermin'. This is the same kind of ambivalent legality regarded by Michel Foucault as paradigmatic of latter-day societies of control, that he termed 'normalisation'.

The 'birth' of Franz Ferdinand occurs precisely there, in the cracks of today's society of control. Their cultural output (by means of which Franz Ferdinand is articulated as the name of a collective) is itself instrumental in that emergence, its very form being that of the traversing of fantasy and the interruption of the drive that breaks it and breaks it up, disturbs it, thereby interrupting the flow of the drive towards its given end. Perhaps it is not altogether coincidental that Franz Ferdinand's songs often sound as the impossible merge between two pieces: one that does not actually know when to end and another that does not know when to begin. All we hear is the in-between, a cut which renders the sound material convertible and amenable to reordering in radically new ways. The image that comes to mind is that of an element at a crossroads, a figure connected with the innovative destiny of narrative and music, and ultimately with everything that is not at all contained in the precedent situation.[3]

Just like a cut that opens up crossroads in the middle of a song, The Castle functions precisely as an interzone that comes to be seen as an end itself. After the repressive stance taken by the Glasgow police, The Castle kept changing location, neither here nor there but in between. The aim of the music and the collective's existence becomes then absolutely clear: *to bring forth out of nothing and always occupy an autonomous zone*. Thus we learn on the band's website that the 'band currently lives in the garden of The Castle'.

In this respect Franz Ferdinand has something in common with other forms of contemporary sound that seek to disrupt the scene of popular music. The literature on the political significance of DIY art, punk, electronic music, micromusic, rave culture and 'get your own label' neo-punk teaches us about the meaning of so-called 'temporary autonomous zones' as actually existing interzones, spaces of rebellion and liberation. This melting of space and time with music and political activism was theorised concurrently by people such as Achim Szepanski and Hakim Bey, who gave name to the temporary autonomous zone (or TAZ).

In a section titled 'Music as an Organizational Principle', Hakim Bey describes the history and meaning of TAZ as follows:

> When escape beyond the frontier proved impossible, the era of revolutionary urban Communes began in Europe. The Communes of Paris, Lyons and Marseilles did not survive long enough to take on any characteristics of permanence, and one wonders if they were meant to. From our point of view the chief matter of fascination is the spirit of the Communes. During and after these years anarchists took up the practice of revolutionary nomadism, drifting from uprising to uprising, looking

to keep alive in themselves the intensity of spirit they experienced in the moment of insurrection (. . .) Makhno's Ukraine and anarchist Spain were meant to have duration, and despite the exigencies of continual war both succeeded to a certain extent: not that they lasted a "long time", but they were successfully organized and could have persisted if not for outside aggression. Therefore from among the experiments of the inter-War period I'll concentrate instead on the madcap Republic of Fiume, which is much less known and was not meant to endure.

(Bey, 2003: 122–4)

Hakim Bey goes on to explain the significance of the extraordinary experiment set up by Gabrielle D'Annunzio after he and the small army known as 'Arditi' emerged from the First World War as heroes, captured the city of Fiume, and declared it independent from Italy and everywhere else. Bey observes: '[D'Annunzio] and one of his anarchist friends wrote the constitution, which declared music to be the central principle of the state' (2003: 123). The liberated city became a refuge to artists, bohemians, adventurers, free women, pirates, anarchists, fugitives and stateless figures, homosexuals, and crank reformers of every stripe. The party went on for eighteen months at the end of which the Italian army finally showed up at its shores and brought the experiment to an end. Although lacking the seriousness of Ukraine or Barcelona, the destiny of Fiume (including D'Annunzio's embrace and later denunciation of Fascism; *Il Duce* had him killed in his old age), deeply rooted in the history of maroon cities and pirate utopias in Europe and the Caribbean, some of whom persist to this day, can be taken, according to Bey, as a blueprint for the contemporary TAZ.

He emphasises the common trends between Fiume and the Paris uprising of May 1968, as well as with the counter-cultural communes in the Americas. Chief among them is the importance of aesthetic theory (from Situationism to Magical Realism), pirate economics, the concept of music as a principle for revolutionary social change and crucially, the shared perception of their own contingency, their capacity to move on (Bey, 2003: 124). From the much misunderstood Munich Council Republic of 1919 and the participation of Gustav Landauer as Minister of Culture to 'networking' as an alternative to hierarchical politics (from ACT UP to today's World Social Forum) and a generalised strategy of 'refusal', the Bartleby-like politics recently recovered by engaged thinkers such as Alain Badiou and Slavoj Žižek, Bey outlines the concept/intervention he termed TAZ not as an escapist strategy of never coming back, but rather as withdrawal, absenting and invisibility, in a sense that comes closer to the mathematical meaning of the term 'catastrophe': a sudden topological change (Bey, 2003: 130).

TAZ was to become a meme across cyberculture, spread by San Francisco magazine *Mondo 2000* and Semiotext(e), BBS relays and eventually the World Wide Web. It resonated with punk, certain strains of hip-hop and electronic music, and cyberculture itself, envisioning digital technology in the service of TAZ, as a means to make possible its emergence. Aware of the fact that the web has nowadays become synonymous with commerce and surveillance, a mirror of global capital, Bey attaches now the constitutional project of music as an organisational principle of the state to the transition from our media-ridden lives (and their 'mediated freedom') to the un-mediated, radical experience of topological change. He writes: 'the TAZ must exist in geographical odorous tactile tasty physical space (...) otherwise it's no more than a blueprint or a dream' (2003: xi).

However, as Tobias Van Veen observes, the long-lasting influence of the TAZ link between digitalisation and topological change has been to provoke innumerable challenges across the planet to laws concerning private property, the commons and the liberty to gather – the organisational principle of music, the cut-up technique – so dreaded by Plato and the Blairites, by granting a theoretical framework to the more adventurous members of a new subculture focused around cyberpunk, rave and spatio-temporal intervention – remember the battle of Genoa in July 2001, the closest thing to a 'tipping point' in anti-capitalist politics in recent European history, unfairly buried under the rubble of the Twin Towers.

Since the end of the 1990s this decade has been the era of warehouse break-ins, of the kind found in Franz Ferdinand's story, and sonic squats. TAZ was 'introduced along with the terror of sampling and the sudden challenge to copyright. Property in all forms was being remixed, theft was creative, and the establishment was at a loss for a good 10 years' (Van Veen, 2003: 4–6). In spite of well-known legal victories (the Napster case, iTunes) and the occasional prosecution of a teenager downloading the latest Kaiser Chiefs in the solitude of her university residence, it is fair to say that the industry is still at a loss. There are at least two particularly telling examples in this respect: on the literary front, the 2004 case of the last book written by Nobel-prize winner Gabriel García Márquez, *Memoria de Mis Putas Tristes*. The hacker version hit the streets well before its much flaunted official launch by the publishing house in Spain. A similar case, this time in cinema, occurred in 2007 with the Brazilian 'shadow market' hit *Tropa de Elite*. This is the case of the cultural artefact that circulated before it was actually produced. The second example is the much debated 2007 launch of Radiohead's album *In Rainbows*, which signalled the definitive demise of the mainstream propietary forms of the music industry.

Whatever you think about Radiohead's stunt and the cheeky kids that bought the ten tracks of their new album for nothing, and whether or not this is really year zero for the industry, the consensus is that the existing music system is failing. Music journalist Adam Webb put it thus: 'There is no denying that the major labels *are* in a pretty bad place. The takeover of EMI by private equity firm Terra Firma and plummeting share values elsewhere were startling evidence of this (...) The truth is, most new acts are still interested in signing a record deal [with a major label] and how such dreams are accommodated into a failing system is where the interesting action will take place' (2007: 41).

There is radical innovation in the challenge posed by the new centrality of information and enunciation without a statement. However, we shall steer clear of exaggerating the liberating potential of the transformation of partial cultural objects into (digitalised) information. On the one hand, as Bey points out, this transformation occurs alongside industrial capitalism's renewal as cultural capitalism, based on the circulation of informational objects. It is well known, for instance, the way in which counter-cultures such as rock, punk and hip-hop, which first emerged as acts of resistance and liberation in the face of law and capital, were quickly normalised and re-appropriated, turned into chic commodities with little or no political leverage. But the reinscription of such counter- and sub-cultures in today's digitalised landscape cannot be described as corresponding to the same cycles of appropriation. Already the resistance music of rave culture fell not only to commercialisation, but was also re-appropriated by an elite avant-garde to the point where, as Van Veen asserts, 'the history of rebellious rhythm was erased from the record' (ibid.). Those who run the workshops on digital music and other forms of autonomous expression in the World Social Forum, focusing on the trans-culturality of rhythm, still believe that these musics can be re-appropriated for the purposes of choice and rebellion insofar as, in their function as substitutes, they remain a challenge to established notions of property and sovereignty.

Law, radical choice and rock 'n' roll

Plato thought of music as the prime cause of unwanted mass behaviour threatening the stability of the republic. In doing so, he inaugurated a long and unfortunate tradition of state interference, control of music and youth's expression that links seventh-century BC classical philosophy with the ban on the *Batuques de Negros* – the dance 'n' drums of black slaves in nineteenth-century Brazil (recently portrayed with a twist in *The Matrix Reloaded*), the Orwellian-sounding 'Aborigenes Protection Board' in twentieth-century Australia and the Brain Police.

The question that concerns us, in these different contexts, is the battle to control *who* gets to disseminate *which* sounds (and information) and to *whom*, and to what extent such a dissemination may count as radical innovation. Thus we are also interested in the dynamics of dissemination: identification, mimesis or over-identification? As we will see in the remainder of this chapter, this is no trivial matter. At stake is the wider question of the relationship between expressive freedom, irruption *ex nihilo* and political action or radical choice.

When rock-maverick Frank Zappa asked the question 'who is the Brain Police?' he was pointing at the centrality of the struggle to censor music, the dissemination of resistant sounds and gathering bringing forth unforeseeable virtualities, in the contemporary slippage from politics to police. He argued that resistant sounds and rebellious forms of gathering are at the core of the relationship between expressivity (the dimension of enunciation without statement) and the political constitution of a collective interrupting the drive to order, against attempts to police the collective and complete the death-drive (Zappa, 1968). He thought it paradoxical that the companies selling 'rebel' music for profit would one day be led by young people called to action by these very same music-products. In doing so, Zappa embarked on a long and sustained reflection on the complex relationship between art, law and ideology that prepared the terrain for the likes of Laibach, the 'Good Wave' of new Latin American cinema and Slavoj Žižek.

Decisively, rather than working against these forces of 'corruption' he ritualistically held out his hand to them and, let us say, collaborated in the work of subversion. It is a common criticism against the rebellious nature of popular music that its generic stereotypes are formed and reinforced by the commercial interests that seek to use expressivity for profit. Musicians themselves have often voiced their concerns about this phenomenon: Zappa, for instance, spoke against the 'monochromonotony' of minimalist and serial electronic music linked to foundation monies. What is different about his stance is that he transformed these phenomena not by working against them in self-righteous mode, but rather by over-identifying with and over-activating the forces of corruption.

Thus, for instance, he took on the Beatles' *Sergeant Pepper* album and the whole of 1960s 'counter-culture' by declaring, brutally, that *We're Only In It For The Money*. Somewhat similarly, in their 2006 album *Volk,* post-Punk band Laibach de-composed the national anthems of America, some of the countries in the Middle East (Israel and the Palestinian Authority), Asia and Europe at a time when the liberal Left fatally embraces Human Rights as the (counter) culture of *imperium*. If in *We're Only . . .* overactivation and de-composition gave Zappa the tools to respond to 'the limits imposed on audiences through the mediations of the musical marketplace, in which stable genres equal stable cash-flows' (Fischlin, 2003: 12), in *Volk* the same strategies allow Laibach to respond to the fatal embrace of globalism, in which stable legal–political genres equal stable governance – and cash-flows, all the while sustaining their focus on the power of music as an enunciation without statement or a radical organising principle.

In order to understand the innovative character of this sort of choice/action and its limitations it is necessary to revise our knowledge of the relationship between command/fascination and ideology that structures global law and governance (stable legal standards = stable governance/cash flows), but also the nature of the peculiar phenomenon that results in the production of fixed endogenous points projected into the future, trans-critical spaces and in-between or fetish objects, that support the radical choice of a collective subject.

In his concept album *Joe's Garage* (1979) Frank Zappa provides a trenchant critique of state intervention and the political forces behind the attempt to limit musical expression in order to consolidate state power. In this critique, he provides us with some fundamental insights concerning the relationship between expression (or 'indirect communication') and ideology that may prove useful in order to better our understanding of radical political choice and the interruption of legal interpellation. He writes in the album liner notes:

> All governments perpetuate themselves through the daily commission of acts which a rational person might find to be stupid, or dangerous, or both. Naturally, our government is no exception . . . for instance if the President – any one of them – went on TV and sat there with the flag in the background – or maybe a rustic scene on a little backdrop, plus the flag – and stared sincerely into the camera and told everybody that all energy problems and all inflationary problems had been traced to and could be solved by the abolition of MUSIC, the chances are that most people would believe him and think that the illegalization of this obnoxious form of noise pollution would be a small price to pay for the chance to buy gas like the good ol' days.
> (Zappa, 1979, quoted by Fischlin, 2003: 34)

The point in this passage is the relationship between expressivity – the flag, the image of a rustic landscape, an anthem – the (legal) regulation of the means of expression, and the beliefs that constitute subjects politically. On the one hand, to say that there is a relation between expressivity – the formal and indirect character of one's own expression – and the political constitution of a collective, conveys the notion that social identities are constituted around diffuse symbols and partial objects, for instance a sound or an image (Laclau, 2005).

On the other hand, to posit the question of the (legal) control of expressivity obliges us to consider the wider problem of the (political) management of beliefs. The latter pertains to: (a) a surface dimension or more or less transparent command, which conceives social actors as constituted around well-defined self-interests and 'rationally' negotiating them with their surrounding environment, and (b) a deeper dimension or 'father's voice', which interpellates the subject into identifying him/herself with the command as if it were the law issued by nature itself or its personification in some 'Big Other'.

These two dimensions are highlighted in Zappa's absurdist reference to a form of cost–benefit analysis operating in the rationality that weighs up a ban on music against the risk of higher gas prices. This probabilistic form of reasoning takes the form of an interpellation-question: 'If you could get cheap gas, like in the good ol' days [and it is important to notice that this 'memory' is actually future-oriented, it acts as a forecast] at the price of prohibiting some rebellious music, what would you choose?' Let us examine this form of voicing the law as a question. The question may seem quite conventional but it is actually quite compelling, even if ultimately ridiculous: on the one hand, the call to become a 'rational' calculating subject is implicit in the very positing of the question. The positing of the question does not simply assume that you are a reasonable person, free to choose, but rather produces you as a 'freely choosing subject' (a subject that is not only out of context but, furthermore, without any concern for her visualisation of herself as carried by her relations to others)[4] on the condition that you respond to the interpellation-question. If you respond, and only after you respond, 'the command' is presented as the result of your (free) negotiations with the environment, that is to say, as rational or reasonable. On the other hand, just in case you do not get it, the excessive background to your 'rational' negotiations is posited in terms of a 'risk'.

What is a risk? A memory turned into a forecast; a memory of the future. Strictly speaking forecast is no anticipation, since what is 'remembered', or simulated, is merely a possibility, that is to say, an abstract simulation whose chance of becoming real is pretty dim, but which can be given in terms of probability. Perhaps it would be more appropriate to speak of prevention, since the object of your 'rational choice' is identified here with an obstacle – the 'transgressive object/subject' whose evil ways stop you from getting your enjoyment. The idea is that your chances to get enjoyment (gas at cheaper prices, in this case) would increase if the obstacle is removed, and would decrease with the presence of the presumed obstacle.

Put otherwise, the cost of your negotiations, the length of time that it would take you to get your enjoyment, would increase because of the presence of some potential evil-doer. The idea is that it is up to you to increase rather than decrease your chances to get enjoyment, if you decide to choose the strategy that would keep at bay the potential evil-doer/obstacle. But notice that in fact you are being persuaded to engage in sacrifice: the obstacle *must* disappear, and it seems reasonable that it must disappear in order to increase your probabilities of enjoyment, but it can only disappear with *your* participation.

In the example, 'music' occupies the place of the sacrificial victim; the ridiculous thing is that it could be occupied by pretty much anyone or anything else: 'music', 'drugs', 'hooded youth on drugs', 'the enemy', 'the red scare', 'immigrants' and so on. Now, when the formal place of the sacrificial victim is provided with an actual sacrificial victim, the ridiculous becomes genocide. And you are an accessory to it, even if you feel you are not; the trick is that in the presentation of this excessive dimension as 'risk' you are allowed to choose a command while at the same time keeping some sort of ironic distance from that command. You are allowed to transfer your responsibility onto the 'big other', the law itself and/or its transgressive evil underside.

The structure of the law or command that we have isolated with the help of Zappa's absurdist reduction could be presented in the following simple manner:

(i) 'You must do X, because it is reasonable to do X.'
(ii) 'In case you don't do X, out of your own free will, Y may (or may not) happen.'
(iii) 'If Y happens it would be costful. If Y doesn't happen (even though it may happen) that is because you've reasonably chosen to do X.'

We must notice several things about this structure. First, as can be seen, the reasonable-ness of 'doing X' is not as autonomous as it seems at first sight. It is dependent upon the possibility, the threat of Y taking place. Y is a 'catastrophic risk', something to be taken very seriously, partly because of the radical uncertainty about its magnitude and its likelihood, partly because the value of its consequences and effects is particularly difficult to calculate or monetarise. Second, the way to take catastrophic risks seriously is to intervene now; but given the radical uncertainty of their magnitude and the difficulty to make sense (causally) of the consequences, the chooser must accept that the intervention itself may be risky and catastrophic. In fact, the more catastrophic the risk, the more an exceptional licence is or should be given in order to intervene in catastrophic ways. The message is clear: the ends justify the means. Only the (causally related) consequences in the future will tell, and the more catastrophic is the potential of these consequences, the more we are allowed to intervene catastrophically – that is, with less or no regard for (counterfactual) effects, others and 'collateral damage'. This is of course nothing more than a political stance – a thoughtless one, whose universalising capacity is questionable – passed on as 'rational' or 'social' choice.[5]

The crucial point is that 'doing X' looks reasonable: choices, hard as they may be, must be made; and the best way to make those hard choices is to fend off any feelings of guilt or responsibility for your fellow men. In this approach you are not choosing out of the goodness of your heart or because you expect others to care for you if you find yourself in the situation of being affected by the hard choices that must be made. You choose alone, you are not tied to anyone; their actions are their own, mine do not cause them. Nevertheless your choice is 'ethical' in the sense that it is all that can be asked from you.[6]

Third, you choose because not to do so would cost you. It is simply a matter of monetary transactions, and monetary transactions leave the seller and buyer free from any ties. Again, according to this line of reasoning there is no causal relationship between what you do and what others do, which also means to say that you are not responsible if others are affected by the hard choices made; these are necessary costs, necessary sacrifices, or as Human Rights scholar Michael Ignatieff would say, 'the lesser evil' (2004). It follows that in terms of the causal consequences of your choice in favour of the command, nobody can blame you.

As can be seen, this command structure allows you to choose X while at the same time keeping an 'ironic' distance from X, first by transferring 'the reasons/causes' of your choice onto Y, and second, by severing any causal connection between your choice and the sacrifices made in order to keep Y at bay.

There is yet another, more complicated dimension involved in this structure: Y and the costs attached to averting/sacrificing the obstacle-enemy Y are a mere possibility. The actualisation or the coming of the enemy/obstacle Y is only one among several, equally possible, paths or events. And there is no reason to choose this possible event over any other. In fact, at this point we can no longer rely on reason to constitute the absolute totality of all possible events, and since we cannot give any specific reason upon which to ground the existence of the universe of possibilities (including the enemy's attack) we cannot legitimately construct any multi-verse within which the foregoing probabilistic survey could make sense (including the estimated costs of the attack). Thus, the inference from the contingency of the risk to its varied but necessary frequency is a mistake. As potentialities, they do not really exist and will remain as potentialities. We must conclude that the other side of the injunction 'all sacrifical victims are innocent', as proposed by René Girard (2003, 2004), is 'all enemies are non-existent'.[7]

What happens then to responsibility? It cannot simply disappear, and since it cannot be transferred to a non-existent domain, then it must be transferred to a virtual but real domain, that of anticipation. Anticipation is neither mere prevention nor an evaluation of actions and/or omissions based only on their direct causal consequences. Strictly speaking, anticipation is the exploration of a time that nothing subtends. It operates at the level of sensuality and virtual presence, and/or the allure of an unreachable object or event. Anticipation entails an enunciation without statement – for instance, a concrete memory of the past/future: 'catastrophe (Z) will happen'. But notice that such an enunciation does not tell you when exactly Z will occur or what you must do in order to avert it or bring it forth. It entails no recipe, no ready-at-hand strategy. It does not tell you that in response, you must forfeit your responsibility and allow the 'father' or 'decider' to intervene in catastrophic ways. Rather, it compels you to provide the statement, to take a stance, to be responsible even in the absence of *a priori* forms of evaluation. It merely implies that your omission to provide the statement or take a stance will have consequences.

What sort of consequences are these? Let us call them virtual consequences or, after Dupuy, 'counterfactual' consequences (2006). Let us now, in the final chapter of this book, examine the nature of the sort of consequences that we have termed above 'virtual' or 'counterfactual', after Dupuy and others, and obtain some conclusions concerning the importance of taking into account these hitherto ignored phenomena with respect to radical choice and transformative political action.

We will do this by means of a reference to the path of the rebel, as expressed in the archetypical story of Orestes. Then we will consider the following question, which arises from the examination of cases like that of Orestes and other, more contemporary examples, such as that of Ernesto Guevara or Butch Cassidy and the Sundance Kid: Is there a right to revolt? The chapter will not aspire to find a definitive answer to that question, rather, and this is perhaps the conclusion, the end-point of this book, to assert that this is the definitive question of our times, the decisive problem haunting our far too limited and complacent notions of freedom.

Notes

1 As is well-known, Germans tested 'carpet-bombing' first during the Spanish Civil War. The uncanny correspondence between this sort of mass ordinary violence and avant-garde techniques became the subject of much exploration among avant-garde artists. 'Guernica', by Pablo Picasso is a well-known example, less well-known, but no less important, is the work of Peruvian poet César Vallejo.
2 See on 'retrogarde' Monroe (2005).
3 For the *topos* of the crossroads as the figure of interstice, novelty, crisis and decision, in relation to literature and space, see Gibson (2005: 84 ff.) and Serres (1972: 67). See also Zubiri (1982: 101–4).
4 See on this Strathern (2004: 232–3). She argues that rather than a deficit in cultural understanding, what is at stake here is a deficit in social analysis. Let us point out that there may be also a deficit in the understanding of cognitive processes. Later on we will see that, according to the findings of cognitive science, this visualisation amounts to 'subjectivity' itself. If so, then this command-form empties subjects and replaces them with a standard of its own.
5 For an example of this sort of shortsighted stance, passed on as 'social scientific' reasoning in relation to risks and catastrophes, see Posner (2004).
6 For a persuasive analysis of contemporary law and politics as an alibi, allowing us to deny our responsibility while keeping an anarchic sense of ethics, see Diamantides (2006–7: 17–32).
7 The 'enemy' referred to here is the inhuman other with whom no relationality is possible at all, the obverse of legal globalism, good-governance and Human Rights: the inert object. In this sense, it could be argued that the structure of today's global governance and human rights is thoroughly perverse-sadistic. For a brief history of the concept of 'the enemy', from Paul of Tarsus and Francisco de Vittoria to Carl Schmitt and the neo-cons, in relation to the obliteration of concrete subjectivities and assemblages, see Rasch (2004: Chapters 7–8).

Chapter 10

Guevara's choice

On revolution as a radical organising principle

With this chapter comes the end of our particular history of the fetish. At the beginning of this book the fetish was a remainder, nothing more than a residue left behind by the operation of critique at the dawn of modernity. Critique, it was suggested early on, should be understood as a way of counting: it takes into account certain things and not others, even if the latter are included in the set. For instance, it discounts the fetish as archaic or obscure. The same goes for those who maintain an engaged subjective stance and make common cause with the fetish. They are all adjudicated against as archaic, and relocated to 'less enlightened' eras, ripe for intervention and developmental transformation. More precisely, as Mladen Dolar says (1991), they become unplaceable.

However, the fetish and the rebels who make common cause with it return: they return in the arts and the sciences, in particular the harder sciences that had been given the task of expelling all the objects that were found obscure or superstitious, but also in the softer sciences that were supposed to police the harder ones. The latter were made powerless by the power of the fetish, while the former became so powerful that in fact were made virtually unrecognisable: they started to speak of such unbelievable things as the ancestrality of a rock, dark matter, or the coming end of all things.

Artists copied ancient rocks and archaic coffins and then smashed them only to infuriate their already confused spectators. Anthropologists declared that in fact it was the archaic peoples and their fetishes that did the work of critical thinking. All the while, critique, in the strictest sense of the term, seems to have run out of steam. Earlier anthropologists brought the fetish from Africa and the rebellious Caribbean to Europe in the eighteenth and nineteenth centuries. Rebellion became contagious and the motif of the fetish 'catches on' in critical language after Feuerbach and Marx. The fetish changed everything: a circle that did not return to its set target. Like women, who do not know how to keep their station, the fetish troubled the founders of psychoanalysis. In anthropology, law and political economy, the fetish shined with divine glory. It became a blinding light, in spite of its darkness. In psychoanalysis it became *objet petit a*, the heart in the chest of narcissistic capital and empire. And so, at the end of it all, it came back to the place it had left in the eighteenth century: to Africa and the Caribbean; to rebellion, to music and revolution.

In this final chapter the fetish returns to the Caribbean where it all began, more precisely to the island of Cuba. There it ignites a fire and becomes an image, the most iconic image of the twentieth century. Think what you will about icons and freedom fighters; perhaps it is true that they and the fetish do very little, almost nothing. But, hell, after their unlikely return, things are not the same.

On virtuality

Following the analysis of the risk-structure of command and the nature of choice vis-à-vis recent attempts to curb expressivity in the realm of the arts – that is, the aesthetic and disruptive form of indirect communication and virtual presence – particularly apparent in the case of rock 'n' roll, digital media and digital sound, the reader of the previous chapter was introduced to the notion of 'virtual' or 'counterfactual' consequences. As pointed out at the end, this notion emerges out of a distinction between direct and indirect causality. Dupuy explains that virtual consequences are the sort of consequences that arise from a comparison between the world as it is and a virtual but not yet actual world (a memory of the future whose genealogy cannot be traced back to the previous situation).

Put otherwise, the sort of reasoning that involves consideration of these consequences entails a judgement of the world as it is against what is more in the world than what there is, what the world is *de suyo* rather than any simulated or possible world. Incidentally, this form of reasoning has more in common with predictive moves, with prophecies and riddles, than with the severe forecasts of our economists and political gurus. As we will see later on, it is nonetheless more powerful than the latter.

Virtual consequences are very different from direct causal consequences in that the latter entail a connection between possible worlds that allegedly exist side-by-side in some actuality beyond experience. One is supposed to choose, among them, the one that maximises essence, perfection or self-interest. However, as stated already in previous chapters, this approach is nonsense. The side-by-side metaphysics that underpins contemporary models of prevention and choice, present in philosophy since at least Leibniz and Hume and pervasive in contemporary law/politics and economics since the days of the Cold War, leads to a conception of transformation that is other-worldly: according to this conception, transformation involves making a difference between different successive actualities or 'possible worlds' (taken as actual). Decisively, in order to 'make a difference' between successive actualities the subject of transformation must be able to observe them all at once and intervene, as it were, from outside.

'Intervention' becomes here the subject's act and/or omission in respect to such successive possibilities, and the causal impact of such an act; however, crucially, that sense of potential catastrophe extends only to the act itself and its immediate effects. Everything else is said to be not (causally) related to the subject's choice or act: for instance, the choices made by other agents and the activity of objects or nature. It is taken as a given that, since the latter do not depend causally upon, say, my actions, then the state of affairs (other people, objects, nature) can be presumed to be counter-factually independent of them.

In such a world, whatever I do would make no difference to what others do or to the activity of objects or nature (which are then presumed inert), and vice versa. Thus we remain at absolute distance from, rather than proximate to, others and the world around us. It is the same as with monetary transactions: the bond between exchange partners is severed (cfr. Anspach, 2001: 3). This postulates an agent of time out of time, incapable of engaging in any significant relationality: a prime engine or a static, invisible meta-law governing change in between successive actualities *out of nowhere*, as in some sort of religious creation *ex nihilo*.

Clearly, this is not how we, timely beings, change the future. In fact, the difference we make is between the actual concrete world and other virtual worlds – between the world as it is and what is more in it than what there is – never between successive actualities (Lewis, 1986). This means that if the law governing change between successive actualities looks 'invisible' or 'hidden' that is because in fact it is not there. The key point is to understand that what is more in the world is not *beyond this world*, that it includes not only immediately caused consequences but also emergent landscapes of objects, effects and values that can be judged only in accordance to such values. What we do in actuality brings about those emergent landscapes. If so, then it is fair to say that there are no *a priori* or static values (a meta-law) preceding choice, and no engine or design preceding action and transformation. It is also fair to say that even if others make choices independently of mine (causally speaking), what I do now 'catches on', it is contagious, transcends myself and becomes normative: part of the norms, rules, conventions and institutions; something that is taken into account, perhaps even interiorised by others when they go about making choices of their own.

Of course the process that connects my choice with the counter-factual reasoning of others is subjectless through and through, and this is why we see no agency, no causal connection in between. This perception is correct, and there is no need to postulate some transcendent, machine-like realm of language or symbols in order to account for the connection-process and its subjectless nature (in the place of the subject). Instead, it may suffice to consider what reality gives to itself of itself: other composite orders of reality – a third order beyond the code of the subject and that of the object, beyond what we can see and hear. Here, the work of Friedrich Hayek meets that of Alexandre Kojève; and they both meet Lacan and Althusser.[1]

Indeed, my action may represent from a causal perspective 'no more than a drop of water in the ocean of human affairs' (Dupuy, 2006: 8) and no object or realm of partial-objects (language, symbols, empty signifiers) can serve as a stand-in for subjective purpose. Posited like that, the existence of a realm of partial objects fails to capture the notion that there is more to reality (more than the code of the subject, more than the code of the object) than what there is. Let us clarify this point: so-called 'partial objects', those entities whose existence seem to violate the golden rule of side-by-side doctrinists and methodological individualists, are no mere stand-ins but real entities on their own right. Their reality is that of the break and the cut, that is to say, of intervention and radical transformation in the sense that phenomenologists would refer as 'transcendence within immanence'.

As Dupuy suggests the correct question is: What is the impact of my action in subjectless processes? Clearly my subjective designs are not causally responsible for these processes; but if we abandon this causal approach we may see action in an entirely different light: we would see it as the process of configuring images of ourselves that we project forwards in time and space and which become powerful in their own right.

The presence of the term 'image' in the previous phrase should not lead towards confusion. This has nothing to do with 'imagination' as a subjective capacity in the common sense of the term, but rather with fantasy as the structural frame of reality. The image referred to here is a thing-image or a thing-sound, the fetish-object, which must be understood as the auto-transcendent exteriority of a myriad, different and causally unrelated individual acts linked to one another through mimesis and contagion. Laughter is an example of this sort of infectious activity; others are dance, a *Voudoun* ceremony, or the singing of a refrain in a rock concert. In all these instances it becomes clear that we may not be causally responsible for the choices of others, but we are responsible in the sense that whatever we do in actuality becomes infectious. Cognitive scientists have identified these phenomena and think they are at the centre of what they call 'predictive moves', allowing segmented operations to be integrated as a totality that is capable of obtaining not only unity but also exteriority or 'uniqueness'. These 'totalities' have been described in the relevant literature as 'circuits' or networks (including human and nonhuman elements) that can represent their own dynamic powers: animals are one example, but also collective entities (for instance 'the people' or 'the electorate' of radical democratic legal theory) and even nonhuman entities such as the World Wide Web (Llinás, 2002: Chapter 12; Clark, 1997).

These scientists tell us that the mimic properties of sound and image are the key to understanding predictive moves and activity through vicar elements. It is because of the self-standing allure of a thing-image or a thing-sound that the totalised entity is capable of choice, but there is no need to confuse these objects with fully self-referential commands or consensual, fixed frameworks or backgrounds of meaning pre-existing the act of communication/interpellation. For we can conceive such an act as 'infectious' and then conclude that 'consensual meaning' (that is, meaning intended for the other party) is in fact an effect of mimesis rather than pre-existing accord.

The argument for infectious activity in relation to cognitive phenomena goes more or less like this: the repetition of certain behaviours associated with the consequences of the behaviour repeated, results in quick and common comprehension. Mimesis is required to associate repetitive behaviour and the consequences of such repetition. It makes sense to engage in mimetic behaviour because it allows me to predict the other's moves and relate them to my moves. They become meaningful, fixed patterns evolving with time. There emerges a third dimension beyond the code of the subject and that of the object: it is populated by trans-subjects and trans-objects with reality of their own: things-sound, things-image. It is in this dimension that prediction is possible, indeed necessary. This is the dimension of ethical–political choice and, as suggested before, the mimetic properties of sound (and image) are the key elements of this dimension. To conclude, it may be true that in the causal dimension my actions may be no more than a drop of water in the ocean, but in the anticipatory, predictive, virtual or counterfactual dimension their consequences can be momentous. I am responsible for these consequences.

This responsible person is what Frank Zappa calls 'rational person' in the quote provided in a previous chapter, and as he says, there is nothing special about being responsible, for it has nothing to do with infinite calculators or Leibnizian gods. The evidence provided by cognitive science seems to support that statement. We must distinguish then between this dimension in which responsibility cannot be avoided, or transferred – an undetermined but compelling call – and the determination of a call as a specified command or the interpellation of a big other. The space in between the two is the space of the political, which cannot be averted/aborted by means of risk-analysis, scenario planning and catastrophic intervention (humanitarian or otherwise), which are in reality purely preventive rather than predictive. The latter, at best, only delay catastrophe and, at worst, make us all complicit in the taking place of catastrophic interventions.

The political dimension is not absolutely outside of the law, but rather, it is its inherent alterity, as Mladen Dolar would put it (2006). As Zappa's example shows, we gain access to it, not by 'keeping our distance' from the specified command and retreating into its underside (this, by the way, is the grey zone that legal commentators have identified with the so-called 'state of exception'), but rather by over-identifying with it, by taking the command as 'personal', as a call to me, in uniqueness (this is the meaning of responsibility) and then taking a stance before it – before the law – without the short-cut provided by the big other.

Over-identification is then the result of a concentrated focus upon the mimetic properties of sound and image. It is related to the logic of sympathetic magic and envy, an oppositional strategy (which may also be a survival strategy, if we accept the evidence provided by cognitive scientists) identified also by anthropologists such as René Girard, Françoise Vergès and Michael Taussig among indigenous populations facing colonial and post-colonial demise, and in so-called 'advanced' societies in which it has taken the form of science, art and – as I have argued throughout the book – radical politics and law. Whenever this logic – the logic of an enunciation without statement – is mistaken as structured like an abstract language and posited as functioning like an automaton or any other figure of the 'Big Other', as a specified command rather than a call, the result is the impoverishment of the political and the transformation of processes of totalisation into homogenisation.

The champions of homogenisation in today's global landscape, political and economic, argue in favour of curbed expressive powers – the deflation of the political realm – under the assumption that this would bring about the more transparent management of relations. The idea is that we need a more programmed collective, able to respond and decide in the face of impending doom. No matter how well intentioned, this is a serious misunderstanding of mimetic communication and prediction, and it results in the very opposite of freedom. We are invited to accept the argument that the more catastrophic the predicted risk, the more our 'deciders' should be allowed to intervene with absolute licence. The aim of such an absolutely licensed intervention would be the construction of a full totality – one which features transparency between itself and its centre, able to respond as a whole, in a homogeneous manner, against the announced threat. As can be seen, the politics of prevention results in the very opposite of freedom: the construction of a homogeneous collective completely identified with its centre and its commands.

Furthermore, that sort of transparency in fact reduces the options present to a collective. With options being reduced if everyone feels exactly the same about any event or given set of values, the assemblage becomes brittle; it might not survive. This is why homogenisation, which abhors failure and dissent, is the opposite of practices of over-activation and prediction, which require negativity – error and noise – in order to operate. Strategies of over-identification and prediction activate error and noise and multiply the options in order to accelerate processes of decomposition and contagion in concrete reality. Rather than being aimed at establishing the relative cost and value of a given set of options, or surveying the entire set of possible futures for the purposes of prevention – a thoroughly unreasonable endeavour – these strategies take into account the fact that the projection of any image of the future (catastrophic or hopeful) must include error and noise as the very element that stops the drive towards the future from becoming fatalistic.

It is not the potential catastrophe, or 'risk', that ensures the closure of the loop that links the future to the past in the practice of projection/ enactment, since it will always remain merely potential. 'Risk' is in fact the potential image of an undesirable future, and if we succeed in preventing it, it would make no sense to state that our collective action was achieved by fixing our sight on that same future (Dupuy, 2002b; 2004: 30–1). The element that stops the drive from achieving its set target has to be actual, something that time gives to itself out of itself. This can only be a radical novelty, a perhaps undesirable (to some, hopeful to others) but inevitable error in our calculations of the future. This element is what we have called 'the remainder' earlier on in this book, after Mazzoldi and Derrida: the rebellious element, unexpected, which cannot be taken into account beforehand (Mazzoldi and Téllez, 2007: 362–88). The problem with our mainstream notion of freedom as choice is that it fails to include the allure of the unexpected or the uncanny, as the foreign but intimate aspect that radicalises choice.

The behaviour of the rebel teaches us something very important in this respect: that this 'irrational' allure of the unexpected is very much an aspect, perhaps the core of freedom. The key to understanding the actions of rebels is to acknowledge that they engage in the act not because of the compelling force of reason or calculation, in the sense of a motif that would result from the careful survey of all possible options, but rather, precisely because they have no options. It is because of the lack of a 'world' of possibilities in which their existence may have a place that rebels act. In fact, they act against such a world. In that sense, their action has the form of an escape from a given set of possibilities and relations that interrupts and disrupts them, thereby transforming the set in unexpected ways.

This is not to say that they lack vision, that their behaviour is sheer madness; on the contrary, their vision is pretty clear: that there should be a world within which they can have a place, and since the present world does not and cannot hold such a place, then the rational option, which they take against all odds, is to stand up against it.

Rebels do not escape in order to never come back, as Hakim Bey observes (2003: 130), but rather, as in the case of Orestes, with the aim of coming back to the existent world, rising against it, and replacing it with another one that features a different principle of organisation. In doing so, rebels offer themselves as a substitute for the widespread violence that holds together the present world, which then becomes concentrated upon them and offers to others – who do not share their position of total exclusion –

the spectacle of an unjustified sacrifice. It is then when their behaviour 'catches on', and their example spreads like fire containing violence and redirecting the latter against the (present) world itself!

The path of the hero: virtuality and the sacrificial

It is important to understand that this behaviour is in no sense the exclusive remit of exceptional individuals or peoples. It is not heroic in the romantic sense. For example, there is nothing romantic about what Orestes does: he is not Oedipus the King but Orestes the Exile (cfr. Kristeva, 2000: 129). Orestes returns to a city that covered the crime of its leaders (his mother Clytemnestra conspired with her lover Aegisthus to assassinate Orestes's father, Agamemnon, and seize power), from which he was exiled, in order to incite revolt among the people who have acquiesced in abject passivity and complacency in order to prevent bad consequences for themselves and their loved ones. As Julia Kristeva points out in her analysis of Jean-Paul Sartre's *The Flies,* a modern adaptation of the Greek tale for the time of occupation in Europe,[2] Orestes redirects the violence at the basis of the present legal–political set of relations against the homogeneous and the identical, against the complacency of the people, their wilful blindness towards the crimes of their leaders and their all too quick identification with their law-givers, all the more because, like our present leaders, Aegisthus and Clytemnestra feel no remorse whatsoever.

While the entire city is awash with feelings of fear out of guilt and remorse, acting out those feelings and becoming murderous, persecuting phantom enemies and producing scapegoats, no responsibility is assumed by the leader, the 'exceptional' decider who is the cause of it. What is real in this situation is not the threat of the enemy but the diffuse and ghostly presence of those feelings, a fetid state of mind that leads our attention towards the traumatic event without revealing it, as Kristeva puts it, 'a crowd concealing the crime of leaders and condemning itself to abjection in passiveness' (2000: 129–30). In Sartre's version of the tale, the Real takes the shape of a swarm of flies, an archetypical figure for the fetish-object contaminating everything and everyone it touches, like the gold-coin in the old tales of revolution and the origin of empire in the Caribbean.

It is important to acknowledge that Orestes's response is in no way moralistic; rather than separating himself from the contamination spreading throughout the city he holds his hands out to the forces of corruption, he over-identifies with the evil corrupting the heart of the city of Argos and commits evil in order to contain it: pushed by his sister Electra he kills not only Aegisthus but also their mother Clytemnestra.

Having committed such an atrocious crime, Orestes the rebel becomes an outlaw and in doing so seals his destiny. However, to avoid misunderstanding, we must realise that his is not the romantic path of the hero, confronting and embracing death as the ultimate sign of humility in order to gain redemption in finitude and long-lasting power over those who are weaker than him. In fact, as we learn by the end of the tale, by becoming an outlaw, Orestes will not be triumphant and reign in peace forever. Again, his path is not heroic, but rather the path of the freedom fighter, the thief and murderer who escapes, who is forced to flee 'for the path he has chosen is unbearable' (Kristeva, 2000: 160).

To put it otherwise, he engages in the cruellest form of self-sacrifice, which is not suicidal: becoming a virtual substitute for the contamination sweeping the city, he ingests and harnesses the forces of corruption redirecting them against himself; in this way he turns into the ultimate fetish, the scapegoat.

There will be no serenity for him, he will be neither adored nor recognised by the crowd who would rather turn against him, and in turning against him – fleeing in panic – will become united once again under a different order, one that is based no longer in complicity, abjection and passivity, in the commonality of a sacrificial crime, a common evil, but rather on the rejection of the founding role of sacrifice and the declaration of innocence and inexistence of all sacrificial emissaries. The latter – the refusal and the pledge – is the moment of collective self-legislation, impure and never transparent since it includes within itself the inevitability of failure, the acknowledgement of the incompleteness of the drive.

'Incompleteness' here means that the object of the drive (the scapegoat and the injunction concerning the innocence of the scapegoat), once postulated, has a reality, and a reality with properties of its own; and this reality is not exhausted by the postulation. In fact, the opposite is true: postulation is generative.[3] Put otherwise, the reality of these objects goes far beyond their construction or postulation, their artificiality if you will; just like the reality of a bridge goes beyond the design of its engineer and that of a Hilbert space and the set of all polynomials of a certain function go beyond the conceptual construction of the mathematician.

In other words, the path of the Oresteian hero and his crowd ends not in finitude, the realisation of the limitation intrinsic to common injunctions and affirmations, but the radical novelty of what is posited in common, what Sartre called 'the pledge' or the constitution, a reality that does not get exhausted by the act of postulation and thus must be repeated (Hardt, 2007; Jefferson, 2007). It is not the case that the crowd reacts in abjection over the clear injustice of the hero's ultimate sacrifice, but rather it steps back in disgust faced with the impossibility of realising to the full its own will to destruction. It learns from its error not because of the sudden realisation of the transcendental evil of its ways, but more simply, because of the impossibility of achieving (the drive's) fullness. In Hegelese, this is the work of the negative: the very thing that threatens the collective becomes its salvation.

This is to say that the path of the rebel is not resolved in ultimate gracious self-sacrifice, giving himself up to satiate the murderous instincts of the crowd. On the contrary, the path of the rebel is to stop the murderous drive of the crowd in its tracks. Orestes is no Christ. For Orestes would not even allow this drive, the crowd's will to destruction to achieve its aim; rather than being crucified, Orestes – disowned by his sister – protests that he is free 'and leaves Argos forever' (Kristeva, 2000: 160).

So, the solution to the potential paradox represented by Orestes as a figure of freedom and revolt is that, in fact, he is not the ultimate scapegoat: unlike Christ or the fundamentalist suicide bomber who dreams of paradise, he does not 'exit the stage', he does not allow the crowd the final pleasure of purification and ultimate cleansing. He traverses violence and chooses freedom not as grace or good, but rather as an obligation that challenges the conventional morality of the victors. Freedom is in this sense, as Kristeva puts it after Sartre, 'antigood, antinature, antiphysis: because nature is the mother, the mother must be killed' (2000: 160–1).

'Nature', or the 'feminine marvellous' as Kristeva puts it (ibid.), are here metaphors for the ultimate, all-embracing totality that we all seek to return to, the figure of ultimate fullness but also, in this respect, a figure for the death-drive, the earlier state of harmony or inertia postulated by Freudian theory that is often identified with the lack of reality attributed to objects in mainstream Western philosophy,[4] and read by Freudo-Lacanians in terms of the primordial duality (the mother/child dyad) 'which supposedly contained all things and every happiness and to which the subject strives throughout life to return' (Copjec, 2003: 33). Therefore, the mother/child final reconciliation functions also as a marker for the most nihilistic will to destruction, and this is precisely what Orestes's act disallows.

The ultimate lesson of the path of the rebel is this one: freedom can only be attained by wrestling oneself out of the world, the city and nature, in the sense of the primordial embrace of the all-encompassing set of relations. This is the meaning of the mother's murder and self-imposed exile. Put otherwise, there is no sacrifice to end all sacrifices, no set of all sets, but only inevitable, obligatory freedom interrupting the quiet flow and embrace of the situation as an unexpected irruption: emergence, more reality, the shattering force of time. Orestes is the archetypal anti-hero because he chooses the unexpected; in doing so he chooses freedom. He withdraws to a temporary autonomous zone (that involves temporary implication in evil and crime) but always in order to come back,[5] not with the aspiration of being perceived as a citizen (unlike Oedipus, Orestes does not seek recognition) for he is always/already an exile, ready to cut any links with the established situation of the social group in the most radical manner (to kill his mother, to avoid crucifixion) by walking away out of his own free will.

Kristeva concludes her reading of Sartre's adaptation of Aeschylus' *Oresteia* with the following lines:

Sartre's Orestes amalgamates certain traits of Oedipus ('plague' for Oedipus, 'flies' for Orestes; like Oedipus, Orestes is ready to 'do himself the greatest harm'). Yet Orestian revolt is far more radical. To kill his mother and cut the ties with the social group by exiling himself of his own free will makes this man 'foreign to himself'. He says to Zeus: 'Foreign to myself – I know it. Outside nature, against nature, without excuse, beyond remedy except what remedy I find within myself. But I shall not return under your law; I am doomed to have no other law but mine.'

(2000: 140, quoting Sartre, 1947: 140)

As she explains, the very foundation of identity – that of the social group and its legislation, that of the individual – is challenged here (Kristeva, 2000: 140–1). The point is that freedom as ultimate self-sacrifice, that is to say, as ultimate egotism and supreme narcissism, makes no sense: there will be more exiles and new sacrifices will be seen as necessary. But the sacrificial form has become minimally different, no longer the sacrifice of an innocent scapegoat but sacrificial self-discipline. It is crucial to distinguish the two, for in fact, the sacrificial self-discipline of the collective, what Varela and Dupuy call 'panic', may be the only weapon left to the collective when the powerful have monopolised all other means of violence, and therefore the last reserve of freedom.

Against those who can only see in self-sacrificial collective discipline a form of latent Fascism, one should argue that this sort of violence is emancipatory, and totally different from Fascism, precisely because it does not achieve its aim; it does not end in ultimate scapegoating, but rather in the realisation of its impossibility. This is to state that not every closure or 'totality' is by itself totalitarian. The point is to postulate a form of closure with a 'minimal difference', a minimal failure or in-closure, and, as Ernesto Guevara proposed, to make this reality by postulation into a method in everyday life: to carry on abstracting.

It must be emphasised, against people like Susan Sontag who mobilises the accusation of 'proto-Fascism' whenever they hear a call to (sacrificial) collective self-discipline, that what is essential to Fascism is its will to mobilise collective sacrifice in the service of Capitalism; nothing like that happens in the case of collective sacrificial self-discipline against IMF-driven globalisation and oppressive capitalist relations. In the case of Sontag's vociferous denunciation of Gabriel García Márquez as being complacent, if not complicit, with the 'proto-Fascist' regime of anti-capitalist Cuba, because of his proximity to Fidel Castro who as a leader is well-renowned for his repeated calls to collective sacrifical discipline in the island of Cuba, one has to take sides with the Colombian novelist.

Sontag denounced García Márquez at a conference at the 2003 International Book Fair in Bogotá after he failed to join the likes of Carlos

Fuentes and Eduardo Galeano in condemning the Cuban leader for the infamous crackdown of at least seventy-five dissidents and the execution of three men who hijacked a ferry in a failed attempt to reach the coast of Florida in April 2003. Crucially, in taking sides with García Márquez over this dispute one does not have to accept any justification of the firing squads against the hijackers (García Márquez himself, in a response to Sontag's criticism as 'an unnecessary and provocative question',[6] insisted on his overall opposition to the death penalty in all circumstances), but neither the ill-intentioned attempt by Sontag to question the continuing relationship between García Márquez and Castro in spite of the latter's crackdown of dissidence in the island. It would be naïve to reduce this issue to one of 'friendship', for the stakes are much higher: the point is that in taking sides, García Márquez maintains, or rather repeats – in the Deleuzian sense of the term – his commitment to revolutionary politics, even after having condemned (in a letter signed with other Colombian intellectuals some years ago) armed struggle as the royal road towards liberation.

That is the real issue behind Sontag's 'discomfort', the fact that she sees no difference between collective self-discipline in the service of capitalism (as in Fascism) and the praise of self-sacrifice as a value against it. For her they both lead, ineluctably, towards 'totalitarianism', after the latter has been made into the ultimate crime. One should react strongly, as strongly as García Márquez did, against this sort of political blackmail. For one can only remain loyal to the thought of an author or the political example of a true revolutionary by repeating it, that is, in the Deleuzian sense, by betraying that thought and example.

Similarly, García Márquez can only remain faithful to the cause of revolutionary politics – to his friend Castro – by betraying him in repetition, bringing out something new from within the cracks of the revolutionary movement itself in Latin America. Here Sontag misses the point, but also Fuentes and Galeano, and García Márquez proves to be the only 'true friend' (of the revolution). García Márquez is Castro's friend not because he's ready to take a bullet *for* him, but rather because he is ready to take a bullet *from* him.[7] In this way, the Colombian novelist brings forth the real meaning of self-sacrifice and discipline, the common cause with the political object in connection to radical politics, and in this respect he is (not Sontag, or Fuentes and Galeano) both the real critic and the true friend.

It is not the case that sacrificial collective self-discipline is by definition 'proto-fascist', since its correct meaning is not that of purification through separation (as in the argument 'now that the revolution has become impossible, all we can do is prevent totalitarianism and/or build and retreat to our little temporary autonomous zones'). On the contrary, as a reserve-violence of the weak against the powerful, collective self-discipline aims at the radical transformation of the present (capitalist) situation. In Badiouian terms, this means to subtract the minimal difference (the nothing that substitutes everything) out of a given multiplicity (Badiou, 2005b: 153–62). To subtract the most unheard and almost silent voice, a voice and nothing more, out of the false totality and read the totality of the world from the position of that voice, thereby forever disrupting the given situation (cfr. Dolar, 2006).

This is precisely what Castro and Guevara pointed at in their repeated references to the sacrificial nature of radical political action, something that, as the latter explains, they learned not from aloof theorisation, but rather from the unheard voices of the peasants themselves.[8] Guevara wrote:

> In our work of revolutionary education we frequently return to this instructive theme (that of sacrifice and the uniqueness of the path of the hero). In the attitude of our fighters could be glimpsed the man of the future. On other occasions in our history the act of total dedication to the revolutionary cause was repeated. During the October [1962 missile crisis] and in the days of Hurricane Flora [in October 1963] we saw exceptional deeds of valor and sacrifice performed by an entire people. *Finding the method to perpetuate this heroic attitude in everyday life is, from the ideological standpoint, one of our fundamental tasks.*
> (Guevara, 1997: 198)

One should read this passage without a gram of romanticism. Like Orestes, Guevara is no Christ, and it probably is the biggest disservice to his example to insist on the construction of Guevara's thought, life and death in the model of some sort of Christ-like figure. Notice first that in the quoted passage catastrophe and sacrifice are linked to the projection of an image of the future. That is the basic theme of the essay on socialism and man in Cuba. The underlying problem is to establish what type of fixed, catastrophic point, what powerful fetish is capable of insuring the closure of the loop that links the future to the past in projected time (cfr. Dupuy, 2004: 31). It is out of the consideration of this seemingly intractable problem that the conclusions concerning responsibility, choice and radical novelty obtained by Guevara in his famous essay will emerge.

Guevara's choice

Remember 8 October, 1967? A group of rebels found themselves cornered in Bolivia. Outgunned and outsmarted, the outlaws faced their destiny. Surrender would be the only reasonable way to save their lives; instead they chose to go down in a blaze. They walked into an ambush, and faced a rain of bullets. They chose freedom.

On that day Ernesto Guevara was seriously wounded and captured by Bolivian troops, trained by US Special Forces and aided and abetted by the CIA. The next day, Guevara and two other captured guerrillas were summarily executed following orders from the Bolivian government and Washington. Here again, the differences with the treatment of former leaders and collaborators of Fascism twenty years ago in Germany and elsewhere in Europe are striking. It is well known that Churchill and others favoured a policy of summary execution for the leaders and collaborators of the Third Reich. American legal common sense triumphed, and some of those men were put on trial, evidence was gathered against them, and then, after their guilt was proven beyond reasonable doubt, they were punished.

Twenty years later, leftist rebels in Latin America did not deserve even the minimal honour of 'American style' justice. This sort of justice may be flawed in more than a few aspects, as revealed by many analyses of the trials at Nuremberg and its more or less refined successors from South Africa to Iraq,[9] but it did serve the purpose of producing and projecting a memory, rather than to allow erasure and forgetfulness. In the case of Guevara and his leftist rebels not even this was allowed. The directive was to effectively and immediately erase them from the face of history. What was their crime, so heinous, that it was judged by the Americans and their Bolivian allies to be undeserving of memory and monumental justice? It has to be one of the greatest ironies of history that the image of Ernesto 'Che' Guevara became the most reproduced and infectious image of the twentieth century. He became the ultimate icon. Whatever one may think about the nature of his deeds, and whether or not they were justified and deserving of forgiveness, the truth remains that history did not forget him.

His example remains; the nature of his choice – that there is a right to revolt; that this right disrupts the quiet flow of legality – became engrained in the collective unconscious. It is part and parcel of our idea of freedom. In *Socialism and Man in Cuba*, Guevara set out to develop the idea of freedom that had emerged out of revolutionary action. 'The revolution is a praxis which forges its ideas in action', the slogan of the Cuban revolution, suggests already the Sartrean tone of this conception of radical organisation and freedom. However, unlike Sartre (and Freud, whose writings Guevara also read profusely), who, as we have seen in the chapters above, started with the individual in the series but gradually moved towards the notion of the necessary fusion of the individuals in the group, ultimately completed in the axiomatic constitutional moment of 'the pledge' that gives origin to the statutory/organised group (Sartre, 1976: 417–504), Guevara insisted on the 'dialectical' relation between the individual in the series and the statutory group. Later on it will be argued that the dialectical relation in Guevara's essay should not be understood along diamat or Engelsian lines, but rather in a more Hegelian manner, along the lines of a repetitious or self-reflexive loop that never achieves complete fullness.[10]

Hegelian Marxists would probably recognise this self-reflexive image, as well as Freudo-Lacanians acquainted with the notions of fantasy and the death-drive; but what seems entirely original in this reading of Guevara's notion of 'repetition' is its uncompromising realism in relation to the object that breaks and breaks up the individual's drive. Rather than making relationality as such (the subject–object relation) absolute, thereby re-injecting the transcendental code of the 'for us' into the 'in-itself' out there, Guevara affirmed, as will be argued in the remainder of this chapter, that intellect or fidelity (to the cause) do not *create* their objects but *postulate* them, that these objects are virtual rather than transcendental and therefore real in the formal sense, and that, insofar as this is the case, objects and individual elements connect with one another at the level of sensuality, that is to say, at the aesthetic level where 'networks', 'meshworks' and 'multi-faceted beings' exist,[11] with full reality, beyond the poles of the transcendental object and the transcendental subject, that is to say, as elements in (indirect) connection without (Sartrean) fusion.

He is probably the only Marxist, with the important exception of Marx himself (cfr. Kemple, 1995: 1), to have developed a notion of revolutionary freedom as radical innovation from the perspective of the individual's sensual freedom, the uncanny ability of the element to escape all relations.

His Freud-like starting point is the incompleteness of the individual (of his drives) because of the incompleteness of reality, as evidenced in historical reality by such (catastrophic) events as the missile crisis of October 1962 or Hurricane Flora in October 1963, which interrupt the fully reflexive flow of the drive. It would seem strange at first to speak of a missile crisis or a hurricane as obstacles that are inherent, rather than external, to the individual's drive. But this is precisely what Guevara does when he connects these two seemingly external events with the 'exceptional deeds of valor and sacrifice performed by an entire people' (1997: 198).

One could read this connection in two different but related ways. First, as a case of radical investment of the individual's affectivity in these seemingly 'external' objects. Second, one could read this connection as the making of a common cause with the object, a postulation that does not strip the latter from its independent reality. Since none of the elements in this relation lose their independent reality, that is, since they are not deemed co-relative to experience, the relationship between them is affected from the very outset by the unexpected entry or withdrawal of the elements involved and/or other elements. This entails bringing to the fore the inevitability of radical innovation within the flow of the drive.

In the first case, having invested emotionally in these objects, the loss or 'void of being' caused as an actual consequence of the forces unleashed (or, in the case of the missile crisis, the counterfactual consequences) is not complete loss. Rather, the drive focuses upon that element, that object, which has been made insignificant by the ensuing situation, so that now it becomes the structuring principle of the whole scene.

Thus, in the case of Guevara's example, it is in the concrete (in)existence of the fighters and peasants hit by the Hurricane, and the virtual consequences of the missile crisis, that one can see, in the present, a glimpse of the future.

Such 'virtual' peasants, the real residue of the present situation, in fact an ensemble between the missile/hurricane and the real peasants, become the fixed point capable of ensuring the closure of the loop that links the future to the past in projected time. 'New man' is not in this perspective just some abstraction in a utopian, possible future, but rather a direct presence embodied in the figure of catastrophe – the missile, the hurricane – as it hits actual people, which sends signals back to the rest of us now, thereby triggering the action that would result in its realisation (or else, that would keep the catastrophic future from being realised).[12]

To be sure, 'realisation' does not pertain here to the coming into actuality of a potentiality already present in some pre-given set of all possibilities, but on the contrary, the perpetuation of this 'attitude', which Guevara calls 'heroic' (to subtract the lowest element from the given situation and read the whole situation from that stance, thereby disrupting it forever) in daily life.

This is a correct and very acute reading of the connection between the 'external' object and the individual's drive, and one that has been put forward to great effect, without reference to Guevara but in the similar context of the analysis of forms of radical political collective action, by people such as Ernesto Laclau, Slavoj Žižek and Alain Badiou, among others.[13]

Notice however, that Guevara emphasises the nonhuman side of the connection (the missile, the hurricane) and the composite object (the missile/hurricane/real peasant ensemble) in a way that cannot be found in any of the authors mentioned above. In Guevara, the real objects (for example, the real missile, the real peasant) are related by means of an ideal/sensual third, namely 'new man'. The condition for this is the split between the object (the real peasant, the real missile) and its quality (for example, victim, weapon) so that it can be reconnected in novel ways, or more precisely, by allusion to the 'gravitational' power of a real object lying beyond: a real new man.

That emphasis is reminiscent of Sartre's ambiguity concerning the distinction between the human and the nonhuman, which, as we saw before, involves also the dimension of future temporality. In addition to that, Guevara seems to notice, in spite of his emphasis on these objects, that neither the missile nor the hurricane can be the fixed point linking the future to the past in projected (revolutionary) time. He shifts, ambiguously, between the poles of the object and the subject, without abandoning them, but also, and this is crucial, without settling for one of them. He chooses the ensemble, the artifice. It could be argued that, conscious of the fact that the deterrent effect of a catastrophe would be self-obliterating and that no individual on its own, given his/her nature, could withstand such an obliterating force,

Guevara moves beyond the poles of the object and the subject, beyond critique, and settles for a different kind of objectivity or reality, one that refuses to be integrated in the web of possibilities and (human) investments linking all cognisable elements to one another, because it indexes a reality that occurs in a time beyond or before the possibility of actual investment or 'experience'.

Let us explain: Catastrophe cannot be the element upon which we fix our sight in order to link the future to the past so as to transform the present. This is so because, as Dupuy and Varela have explained, the signals it would send back to the past would trigger actions that would keep the catastrophic future from being realised. Again, 'if the deterrent effect of the catastrophe worked perfectly, it would be self-obliterating' (Dupuy, 2004: 31). Notice that, in point of fact, Guevara cannot speak about the missile crisis and Hurricane Flora as objects sending signals to the past from some possible future, but only as events that have already occurred. It is because the unexpected is inevitable that we can use it as an index of reality for the future and thus as the basis of our predictive moves.

To put it otherwise, what must subsist, inscribed in the future, and therefore in the reality of a time beyond (or before) the possibility of actual investment, that is to say, as something that persists on its own, independent of our direct, actual, subjectively affective relation, is the inevitability of the unexpected and the improbable, or the imperfection in the closure of the loop. As Guevara puts it, these are the (other) occasions in 'our history' when 'the act of total dedication to the revolutionary cause was repeated' (1997: 198).

One should read the term 'repeated' in this passage strictly in the Sartrean/ Deleuzian sense, as novelty, split or 'cut'. That is the first key term in the passage. The second key term is 'to perpetuate' (ibid.) and, finally, less important ontologically but perhaps no less so in sociological terms, the phrase 'an entire people'. 'People' is the collective that has included within its own organisation the object/obstacle of its drive. Therefore, it is an 'impure' object, never fully self-reflexive: it knows that it will be faced with the task of repeating/betraying the revolution again and again, as Guevara puts it, 'in daily life' (ibid.). But this knowledge does not come from some abstract utopianism, or out of fidelity to a purely subjective ideal. It comes from the innovative/disruptive element the people themselves have placed at the centre of their organisation. In more technical terms, the source of this knowledge is sentient intellection of a postulated reality.

Sentient intellection or 'arche-prehension' has been posited by writers such as Zubiri and Ellacuría as the structural and systematic unity between sense and intellect, against the scholastic wisdom according to which 'there can be nothing more in intellect that did not start in the senses' but also against the continuity of such medievalism in the modern, Kantian, sharp distinction between the transcendental (*a priori*) and the physical (a posteriori), in which the first becomes the condition of intelligibility of the second, that is to say, the condition for the constitution of the unity of perceived objects.

From the perspective of arche-prehension, the intelligible and the sensible are not opposites, but rather they are both formally physical and material. What has been called the transcendental dimension is inscribed in the objects themselves: each object opens itself to itself and other objects in proximity, and is never in full contact. In this sense, what is often called 'the content' of an object can never be sensed in solitude, simplicity or just as content (the traditional notion of 'essence') but actually only in a determinate and composite form, as something other or artificial, and this artificiality of otherness, irreducible to content, is formality. In this sense content and form, although different, are always sensed as a unity, that of the real *qua* real. That is why throughout this book we have used such terms as 'fantasy', 'sensuality' and 'proximity' in order to refer to a realm of connections that does not exhaust the reality of the elements in the fact of their connectivity. The point is communication without fusion.

Another way to put this would be to state that in arche-prehension one is open not to transcendence in the traditional sense of the term, but rather to something primordial and more radical; to be in reality, as formality, transcending towards that which reality can or could be in its own right. In this sense, knowledge entails neither mirroring the real nor performing a *salto mortale* from what is perceived to the real, from immanence to transcendence, as conceived in (post-Kantian) critical realism, but rather the sense of the unfolding of a reality within which we are immersed already. Cut-up techniques, assembling and disassembling, become the very form of knowledge.

Thus, we remain open, not only to what is there but also to the actuality of reality in all its actual possibilities, to reality in apprehension as well as to reality beyond apprehension. The reality in question is always physical (and not merely conceptual in the second case) because of its formality, its character 'of itself'. This is to say that the reality of objects is independent of the subject, it is not a subjective imaging or self-positing, but something imposed upon the subject, something which is here-and-now before the subject even if it cannot be perceived immediately; and this holds equally among different types of reality, whether we are talking about colours or photons, individuals or political entities. In 'praxis', as Guevara would say, we are in contact with reality, but not with all of reality. Rather, praxis or technics leaves us open to all reality; and it is this openness (the 'heroic attitude') that, Guevara tells us, must become perpetuated in daily life against the mainstream view that equates 'reality' with what is there or what is possible. In conclusion, reality itself remains an 'open system' in the sense that we cannot deduce *a priori* what reality can give to itself out of itself, but also in the sense that each new form of reality that emerges brings with itself a new mode of reality.

The object of philosophy is reality as a dynamic totality, radical novelty; and in the case of rebellious political practice, the focus is upon 'historical' reality, the unfolding of reality as it is opened up to its maximal virtualities. In this totality there is no place for the complete absorption of the realities that configure it as its structural moments. Otherwise one could not speak of 'structure' or 'relation', formally and properly. A structure implies co-determination, in which the elements related have a constitution of their own and do not lose it or cease to exist outside of the system of relations. This relation or co-determination does not have to be causal in the more direct sense of the term, that is to say, it does not have to deny the characteristics and actions of each part in the whole. Thus, the sort of totalisation that seems to be part and parcel of the postulation of political objects in historical reality (what Guevara calls 'the method') does not have to mean the negation of individual elements or 'plurality in proximity'.

On the contrary, the latter, plurality in proximity, appears as an exigency of historical reality since, otherwise, there would be no structures but only contradiction between the parts and the whole. Finally, a historical reality that is a totality qualified by its constitutive parts is configured and constructed (not created) in praxis, rather than being activated by a metaprinciple (Reason or any such abstractions as Matter, Spirit and so on).

It is a complex, self-reflexive but in-closed totality, whose concrete contents and forms are not given in advance by a teleological principle or in some set of all possibilities. These contents and forms depend upon human and nonhuman options, that is, on the dynamism unleashed by these options, connections and disconnections, once they are postulated, instantiated in historical (retentive or anticipatory) structures. Because of this, because of the central role of these postulated objects in history, political and otherwise, it cannot be said that the totality contains an immanent law that would rule over its process of unfolding all the way to some final point of closure without accident. Only by denying reality to postulated objects in politics can we reduce the totality of history to a simple and undifferentiated process that would absorb all complexity, including its own, nihilistically obliterating the specificity of its constitutive elements (cfr. Ellacuría, 1990: 977 ff.).

Postulated objects or *objets petit a,* as psychoanalysts call them, belong neither to the order of the transcendental object nor to that of the transcendental subject. *Objet petit a* is neither the ordinary object (practico-inert) invested upon by the individual's drive, around which the drive moves, and which may be summoned up by him/her in order to perform the role of substitute nor, as Slavoj Žižek argues, merely the circular movement around, that is, relationality as such (between the thinking subject and objective being). Incidentally, by absolutising relationality as such in this way, Žižek's definition of objectivity insists on the necessary isomorphism between thinking and being, leaving no room whatsoever for a thought of the real and unexpected remainder or the imperfection or novelty in the closure of the loop.

In contrast, in Guevara's example the postulated but real object, existing with independence from our (the people's) relation to it, stands for the inevitable imperfection (in the closure of the loop between the people and the original revolutionary event) that causes them to repeat/betray the revolution. Put simply, the true test of the revolution comes after the revolutionary event, when the people face their destiny *in the absence of their revolutionary leaders*. Political objects are postulated objects, and not subjective or intersubjective idealisations; ultimately, they are imposed upon the subject. The object is what links the future to the past in projected time. It stands simultaneously for sensuality and proximity (allure, fascination) on the one hand, and for that which this allure is obfuscating or masking, for the void, the inaccessible real object behind fascination, on the other. When the time comes, the revolutionary agent will reduce himself to the void and provoke the collective into confronting the truth of its desire.

This explains Guevara's choice: he left his ministerial position in Cuba not because of supposed rivalries with Fidel Castro or as an act of cowardice, fleeing the difficult task of nation-building, the sobriety of the morning after, for the easier task of hell-raising. First, no such rivalry ever existed,[14] and second, to provoke a revolution in Bolivia could not be reasonably described as easier than the (re)construction of Cuba's economy. The actual outcome of Guevara's adventure in South America is sufficient proof. Rather, Guevara's choice is similar to that of the analyst who reduces himself to the void (when we pass from perversion to analytic discourse in Lacan's formula of the 'discourse of the analyst' in *Seminar XVII*).[15]

It is crucial to notice that what is at stake in the discourse of the analyst is the analyst's withdrawal, or more generally, *the withdrawal of the object as truth*. Knowledge in the position of truth (below the bar under the 'agent', in Lacan's formula) is neither the truth of naïve realism (*adequatio*) nor that of critical realism (self-positing), but rather the truth of postulation as radical novelty independent of one's or anybody's subjective position. For Guevara the subject, to avoid becoming the big Other of the Cuban people, he must function precisely as a substitute for the ultimate inconsistency and failure of the big Other (the perfect identification between the people and its cause, represented in its leaders). Enter Guevara the object, which not only emerges at the very moment of its loss but also is the loss itself, *withdrawal itself as an object*.

Here withdrawal is not a relation but rather the lack of relation as such, the cut; not just a spatial separation or a fault but, more radically, the point where the spatial order breaks down, the missing mass of the universe, withdrawn and invisible but with enormous gravitational effect, like 'dark matter' and 'dark energy' in physics and cosmology.[16] At this point Guevara and the island of Cuba become not only the lost object cause of desire but also, and much more important, the circular movement of the drive obeying the weird logic of curved space. Notice however that if there is curved space then there must be something beyond causing the curvature; it may be an object beyond perception but its existence is revealed by its gravitational pull on other massive bodies (in this case, what Guevara calls 'the entire people'). Enter the political object, with reality by postulation, and in that sense, something with reality in its own right.[17]

In *Socialism and Man in Cuba*, Guevara is inviting the Cuban people, and more generally 'the entire people' to enact the cut and not to succumb to the fantasy of unconstrained productivity or pure self-rule. The catastrophes of 1962 and 1963 have shown not only that the suffering of the lowest among the low is the sign of the future but also, the much more crucial point that incompleteness (that of the individual, of reality itself) does not mean finitude and the limitation of any system of rules wishing to replace the old order, but rather its radical originality, its novelty in the face of the past, the impossibility of tracing its genealogy to the possibilities inherent in the previous situation, and thus the task of doing away with the innermost fantasy of capitalist society (which is no different from that of the ultimate communist society): permanent self-enhancing productivity and self-regulation. This is what Guevara called 'commodity as the economic cell of capitalist society', and he warned that 'so long as it exists its effects will make themselves felt in the organisation of production and, consequently, in consciousness' (1997: 201). Ultimately, he opposed 'radical novelty', incompleteness, new man, the political object, to permanent, inherently transgressive productivity, and the injunction to enjoy oneself that underlies pure self-regulation, the economic object.

This also explains why, continuing from where Guevara left off, Fidel Castro has periodically summoned the 'valor and sacrifice' of the entire people of Cuba in the face of new 'catastrophes' such as the US embargo, the repeated attempts by the Cuban *creole* elite in Miami to infiltrate the island with the excuse of defending dissent, or the fall of the Soviet Union. In this aspect, Guevara's writings proved to be prophetic, since the 'heroic attitude' became perpetuated in daily life, as the substitution of 'missile crisis' and 'Hurricane Flora' for 'US embargo' demonstrates, no less than the fact of the survival of the Cuban people and their revolution in the face of almost complete isolation, not only from the US but also from the former 'Soviet camp' itself. This is the source of the strength and dignity of the island. In this respect, the island offers to others the spectacle of an unjustified sacrifice; it is not an object belonging to a reprehensible past, but rather, it sends signals back to the past/present that would trigger actions aimed at radical innovation and freedom (as it has done, for instance, to people such as Hugo Chávez, Evo Morales and others in Latin America). In that sense, the future is an island.

Coda: in freedom

To conclude: freedom is an endless path, it is the very figure of infinity in the sense of radical novelty and in opposition to the notion of an all-encompassing world, world of worlds, or set of sets, that underpins our fraudulent mainstream acknowledgements of finitude.

Once again, writing about Orestes, Julia Kristeva points out that:

> Whether the critical state of Greek legislation, or the critical state of European states during World War II, or even the internal crisis of a technological and media-driven society, we are differently and conjointly confronted with a demand. When the symbolic link (political law, as in sated Aegisthus, or divine law, as in mocking Zeus) fails, oedipal revolt is impossible and fails in its dialectical function to construct the subject's autonomy. Condemned henceforth to shatter the most archaic links – those of desire for the mother and even the attachment to natural biological survival – the subject reaches these zones of turbulence that are discord or war: turbulence in oneself, the family, the city, and at the core of being.
>
> (Kristeva, 2000: 162)

Her point is well taken. She fails to notice however, that for the subject to withdraw from archaic and oppressive links, he must be able to relate to them, to communicate to himself and others the reality of a world or an object that is truly archaic, subsisting independently of our relation to it. The postulation of this sort of archaic objects or statements, the fetish, of an experience before the conditions for our experience had emerged at all, or beyond it, seems repugnant to the philosophical common sense of our age according to which there can be no cognisable reality outside the network of our relations with nature.

Since these postulated objects or experiences (the fetishes and ultimately, the experience of freedom) seem to index a reality that is not a case falling under the rules of the transcendental subject or the transcendental object, and refuses to be integrated under such a set, because it either occurred at a time anterior to the possibility of transcendental experience, or takes place beyond it, in a projected, postulated or virtual but real future, they seem to point towards a cognisable reality which is not given in the transcendental object of possible experience.[18]

In this sense, the Oresteian revolt takes us not only beyond the laws of the social, rightful and divine, but also beyond critique in the strictly philosophical sense of the word. That beyond is the future of the fetish. It entails yet another sort of revolution.

Notes

1 For society and its rules as a third type of order, see Hayek (1973: 20 ff.). For 'the third' as an emergent entity, with powers of intervention of its own, whose emergence brings about the existence of law and society, see Kojève (2000: §14, §15, at 77–94). See also Althusser (1996: 151 ff.).
2 See Kristeva (2000: 129) and Sartre (1947). For the ancient Greek trilogy, see Aeschylus (1991).
3 For this reference to 'reality by postulation' and its relationship to mathematics, see Diaz Muñoz (2000: 57–66) and Fowler (2006). See also Zubiri (1982: 144) and Ellacuría (1988).
4 In philosophy, this denial takes the form of the traditional notion of reality as a determined zone of things 'out there' for us. In that scheme reality can only be discovered, and even ultimately discovered to exhaustion (as in Whitehead and Russell's *Principia Mathematica*, or in the motif behind the search for a 'theory of everything' in physics). However, this notion creates many problems in relation to objects such as dreams, mathematical objects, laws, literary figures, historico-political realities and scientific theories that are known to utilise simplifying or incomplete assumptions. Against this notion, one should affirm that reality in the fundamental sense is not a determined zone of things but a formality: objects withdraw from any relationship to us and appear as something other, in a determinate form.
5 Therefore, this sort of withdrawal entails neither the acceptance of the background situation as fixed and fundamentally unchangeable, nor escapism to an authentic elsewhere, untouched by the situation. On the contrary, the figure of this withdrawal is that of the loop, the auto-transcendence of reality. See on TAZ and 'coming back' Bey (2003: 30).
6 'García Márquez Responde a Susan Sontag', in *El Tiempo*, 29 April 2003. Quoted by Jason Webb in 'Gabriel García Márquez Stays True to Beleaguered Castro', in *Guardian Unlimited, Guardian Newspapers,* posted on the web on 5 April 2003.
7 I am indebted to Slavoj Žižek for this critical point.
8 'And the peasant showed us the tricks of the Sierra, the strength necessary to live and triumph in it, and the dose of tenacity, the willingness to sacrifice, that is necessary to have in order to carry forward a people's destiny'. See Guevara (1997: 115).
9 See for instance Douzinas (2006: 13–27). Douzinas's argument gives support to the suggestion at the basis of this book: that the problem with this sort of justice is that it contains an implicit metaphysics of temporality that conceives the future as indeterminate and, hence, not real but merely possible. Building upon Douzinas's insight, it could be argued that this metaphysical structure is what connects the law of the Human at the time of empire (for instance, the doctrine of pre-emption) as law (barred) and the widespread de-normalisation (or renovation, re-fictionalising) of desire.
10 In Latin American philosophy this line connects Hegelianism and Heidegger, including Sartre and Fanon, with Guevara and Ignacio Ellacuría via the thought of Xavier Zubiri. For this connection and Ellacuría's criticism of dialectic materialism vis-à-vis historical materialism, see Ellacuría (1981: 970; 1970: 522).

11 For 'multi-faceted beings' see Guevara (1997: 199).
12 See Guevara (1997: 201–6). On 'fixed points' and the deterrent effect of catastrophe, see Dupuy (2004: 31).
13 See Laclau (2005: 110–17), Žižek (2006a) and Badiou (2005b: 117 ff).
14 The evidence to back up this assertion is contained in the documents written by Guevara after his departure from Cuba in April 1965. See Guevara (1997: 4–5). See also Castro (2005).
15 See Lacan (1991).
16 See on 'dark matter' Trotta (2007: 83–169). For a similar but crucially different analogy see Žižek (2006e).
17 See on this Zubiri (1980: 172). English version in *Sentient Intelligence*. Translated by T. Fowler. Washington DC: Xavier Zubiri Foundation of North America, 1999, 63.
18 For neuroscientist Rodolfo Llinás on cognition beyond/before experience, or 'predictive moves', see 2002, Chapter 12. For objects anterior to the possibility of experience or 'arche-objects', see Meillassoux (2006). See also Brassier (2007b: 15–54, at 20). He quotes Kant's critical denial of the possibility of such objects in *Critique of Pure Reason*. Translated by Norman Kemp-Smith. London: Macmillan, 1929, A495.

Bibliography

Abímbólá, Kólá (2006) *Yorùbá Culture: A Philosophical Account*. Birmingham: Ìrókò Academic Publishers.
Aeschylus (1991) 'Oresteia', in *The Complete Greek Tragedies*, edited by David Grene and Richmond Lattimore, vol. 1, Chicago, IL: University of Chicago Press.
Agamben, G. (1998) *Homo Sacer. Sovereign Power and Bare Life*. Translated by Daniel Heller-Rozen. Stanford: Stanford University Press.
Albiac, G. (1997) *La Sinagoga Vacía. Un Estudio de las Fuentes Marranas del Spinozismo*. Madrid: Hiperión.
Althusser, L. (1996) *Writings on Psychoanalysis*. Translated by J. Mehlman. New York: Columbia University Press.
Anspach, M. (2001) *Global Markets, Anonymous Victims*. Available online at http://europa.sim.ucm.es/compludoc/AA?a=Anspach%2c+Mark&donde=castellano&zfr=0 (Accessed 25 May 2007).
—— (2004) 'Introduction: Imitating Oedipus', in René Girard's *Oedipus Unbound. Selected Writings on Rivalry and Desire*. Stanford: Stanford University Press.
Arendt, H. (1951) *The Origins of Totalitarianism*. New York: Harcourt Brace.
—— (1958) *The Human Condition*. Chicago, IL: The University of Chicago Press.
—— (1994) *Eichmann in Jerusalem. A Report on the Banality of Evil*. 2nd edition, London and New York: Penguin.
Arias, A. (ed.) (2001) *The Rigoberta Menchú Controversy*. Minneapolis, MN: The University of Minnesota Press.
Badiou, A. (1990) *Le Nombre et les nombres*. Paris: Editions du Seuil.
—— (2002) *Ethics*. London: Verso.
—— (2003) ' The Caesura of Nihilism'. Lecture delivered at the University of Essex, September 2003.
—— (2005a) 'Politics: A Non-expressive Dialectics'. Lecture delivered at Birkbeck College, University of London, November 2005.
—— (2005b) 'Politics as truth Procedure', in *Theoretical Writings*. Translated by Ray Brassier and Alberto Toscano. London: Continuum.
—— (2007a) *L'Etre et L'événement, 2: Logiques des Mondes*. Paris: Seuil.
—— (2007b) 'Homage to Jacques Derrida', in *Adieu Derrida*. Edited by Costas Douzinas. Basingstoke and New York: Palgrave Macmillan.
Ballvé, T. (2005a) 'Bolivia's Separatist Movement', in *NACLA Report on the Americas*, 38(5), March/April 2005, pp. 16–17.

—— (2005b) 'Far From Over: Bolivia on the Brink of Civil War – or Revolution', posted on June 10, 2005. www.americas.org/item_19790 (Accessed on 19 June, 2005).
Baudrillard, J. (1975) *The Mirror of Production*. Translated by M. Poster. St Louis: Telos.
Becchi, P. (1986) 'Hegelsche Vorlesungsnachschriften und noch kein Ende?', in *Materialli per una storia della cultura giuridica* 16.1, 251–61.
Benjamin, W. (1985) *The Origin of German Tragic Drama*. Translated by J. Osborne. London: Verso.
—— (1986) 'Critique of Violence', in *Reflections: Essays, Aphorisms, Autobiographical Writings*. Translated by E. Jephcott. New York: Shocken.
—— (1999) *The Arcades Project*. Translated by H. Eiland and K. McLaughlin.
Benton, L. (2002) *Law and Colonial Cultures. Legal Regimes in World History: 1400–1900*. Cambridge: Cambridge University Press.
Berger, P. L. (1974) *Pyramids of Sacrifice. Political Ethics and Social Change*. New York: Anchor Books.
Bey, H. (2003) *T.A.Z. The Temporal Autonomous Zone, Ontological Anarchy, Poetic Terrorism*. First edition in 1985. New York: Autonomedia.
Bhaskar, R. (1990) *Harré and his Critics. Essays in Honour of Rom Harré with his Commentary on Them*. Oxford: Blackwell.
—— (1997) *A Realist Theory of Science*. 2nd edition. London: Verso.
Blanchot, M. (1981) *The Gaze of Orpheus and Other Literary Essays*. Edited by P. Adams Stirney and translated by Lydia Davis. New York: Station Hill.
Bloor, David. (1991) *Knowledge and Social Imagery*. London: Routledge, 1976; 2nd edition by the University of Chicago Press.
Borges, J. L. (1970) 'Tlön, Uqbar, Orbis Tertius', in *Labyrinths*. Edited by D. Yates and J. Irby, London: Penguin.
Bowers, M. A. (2004) *Magic(al) Realism*. London: Routledge.
Bracht, B. R. (1996) 'Defacing the Currency: Diogenes' Rhetoric and the Invention of Cynicism', in *The Cynics. The Cynic Movement in Antiquity and Its Legacy*. Edited by R. Bracht Branham and Marie-Odile Goulet-Cazé. Berkeley and Los Angeles: University of California Press.
Bracken, C. (1997) *The Potlatch Papers: A Colonial Case History*. Chicago, IL: The University of Chicago Press.
—— (2007) *Magical Criticism. The Recourse of Savage Philosophy*. Chicago, IL: The University of Chicago Press.
Braidotti, R. (2006) *Transpositions*. Cambridge: Polity Press.
Brassier, R. (2007a) *Nihil Unbound: Enlightenment and Extinction*. Basingstoke and New York: Palgrave Macmillan.
—— (2007b) 'The Enigma of Realism: On Quentin Meillassoux's *After Finitude*', in *Collapse: Philosophical Research and Development*. Oxford: Urbanomics.
Breckman, W. (2001) *Marx, The Young Hegelians and the Origins of Radical Social Theory*. Cambridge: Cambridge University Press.
Bronkhorst, D. (2003) *The Human Rights Film: Reflections on its History, Principles and Practices*. International Amsterdam Film Festival. Available online at www.oneworld.cz/ow/2004/en/workshops/index2.php (Accessed 11 April 2007).
Buck-Morss, S. (2000) 'Hegel and Haiti', in *Critical Inquiry*, Vol. 26, No. 4, Summer.

Butler, J. Laclau, E. and Žižek, S. (2000) *Hegemony, Contingency, Universality*. London: Verso.
Calasso, R. (1994) *The Marriage of Cadmus and Harmony*. Translated by Tim Parks. London: Vintage.
Carotenuto, A. (1984) *A Secret Symmetry: Sabina Spielrein Between Jung and Freud*. Translated by A. Pomerans, J. Shepley and K. Winston with a commentary by Bruno Bettelheim. New York: Pantheon.
Carpentier, A. (1976) *Reasons of State/El Recurso del Método*. London: Writers and Readers Publications.
—— (1987) *Guerra del tiempo y otros relatos*, Madrid: Alianza.
—— (2001) *Music in Cuba*. Translated by Alan West-Durán. Edited by Timothy Brennan. Minneapolis, MN: University of Minnesota Press.
Castro, F. (2005) *Che: A Memoir by Fidel Castro*. New York and Melbourne: Ocean.
Castro-Klarén, Sara (2000) 'A Genealogy for the "Manifiesto Antropófago"', in *Nepantla. Views from South*, vol. I, issue 2. Durham: Duke University Press.
Cerón, Jaime (2007) 'Translating Hegemony: Art Practices in Latin America', in *Naked Punch. An Engaged Review of Contemporary Art and Thought*. Issue 09, Summer/Fall 2007. London: Naked Punch Collective.
Chase, A. (1997) *Law and History. The Evolution of the American Legal System*. New York: The New Press.
Cheah, P. (2003) *Spectral Nationality. Passages of Freedom from Kant to Postcolonial Literatures of Liberation*. New York: Columbia University Press.
Clark, A. (1997) *Being There. Putting Brain, Body and World Together Again*. Cambridge, MA: MIT Press.
Clastres, P. (1994) *Archeology of Violence*. New York: Semiotext(e).
Clavero, B. (2000) *Ama Llunku, Abya Yala: Constituyencia Indígena y Código Ladino por América*. Madrid: Centro de Estudios Políticos y Constitucionales.
Cook, N. (1998) *Analysing Musical Multimedia*. Oxford and New York: Oxford University Press.
Copjec, J. (2003) *Imagine There's No Woman: Ethics and Sublimation*. Cambridge, MA: MIT Press.
Coronil, F. (1995) 'Transculturation and the Politics of Theory: Countering the Center, Cuban Counterpoint'. Introduction to Fernando Ortiz's *Cuban Counterpoint. Tobacco and Sugar*. Durham: Duke University Press.
—— (1997) *The Magical State. Nature, Money and Modernity in Venezuela*. Chicago, IL: Chicago University Press.
—— (2000a) 'Towards a Critique of Globalcentrism: Speculations on Capitalism's Nature', in *Public Culture*, vol. 12, n. 2. *Milennial Capitalism and the Culture of Neoliberalism*. Edited by Jean and John Comaroff. Society for Transnational Cultural Studies. Durham: Duke University Press.
—— (2000b) 'Del Eurocentrismo al Globocentrismo: La Naturaleza del Poscolonialismo', in *La Colonialidad del Saber*. Edited by Edgardo Lander. Buenos Aires: CLACSO.
Crawford, H. T. (2007) 'An Interview With Bruno Latour'. Available online at http://muse.jhu.edu/journal/configurations/v001/1.2crawford.html (Accessed 24 April 2007).
Davies, H. (1996) 'A History of Sampling' in *Organised Sound*, 1: 3-11. Cambridge: Cambridge University Press.

Davis, M. (2007) *Buda's Wagon. A Short History of the Car Bomb*. London: Verso.
De Andrade, O. (1981) [1928]. 'Manifiesto Antropófago', in *Obra Escogida*. Edited by Haroldo de Campos. Caracas: Biblioteca Ayacucho.
De Landa, M. (1999) *The Geology of Morals. A Neo-Materialist Interpretation*. Available online at www.t0.or.at/delanda/geology.htm (Accessed 23/6/06).
De Las Casas, B. (1957) *Obras Escogidas*, I–IV. Madrid: BAE.
Dedekind, R. (1909) *Continuity and Irrational Numbers*, in *Essays on the Theory of Numbers*. Translated by W. W. Beman, Chicago, IL: Open Court.
Deleuze, G. and Guattari, F. (1987) *A Thousand Plateaus*. Minneapolis: University of Minnesota Press.
Derrida, J. (1987a) *The Truth in Painting*. Translated by G. Bennington and I. McLeod, Chicago, IL: The University of Chicago Press.
—— (1987b) 'The Laws of Reflection: Nelson Mandela, in Admiration', in *For Nelson Mandela*. Translated by M. A. Caws and I. Lorenz, edited by J. Derrida and M. Tlili. New York: Henry Holt & Co.
—— (1987c) 'To Speculate – On "Freud"', in *The Postcard: From Socrates to Freud and Beyond*. Translated by Alan Bass. Chicago: The University of Chicago Press.
—— (1994) *Spectres of Marx*. Translated by P. Kamuf. London and New York: Routledge.
—— (2002) 'Force of Law: The Mystical Foundation of Authority', in *Deconstruction and the Possibility of Justice*. Edited By Drucilla Cornell, Michael Rosenfeld and David Gray Carlson. New York: Routledge, 1992. Reprinted (complete English version) in *Acts of Religion*. New York and London: Routledge.
—— and Stiegler, B. (2002) *Ecographies of Television*. London: Polity Press.
Dhanvantari, S. (2004) 'French Revolutionary Song in the Haitian Revolution', in *African Diasporas in the New and Old Worlds. Consciousness and Imagination*. Edited by G. Fabre and K. Benesch. Amsterdam/New York: Rodopi.
Díaz Muñoz, G. (2000) 'Aproximación del Realismo Matemático de Gödel al Realismo Constructivo de Zubiri', in *The Xavier Zubiri Review*, 3: 7–28.
Diamantides, M. (2006–7) 'The Rule of Law and Its Discontents' in *Constitutional & Administrative Law. Student Handbook*. Edited by M. Diamantides and O. Guardiola-Rivera, London: Birkbeck Law School.
Dickey, L. (1998) *Hegel. Religion, Economic, and the Politics of Spirit, 1770–1807*. Cambridge: Cambridge University Press.
Dolar, M. (1991) 'I Shall Be With You on Your Wedding-night: Lacan and the Uncanny', in *October*, 58.
—— (2006) *A Voice and Nothing More*. Cambridge, MA: MIT Press.
Dollimore, J. (1998) *Death, Desire and Loss in Western Culture*. London: Allen Lane & The Penguin Press.
Donzelot, J. (1981) 'Pleasure in Work', in *Ideology and Consciousness*, Winter issue, 3–28.
Douzinas, C. (1998) *Law and the Emotions. Prolegomena for a Psychoanalytical Approach to Legal Study*. Florence: European University Institute.
—— (2000) *The End of Human Rights*. London: Hart Publishing.
—— (2006) 'Theses on Law, History and Time', in *Melbourne Journal of International Law 7*, Issue 1.

—— (2007) *Human Rights and Empire. The Political Philosophy of Cosmopolitanism*. London and New York: Routledge-Cavendish.
—— and Nead, L. (1999) *Law and The Image: The Authority of Art and the Aesthetics of the Law*. Chicago, IL: Chicago University Press.
——, Goodrich, P. and Hachamovitch, Y. (1994) *Politics, Postmodernity and Critical Legal Studies*. London: Routledge.
D'Spagnat, B. (2006) *On Physics and Philosophy*. Princeton, NJ: Princeton University Press.
Duffield, M. (2001) *Global Governance and the New Wars. The Merging of Development and Security*. London and New York: Zed Books.
Dupuy, J. P. (1992) *Le sacrifice et l'envie*. Paris: Fondation Saint-Simon/Calmann-Lévy.
—— (1998) *El Sacrificio y la Envidia: El Liberalismo Frente a la Justicia Social*. Translated from the French original by J. Gutierrez and J. C. Martins. Barcelona: Gedisa.
—— (2000a) *The Mechanization of the Mind. On the Origins of Cognitive Science*. Translated by M. B. DeBevoise. Princeton, NJ: Princeton University Press.
—— (2000b) 'Philosophical Foundations of a New Concept of Equilibrium in the Social Sciences', in *Philosophical Studies* 100: 323–45.
—— (2002a) *Pour un Catastrophisme Éclairé*. Paris: Seuil.
—— (2002b) *Avions-nous Oublié le Mal?* Paris: Bayard.
—— (2004) *Complexity and Uncertainty. A Contibution to the Work in Progress of the 'Foresighting the New Technology Wave' High-Level Expert Group*. Brussels: European Commission.
—— (2005) *Petite Métaphysique des Tsunamis*. Paris: Seuil.
—— (2006) *Counterfactual Consequences*. Presented at the Workshop on Rationality and Change, Cambridge, UK, 6/8 September.
Durand-Barthez, M. (2002) 'West Africa/Haiti: The Voodooic Bridge', in *Internet Zeitschrift für Kulturwissenschaften 14*. Available online at www.inst.at/trans/14Nr/barnes14.htm. (Accessed 2 March 2008).
Dussel, E. (1998) *Ética de la Liberación en la Edad de la Globalización*. Madrid: Trotta.
—— (2001a) *Hacia Una Filosofía Política Crítica*. Bilbao: Descleé de Brouwer.
—— (2001b) 'Ethics is the Original Philosophy, or The Barbarian Words Coming from the Third World: An Interview with Enrique Dussel', in *Boundary 2. An International Journal of Literature and Culture*, 28: 19–73. Durham: Duke University Press.
—— (2003) 'Philosophy in Latin America in the Twentieth Century: Currents and Problems', in *Latin American Philosophy: Currents, Issues, Debates*. Edited by Eduardo Mendieta. Bloomington and Indianapolis: Indiana University Press.
—— (2006) *20 Tesis Sobre Política*. Méjico: Fondo de Cultura Económica.
Ellacuría, I. (1970) 'La Idea de Filosofía en Xavier Zubiri', in *Homenaje a Xavier Zubiri II*, Madrid: Editorial Moneda y Crédito.
—— (1981) 'El Objeto de la Filosofía', in *Estudios Centroamericanos ECA*, n. 396–7, vol. 1, San Salvador: Universidad Centro Americana.
—— (1988) 'Superación del Reduccionismo Idealista', in *Estudios Centroamericanos (ECA)*, n. 477, San Salvador: Universidad Centro Americana Editores.
—— (1990) *Filosofía de la Realidad Histórica*. San Salvador: UCA Editores.

Engels, F. (1944) *Ludwig Feuerbach and the Outcome of Classical German Philosophy*, People's Publishing House.
Epstein, R. (2005) *Takings: Private Property and the Power of Eminent Domain*. Cambridge, MA: Harvard University Press.
Escobar, A. (1995) *Encountering Development: The Making and Unmaking of the Third World*. Princeton: Princeton University Press.
—— (Forthcoming) 'Actors, Networks, and New Knowledge Producers: Social Movements and the Paradigmatic Transition in the Sciences', in *Para Além das Guerras da Ciência: Um Discurso sobre as Ciências Revisitado*. Edited by Boaventura de Sousa Santos. Porto: Afrontamiento.
Ferguson, A. (1792) *Principles of Moral and Political Science*. Vol. 1. Edinburgh: A. Strahan.
Feuerbach, L. (1957) *The Essence of Christianity*. Translated by G. Eliot. New York: Harper Row.
—— (1973) *Das Wesen des Christentums*, 71, included in the *Gesammelte Werke*, 19 vols, vol. V, edited by Werner Schuffenhauer and Wolfgang Harich, Berlin: Akademie-Verlag.
Feyerabend, P. (1993) *Against Method*. London and New York: Verso.
Fischer, S. (2004) *Modernity Disavowed. Haiti and the Cultures of Slavery in the Age of Revolution*. Durham: Duke University Press.
Fischlin, D. (2003) 'Rebel Musics: Human Rights, resistant Sounds, and the Politics of Music Making', in *Rebel Musics*. Edited by Daniel Fischlin and Ajay Heble. Montréal: Black Rose Books.
Fitzpatrick, P. (2000) 'Magnified Features: The Underdevelopment of Law and Legitimation', in *Journal of South Pacific Law*, vol. 4.
—— (2001) *Modernism and the Grounds of Law*. Cambridge: Cambridge University Press.
—— (2006) 'Bare Sovereignty: *Homo Sacer* and the Insistence of law' Available online at http://muse.jhu.edu/journals/theory_and_event/v005/5.2fitzpatrick.html (Accessed 3 August 2006).
—— and Mostert, H. (2006) 'Law Against Law: Indigenous Rights and the Richtersveld Cases'. Available online at www.2.warwick.ac.uk/fac/soc/law/elj/lgd/2004_2/mostertfitzpatrick/ (Accessed 3 August 2006).
Forman, F. N. (2003) *Constitutional Change in the United Kingdom*. London and New York: Routledge.
Foucault, M. (1994) *The Order of Things. An Archeology of the Human Sciences* [1966]. First English edition printed by Tavistock Press, 1970. Reprinted, London: Routledge.
Fowler, T. B. (2002) 'A Framework for Political Theory Based on Zubiri's Concept of Reality', in *The Xavier Zubiri Review*, 4: 109–32. Washington: The Xavier Zubiri Foundation of North America.
—— (2006) *Zubiri's Reality by Postulation and Its Implication for the Relationship Between Science and Religion*. Delivered at the 'Continuity + Change: Perspectives on Science and Religion', June 3–7, 2006, in Philadelphia, PA, USA. Available online at www.metanexus.net. Accessed 13 November 2006.
Freud, S. (1953–74) 'The Uncanny' [1919], in *The Standard edition of the Complete Works of Sigmund Freud*, vol. 17: 247 ff. London: Hogarth Press and the Institute of Psycho-Analysis.

—— (1953–74) 'Observations on Transference Love (Further Recommendations on the Technique of Psycho-Analysis III' [1914] in *Papers on Technique*, included in *The Standard Edition of the Complete Works of Sigmund Freud*, vol. 12. London: Hogarth Press and the Institute of Psycho-Analysis.

—— (1953–74) 'The Unconscious' [1915], in *The Standard Edition of the Complete Works of Sigmund Freud*, vol. 18. London: Hogarth Press and the Institute of Psycho-Analysis.

—— (1953–74) 'Introduction to *Psycho-Analysis and the War Neuroses*'. London: International Psycho-Analytic Press, [1919] 1921; reprinted in *The Standard Edition of the Complete Works of Sigmund Freud*, vol. 17, pp. 205–10. London: Hogarth Press and the Institute of Psycho-Analysis.

—— (1975) [1922] *Group Psychology and the Analysis of the Ego* [1922]. W. W. Norton & Company.

—— (1973–86) 'Beyond the Pleasure Principle', in *The Pelican Freud Library*. Translated by James Strachey, Alix Strachey and Alan Tyson. Vol. 11, Harmondsworth: Penguin.

Friedmann, M. (1981) *Free to Choose*. Avon. Spanish edition: *Libertad de Elegir* (1982) Barcelona: Grijalbo.

Fuentes, Federico (2007). 'The Battle for Bolivia's Future', posted on 15 June 2007 Available online at http://boliviarising.blogspot.com/2007/06/battle-for-bolivias-future.html (Accessed 16/6/07).

Fukushima, M. (2005) 'On Small Devices of Thought. Concepts, Etymology and the Problem of Translation', in *Making Things Public. Atmospheres of Democracy*. Edited by Bruno Latour and Peter Weibel, ZKM/Center for Art & Media Karlsruhe, Cambridge, MA: MIT Press.

Galeano, E. (1978) *Open Veins of Latin America: Five Centuries of the Pillage of a Continent*. Translated by C. Belfrage. New York: Monthly Review Press.

Garavito, E. (1991) 'Tiempo y Espacio en el Discurso de Michel Foucault', in Foucault, Michel. *El Sujeto y el Poder*. Bogotá: Carpe Diem Ediciones.

Geary, A. (2005) 'JG Ballard's Jurisprudence', in *Law and Popular Culture*. Edited by Michael Freedman. Oxford: Oxford University Press.

Gibson, A. (2005) 'Serres at the Crossroads', in *Mapping Serres*. Edited by N. Abbas. Ann Arbor: The University of Michigan Press.

Gil, J. (1998) *Metamorphoses of the Body*. Minneapolis, MN: University of Minnesota Press.

Girard, R. (1977) *Violence and the Sacred*. Translated by P. Gregory. Baltimore, MD: Johns Hopkins Press.

—— (2003) *Things Hidden Since the Foundation of the World*. London and New York: Continuum.

—— (2004) *Oedipus Unbound. Selected Writings on Rivalry and Desire*. Edited by M. A. Anspach. Stanford, CA: Stanford University Press.

—— (2005) 'From Ritual to Science', in *Mapping Serres*. Edited by Niran Abbas, Ann Arbor: The University of Michigan Press.

Goodchild, P. (2005) 'Capital and Kingdom. An Eschatological Ontology' in *Theology and the Political. The New Debate*. Edited by Creston Davis, John Milbank and Slavoj Žižek, with and introduction by Rowan Williams. Durham: Duke University Press.

Gordon, A. F. (2004) *Ghostly Matters: Haunting and the Sociological Imagination*. 4th edition. Minneapolis, MN: Minnesota University Press.

Gordon, P. E. (2005) 'Self-authorizing Modernity: Problems of Interpretation in the History of German Idealism', in *History and Theory* 44: 121–37. Wesleyan University Press.

Grosfoguel, R. (2000) 'Developmentalism, Modernity, and Dependency Theory in Latin America', in *Nepantla. Views from South*, vol. I, issue 2. Durham: Duke University Press.

Grosfoguel, Ramón and Cervantes-Rodríguez, Ana (2002) 'Introduction: Unthinking Twentieth Century Mythologies', in *The Modern/Colonial/Capitalist World-System in the Twentieth Century*. Westport, Conn.: Praeger.

Guardiola-Rivera, O. (2006a) 'The Most Sublime of Fetishists', in *Naked Punch. An Engaged Review of Contemporary Art and Thought*. Issue 8. London: Naked Punch Collective/Arts Council England/The European Forum for Philosophy.

—— (2006b) 'Paradise Lost...The Meaning of Modernity and the Antinomy of the Law', in *Law and Critique* 17, Berlin: Springer.

—— (2006c) 'A Politics of Inexistence. On Santos' Sociology of Emergence', in *King's College Law Journal*, 17(1). London: Hart Publishing.

—— (2007a) 'Return of the Fetish: A Plea for a New Materialism', in *Law and Critique* 18, Berlin: Springer.

—— (2007b) 'The Image-Space', in *Naked Punch. An Engaged Review of Contemporary Art and Thought*. Issue 09, Summer/Fall 2007. London: Naked Punch Collective.

——, Castro-Gómez, S. and Millán, C. (1999) *Pensar (en) los Intersticios. Teoría y Práctica de la Crítica Poscolonial*. Bogotá: Universidad Javeriana.

Guattari, F. (1993) 'La Construcción Filosófico-Ecosófica', in *El Constructivismo Guattariano*. Cali, COL: Universidad del Valle.

Guéguen, P. G. (2006) 'The Intimate, The Extimate and Psychoanalytic Discourse', in *Jacques Lacan and the Other Side of Psychoanalysis*. Edited by J. Clemens and R. Grigg. Durham and London: Duke University Press.

Guevara, E. (1997) 'What We Have Learned and What We Have Taught' [December 1958], 'Notes for the Study of the Ideology of the Cuban Revolution', and 'Socialism and Man in Cuba' [1965], in *Che Guevara Reader: Writings on Guerrilla Strategy, Politics and Revolution*. Edited by David Deutschmann. Melbourne and London: Ocean Books.

Gunning, T. (1995) 'Phantom Images and Modern Manifestations: Spirit, Photography, Magic Theater, Trick Films and Photography's Uncanny', in *Fugitive Images: From Photography to Video*. Edited by Patrice Petro. Bloomington, IN: Indiana University Press.

Habermas, J. (1975) [1973] *Legitimation Crisis*. Translated by T. McCarthy. Boston: Beacon Press.

—— (1994) *The Past as Future*. Cambridge: Polity.

—— (2001) *The Postnational Constellation*. Cambridge: Polity.

Haidar, A. Esposito, P. and Lekhal, M. (2007) 'Breaking the Silence. The Impact of the Moroccan Occupation on Human and Cultural Rights'. Roundtable at the Sandblast Festival, 3–4 November London.

Hallward, P. (2001) *Absolutely Postcolonial*. Manchester: Manchester University Press.

—— (2002) 'Translator's Introduction', in Alain Badiou's *Ethics. An Essay on the Understanding of Evil*. London: Verso.
—— (2003) *Badiou. A Subject to Truth*. Minneapolis: Minnesota University Press.
—— (2005a) 'Where Is a Political World?'. Conference delivered at Birkbeck College, University of London. 25 November 2005.
—— (2005b) 'The Politics of Prescription', in *The South Atlantic Quarterly* 104: 4. Durham: Duke University Press.
—— (2006) 'Retreatment' in *Radical Philosophy* 139, September/October.
Hanssen, B. (1998) *Walter Benjamin's Other History. Of Stones, Animals, Human Beings and Angels*. Berkeley, CA: University of California Press.
—— (2000) *Critique of Violence. Between Poststructuralism and Critical Theory*. London: Routledge.
Haraway, D. (2000) 'A Cyborg Manifesto: Science, Technology and Socialist Feminism in the Late Twentieth Century', in *The Cybercultures Reader*. Edited by David Bell and Barbara Kennedy. New York and London: Routledge.
Hardt, M. (2007) 'Thomas Jefferson, or, the Transition of Democracy', in *Thomas Jefferson: The Declaration of Independence*. London and New York: Verso.
—— and Negri, A. (1994) *Labour of Dionysus. A Critique of the State-Form*. Minneapolis: University of Minnesota Press.
—— (2000) *Empire*. Cambridge, MA: Harvard University Press.
Harman, G. (2002) *Tool-Being. Heidegger and the Metaphysics of Objects*. Chicago and La Salle: Open Court.
—— (2003) *The Metaphysics of Objects: Latour and its Aftermath*. Manuscript with the author.
—— (2005) *Guerrilla Metaphysics. Phenomenology and the Carpentry of Things*. Chicago, IL: Open Court.
—— (2006) 'Quentin Meillassoux: A New French Philosopher', in *Philosophy Today*, Spring 2007, Chicago: De Paul University. Manuscript with the author.
—— (2007a) 'On Vicarious Causation', in *Collapse. Philosophical Research and Development*, vol. II: 171–205. Oxford: Urbanomics.
—— (2007b) 'Aesthetics as First Philosophy. Levinas and the Nonhuman', in *Naked Punch. The Engaged Review of Contemporary Art and Thought*, issue 9. London: Naked Punch Collective.
—— (2007c) 'Heidegger's Numerology', in *Heidegger Explained: From Phenomenon to Thing*. Chicago, IL: Open Court.
Hart, H. L. A. (1961) *The Concept of Law*. Oxford: Oxford University Press.
Hart, S. 'Review. Selected Poems by César Vallejo', in *The Liberal*, October/November 2006, 41.
Hayek, F. v. (1973) *Law, Legislation, and Liberty. Volume 1: Rules and Order*. Chicago, IL: Chicago University Press.
Hegel, G. W. F. (1941) *Sämtliche Werke: Jubiläumsausgabe in zwanzig Bänden*. Edited by H. Glockner. Stuttgart: Frommann.
—— (1969) *The Science of Logic* [1812]. Translated by A. V. Miller. New Jersey: Humanities Press International.
—— (1973–4) *Vorlesungen über Rechtsphilosophie* [1824–5]. Edited by Karl-Heinz Ilting. Stuttgart.

—— (1977) *Phenomenology of Spirit*. Translated by A. V. Miller. Oxford: Oxford University Press.
—— (1979) 'The System of Ethical Life', in *System of Ethical Life and First Philosophy of Spirit*. Edited and translated by H. Harris and T. Knox. Albany: State University of New York Press.
—— (1981) *Philosophy of Right*. Translated and edited by T. M. Knox. Oxford: Oxford University Press.
—— (1983) *Philosophie des Rechts: Die Vorlesung von 1819–20 in einer Nachschrift*. Ed. D. Heinrich, Frankfurt: n.p.
—— (1988) *Phenomenology of Spirit*. Translated by A. V. Miller. India: Motilal Banarsidass.
—— (1991) *Encyclopedia of the Philosophical Sciences I: Logic*. T. F. Geraets, W. A. Suchting and H. S. Harris. Indianapolis: Hackett.
—— (1999) *Haptwerke in sechs Bänden*, Hamburg: Felix Meiner.
Heidegger, M. (1959) *An Introduction to Metaphysics*. Translated by R. Manheim. New Haven, CT: Yale University Press.
—— (1967) *Being and Time*. Translated by J. Macquarrie and E. Robinson, Oxford: Blackwell.
—— (1975) 'The Origin of the Work of Art', in *Poetry, Language, Thought*. Translated by Albert Hofstader. New York: Harper Colophon Books.
—— (1993) 'The Way to Language', in *Basic Writings: From Being and Time (1927) to The Task of Thinking (1964)*. Edited by David Farrell Krell. London: Routledge.
Hernández, J. A. (2005) *Hacia Una Historia de lo Imposible. La Revolución Haitiana y el 'Libro de Pinturas' de José Antonio Aponte*. PhD Dissertation. University of Pittsburgh. Faculty of Arts and Sciences.
Hirst, P. and Thompson, G. (1996) *Globalisation in Question*. Cambridge: Polity Press.
Hoogvelt, A. (1997) *Globalization and the Postcolonial World*. Baltimore, MA: Johns Hopkins University Press.
Hopkins, T. and Wallerstein, I. eds. (1996) *The Age of Transition. Trajectory of the World-System – 1945–2025*. London: Zed Books.
Houllebeq, M. (2006) *H. P. Lovecraft. Against the World, Against Life*. London: Weidenfeld & Nicolson.
Humphreys, M. and Weinstein, J. (2007) 'Demobilization and Reintegration', in *Journal of Conflict Resolution*, vol. 51, n. 4, 531–67. Sage Publications.
Ignatieff, M. (2004) *The Lesser Evil. Political Ethics in an Age of Terror*. Princeton: Princeton University Press.
Jefferson, T. [1787–1824] (2007) *The Declaration of Independence*. Edited with an introductory study by Michael Hardt. London and New York: Verso.
Jonas, H. (1985) *The Imperative of Responsibility. In Search for an Ethics for the Technological Age*. Chicago, IL: University of Chicago Press.
Kaiser, M. (2006) 'Defining the Precautionary Principle: Uncertainties and Values in Science for Policy', in *Dilemmata. Jahrbuch der Altonaer Stiftung für Philosophische Grundlagenforschung (ASFPG)* I: 1–11.Töning, Lübeck and Marburg: Der Andere Verlag.
Kant, I. (1929) *Critique of Pure Reason*. Translated by Norman Kemp Smith, London: Macmillan.

—— (1993) *Opus Postumum*. Edited by Eckart Forster. Translated by E. Forster and M. Rosen. Cambridge: Cambridge University Press.
—— (1996) *Critique of Pure Reason*. Translated by Werner S. Pluhar. Indianapolis: Hackett.
Karatani, K. (2005) *Trans-Critique. On Kant and Marx*. Translated by Sabu Kohso. Cambridge, MA: MIT Press.
Kaufman, E. (2005) 'To Cut Too Deeply and Not Enough: Violence and the Incorporeal', in *Theology and the Political. The New Debate*. Edited by Creston Davis, John Milbank and Slavoj Zizek. Durham: Duke University Press.
Kemple, T. (1995) *Reading Marx Writing. Melodrama, the Market, and the 'Grundrisse'*. Stanford, CA: Stanford University Press.
Kermode, M. (2006) 'Pain should not be sought – but it should never be avoided', *The Observer*, Review, 5 November 2006, 11.
Kerr, J. (1995) *La Historia Secreta del Psicoanálisis: Jung, Freud y Sabina Spielrein*. Barcelona: Crítica. Original English edition (1993) *A Most Dangerous Method: The Story of Jung, Freud and Sabina Spielrein*. New York: Alfred A. Knopf.
Kerruish, V. (2006) 'On Re-Staging the Universal: Butler, Hegel and Contesting the Closure of Logic', in *Dilemmatta. Jahrbuch der ASFPG*, I: 23–60. Marburg: Der Andere Verlag.
—— and Petersen, U. (2006) 'Philosophical Sanity, Mysteries of the Understanding, and Dialectical Logic', in *Dilemmatta. Jahrbuch der ASFPG*, I: 61–91. Marburg: Der Andere Verlag.
Klein, N. (2007) *The Shock Doctrine. The Rise of Disaster Capitalism*. London and New York: Allen Lane.
Klossowski, P. (1969) *Nietszche et le Cercle Vicieux*. Paris: Mercure de France.
Kojève, A. (1969) *Introduction to the Reading of Hegel. Lectures on the Phenomenology of Spirit*. Edited by A. Bloom and translated by J. H. Nichols Jr. Ithaca, IL: Cornell University Press.
—— (2000) *Outline of a Phenomenology of Right*. Translated by B. Frost and R. Howse. Oxford: Rowman and Littlefield.
Kramer, L. D. (2004) *The People Themselves. Popular Constitutionalism and Judicial Review*. Oxford: Oxford University Press.
Kristeva, J. (1982) *Black Sun: Depression and Melancholia*. Translated by L. S. Roudez. New York: Columbia University Press.
—— (2000) *The Sense and Non-sense of Revolt*. New York: Columbia University Press.
Küchler, T. (1994) *Postmodern Gaming: Heidegger, Duchamp, Derrida*. New York: Lang.
Lacan, J. (1991) *Le Séminaire, Livre XVII: L'envers de la Psychanalyse*. Edited by J. A. Miller. Paris: Seuil.
—— (1997) *The Ethics of Psychoanalysis. The Seminar of Jacques Lacan Book VII*. Translated by D. Porter. London: W. W. Norton.
—— (2001) 'La Logique du Fantasme', in *Autres Écrits*. Paris: Seuil.
Lacey, N. (2004) *A Life of H. L. A. Hart: The Nightmare and the Noble Dream*. Oxford: Oxford University Press.
Laclau, E. (1980) 'Populist Rupture and Discourse', in *Screen Education* 34, Spring.
—— (1996) *Emancipation(s)*, London: Verso.
—— (2005) *On Populist Reason*. London: Verso.

—— (2006) 'Why Constructing a People is the Main Task of Radical Politics', in *Critical Inquiry* 32, Summer. Chicago, IL: Chicago University Press.
Langer, Suzanne K. (1942) *Philosophy in a New Key: A Study of the Symbolism of Reason, Rite and Art*. Cambridge, MA: Harvard University Press.
Latour, Bruno (2002) *La Fabrique du droit: Une Ethnographie du Conseil D'État*, Paris: La Découverte.
—— (2004a). 'Why Has Critique Run Out of Steam? From Matters of Fact to Matters of Concern', in *Critical Inquiry* 30, Chicago, IL: Chicago University Press.
—— (2004b) *Politics of Nature*. Cambridge, MA: Harvard University Press.
Le Bon, G. (1895) *La Psychologie des Foules*. Paris: Édition Félix Alcan.
Legendre, P. (1988) *Ecrits Juridiques de Moyen Age Occidental*. Paris: Variorum.
—— (1997) *Law and the Unconscious: A Pierre Legendre Reader*. Edited by A. Pottage and A. Schutz. London: Palgrave McMillan.
Lehmann, William C. (1979) *John Millar of Glasgow, 1735–1801*. Cambridge: Cambridge University Press, 1960, reprinted by Arno Press.
Leibniz, G. W. (1966) *Logical Papers. A Selection*. Edited and translated by G. H. R. Parkinson. Oxford: Oxford at Clarendon Press.
Lenin, V. I. (1961) *Philosophical Notebooks*, in *Collected Works*, vol. 38. Translated by C. Dutt, Moscow: Foreign Languages Publications.
Leroi-Gourhan, A. (1993) *Gesture and Speech*. Translated by Anna Bostock Berger. Cambridge, MA: MIT Press.
Levinas, E. (1997) *Otherwise than Being, or Beyond Essence*. Translated by A. Lingis. Pittsburgh: Duquesne University Press.
Lévi-Strauss, C. (1973) 'Introduction à l'oeuvre de Marcel Mauss', in Marcel Mauss' *Sociologie et anthropologie*, Paris: PUF.
Lewis, D. K. (1986) 'Counterfactual Dependence and Time's Arrow', in *Philosophical Papers*, vol. II. Oxford: Oxford University Press.
Lifshitz, M. (1973) *The Philosophy of Art of Karl Marx*. London: Pluto Press.
Lindahl, H. (2006) 'Give and Take: Arendt and the *Nomos* of Political Community', in *Philosophy and Social Criticism*, 32(7): 881–901.
—— (2007) *Collective Self-Legislation as an Actus Impurus. A Response to Heidegger's Critique of European Nihilism*. Paper delivered at the Thematics Workshop series on secular theology, 9 February 2007, Birkbeck School of Law, University of London
Linebaugh, P. and Rediker, M. (2000) *The Many-Headed Hydra. Sailors, Slaves, Commoners and the Hidden History of the Revolutionary Atlantic*. Boston, MA: Beacon Press.
Llinás, R. R. (2002) *I of the Vortex*. Cambridge, MA: MIT Press. Spanish Edition (2003) *El Cerebro y el Mito del Yo*. Prologue by Gabriel García Márquez. Bogotá: Norma.
Lloyd Smith, A. (1992) 'The Phantoms of *Drood* and *Rebecca*', in *Poetics Today*, 13(2): 285–308.
Lora, M. (2005) 'Los capitanes del Comando Camba', in *Juguete Rabioso*, 5 February 2005, 8–10.
Losurdo, D. (2004) *Hegel and the Freedom of Moderns*. Durham: Duke University Press.
Luckmann, T. and Berger, P. (1966) *The Social Construction of Reality: A Treatise in the Sociology of Knowledge*. New York: Anchor Books.

Luhmann, N. (1990) 'The Cognitive Program of Constructivism and a reality that remains Unknown', in *Self-organization: Portrait of a Scientific Revolution*. Edited by Wolfgang Krohn et al. Dordrecht: Kluwer.
—— (2000) *Art as Social System*. Translated by Eva M. Knodt. Stanford, CA: Stanford University Press.
McDowell, J. (2007) 'Disputed Ground: Battle Between Left and Right Becomes Territorial in the Plaza de Cochabamba', posted on 12 June 2007 Available online at www.ubnoticias.org/en/article/disputed-ground (Accessed 17 June 2007).
McGowan, T. (2007) *The Impossible David Lynch*. New York: Columbia University Press.
Mack, A. Humphreys, M. and Weinstein, J. (2004) *Understanding Civil War: Quantity versus Quality? Toward More Effective Collaboration between Qualitative and Quantitative Conflict Research Communities*. Available online at www.hsrgroup.org/workshops/bellagio1/bellagio1concept.pdf. (Accessed 21 February 2008).
Mahmood, S. (2004) *Politics of Piety: Islamic Revival and the Feminist Subject*. Princeton, NJ: Princeton University Press.
—— (2007) 'Objectivity and Moral Claims'. Paper delivered at the *Thematics* workshop, Birkbeck College School of Law, University of London, 9 February 2007.
Malabou, C. (2004) *Que Faire de Notre Cerveau*. Paris: Bayard.
—— (2005) *The Future of Hegel: Plasticity, Temporality and Dialectic*. With a preface by Jacques Derrida. New York and London: Routledge.
Mariátegui, J. C. (1979) 'El Hombre y el Mito', in *El Alma Matinal*. Lima: Biblioteca Amauta.
—— (1980) 'Prólogo a "Tempestad en Los Andes" de E. Valcárcel', in *El Marxismo en América Latina (De 1909 a Nuestros Días), Antología*. Edited by M. Löwy. Méjico: Era.
Martin, R. P. (1996) 'The Scythian Accent: Anacharsis and the Cynics', in *The Cynics*. Edited by R. Bracht Branham and M. O. Goulet-Cazé. Berkeley and LA: California University Press.
Marx, K. (1973) *Grundrisse*. Translated by Martin Nicolaus. New York: Vintage Books.
—— (1975) [1842] *On Freedom of the Press. Proceedings of the Sixth Rhine Province Assembly. Debates on Freedom of the Press and Publication of the Proceedings of the Assembly of the Estates*. First published in 10 May 1842, in the *Rheinische Zeitung*. Included in: Marx, K. and Engels, F. *Collected Works* [normally cited as MECW], vol. 1, Chapter III, pp. 132–81. New York: International Publishers.
—— (2007) *Dispatches for the New York Tribune: Selected Journalism of Karl Marx*. Edited by James Ledbetter with a foreword by Francis Wheen. London and New York: Penguin Classics.
—— and Engels, F. (1976) 'Exzerpte und Notizen bis 1842', in *Gesamtausgabe* (new MEGA), vol. 4/1. Berlin: Dieta Verlag.
May, L. Friedman, M. and Clark, A. (eds) (1996) *Mind and Morals. Essays on Ethics and Cognitive Science*. Cambridge, MA: MIT Press.
Mazzoldi, B. and Téllez, F. (2007) 'The Pocket-Size Interview with Jacques Derrida', in *Critical Inquiry*, 33: 362–88. Chicago, IL: Chicago University Press.

Medrazza, S. and Rahola, F. (2006) 'The Postcolonial Condition. A Few Notes on the Quality of Historical Time in the Global Present', in *Postcolonial Text* 11, 1.
Meek, R. (1976) *Social Science and the Ignoble Savage*. Cambridge: Cambridge University Press.
Meillassoux, Q. (2006) *Après la finitude: Essai sur la nécessité de la contingence*, with a Preface by Alain Badiou. Paris: Editions de Seuil.
—— (2007) 'Potentiality & Virtuality', in *Collapse. Philosophical Research and Development*, vol. II, Spring 2007, Oxford: Urbanomics.
Menchú, R. (1985) *I, Rigoberta Menchú. An Indian Woman in Guatemala*. Edited by Elisabeth Burgos-Debray. London and New York: Verso.
Merleau-Ponty, M. (1968) 'The Intertwining – The Chiasm', in *The Visible and the Invisible*. Translated by Alphonso Lingis. Evanston, IL: Northwestern University Press.
Métraux, A. (1989) *Le Vaudou Haïtien*. Paris: Gallimard.
Mignolo, W. (1995) *The Darker Side of the Renaissance*. Ann Arbor, MI: Michigan University Press.
—— (2005) *The Idea of Latin America*. Oxford: Blackwell.
Milbank, J. (2005) 'Materialism and Transcendence', in *Theology and the Political. The New Debate*. Edited by Creston Davis, John Milbank and Slavoj Žižek. Durham: Duke University Press.
—— (2007) *Only Theology Saves Metaphysics: On the Modalities of Terror*. Available online at www.theologyphilosophycentre.co.uk/papers/Milbank_Only TheologySavesMetaphysics_final.doc (Accessed 8 August 2007).
Monroe, A. (2005) *Interrogation Machine. Laibach and the NSK*. Cambridge, MA: MIT Press.
Montag, W. (1999) *Bodies, Masses, Power. Spinoza and his Contemporaries*. London: Verso.
Moreiras, A. (2003) 'A Thinking Relationship. The End of Subalternity', in *The South Atlantic Quarterly* 101: 1, Winter. Durham: Duke University Press.
Múnera, A. (1995) *Failing to Construct the Colombian Nation: Race and Class in the Andean Caribbean Conflict, 1717–1816*. Ph.D. dissertation, University of Connecticut.
—— (1998) *El Fracaso de la Nación. Región, clase y raza en el Caribe Colombiano*: 1717–1810. Bogotá: Banco de la República y El Ancora Editores.
—— (2005) *Fronteras Imaginadas. La Construcción de la Geografía y de las Razas en el Siglo XIX*. Bogotá: Planeta Editores.
Murphy, J. (1994) *Working the Spirit: Ceremonies of the African Diaspora*. Boston, MA: Beacon Press.
Nancy, J. L. (2001) 'The Two Secrets of the Fetish', in *Diacritics* 31(2): Summer issue.
Negri, A. (1984) *Marx Beyond Marx. Lessons on the Grundrisse*. Edited by J. Fleming and translated by H. Cleaver, M. Ryan and M. Viano. South Hadley, MA: Bergin and Garvey.
Niehues-Pröbsting, H. (1996) 'The Modern Reception of Cynicism: Diogenes in the Enlightenment', in *The Cynics*. Edited by R. Bracht Branham and M. Goulet-Cazé. Berkeley, CA: University of California Press.
Nimtz jr. A. H. (2003) *Marx, Tocqueville and Race in America*. Lanham/New York: Lexington Books.

Nucetelli, S. (2002) *Latin American Thought. Philosophical Problems and Arguments*. Cambridge, MA.: Westview Publishers.
Offe, C. (1984) 'Crises of Crisis Management: Elements of a Political Crisis Theory', in *Contradictions of the Welfare State*. Edited by J. Keane. Cambridge, MA: MIT Press.
Ortiz, F. (1995) *Cuban Counterpoint: Tobacco and Sugar*. Translated by Harriet de Onís. Durham: Duke University Press.
Otero, L. M. (ed.) (1965). *Constituciones de Venezuela*. Madrid: Instituto de Estudios Políticos y Constitucionales, 1965, *Constitución de 1811*, *Disposiciones Generales*
Paternosto, C. (1989) *Piedra Abstracta. La Escultura Inca: Visión Contemporánea*. México: Fondo de Cultura Económica.
Petersen, U. (2000) 'Logic Without Contraction as Based on Inclusion and Unrestricted Abstraction', in *Studia Logica*, 64: 365–403.
Petit, P. (2001) *A Theory of Freedom*. Cambridge: Polity.
Pol-Fuchet, M. (1989) *Wilfredo Lam*. Barcelona: Ediciones Polígrafa.
Posner, R. A. (2004) *Catastrophe: Risk and Response*. Oxford: Oxford University Press.
Pratt, F. (2007) 'Michael Kidner: The Big Bang, Chaos and the Butterfly', in *Michael Kidner*. London: Flowers.
Priest, G. (2002) *Beyond the Limits of Thought*. Oxford: Oxford University at Clarendon Press.
Prigogine, I. (1983) *La lecture du complexe*, included in *Le Genre Humain* 7–8, pp. 221–3.
—— and Nicolis, G. (1997) *Self-organization in nonequilibrium systems. From dissipative structures to order through fluctuations*. New York: Wiley.
Protevi, J. (2005) *Beyond Neo-Cybernetics: Inflections of Emergence and Politics in the Work of Francisco Varela*. Available online at www.protevi.com/john/Varela_draft_18_September_2005.pdf (Accessed 5 July 2006).
Puma de Ayala, W. (1993) [1615] *Nueva Corónica y Buen Gobierno*. México: Fondo de Cultura Económica.
Quijano, A. and Wallerstein, I. (1992) 'Americanity as a Concept or the Americas in the Modern World-System', in *International Social Science Journal* 134, Paris: UNESCO.
Rasch, W. (2004) *Sovereignty and Its Discontents. On the Primacy of Conflict and the Structure of the Political*. London: Cavendish/Birkbeck Law Press.
Rediker, M. (2006) 'Thomas Clarkson and History From Below', in *Naked Punch. An Engaged Journal on Contemporary Art and Thought*. Issue 08, Autumn, pp. 16–23. London: Naked Punch Collective.
—— (2007) *The Slave-Ship. A Human History*. London: John Murray/Hachette Livre UK.
Roermund, B. v. (2003) 'First-person Plural Legislature: Political Reflexivity and Representation', in *Philosophical Explorations* 6(3): 235–52.
Rose, G. (1990) *Dialéctica del Nihilismo. La Idea de la Ley en el Pensamiento Postestructuralista*. Méjico: FCE. For the English edition, *Dialectic of Nihilism. Postestructuralism and Law*, Oxford: Basil Blackwell, 1984.
Rose, J. (1986) *Sexuality in the Field of Vision*. London: Verso.
Rose, M. A. (1989) *Marx's Lost Aesthetic. Karl Marx and The Visual Arts*. Cambridge: Cambridge University Press.

Rousseau, J. J. (1817) *Rousseau juge de Jean-Jacques. Dialogues*, in *Oeuvres de J. J. Rousseau*. Tome Quinziéme. Premier Dialogue. Paris: Deterville.
—— (1979) *Reveries of the Solitary Walker*. London: Penguin.
Royle, N. (2003) *The Uncanny*. Manchester: Manchester University Press.
Russel, B. (1921) *The Analysis of Mind*. New edition 1989. London: Routledge.
Sainsbury, R. M. (1990) 'Concepts Without Boundaries', in *Vagueness: A Reader*. Cambridge, MA: MIT Press.
Sakolsky, R. and Ho, F. (eds) (1995) *Sounding Off! Music as Subversion/ Resistance/ Revolution*. Brooklyn: Autonomedia.
Salcedo, D. (2007) 'It Will Be Incredibly Angry. An Interview By Richard Cork'. Available online at www.ft.com/cms/s/0/632d6fae-6e64-11dc-b818-0000779fd2ac.html (accessed 29 September 2007).
Samour, H. (2006) *Zubiri y la Filosofía de la Liberación*. Available online at www.uca.edu.sv/facultad/chn/c1170/samour2.html (Accessed 2 February 2006).
Santos, B. de Sousa (2003). *Toward a new Common Sense: Law, Science and Politics in Paradigmatic Transition* [1995], 2nd edition. London: Butterworths.
Sarmiento De Gamboa, P. (1999) *History of the Incas*. New York: Courier Dover Publications.
Sartre, J. P. (1947) *The Flies*. Translated by Stuart Gilbert. New York: Knopf.
—— (1957) *Existentialism and Human Emotions*. New York: Philosophical Library.
—— (1964) *Nausea*. New York: New Directions.
—— (1969) *Being and Nothingness*. Translated by H. E. Barnes. London: Routledge.
—— (1976) *Critique of Dialectical Reason*. Translated by A. Sheridan-Smith. London: NLB.
—— (1998) [1948] *What Is Literature?* [1948] Translated by B. Frechtman, London: Routledge.
—— (2004) *Critique of Dialectical Reason. Volume One*. Translated by A. Sheridan-Smith. Edited by J. Reé. Foreword by F. Jameson. London and New York: Verso.
—— (2006) *Colonialism and Neocolonialism*. Translated by A. Haddour, S. Brewer and T. McWilliams, with a preface by Robert Young and an introduction by Azzedine Haddour. 1st edition in 1964. London and New York: Routledge.
Schmitt, C. (1996) *The Concept of the Political*. Chicago, IL: Chicago University Press.
Schotter, A. (1983) 'Why Take a Game Theoretical Approach to Economics? Institutions, Economics and Game Theory', in *Economie Appliquée*, 36.
Schumpeter, J. (1951) 'The Sociology of Imperialism', in *Imperialism and Social Classes*. Edited by B. Hoselitz and translated by H. Norden. New York: New American Library.
Serres, M. (1972) *Hermès II: L'Interférence*. Paris: Minuit.
—— (1982) *The Parasite*. Transllated by Lawrence R. Schehr. Baltimore, MD: Johns Hopkins University Press.
—— (1983) *Rome, le livre des foundations*. Paris: Grasset.
—— (1993) *Les Origines de la géométrie*. Paris: Flammarion.
—— (1994) *Angels*. Paris/New York: Flammarion.
—— (1995a) *The Natural Contract*. Trans. Elizabeth MacArthur and William Paulson. Ann Arbor, MI: University of Michigan Press.
—— (1995b) *Atlas*. Madrid: Cátedra.

—— (1996) *Eloge de la philosophie en langue française*. Paris: Fayard.
Shields, R. (2003) *The Virtual*. London: Routledge.
Simondon, G. (1958) *Du Mode d'existence des objets techniques*. Paris: Aubier.
—— (1964) *L'individu et sa genèse physico-biologique*. Paris: Presses Universitaires de France.
Smolin, L. (2006) 'Never Say Always' in *New Scientist*, 23 September, 30–5.
Simpson Ross, I. (1995) *The Life of Adam Smith*. Oxford: Oxford University Press.
Spielrein, S. (1983) 'Extraits inédits d'un journal: D l'Amour, la mort et la transformation', translated by Jeanne Moll, in *Le Bloc-Notes de la Psychanalyse, 3*.
Spinoza, B. (2000) *Ethics*. Translated by G. H. R. Parkinson. Oxford: Oxford University Press.
Spivak, G. C. (1995) 'Supplementing Marxism', in *Whither Marxism? Global Crises in International Perspective*. Edited by B. Magnus and S. Cullenberg. London and New York: Routledge.
Stengers, I. (2007) 'Diderot's Egg: Divorcing Materialism from Eliminativism', in *Radical Philosophy 144*, July/August 2007, London: Radical Philosophy.
Stiegler, B. (1998) *Technics and Time, 1. The Fault of Epimetheus*, Translated by Richard Beardsworth and George Collins. Stanford, CA: Stanford University Press.
—— (1996) *La technique et le temps. Tome 2: La désorientation*. Paris: Galileé.
—— (2001) *La technique et le temps. Tome 3: le temps du cinema et la question du mal-être*. Paris: Galileé.
Strathern, M. (2004) 'Losing (Out On) Intellectual Resources', in *Law, Anthropology, and the Constitution of the Social*. Edited by Alain Pottage and Martha Mundy, Cambridge: Cambridge University Press.
Szepanski, A. (2002) 'Digital Music and Media Theory.' *Parachute* 107.
Taubes, J. (2007) *La Teología Política de San Pablo*. Madrid: Trotta.
Taussig, M. (1983) *The Devil and Commodity Fetishism in South America*. Chapel Hill: University of North Carolina Press.
—— (1996) *The Magic of the State*. London and New York: Routledge.
—— (1992) *Mimesis and Alterity. A Particular Study of the Senses*. New York: Routledge.
—— (2003a) *Law in a Lawless Land. Diary of a Limpieza in Colombia*. New York: New Press.
—— (2003b) 'The Adult's Imagination of the Child's Imagination', in *Aesthetic Subjects*. Edited by Pamela R. Matthews and David McWhirter. Minneapolis and London: University of Minnesota Press.
—— (2006) 'Diary' in *London Review of Books*, 28(19), 5 October.
—— (2008) 'Zoology, Magic and Surrealism in the War on Terror'. in *Critical Inquiry*, vol. 34, n. S32, Winter 2007–8. Chicago: The University of Chicago Press.
Trotta, R. (2007) 'Dark Matter', in *Collapse: Philosophical Research and Development*, vol. II, March 2007. Oxford: Urbanomic.
Tucker, St G. (1999) [1803] 'On Sovereignty and Legislature', in *Blackstone's Commentaries*, appendix A, Philadelphia, 1803, reprinted in St George Tucker (1999) *A View of the Constitution of the United States with Selected Writings* 19, Indianapolis, IN: Liberty Fund.
Twining, W. (2003) 'A Post-Westphalian Conception of Law. On Boaventura De Sousa Santos', in *37 Law and Society Review*: 199.

—— (2005) *General Jurisprudence*. XXII World Congress of Philosophy of Law and Social Philosophy. Draft for Comment.

Unger, R. (1987) *Politics: A Work in Constructive Social Theory*. Cambridge: Cambridge University Press.

—— (1996) *What Should Legal Analysis Become?* London: Verso.

—— and Smolin L. (2005) 'Changing Laws', audio recording. Available online at www.perimeterinstitute.ca/activities/scientific/cws/evolving_laws/agenda.php

Vallejo, C. (2006) *Selected Poems*. Edited and translated by Valentino Gianuzzi and Michael Smith. London: Shearsman.

Van Veen, T. C. (2002) 'Laptops & Loops: The Advent of New Forms of Experimentation and the Question of Technology in Experimental Music and Performance'. Delivered on 1 November 2002 at the University Art Association of Canada, Calgary. Available online at: www.quadrantcrossing.org/papers.htm (Accessed 15 July 2006).

—— (2003) 'Hearing Difference: The Seme.' Delivered on 6 July 2003 at the International Conference of the International Association for the Study of Popular Music (IASPM), Montreal. Available online at: www.quadrantcrossing.org/papers.htm. (Posted to Nettime, July 7, 2003. Accessed 8 September 2007).

Varela, F. and Depraz, N. (2000) 'At the Source of Time: Valence and the Consitutional Dynamics of Affect', in *Ipseity and Alterity: Interdisciplinary Approaches to Intersubjectivity*. Edited by S. Gallagher and S. Watson. Rouen: Publications de l'Université de Rouen.

—— and Dupuy, J. P. (1992) 'Understanding Origins: An Introduction', in *Understanding Origins: Creative Circles*. Edited by F. Varela and J.P. Dupuy. Dordrecht: Kluwer.

—— and Thompson, E. (2001) 'Radical Embodiment, Neural Dynamics and Consciousness', in *Trends in Cognitive Science*, 5(10) October 2001, 424.

——, Maturana, H. and Uribe, R. (1974) 'Autopoiesis: The Organization of Living Systems, Its Characterization and a Model', *Biosystems*, 5: 187–96.

Vargas Llosa, M. (2007) *'Izquierda Vegetariana' versus 'Izquierda Carnívora': Enfrentamiento que Toma Fuerza en América Latina*, in *Lecturas Dominicales*. *El Tiempo*, 15 June 2007. The article is a rendition of his prologue to Montaner, C., Mendoza, P. A. and Vargas Llosa Jr., M. (2007) *El Regreso del Idiota*. Madrid: Random House/Mondadori.

Vergès, F. (1999) *Monsters and Revolutionaries*. Durham: Duke University Press.

Vernes, J. R. (1981) *Critique de la Raison Aléatoire*. Paris: Aubier.

Verstraeten, P. (1972) *Violence et éthique: Esquisee d'une critique de la morale dialectique á partir du théâtre du Sartre*. Paris: Gallimard.

Virno, P. (2004) *A Grammar of the Multitude. For an Analysis of Contemporary Forms of Life*. Los Angeles and New York: Semiotext(e).

Wallerstein, I. (2002) 'The Twentieth Century: Darkness at Noon?', in *The Modern, Colonial, Capitalist World-System in the Twentieth Century. Global processes, Antisystemic Movements and the Geopolitics of Knowledge*. Edited by R. Grosfoguel and A. M. Cervantes-Rodríguez. Westport: Praeger.

Watson, G. van Noord, G. and Everall, G. (eds) (2007) *Making Everything New: A Project on Communism*. London: Bookworks/Project Arts Centre.

Webb, A. (2007) 'Year Zero for the Industry', in *The Observer Music Monthly*, December 2007, London: Guardian/Observer.
Weber, M. (1954) *On Law in Economy and Society*. Edited by Max Rheinstein. Cambridge, MA: Harvard University Press.
Weiner, A. D. and Hansard-Weiner, S. (1992) *Forcing the Real: Gérard Titus-Carmel and the Art of Renewal*. Madison: Wisconsin.
Wiebering, J. (1971) 'Kreatur', in *Historisches Wörterbuch der Philosophie*, vol. 4. Darmstadt: Wissenschaftliche Bugesellschaft.
Winch, P. (1990) *The Idea of a Social Science: And Its Relation to Philosophy*, 2nd edition. London: Routledge.
Wright, G. von (1980) ' Problems and Prospects of Deontic Logic', in *Modern Logic. A Survey*. Edited by E. Agazzi. Dordrecht: D. Reidel.
Yatabe, S. I. (2006a) Concepts with Unstable Boundaries. Available online at http://cogprints.org/5333/1/Sainsbury_PR3_1228.pdf Accessed 13 August 2007.
—— (2006b) 'On Evans's Vague Object from a Set Theoretic Viewpoint', in *Journal of Philosophical Logic*, 35: 423–34.
Young, R. J. C. (2001) *Postcolonialism. A Historical Introduction*. Oxford: Blackwell.
Zappa, F. (1968) 'The Oracle Has It All Psyched Out', in *Life Magazine*, June 28.
—— (1979) *Joe's garage*. Liner notes.
Žižek, Slavoj. (1991) *For They Know Not What They Do. Enjoyment as a Political Factor*. London: Verso.
—— (1997) 'The Abyss of Freedom', in *The Abyss of Freedom/Ages of the World*. Edited by S. Žižek and F. W. J. Schelling. Ann Arbor, MI: The University of Michigan Press.
—— (1999) *The Ticklish Subject*. London and New York: Verso.
—— (2000) *The Fragile Absolute*. London: Verso.
—— (2003) *The Puppet and the Dwarf*, Cambridge, MA: MIT Press.
—— (2004) *Organs Without Bodies. On Deleuze and Consequences*. London: Routledge.
—— (2006a) *The Parallax View*. Cambridge, MA: MIT Press.
—— (2006b) *A Plea for Ethical Violence*. Delivered at Birkbeck College in June 2006.
—— (2006c) *Master Class*. Birkbeck Institute for the Humanities, Birkbeck College, University of London. Session of 20 June 2006.
—— (2006d) 'Schlagend, aber nicht Treffend', in *Critical Inquiry* 33, Autumn. Chicago, IL: The University of Chicago Press.
—— (2006e) 'Objet a in Social Links', in *Jacques Lacan and the Other Side of Psychoanalysis*. Edited by Justin Clemens and Russell Griggs. Durham: Duke University Press.
—— (2007a) *How to Read Lacan*. London and New York: Granta.
—— (2007b) 'Mao-Tse Tung, the Marxist Lord of Misrule', introduction to *On Practice and Contradiction* by Mao-Tse Tung. London: Verso.
—— (2007c) 'An Ode Too Turkish for Europe', in *The Drawbridge*, Issue 4, Spring, 3.
Zubiri, X. (1963) *Sobre la Esencia*. Madrid: Sociedad de Estudios y Publicaciones.
—— (1974) 'La Dimensión Histórica del Ser Humano', in *Realitas*, vol. 1, Madrid: Sociedad de Estudios y Publicaciones.
—— (1980) *On Essence*. Translated by A. R. Caponigri. Washington DC: Catholic University Press.

—— (1982) *Inteligencia y Logos*. Madrid: Alianza Editorial.
—— (1992) *Sobre el Sentimiento y la Volición*, Madrid: Alianza Editorial.
—— (1999) *Sentient Intelligence*. Translated by Thomas Fowler. Washington DC: Xavier Zubiri Foundation of North America.
Zupančič, A. (2000) *Ethics of the Real. Kant, Lacan*. London: Verso.

Index

absence and presence 26–7, 34, 203
access 34, 81, 84, 90, 117, 118, 132
accidents 53, 54
action 205, 238, 239
actuality 97, 99
aesthetics 19, 34, 46, 129
affective perception 39
Africa 107, 235, 236; *see also* Afrological religious forms; Saharawi people; West Africa
Afrological religious forms 63, 70, 95, 96, 101
aid policy 210, 211, 213
AK-47s 140
algorithmic 2–3, 4, 10
alienation 70, 102, 194
allure 53, 54, 104, 120, 129, 241
alteration 196, 202, 206, 217
alterity 119, 134, 178
(am)bivalent objects 142, 143, 144, 145, 146, 181
American Revolution 78, 79, 173
Americas 66, 99, 102, 149, 159, 168, 226; *see also* Latin America; United States
Andean countries 14, 15, 19, 59–61, 81
Andrade, Oswald de 71
anthropocentrism 201, 203, 205–6
anthropology 43, 235
anthropophagy 71
anti-capitalism 227, 245
anticipation 66–70, 102, 103, 172, 173, 204; anticipatory use of reason 66; inevitability of failure 72; in *Nueva Corónica* 81; obligation to anticipate the future 200, 233; reality affected by 53; speculation 78
anti-fetishism 67, 170, 199, 217

anti-heroes 244
antinomies 65–6
anti-slavery 141
appearance 29, 88, 129, 142
archaic level of reality 111
archaic objects 9, 18, 24–36, 256; *The Pocket-Size Tlingit Coffin et les 61 premiers dessins qui s'ensuivrent* (Titus-Carmel) 26–9, 55n1
arche-prehension 251, 252
a-referentiality 221, 222
Arendt, Hannah 61, 121, 148
Aristotle 219n20
Arp, Hans 220
art 101, 110, 113, 202–3, 235; *see also* cinema; music
artifices 63–4, 70, 112
At World's End (Verbinski) 152, 158, 165
Australia 228
authority 144, 145, 151
autonomous zones *see* temporary autonomous zones (TAZs)
(auto)transcendence 33, 41, 175, 184, 189, 195
avant-garde 220, 221, 222, 223, 228, 234n1
Aztlán 224

Badiou, Alain 191, 226, 246–7, 250
bastones de mando 140
Battle of Algiers, The (Pontecorvo) 42
behetrías 159, 160, 161
Being against the world, how to think 6
Benjamin, Walter 139
Berger, Peter 161–2
Bey, Hakim 135–6, 225–6, 227

Beyond the Pleasure Principle (Freud) 107, 111, 114
Blanchot, M. 79
blindness 60, 100, 121, 122, 123, 130, 146, 163, 169
body–mind problem 28–9, 39, 65
Bolivia 3, 19, 59, 90n2, n3, 91n4, 247–8, 254
books 169, 170; *see also* sacred texts
Borges, J. L. 202, 218n16
boundary-crossing 121, 124, 125, 129, 133, 175
boundary drawing 143, 146
Bracken, Christopher 6–7
Brazil 227, 228
breakdown 40, 42, 55, 158
Britain 165, 199, 224
Burroughs, William S. 220, 221
bus example to explain notion of series 177–9, 180, 181
Butch Cassidy and the Sundance Kid (Hill) 3, 24, 46, 135
Butler, Judith 167n6

Calasso, Roberto 112
cameras 139, 140, 180
Cantorian revolution 215
capitalism 191–2; anti- 227, 245; cultural 228; Cuna peoples and 72; emergence of 13, 76, 141, 152, 163, 164, 166; fantasy and 164; future and 198–200; globalisation and 206–9, 210, 211, 212–14; money and 161, 162, 163; nihilistic tendencies of 207; in *Pirates of the Caribbean* 153, 163, 164–5, 166; resistance and 39; Scottish enlightenment on 94; slavery and 159, 160; turbo- 119; violence and 142, 172, 206
car bombs 139–40, 180
Caribbean 47, 48, 103, 185, 226; history of fetish in 20, 63, 70, 94, 95, 100, 107, 120, 235; Marx's study of religious forms in 101, 120; *see also* Cuba; Haiti; *Pirates of the Caribbean* (Verbinski)
Carpentier, Alejo 174, 176–7, 183, 184, 185
Castle, The 223–5
Castro, Fidel 245, 246, 247, 254, 255
catastrophe 226, 250, 251, 255
catastrophic intervention 239
catastrophic risk 232

causal being 47
causality 16, 27, 28, 31, 34, 35, 37, 38, 205; formal 49; intermediary 49, 54
censorship of music 228, 229, 230–1
chance, metaphysics of 188
Charles River Bridge case 71, 95–7, 100
charms 18, 28, 31, 46; role of 29
Chase, Anthony 96
Chicanos in the US 224
choice 25, 46, 71, 75, 150; Guevara's 248, 254; radical 149, 228, 230, 232–3, 234, 241; *see also* either/or propositions
Christian art 101
cinema 100, 152, 153, 156–8, 164; *The Battle of Algiers* 42; *Butch Cassidy and the Sundance Kid* 3, 24, 46, 135; *1871* 100; *The Fight Club* 200; film studies 131n4; *Les Maîtres Fous* 75; *The Matrix* 89; New Latin American 199, 229; *Trobriand Cricket: An Ingenious Response to Colonialism* 75; *Vertigo* 118–19; *Zeyna* 113; see also *Pirates of the Caribbean* (Verbinski)
circles, incomplete 110, 115
Clark, Andy 39
Clastres, Pierre 13
climate change 199–200
cognitive science 39, 234n4, 238
collectives 14, 30, 38, 39, 80, 90, 136, 138; establishment of value by 194; homogeneous 240; radical attachments of 171, 196; sacrificial self-discipline of 245, 246; self-legislation 20, 57, 196, 243; sexuality and 113
Colombia 72, 140, 211, 212; pre-Columbian objects 18, 19
colonialism 6–7, 12, 26, 47, 59–60, 71, 72–3, 121, 185; coloniality of power 142; *Trobriand Cricket: An Ingenious Response to Colonialism* 75
commodities 6, 69, 72, 154–5, 161
common citizenship 60, 72, 91n7
communes 225, 226
communication, problem of 130, 132, 134
community of default 80, 81
comparativism 46–7
complexity 147, 148–9, 179, 193
concrete universality 189
concretisation 89, 92n24

conflict resolution 209, 210, 211, 213
consensus 41
consequences, virtual or counterfactual 234, 236, 239, 249, 250
consistency 124, 125–7
constitution 80–1, 88, 89, 138, 139; connection between rebellion and 11, 145; eternal revision of 12, 14; re-constitution 82; relationship between rebellion and 145; of the United States 96; of Venezuela 91n7
constructivist subjectivism 24
constitutionalism 60, 77, 99; popular 77, 94, 95, 100, 105; projected 85, 99
constitutional law 77
contagion 25, 30, 71, 72–6, 120, 195, 238
contingency 40, 45, 47, 48, 116, 188; improbable 127
continuity 186n5; between human and nonhuman 20, 107, 174, 180, 182–3, 187, 188; temporal 183, 184, 185, 187
contradiction 10, 24, 65–6, 124, 125–6, 127–8
contradictory objects 120, 124, 125, 128, 129, 149
conviction 88, 89, 118
Copjec, Joan 123, 128, 131n9, 135, 137, 244
Coronil, F. 17
counter-cultures 221, 223, 226, 228, 229
counterfactual consequences 234, 236, 239, 249
counterfactual reasoning 218n5, 237
counter-fetishes 169, 170, 171
counting 32, 235
createdness 189, 190
creature 6
criticism, two tasks of 4
critique 235
crossroads 225
crowd theory 45, 76, 178
Cuba 236, 245–6, 247, 248, 254, 255
Cuna peoples 72
cut 20, 68, 186n5, 188, 251; cutting fetishes 185; fantasy as a 51, 54; in Sartre's usage 181–4
cut-up technique 33, 74, 216; in music 220
cyberculture 226–7

D'Annunzio, Gabrielle 226
Davis, Mike 139
Dead Man's Chest (Verbinski) 21, 133, 152, 153, 157, 162, 164
death 110, 111, 112, 113, 114–15, 119; proper 148, 153–4
death-drive 107–8, 114–15, 133, 152, 153; desire and 166; Lacanian revolution and 120; link between law of the proper and 148; mother/child dyad and 123, 128, 244; Spielrein on 111, 112–13
debt 14, 164, 165, 166, 200, 207, 209
decolonisation 16, 18, 35, 47, 59, 60, 141
Dedekind, Richard 174, 182, 184, 186n5
deduction 9–10
default of community 80, 81
delirious phenomena 109, 111
demystification 63–4
Derrida, Jacques 17–18, 19, 26, 28; commodities 155; duplicity 122; hauntology 88; proper death 148, 153–4; *restance* 19, 37
Des Brosses, Charles 100–1, 102
desire 103–4, 108, 111, 119, 156, 157–8, 165, 166; *see also* love; sexuality
development 209–11, 219n21
Dickey, Laurence 105n1
digital technology 221–2, 226–8
discourse of the analyst 254
Dolar, Mladen 43, 57, 151, 220, 235
Dollimore, Jonathan 152–3
donations 14, 73; *see also* gifts
double 122, 123, 125, 126
double aspect of the fetish 55, 84, 98, 167n6, 194
Douzinas, C. 257n9
Duffield, Mark 209–10, 211, 212, 213
duplicity 122, 123
Dupuy, Jean-Pierre: action 238; catastrophe 251; counterfactual or virtual consequences 234, 236; counterfactual reasoning 218n5; future 173, 200; human-nonhuman continuum 188; ongoing normative assessment 181, 183; preventive hope 213; prophets 86, 151; time 12, 85, 148–50
Durand-Barthez, Manuel 71
Dussel, Enrique 77

East India Company 153, 157, 164–5
economic equilibrium 194
economics 13, 14, 73, 162; consequences of realism in politics and 191–200; of life and death 148; *see also* money
egalitarian circuit of exchanges 14
ego 113
1871 (McMullen) 100
either/or propositions 67, 69, 98, 125, 143
Ellacuría, Ignacio 23n12, 251, 257n10
empire 1, 13, 141, 152, 157, 163, 164–5, 166
enactment 29, 129, 171
enclosures 141
enemies 233, 234n7
Enlightenment 16, 18, 26, 27, 43, 57, 60; Scottish 93–4, 105n1
enunciation without statement 220, 221, 223, 228, 229, 233, 240
environment 39–40
envy 1, 14, 28, 37, 100, 121, 211, 240; empire and 13
epidemiology, analogy between contemporary capitalism and 209, 211, 213
Epstein, Richard 95
equality 90
Escobar, Eduardo 219n21
Esposito, Patrizio 140
Essence of Christianity, The (Feuerbach) 99, 102, 105
Eternal Presence (Lam) 185–6
ethics 4, 15, 105n1; ethical aporia 199–200
ethnology 46, 106n6
evental bodies 39, 114
evil 60, 121, 231, 243
exemplarity 19, 40
existence/essence distinction 189, 190
exposure 135–6
expressive freedom 228, 229, 230–1, 236, 240
exteriorisation 30, 68, 69, 70, 204
eye-witnesses 122, 153

Fanon, Franz 18, 105, 107, 121, 257n10
fantasy or fantasmatic objects 50, 51, 52, 53, 54, 55, 92n23, 158, 161, 163–4

fascination 45–6, 52, 104, 120, 122, 123, 129, 132–3
Fascism 245, 246, 248
Ferguson, A. 93, 105n1
fetishes 2, 9, 20, 100, 119, 144, 257; archaic objects 18, 256; brief history of 70–2; 'call without meaning' 72; commodity 6, 72, 85; counter- 169, 170, 171; in Cuba 236; cutting 185; double aspect of 55, 84, 98, 167n6, 194; explaining the coming-to-presence of 69; false and true aspects of 102–3; in legal language 71, 95; objects between 46; in *Pirates of the Caribbean* 152, 156, 157; in psychoanalysis 107–8; return of 4, 61, 64, 235; scapegoats 243; slave revolt through power of 96; of slaves 155, 171; two aspects of 63–4; unplaceable 116
fetishism: anti- 67, 170, 199, 217; error in 90; Marx's interest in 76–7, 85, 87, 94–5, 100–2, 120; the 'original' religion 101; sublime 21, 69, 104
Feuerbach, Ludwig 47, 90, 99, 102–5
fidelity 78, 79, 80, 249, 251
Fight Club, The (Fincher) 200
film studies 131n4; *see also* cinema
Fischlin, D. 229, 230
Fiume 226
The Flies (Sartre) 242, 244–5
flux, historical 82
flux, infinite 168
foreign elements 41–2
formal cause 49
formality 103, 117
Forman, F. N. 12
form-materialism 20, 34, 105, 167n6
Foucault, Michel 46, 106n6, 225
frames 92n23
France 83–4, 140, 169, 225, 226
Franz Ferdinand 220, 221, 222, 223–5
freedom: allure of the unexpected as core of 241; 'caged' 188, 189, 218n4; contradiction between necessity and 66; expressive 228, 229, 230–1, 236, 240; idea of 25, 205, 248, 256; loss of 160; Orestes and 244; in *Pirates of the Caribbean* 165; of the press 77, 93, 94, 97, 99, 100, 101, 149; as total distance from others 195
free will 172–3

Freud, Sigmund 107–9, 111, 114, 117, 119, 123; crowds 76, 178; death-drive 153, 244; Guevara's familiarity with writings of 248; repetitiveness 152; Spielrein and 115, 116
Fuentes, Carlos 245–6
Fukushima, Masato 46
future 77–9, 81, 87, 90, 172–3, 177, 180–1, 184, 187, 206; capitalism and 192–3, 198–200, 214
futuribles 149, 184, 192, 200

Galeano, Eduardo 246
García Márquez, Gabriel 227, 245, 246
gathering 15–16
Genoa, 2001 battle of 227
Germany 234n1, 248
gifts 6, 14, 15, 48, 73–4
Gil, José 14
Girard, René 133, 233, 240
Glasgow 220, 223–5
globalisation 120, 162, 206–17
Gödel, Kurt 8, 22n10
gods, making of 90, 102, 156–7, 166
gold 85, 94, 103, 120, 133, 158
gold-coin 94, 158, 161, 162, 197, 242
gold-fetish 6, 150, 151, 152, 153, 156
Goodchild, Phillip 198–9
Gordon, Avery 108, 115, 116, 117
Gore, Al 199
Gothic literature 95
government 12–14, 77, 93
grievances, role in conflicts of 211, 212
groups 32, 38, 45, 124, 136, 150, 174, 177–8, 196, 248
Guatemala 122–3
Guéguen, P. G. 122
'Guernica' (Picasso) 234n1
Guerra del tiempo, La (Carpentier) 174, 176–7, 183, 184, 185
Guevara, Ernesto 'Che' 11, 24, 245, 247–51, 252, 253, 254–5
Gunning, T. 153

Haidar, Aminattou 140
Haiti 7, 83–4, 94, 96, 104, 185
Hamilton, Alexander 89
Hansard-Weiner, Sonja 26, 27
Hanssen, B. 139

Hardt, Michael 11–12
Harman, Graham: allure 53; causality 16, 54; cut-up technique 216; first aesthetics 34; formal cause 49; probabilistic fallacy 218n3; problem of communication 130, 132; proximity 132, 134; retroviruses 92n22; sensual objects 50, 52, 53; sensual realm 44, 51, 53
hauntology 88
heart in the chest 94, 120, 133, 152, 153, 156, 157, 158, 161, 164, 235
Hegel, G. W. F.: actuality 97, 99; concrete universality 189; ethical principle 105n1; Feuerbach and 103; influence on Marx of 93, 97, 102; limits and boundaries 145, 146; technics 146; time-matter 94; 'to know the infinite' 143; world-historical 98; writing 79
hegemonic relation 139
Heidegger, Martin: being and logic 125; constitution 80; heritage 79; history 82, 91n19, 98; language 58; technical–practical relation 50; the uncanny 44; world 29, 36n7, 49, 124
Hera 111–12
heritage 79, 80, 81, 82, 83
heroes 81, 111, 112, 242–3, 247
heroic attitude 247, 250, 252, 255
hidden necessity 66, 67, 194, 205
historical reality 249, 253
homogenisation 240
Hondo, Med 100
hubris: humanist 1; imperial 120, 152, 153, 165
human, continuity between nonhuman and 20, 107, 174, 180, 182–3, 187–8
humanitarianism 211, 213
Hurricane Flora 247, 249, 250, 251, 255
Husserl, Edmund 44, 50
hysteria 108–9, 110

icons 30, 63, 248; *see also* religious symbols
identification 76; *see also* over-identification
identity 73, 224, 245
Ignatieff, Michael 233

immortality 68, 153, 164
improbable 7, 83, 86, 145, 149
in-between-ness of objects 124
incest 112, 113
in-closure structures 23n10, 191
incompleteness theorem, Gödel's 8, 22n10
Inconvenient Truth, An (Guggenheim) 199
indigenous peoples 59–60, 73–4, 85, 91n7, 120, 240; Colombian 140; Guatemalan 122–3; Pact for Indigenous and Peasant Unity 59, 91n4
indirect relations 46, 49
infectious activity 238, 239
infinite critique 3, 8
infinities 67
inner conviction 88, 89, 118
intentionality of consciousness 44–5
intentional relation 44–5
interiority 69–70, 115, 204
interrupted talk 220, 221
inter-subjectivity 5, 83
intervention 211, 235, 237, 238, 239, 240
intimacy 116, 117, 118, 122, 124
intuition 203, 215
Italy 226, 227

Jefferson, Thomas 12–13, 15, 79, 80, 149
Joe's Garage (Zappa) 230
Jones, Davy 157–8, 163, 164
Jung, Carl G. 107, 108, 109, 111, 112, 114, 115
justice 155, 197, 248

Kaiser, Matthias 25, 35n2
Kant, Immanuel 62, 64–9, 201, 203, 205
Karatani, Kojin 129
Kaufman, Eleanor 62–3, 174, 177, 182, 183
Kemple, Thomas 158, 161, 162, 207, 208
Kerr, J. 113
Kerruish, V. 1, 144, 145, 146, 167n6, 205
knowledge 6, 7, 8
Kojève, Alexandre 105, 106n7, 107, 238
Krafft-Ebing, R. F. von 108, 109

Kramer, Larry D. 77–8, 95
Kristeva, Julia 48–9, 55, 56n12, 171–2, 179–80; on Orestes 242, 243, 244–5, 256
Kurrish, Valerie 125

Lacan, Jacques 116, 120, 121, 122, 131n4, n9, 254
Lacan effect 122, 131n4
Laclau, Ernesto 76, 128, 133, 136–7, 138–9, 250
Laibach 74–5, 229
Lam, Wilfredo 185
Landa, Manuel de 167n4
Langer, Suzanne K. 170
language 58; fetish in legal 71, 95; metaphors in legal 95, 96; of popular sovereignty 85
Latin America 16–17, 60, 70, 199, 229, 246, 248, 256; *see also individual countries by name*
Latin American philosophy 257n10
Latinos in the US 224
law(s) 13, 15, 169, 171; *Charles River Bridge case* 71, 95–7, 100; consequences of realism for the study of 201–6; constitutional 77; fetish in legal language 71, 95; letter of the 151; necessity of 194; prohibiting rebellious music 230–1; of the proper 147, 148, 153, 154; *see also* legality; self-legislation
lawyers 93
Leach, Jerry 75
leaders 40, 195, 196, 242, 248; Fidel Castro 245, 246, 247, 254, 255; Ernesto 'Che' Guevara 11, 24, 245, 247–51, 252, 253, 254–5
legality 188, 189, 193, 194, 195, 201, 202
Lehmann, William C. 93
Leiris, Michel 185
Levinas, Emmanuel 132
liberal imperial command 214
Lifshitz, Mikhail 101
Lisbon earthquake of 1775 40–1
logic 2, 9–10, 167n6; of abstraction 19; consistency and contradiction 125–7; dialectical 98; relation between world and 145
Losurdo, Domenico 97, 99
love 13–14, 52, 104, 114; allure and 53; narcissism of the leader 195, 196;

that seeks no other 133, 134; *see also* desire; sexuality
Löwenfeld, Leopold 108–9
Luhmann, Niklas 5

McGowan, Todd 164
McMullen, Ken 100, 113
magic 27–8, 31, 42, 43, 57, 155
magical realism 153, 174, 183, 187
Mahmood, Saba 58, 61, 76, 171
Maîtres Fous, Les (Rouch) 75
maker 201, 203–4, 206
Man, distinction between Nature and 201
Martin, R. P. 70
Marx, Karl 63, 86–9; fetishism 76–7, 85, 87, 94–5, 100–2, 120; freedom of the press 77, 93, 94, 99, 100, 101, 149; influences on 93–4, 97, 100–2; money 162; projection and enactment 171; rights 154; value 158–9; work as sacrifice 161
materialism 61–3, 69
materiality 57, 58, 61
mathematical objects 9
Matrix, The (Wachowski and Wachowski) 89
matter 62, 63, 69, 85; *see also* time-matter
Mazzoldi, Bruno 17–19, 26, 27–8, 32, 38, 55n1, 122
medicalisation of politics and policy 209, 211, 213
Meek, Ronald 93
Meillassoux, Quentin 18, 67, 188, 190, 192, 193–4, 204–5, 215
melancholia 48, 49, 56n12, 71, 72
Menchú, Rigoberta 123, 125
meshwork 78, 139, 140, 142, 167n4, 249
mestizaje (common citizenship) 60, 72, 91n7
metaphysics of projected time 85
métissage (miscegenation) 72–3, 176, 185
Métraux, A. 104
Mexica 136, 158, 160, 161–2, 163
Mignolo, Walter 47
Milbank, John 32, 33
Millar, John 93, 105n1
mimesis 40, 49, 71, 119, 120, 136, 196, 228, 238, 239
mind, self-positing of human 62

mind–body problem 28–9, 39, 65
minimal distance 127
minimal failure 125, 126, 149, 150, 174, 181, 216, 222, 245
miscegenation 72–3, 176, 185
missile crisis of October 1962 247, 249, 250, 251, 255
mobile phones 139, 140
modernity 18, 26, 57, 60, 100
money 69, 85, 140, 160, 161, 162, 163; debt and 200; in the music industry 229; personified by Jack Sparrow 157; religious faith in 198–9; *see also* gold; gold-coin; gold-fetish
'mono' 46, 48
Montag, Warren 169
monumental architecture 161–2; *see also* pyramids
Moreiras, A. 197
mother/child dyad 21, 107–8, 123, 128, 244
music 33, 220–31; appropriation of counter-cultural 228; Franz Ferdinand 220, 221, 222, 223–5; Laibach 74–5, 229; as organisational principle 226, 227; Plato on 228; property theft 227; rock stars 166; Frank Zappa 229, 230, 239
Muslims 59, 60, 61, 75
myth 111, 114

Nancy, Jean-Luc 63–4, 84, 85, 120
narrative 66, 68, 174
NATO 74–5
naturalists 3
natural sciences 4, 15
Nature, distinction between Man and 201
nausea 48, 49, 56n12, 71, 72, 76
necessary being 47, 83, 85, 129
necessity 8, 9; hidden 66, 67, 194, 205; wheel of 112
nonhuman, continuity between human and 20, 107, 174, 180, 182–3, 187–8
non-realism 65, 173, 187, 190, 206
normalisation 225
nothing 175, 176, 183, 184
novelty 184–5, 186, 188, 189, 190, 191, 221, 241, 251, 256
NSK/Laibach 74–5, 229
Nueva Corónica y Buen Gobierno (Puma de Ayala) 13, 14, 73, 81

objectivity 3, 4, 9, 10, 70, 102, 109, 144–5; mainstream definition of 22n6; of phantasms and fantasies 51, 52, 161
objects-between 46, 47, 48
objects of inscription 119, 121
objet petit a 53, 120, 235, 253
obscure objects 2, 6, 7, 9, 15, 24, 25, 97; death-drive and 112; in psychoanalysis 108; *see also* quasi-objects
observation 5–6, 7, 8
Oedipus 242, 244, 245
On Freedom of the Press (Marx) 77, 93, 94, 101
ongoing normative assessment 181, 183
ontological indeterminacy 150, 187, 200
order 3
Orestes 112, 241, 242–5, 256
origins 26–7, 31, 32, 33, 34
Ortíz, Fernando 71
other 6, 22n6, 41–2, 73, 79, 103, 104, 116–17, 118
outlaws 3, 153, 197, 242–3, 247
over-identification 7, 30, 72, 73, 74, 75, 240, 242

Pact for Indigenous and Peasant Unity 59, 91n4
panic 42, 136, 154, 195, 245
paradoxes 10, 38, 65
Paris 225, 226
partial objects 30, 128, 133, 135, 138, 196, 224, 238
peasants 59, 91n4, 247, 250, 257n8
people, the 80–2, 89, 90, 105n1, 141, 238, 251, 255
Peru 13, 14, 15, 26, 27
Petersen, Uwe 1, 125
Picasso, Pablo 234n1
Pirates of the Caribbean (Verbinski) 21, 133, 148, 150, 152, 156–8, 162, 163–6; *At World's End* 152, 158, 165; *Dead Man's Chest* 21, 133, 152, 153, 157, 162, 164
Plato 217, 223, 227, 228
pleasure 123
pledge 243, 248
plurality in proximity 253
Pocket-Size Tlingit Coffin et les 61 premiers dessins qui s'ensuivent, The (Titus-Carmel) 26–9, 55n1

political meaning 220
political philosophy 38
politicians 1, 2, 90
politics 1–2; beyond critique 2, 4, 11, 19, 20, 21; as a branch of aesthetics 46; consequences of realism in economics and 191–200; convergence between geometry and 32; 'conviction' 118; of distance 74; either/or choices 143; gathering and 15; Laclau's theory on 136–7; of liberation 73, 140; medicalisation of 209, 211, 213; objects at centre of 15, 24; promises made in 12; 'proper deaths' and 148; reduced to prevention policy 207, 240; role of objects in 140; task of 'modern' 60; truth as a principle of 41–2
Politics of Piety (Mahmood) 76
Pontecorvo, Gillo 42
popular constitutionalism 77, 94, 95, 100, 105
popular education 14
popular sovereignty 85
populism 76
Portugal 70, 76, 169
postulated objects 8, 10, 111, 133, 134, 253–4, 256
postulation 4, 8, 9–10, 19, 23n10, 103, 110, 249
potentialism 184
potlatch 6, 159
power 19, 31, 37; coloniality of 142; constituent 38; will to 102, 119, 123, 137, 146, 153
powerful objects 25, 60, 61, 76; books 169, 170
practical relations 50–1
pre-Columbian objects 18, 19
predictive moves 236, 238, 251
presence and absence 26–7, 34, 203
present, notions of the 16, 25–6, 207
prevention and precaution 4
prevention policy 207, 209, 213, 240
preventive hope 213
Priest, Graham 125, 175
Prigogine, Ilya 218n19
privilege 99, 100, 105
probabilism, fallacious 200, 218n3
probabilistic reasoning 189, 192, 193–4, 196, 197, 201, 203, 231
productivity, unconstrained 119
progress, belief in 16, 25, 26, 35n2

projection 52, 71, 99, 102–3, 122, 130, 171; reciprocal 29, 39
projects 181, 183
proper, law of the 147, 148, 153, 154
property 105n1, 153, 176; *Charles River Bridge case* 71, 95–7, 100; right to 48, 93, 94; theft 28, 37, 155, 227
prophecies 150–1, 236
prophetics 86
prosthesis 34
Protevi, John 39
providence 99, 105, 154
proximity 74, 126, 132–4, 195, 253
psychoanalysis 43, 51, 105, 107, 119; *objet petit a* 53, 120, 235, 253; prehistory of 102; role of Jacques Lacan in 121; role of Sabina Spielrein in 108, 109–11, 112–17; theory of the drives 128–30, 133, 144
publicity 83, 84, 86, 89, 118, 151
Puma de Ayala, Waman 13, 14, 15, 73–4, 81, 149
pyramids 158–9, 161–2, 163

quasi-objects 4–5, 6, 9, 10, 11, 17, 20, 24, 29; *see also* obscure objects; simulacra
Quijano, Aníbal 142

race 59, 72–3, 142
radical attachments 35; between Indigenous and Peasant Unity and its objects 59; collective 171, 196; identification 76; role played by objects in 25, 28, 57, 61; substitution and 136, 138
radical choice 149, 228, 230, 232–3, 234, 241
Radiohead 227
Radziwill, Franz 220
randomness 220, 221
realism: consequences of for the study of globalisation 206–17; consequences of for the study of laws 201–6; consequences of in politics and economics 191–200; ontological consequences of 187–91; substantialist 24
reality 5, 11, 252–3, 257n4; archaic level of 111; of archaic objects 24; existence/essence distinction 189, 190; fantasy and 53; formality as 103, 117; historical 249, 253; incompleteness of 53, 65, 67, 68, 69; modern conception of 58; physical 189; by postulation 4; power of 8; sensual character of 29; *see also* realism; real objects
real objects 30, 44, 48–54, 63–4, 215, 250, 254
reason 144–5, 160, 167n6; embodied in books 169; relationship between theoretical and practical 145; technical–practical and moral–practical 66–7, 69; tribunal of 65, 68
rebellion: breakdown 42; defined 32; interpretations of 3, 9, 10–11; relationship between constitution and 11, 145; return of 12, 13, 14, 79; right to 94, 234, 248; *see also* revolution
rebels 24, 197, 241–2; Ernesto 'Che' Guevara 11, 24, 245, 247–51, 252, 253, 254–5; Orestes 112, 241, 242–5, 256
reciprocal projection 29, 39
reciprocity 14, 15, 48, 132, 137, 139
re-constitution 82
Rediker, Marcus 141, 142, 143, 144, 150
refrain 220, 222
relations, withdrawal of real objects behind all 44–6
religion 47, 157, 199; Afrological religious forms 63, 70, 95, 96, 101
religious forms, study of 70–1, 85, 95, 99, 101–2, 103, 149
religious symbols 58–9, 63; *see also* icons
remainder 32, 33, 73, 241; ghost in the machine 222; invisibility of 5; magic and the uncanny 42; in natural and social sciences 15; Orestes and 112; outcasts of the world 169; produced by the experience of modernity 18–19, 26; rebels, outlaws and freedom fighters 197; *restance* 19, 37; thought of the 18, 19, 20, 28, 35, 55, 57, 61, 171, 173; *see also* residue
remembering 31, 33
repetitiveness 152, 205, 239, 251
representation 135
repression 109, 110, 113
residue 5, 8, 18, 37; residual parts of real objects 54; *see also* remainder

resistance 39, 74
resoluteness 78, 79, 80, 81, 91n18
responsibility 133–4, 136, 233, 239, 240
responsiveness 20
restance 19, 37
retro-garde 221, 222
Réunion Island 72
revolt 48–9; right to 234, 248
revolution 11–12, 13, 254; American 78, 79, 173; Cuban 248; French 84; Haitian 83–4, 96
Rhine Diet 86–7, 93, 94
riddles 150, 151, 236
rights 12; equality 90; human well-being 99–100, 105, 154; privileges and 88; progression from technics to 66; to property 48, 93, 94; of the province 77, 86, 87; to rebellion 94, 234, 248; redefinition of liberal and radical 208; using force to defend human 75
risk and risk prevention 149, 162, 208, 211, 241; catastrophic risk 232
Roberts, Bartholomew 166
rock stars 166
Rose, J. 115
Rouch, Jean 75
Rousseau, Jean-Jacques 91n6, 118
Royle, Nicholas 43, 44, 64, 131n4, 153

sacred 57, 151
sacred objects 6
sacred texts 40; *see also* books
sacrifice 137–9, 158, 161–2, 231, 233, 247, 255; Orestes 242, 243, 244, 245; sacrificial self-discipline 245, 246
Saharawi people 137, 140
sailors 142–3, 144
Santa Cruz Civic Committee 59
Sartre, Jean-Paul 48, 71, 107, 172, 174, 187; cut 181–4; *The Flies* 242, 244–5; intentional relation 44–5; 'the pledge' 243, 248; series and groups 32, 45, 124, 134, 150, 174, 177–81, 196, 248
satisfaction, right to unending 208
scapegoats 35, 136, 137, 242, 243, 244, 245
schizophrenia 113
Schumpeter, Joseph 207
science 4, 110, 113, 155, 202–3, 235; *see also* cognitive science; natural sciences; social sciences
scientification of risk 208

Scotland 220, 223–5
Scottish enlightenment 93–4, 105n1
security 210, 212
self-authorisation 38, 41, 57, 60
self-discipline, sacrificial 245, 246
self-legislation 20, 38, 39, 57, 196, 243
self-reflexive closure 175
self-reflexivity 17, 19, 22n10, 29, 38, 40, 78, 185, 188
self rule without a master 14
self-sacrifice 111, 112, 114, 246
sense, metaphysical and common 1–2
sensuality 34, 147, 179–80, 195, 215–16; appearance and 29; intentional relation and 45, 46; objectivity of 161; simulation and 30
sensual objects 50, 52–4
sensual realm 44, 51, 53
sentient intellection 251
series 32, 38, 45, 124, 134, 150, 174, 177–81, 196, 248
Serres, Michel 2, 4–5, 6, 7
sets 7, 92n23, 143–4, 146, 201
sexuality 104, 108–13, 156, 163; *see also* desire; love
short-sightedness 61, 100, 121, 124, 137; *see also* blindness
Simondon, Gilbert 89, 92n24
Simpson Ross, I. 93
simulacra 30, 31, 33, 34
simulation 29–30
sincerity 52
slaves and slavery: body and 154, 155–6; capitalism and 158–9, 160; in *Eternal Presence* 185; in Haiti 83, 96; legal language and 95; music and 228; in *Pirates of the Caribbean* 166; right to rebellion 94; 'slave rebellion of technology' 139; slave-ships 141–3, 144, 150, 155; in Spinoza's dream 168–71; in the US 96–7
Smith, Adam 93
Smolin, Lee 215, 218n5
snake image 111
social contract 1, 2, 5, 92n23; new 207–8
Socialism and Man in Cuba (Guevara) 248, 255
social sciences 4, 15
sociologists 3
solitude 118
Sontag, Susan 245, 246

South ('Global South') 16–17, 23n14, 210, 211–12; see also Latin America
sovereign 80, 81, 151, 160, 161
Spain 14, 74, 76, 168, 169, 226, 227, 234n1
Sparrow, Jack 156–7, 158, 163, 165
Spielrein, Sabina 108, 109–11, 112–17
Spinoza, Baruch 168–71
'spoken cough' ('*toz*') 220
stability 189, 201
Stengers, I. 1
Stiegler, Bernard 34, 70, 78–9, 80, 83, 84, 218n20
Strathern, M. 234n4
subjectivity 3, 31, 56n12, 83, 154, 234n4; inter-subjectivity 5, 83
sublimation 110, 113, 131n9
substantialist realism 24
substitution 48, 133, 135–8; alteration and 196; concrete instances of 136; distinction between exchange and 129; escaping blindness through 130; freedom and 195; Incan donation 73–4; Orestes as substitute 243; sublimation and 110, 131n9; in *Vertigo* 119
superstition 4, 155; thought of 19, 20, 28, 32, 34, 37, 38, 41, 55, 57, 61, 171
surprises 22n10, 42
symbols 58–9, 63, 111, 161, 162, 170
systemic effect 197

Take Me Out (Franz Ferdinand) 220, 222
Taney, Roger B. 95, 96, 97, 100, 166
Taussig, Michael 72, 84, 119, 122
technical objects 65, 66, 67, 68, 88, 90, 147, 150; Aristotelian assessment of 204; bad copies 50; car bombs 139; constitutions 88, 89; logic and mathematics 167n6; nothing 184; Orestes and 112; slave-ships 141–2
technical–practical relation 50, 65, 66, 67, 69, 164
technics 50–1, 66, 112, 146, 147, 167n6, 204, 218n20, 252
technology 25, 79–80, 139, 155, 184; digital 221–2, 226–8
Téllez, Freddy 17–18, 26, 28
temporary autonomous zones (TAZs) 136, 142, 223, 225, 226–7, 244, 246
terror 13, 62, 142–3

theft 28, 37, 155, 227
Thompson, Evan 39
thought 188, 215–16
time 12, 17, 21, 86–7, 98, 123, 124; economic operations and 162; metaphysics of 148, 149, 150, 184, 188; notion of 'cut' central to understanding of 188; running backwards 174; temporal continuity 183, 184, 185, 187; see also future; present, notions of the; time-matter
time-matter 85, 87, 90, 94, 188
Titus-Carmel, Gérard 26–8, 30, 55n1
Tlingit coffins 26–9, 37, 55n1
Tlön, Uqbar, Orbis Tertius (Borges) 202
Todëstriebe (death-drive) 107, 133, 152; see also death-drive
tools 40, 50, 79, 80, 83, 130, 182
topological change 226, 227
totalitarianism 22n10, 246
totalities 24, 175, 216–17; hidden functions 32; infectious activities 238; totalitarianism and 22n10; *Totalität* 160; uniqueness and 136; world 36n7, 40, 123–4
transcendence within immanence 238
transculturation 71
transference 104–5, 115–16, 120, 131n9
transformation 109, 110, 209, 211, 235, 236, 238
tree, encounter with a 45, 52
tribunal of reason 65, 68
Trobriand Cricket: An Ingenious Response to Colonialism (Leach) 75
Trotta, R. 127
truth 41–2, 74, 118, 122, 214–15, 254; aesthetics and 46; appearance as 88; transformation in the essence of 58, 61
Tucker, St George 78, 80, 81, 86, 87, 99, 103, 149, 173

Ukraine 226
uncanny 19, 42–4, 64, 152; cinema and 153; defined 43, 116; objects in philosophy 44–9; in psychoanalysis 108, 117; unplaceable in modernity 57
Uncanny, The (Freud) 107, 111
unconscious 113, 117
Unger, Roberto 190, 191, 215, 218n5
uniqueness 130, 136, 205, 238, 240

United Kingdom 93–4, 105n1, 165, 199, 220, 223–5
United States 99; American Revolution 78, 79, 173; Aztlán 224; capture and execution of Ernesto 'Che' Guevara 148; embargo of Cuba 255; Supreme Court 95–6, 97, 100
unity of experience 66
universal 167n6
use value 158–9, 161

Vallejo, César 220, 234n1
value 104–5, 154, 158–9, 197; emphasis on Value 206; financial 192, 193, 194, 196, 198–9; necessity 194
Van Veen, Tobias 221–2, 223, 227, 228
Varela, Francisco 39–40, 197
Vargas Llosa, Mario 59–60, 91n5
Venezuela 91n7
Vergès, Françoise 72–3, 84, 176
Vertigo (Hitchcock) 118–19
vicarious connections 49, 120
victims 122, 123, 142, 143, 146, 231, 233
violence 54–5, 62–3, 130, 139–40, 154, 171–2; blindness, short-sightedness and 121; breakdown and 42, 55; capitalism and 172, 206; mythic 139; ordinary and avant-garde 234n1; rebels and 241–2; sacrificial self-discipline 245, 246; in Sarajevo 74; slavery and 141–3, 155, 169; substitution and 130, 137–8; thought of the remainder and 20, 55; *see also* war
virtual consequences 234, 236, 250
virtuality 236, 242
virtual presence 135–6
virtual space 155

Volk (Laibach) 229
voudoun 48, 70, 96, 104, 166, 185, 238

Walras, Leon 194, 195
war: civil 59, 234n1; in development discourse 209, 210; perpetual 16; risk and 211; *see also* revolution
Webb, Adam 227–8
Weberians 3
Weiner, Andrew 26, 27
We're Only In It For The Money (Zappa and The Mothers of Invention) 229
West Africa 70, 76, 83, 96, 100, 101
wheel of necessity 112
withdrawal 6, 118, 124, 197, 216, 254, 257n5; of consciousness 182; of real objects behind all relations 44–6; temporary autonomous zones as 226
world: distinction between environment and 39–40; Heidegger's idea of 29, 36n7, 49, 124; relation between logic and 145
world-historical 80, 81, 82, 84, 98, 117, 121, 149
World Social Forum 16, 226, 228
World Wide Web 226–7, 238
writing 79, 80

Yugoslavia 74–5

Zappa, Frank 229, 230, 239
Zeus 111, 112
Zeyna (McMullen) 113
Žižek, Slavoj 74, 170, 192, 198, 217, 229, 250, 253
Zubiri, Xavier 4, 8, 9, 189, 190, 251, 257n10